The Heaven of Invention

O for a Muse of fire, that would ascend
The brightest heaven of invention!

SHAKESPEARE'S HENRY V.

6 00 129555 5

TELEPEN

Students and External Readers

S

DUE FOR RETURN

The
Heaven
of Invention

UNIVERSITY LIBRARY
NOTTINGHAM

by George Boas

The Johns Hopkins Press, Baltimore 1962

© 1962, The Johns Hopkins Press, Baltimore 18, Maryland
Library of Congress Catalog Card Number 63-8810
Printed in the United States
by Vail-Ballou Press, Inc., Binghamton, N.Y.

This book has been brought to publication
with the assistance of a grant from the Ford Foundation.

To A. B. GRISWOLD

600295555

Preface

THERE IS scarcely a word in English which is not ambiguous, but the hardest ambiguities to deal with are in those terms which are both descriptive and normative. When they are the names for human practices, the ambiguity becomes even more difficult to eliminate, for those who use the term in a eulogistic sense refuse to allow others to use it in a purely descriptive sense. Scientists, for instance, are proud of their specialty, and they want to distinguish it from anything of which they would not be proud. Pure science, for instance, must be sheltered from any contamination of applied science, technology, or engineering, in spite of the demonstrable fact that applied science has made important contributions to pure science and that the verification of pure science lies in the field of applied. So humble a discipline as horticulture, to say nothing of animal breeding, provided some of the evidence needed by Darwin. Pharmacology has aided biochemistry. And if men interested in aerodynamics had relied exclusively on what was known of hydrodynamics, not a plane would be flying today. Moreover, the scientist wants to reserve the name science for what he believes to have been proved, though he knows that many of his conclusions will be rejected in the future and that pseudo science is simply the science of the past. No one will deny that Dalton was a scientist and a great one too; but his atom is no longer our atom. No one today accepts Darwin's explanation of the origin of species, but everyone accepts the fact that they did evolve. The physicist no longer talks of heat as a fluid, but he retains a certain respect for Carnot nevertheless.

When one comes to the word *art*, the trouble is even worse. Everyone, said Collingwood, knows a work of art when he sees one and, he suggests, there is therefore no need to ask what art is. But, we might add, everyone can tell whether a cat is dead or alive, but that prevents no one from trying to discover the nature of life and death. All investigations start from recognized beings, perceived differences in qualities and peculiarities of behavior, and the task of the student is to see whether or not he can organize them into a larger pattern, explain their origin, codify their laws, and clarify their composition. It is precisely because we can recognize generic differences among things that we are beset by intellectual problems. Hence it is incumbent upon us to begin by indicating as clearly as we can just what we propose to talk about.

The word *art*, like all words, is used to point to a distinction among human activities. Works of art, all will agree, are made by human beings, not by Nature or God. It is, we shall contend in this book, one of the differentiae of man that he makes works of art. We propose to use the term in this sense alone, not in the sense which distinguishes between art and science, or arts and crafts, or works of art and artifacts, or liberal and manual arts. The relation, which I believe to be historical, between these antitheses will be discussed in the chapters which follow. We shall not, moreover, use the word in any eulogistic sense, as is sometimes done when a person says in admiration, "This is a true work of art," or in condemnation, "This is inartistic." Eulogistic terms acquire their connotations through historical associations: the British still give one title to surgeons and another to physicians. Anglo-Saxon terms have become indecent, whereas Greek and Latin derivatives with exactly the same denotation are decent. Our point of view in this book, as I hope will become clear, is that while all arts are valuable, some works of art have become less so and others more so as time has gone on, and furthermore that the types of value which they have sometimes change. This is a point which my critics have disputed, but I have found no good reason so far to drop it. For I am thinking of art and artistry in the total complex of the artist and the society in which he is working. Since neither term of the relation is above the world of time, I could not very well ignore the effects of history.

My general purpose has been to indicate some of the questions which a critic should take into consideration before passing judgment on either artistry or works of art and which, I feel, have been neglected by them. In two earlier books, A *Primer for Critics* and *Wingless Pegasus*, I tried to analyze some of these, though with no appreciable effect. Now some twenty years later I return to the problem and tackle it from a somewhat different point of view. Whether this will prove to be an advantage or not remains to be seen, but I have been encouraged to re-enter the field by friends who seemed to be interested in my arguments. All that is needed for a man enamored of writing is but the slightest tap on the shoulder to send him back to his typewriter.

It should be said that my preparation for this sort of work began years ago when I studied design at the Rhode Island School of Design under Henry Hunt Clark. His influence and that of my sister and my wife have been enduring. I have never been able to look at pictures, read poetry, listen to music without a passionate response. But, though I still feel that the love for a work of art is prior to all comment on it, I have also been deeply influenced by such men as Berenson, Lionello Venturi, Focillon, and the various members past and present of the Warburg Institute. To all these I owe a heavy debt of gratitude. If their influence is so apparent that it requires no mention, I shall be most happy, though I realize that none of them, could they read these pages, would agree with everything in them. They have not always agreed with one another. All of them, regardless of their profound differences, have illuminated works of art for me and shown me how much more complex they are than I should otherwise have known. What I have written would have profited from a deeper knowledge of psychoanalysis. What I know of that subject is simply what I have found out in the literature and from conversations with psychiatrists. I think naturally that what use I have occasionally made of it is sound, but I confess that I could have gone more deeply into it without loss.

I cannot end this preface without special thanks to institutions and persons who have given me help. First of all, I want to thank Wesleyan University which, by appointing me a Fellow of its Center for Advanced Studies, gave me the leisure, the facilities of a good library, secretarial help, the stimulation of wise associates, and a delightful office in which to work. Also I want to thank President Victor Butterfield, Dr. Sigmund Neumann, and Dr. Edward Williamson who have co-operated in making my stay at Wesleyan a happy one; Mr. Wyman W. Parker, librarian of the university, and his indefatigable staff; Drs. Cornelius Krusé, Heinrich Schwarz, director of the Davison Art Center, Rosalie L. Colie, and Mr. Tom Tashiro, all of whom helped me to clarify my ideas. I owe special thanks to friends, Mr. and Mrs. Harold Holmes Wrenn, the late Mr. William M. Ivins, Jr., Mr. F. L. Lucas, Dr. Frederick Dorian, and in addition to all the students who for years have listened to me with patience and trust. An outstanding debt of gratitude, which will never be paid in full, is owing to Mr. A. B. Griswold, to whom this book is dedicated; for he revealed to me many of the beauties of Siamese sculpture and encouraged me to study Buddhist art more thoroughly than I should have done if left to my own initiative.

G.B.
Middletown, 1962

Contents

The Heaven of Invention

CHAPTER I

Art and Nature

ONE OF THE peculiarities of the human race is
its ability to improve on nature. As far as we know, most of the
animals follow a routine established, one supposes, at a remote
period of their history, a routine which determines how they
should live in every detail. This routine is sometimes referred
to as the operations of instinct and is praised or belittled by
writers according to their approval or disapproval of intelligence.
The animals apparently know what to eat and what to avoid
eating, how to build their nests and other shelters, how to store
food, when to procreate their kind, how to govern their societies
when they live in societies, what are their natural enemies and
what their natural friends, where to go when it is time to migrate
and how to get there, when to crawl underground or into a cave
or hollow tree when it is time to hibernate, how to gather food
for their young and when to start them off on their own and
independent careers, and they need no education in these practices. We shall not list all the so-called wonders of instinct, for
not only has the topic been spun out for generations, but also
it gains in persuasive force if the details are omitted. The behavior
of the social insects, for instance, has been dwelt upon by
competent entomologists in both learned and popular treatises;
the reasoning powers of the higher mammals have been debated
ever since the fourth century B.C., if not before. Writers who
dislike the human race contrast our follies with the wisdom of

1

the beasts, and even the Proverbs of Solomon suggest that we go to the ant for lessons. Those cultural primitivists who think that innate characters are somehow better than the characters which are acquired usually hold up the beasts as exemplars, but none of them seem to believe that the animals make works of art, though they do of course make artifacts.[1]

One does not have to dislike the beasts to hold the thesis that their instincts fail them in certain situations. These situations arise when their habitual modes of conduct are blocked. There are ants that grow food and others that keep cows; there are still others that collect and store food against the coming of bad times, as in La Fontaine's fable. Squirrels hoard nuts, and bears accumulate fat on which to live while hibernating. Such knowledge is commonplace. One could write volumes on the economy of the animals, on their morals, and on their politics, but it would be impossible, as far as present information goes, to write more than a few pages on their art. The beehive is to be sure an exquisite device for rearing children, and the sexual specialization of the three apian sexes is something which only an Aldous Huxley could have invented. The oriole's nest is an amazing artifact to be made by a creature without hands, and the skunk has developed a defensive weapon which is almost perfect. But nevertheless all of these things work well only so long as the usual course of events is not obstructed. In contrast to such ritualism, men have perfected in the short space of a few thousand years their traditional ways of satisfying their needs and, when they are confronted with potential frustrations, they have been able, if not always willing, to sit down and think out new ways of overcoming them.

It would be absurd to attempt a catalogue of those desires which all men have had and which they have learned to fulfill. The desire for sexual gratification, for alleviating hunger, for avoiding extremes of heat and cold, for defeating their enemies both human and nonhuman, for preventing and curing sickness, for acquiring status in society, for imposing their will on others, for forcing the natural order to conform to their appetites, is so normal and so obvious that no argument is needed to prove its existence. I am not saying that all desires are equally justified or even excusable, nor am I denying their equal justification or reasonableness. I am simply pointing out that they are there and that they orient our behavior. I am not, moreover, saying that all men feel these and other desires with equal intensity. It is clear, for instance, that some men are more submissive than others, more willing to take whatever happens to them without rebellion, more quietistic than others. To justify the ways of God to man in the sense of accepting whatever hardship, whatever suffering, whatever disaster, whatever disappointment occurs to us is an ancient procedure in religious philosophy. Whether it springs from a feeling of incompetence which is congenital, I do not know, nor do I see any way of finding out. But I do know that just as some men are submissive, so others are rebellious. The rebels are those who refuse to accept things as they are, who deny that whatever is is right, who insist that there are no insoluble problems. It is from their ranks that the great artists arise.

When I use the adjective "great," I mean simply "inventive." [2] I mean the man who sees the opportunity to do something better than his predecessors have done it and works out a process for realizing his idea. Sometimes the better is merely the different, for in the eyes of some men to continue the habitual is evil. It is easy enough to tell such people that the ways of our fathers are the best ways. The fact that they are the ways of our fathers may in itself be enough to prove that they are undesirable, for it would be absurd to deny the efficacy of man's desire for novelty in changing the course of history. I shall have more to say of this below and here shall merely advance the argument that if a man finds the persistence of the past tiresome to the point of annoyance, he may set out to change it. The history of decoration in costume and architecture and even the invention of new forms of slang furnish plenty of examples to show that the innovations are not always in the direction of improvement, though some-times improvement consists in not doing what has always been done. Changes in architecture are not all made for increased efficiency; some are made simply because they are novel. To the lover of the new, that suffices to justify them; to the lover of the past, it is folly. Some languages, German for instance, have re-tained a primitive complexity of grammatical forms, whereas others, English and French, have discarded a large percentage of them as useless. No one really knows why this should have happened. But one could imagine some Englishman saying to himself, "Why change the ending of a word when a preposition can express the same meaning just as well? Why have three genders when one, or in a few cases two, will work?" No one ever did this, to be sure; the changes just evolved in the darkness of the unconscious. And if someone had done it, he could be answered, "The Germans seem able to conform to their complex grammar without any more trouble than the English find in their aphonetic spelling."

To look for the origins of very ancient human customs is as fruitless as to look for the origin of horses eating grass and dogs eating meat. There are certain organic obstacles perhaps which determine the diet of all the animals in a state of nature. There are accounts of carnivorous horses, to be sure, but as far as any-one knows they are by nature herbivorous.[3] As a matter of cold fact, we have no way of knowing whether everything has had an origin or not. For an origin implies a previous condition which was different from the condition which we actually discover. In view of the helplessness of human infants, it seems unwise to look for the origin of human societies; it is more likely that as soon as men appeared on earth they lived in groups, if only small ones. Again, we may find the origin of the human thumb in the hands of the great apes, but the great apes do not use their thumbs as we do; and as soon as genuine human beings are found, they seem to have thumbs. When you come upon an animal which you are willing to call a horse, you find that it is a grass eater. And when you find another which you are willing to call a beaver, you find that it builds a beaver dam. Dietary habits, as well as economy, are among the traits of animals and plants which differentiate them from others and they do this as much as anatomical traits do. So in the case of men, we have no evidence that there was ever a time when they lived entirely by what it was once customary to call instinct. The popularity of theories of evolution has led us all to assume that everything must have had a beginning at some determinable date and has progressed either toward greater complexity or toward greater simplicity. But this is an assumption. It may be true, for all any-one knows, that the primate from which *homo sapiens* evolved had no tools, no shelters, no fire, no social organization, no clothing, no magic, nothing which the earliest known men seem to have had. One can scarcely judge the culture of a man if all you have to go on is a lower jaw and a brain pan. When we come to the men who are admittedly men and who lived in the very early period of the Valley of the Vézère, we find evidence that they had the usual problems to solve, though they solved them in ways somewhat different from ours. It has often been pointed out that the Australian savage, who gathers his food where he can find it, goes about naked, and has no fixed habitation, is well-adjusted to a climate where there are extremes of heat and cold during twenty-four hours.[4] Clothing during the day would be unbearable because of the heat, though we should find it desirable if we were in their place during the night. But in view of the impossibility of finding enough food in one fixed spot and therefore the uselessness of houses, what would they do with the clothing in the daytime? These men have accepted their condition and have made no attempt to change it. They are a beautiful example of submission to the laws of nature. They have learned to withstand both heat and cold and seem none the worse for it. To be able to eat small lizards, mice, and grubs is a triumph over the poverty of the soil and the drought. Those of us who have been taught that a good adjustment, as it is called, is the human ideal might well take the Australian aborigines for our model. Far be it from me to proclaim any archetypal human ideal. An ideal, as far as I know, is always the product of some individual's dream or else of a social tradition. If we Americans lived in the Australian deserts, the ideal might be to live like the Australian natives. But we do not live in the desert.

Assuming that everything in human history had an origin, we still do not know why European man started out to live in shelters and caves, to use fire and make clothes. But we do know that if he was to live north of the Mediterranean, he would die if he went about naked and ate nothing but what he could pick up on the ground. For after all there happen to be four seasons in most of Europe and there also happen to be very few edible things on the ground after, let us say, November. Primitive man could of course have lain down and died. That would have been the way of submission. But the fact remains that he refused to lie down and die. Somehow or other he discovered how to make fire and to fashion bones and stones with which he could kill animals at a distance, animals which would have run away had he tried to catch them barehanded. The moment such things were dreamt of, the artistic spirit flared up. For it requires just as much skill to chip stone and make arrowheads, axes, and knives, as it does to pick up a brush and a tube of paint and draw a picture.[5] Skeptics might try it, if they need conviction. The manual skill of the Cro-Magnon men, as well as of their predecessors, was certainly very great, for skill has to be measured in terms of equipment. Even the killing of a bird or rabbit by throwing a stone demands the greatest dexterity. To change the shape of stones so that they will do the job better, to fasten them to the end of sticks and propel them through the air by releasing a tense cord, thus making it possible to kill your prey without frightening it away, is surely no mean exercise of the imagination. How was a man to bring down a bird in flight if he could not take pretty accurate aim and operate from a distance?

Along with the practical method of getting food, which seems to have been only part of man's problem, there seems also to have been a desire to extend his power over nature by magic. Here we enter into the most debatable of subjects and what I say about this can only be conjecture, for we have no documents to tell us what these people thought about anything. We have simply their artifacts to reveal what little an artifact can reveal. Symbols and symbolic gestures are retained long after people have forgotten their original significance, and we may be reading into what is left in the caves and shelters ideas which we think we would have had if we had made these things. With this as a caution, we can begin to speculate. We tend to assert that just as some nonliterate peoples of our own era utilize images as if they were the things represented in them, so did the cavemen. Thus if he painted pictures of edible animals on the walls of the caves with arrows flying at them or spears sticking into them or human beings chasing them or traps waiting for them to fall into, this was because he thought he could exercise his power over the real animals in this way. We all have read of tribes which make images of their enemies which they throw in the fire or stick with thorns, in the hope, it is said, of magically injuring the people for whom the images stand. This is probably accurate enough. We can all imagine the feelings we might have if we saw photographs of our mothers, wives, fathers, and husbands being mutilated. There are still people who in their hatred of a book throw it in the fire, as if that would harm the author of the book. We also know the respect which we pay to symbolic substitutes for our country (the flag), for our religious beliefs (the Cross, the Star of David, the Crescent), for our dead (their letters, locks of their hair, their personal possessions). Bibliophiles have been known to value association copies of books more than ordinary copies of them, manuscript copies of famous poems, and simple autographs. Rationally we know that the flag is only so much cloth, but we treat it with the care which we would take of a living being. Consequently it should be remembered that the paintings of animals in the caves may well have had magical significance and yet not have been put there with the express purpose of producing a successful hunt. They may have been pictures of gods chasing animals or even of animal-gods.[6] Anyone who has attended a number of commencement exercises year after year has heard prayers for wisdom and guidance in our pursuit of truth. Anyone reflecting on such exercises must have waked up to the fact that the university men of 1960 are not any wiser or better guided than those of 1900 or 1800. In short the prayers *in themselves* have been inefficacious. Yet no college president would think of opening the ceremonies without a prayer for the very things which he might know in his heart of hearts would not be granted.

One thing is certain: these paintings were not made to be looked at. First, they were in the dark recesses of the caves where no one lived and indeed how the artists illuminated the walls to see what they were doing is still not certain. Second, the paintings overlap and, in some of the older caves, one has some difficulty in following the outlines of the individual drawings. It hardly seems likely that an artist who wanted others to see his paintings would fail to erase those surfaces which he needed for his own work. Hence it cannot be denied at the outset that the purpose of these artists was not to provide purely visual delight for their fellows. It is in fact possible that their purpose lay in doing the painting and not in having any painting whatsoever as an end-product. If this seems strange, one has only to think of the art of improvising music: once it is played, it is gone for good. The act of painting, I am saying, might have been more important than the work of art. But whether we know precisely to what end they were painted or not, we may reasonably say that it was a magical or religious end. But this seems to have been the sort of purpose which guided artistry in every field, even in much later times. Music was surely religious or composed to accompany religious or magical dances and other forms of ritual. The Greek drama in its origin seems to have been written and performed in honor of some god, in Athens of Dionysos.[7] The

Iliad and the *Odyssey* may not have had overt religious reference, though religious symbolism was read into them well down into Christian times, but the poems of Hesiod surely did and so obviously did the Homeric hymns. Greek sculpture in its earliest form was made in honor of the various divinities and heroes. And to this day "The Song of Songs" is interpreted as a religious allegory, the bride being the Church and the groom being Christ. Such works of art are, of course, at least twenty millennia later than the paintings and carvings in the caves, but they are the earliest works of art in our tradition which have survived. And should one object and wish to push back to Egypt and Mesopotamia to find earlier works, one still finds the religious motivation pre-eminent.

As far as literature other than Greek is concerned, the same is true. The most obvious example is that anthology of Hebrew literature which has had more influence on our thought than any other, the Bible. Along with it, one may classify the various Egyptian and Indian scriptures. I shall not be so brash as to assert just what was the purpose of religious writing, but one can hardly doubt that it existed to change men's minds, to fortify their faith, to edify them, to point a moral, and to communicate with God. It was never "pure" literature written for entertainment. I am neither deprecating entertainment when I say this nor am I saying that one should not read religious writings for one's personal pleasure. That would be irrelevant to our argument. Indeed one of the theses of this study is the multivalence of works of art and of artistry. The fact that fireplaces were originally made for heating rooms does not imply that they are out of place in a modern apartment which has central heating, and that therefore one should not sit before an open fire and enjoy it. Again, the fact that the Book of Job was written as a theological poem need prevent no one from reading it as a human drama if one so wishes. There is enough beauty in the English version, and doubtless in the Hebrew too, to make such an attitude toward it reasonable.

But when one writes a book, carves a statue, paints a picture, dances a dance, or sings a song to praise God, to edify one's fellows, to point a moral, or even to purge people of pity and fear, one is doing something which one thinks is of some use. One is supplementing the artifices of nature by human invention. If one is cold, one can either sit in the sun—if the sun is shining —or build a fire. Unaided, nature provides the warmth of the sun; art adds the heat of the fire, thus supplying the deficiencies of nature. Similarly, if one is sick, one can submit to the aches and pains and fevers, relying on the *vis medicatrix naturae*, or one can consult a physician. If one's fields are drying up in the drought, one can patiently wait for rain to fall or pray for rain or irrigate them. The conflict between nature and art is the conflict between submission and rebellion, between ignorance and knowledge, between animality and humanity.[8] One is not forced to use one's intelligence to solve one's problems; one can always take a chance and see what happens. For sometimes by sheer accident things turn out well and, since we have a happy faculty of forgetting that which contradicts our wishes, we tend to magnify good luck as if it were a god.

My argument briefly, for there is no need to multiply examples, is that the arts originate in man's application of intelligence to the satisfaction of his needs. This does not involve any appraisal of the needs in question, for there is no necessity of proving that all arts are beneficial in any sense other than that they satisfy someone. Our desires are usually criticized by other people, not by ourselves, and are subjected by us to criticism only when they have turned out to be unsatisfactory for some reason or other. We then stand as outsiders looking into our souls. But in the first instance, any desire is self-justified by the simple fact of its existence. Yet we do learn that there are better and worse ways of reaching satisfaction, whatever the criterion of value may be. We then say that we have learned how to improve our technique. This is true even of those desires most intimately associated with our biological nature. There have been manuals, it should not be forgotten, both on the art of cooking and on the art of love. If these exercises are ranked lower in the scale of values than the arts of painting and of music, that is not because of their unimportance, but rather because of a tradition which rests upon contempt for whatever man shares with the beasts. It is a tradition which would prefer that man neither eat nor copulate, in which case the death-wish would become a program.[9] Painting too in its origin, if we are right about its origin, is a tool of superstition and the music of tom-toms and rattles no less so. And, as I hope we shall see, there are residues of magic in the most sophisticated arts.[10] But we can postpone all discussion of heights and depths for the time being if we are agreed that an art comes into being when intelligence is applied to practical problems.

The acceptance of this, however, means the acceptance of communication, fighting, building, swimming, and other day-by-day practices as arts. No art could be more complicated than that of communication; it seems simple only because we begin practicing it so soon after birth. The organization of speech, for instance, with all the rules of grammar and syntax, standardized pronunciation and polite vocabulary, is far from natural in the sense that any child can master it without teaching. When to speech is added writing, a relatively late acquisition of the human race, the difficulties are seriously increased. To speak and write a paragraph in English which makes sense, is clear, and conforms to customary usage is surely as hard as to compose a minuet, one of the more stilted forms of musical composition, or to draw a man in pencil. If this seems like an extravagant exaggeration, it is because all of us speak and write and only a few of us draw or compose music. Verbal communication has all the marks of the other arts and is in fact the most generally practiced. It has its rules, its rituals, its goodness and badness, its teachers, its critics, and one fails to see in what respect it differs from any other art. That it also has its practitioners who engage in it for its own sake and not really to communicate anything which requires communication is proved every day. And what has been said of it could be said of the other "lowly" arts. All one has to do to appreciate the seriousness with which we take any art, however high or low, is to listen to the people who practice it.

Good form in riding, in playing games, in social etiquette, in table manners, as Huizinga has shown in his *Homo Ludens*, is analogous to the rules which surround religious, academic, juristic ceremonies.[11] Whatever the origin of these rules, they have survived not because of their utility but because of their beauty. As soon as the aura of sanctity with which they are enveloped evaporates, obedience to these rules becomes absurd, old-fashioned, stilted, reactionary, according to the linguistic tastes of the critic. To paint a picture or compose a piece of music is not play in the sense that wrestling puppies or gurgling babies are playing, but it is play in the sense that it is behavior guided by formal rules which have lost whatever practical purpose they may once have had and are observed because they are felt to be good-in-themselves.

A second consequence of our point of view is that the distinction between the fine and applied arts becomes purely historical. All arts originate in utility, but that in no way implies that they disappear when their original utility is obsolete. On the contrary, a good case can be made for the thesis that an art becomes fine when it loses its utility. One can be fairly sure that the man who talks about "the Bible as literature" no longer believes in its divine authorship. One wonders, and I for one shall let it stop at wonderment, whether the priests who worry about the correctness of their liturgy have not also lost their faith, but that is a terrain upon which we shall engage in no skirmishes. To cite an example which will arouse less hostility, let us take the case of painting. The collector who buys a portrait of someone else's ancestor is surely not interested in preserving the memory of the person portrayed, any more than the epicure who gloats over a perfect *sauce Béarnaise* is eating to ward off starvation.

That instruments may be retained long after their original utility is gone is proved every day in our houses. Open fires, electric lamps in the form of vases which supplant the old kerosene lamps, windows which are neither needed for light nor air, such things are preserved not for their primordial usefulness but for their beauty. Architecture gives us the most obvious examples of this principle. Crenelations, drawbridges, loopholes, and other vestiges of mediaeval castles, all can be found in modern American college buildings where no one other than a band of rowdy sophomores would dream of using them as they were designed to be used. Wedding invitations engraved to look like handwriting, buttons which button nothing, dead languages which few can understand used in religious and academic ceremonies, all are retained as good-in-themselves, since it is admitted that they are good for nothing else. Utility must not be defined too narrowly nor in terms of historical priority, for things can change their purposes and purposes are not always crudely practical. On that we shall have something to say later. Here we are interested solely in the original purpose of the instrument. It will be granted, I think, that no one would write a wedding invitation by hand nor would he have one typewritten.[12]

The shift in value from utility to beauty goes hand in hand with other shifts in value to be discussed later, such as shifts from the serious to the comic in both painting and the drama, or from the serious to the picturesque or quaint, as in costume, manners, and architecture. The status of what it is now fashionable to call "values" is one of the most mutable things in human culture and its significance for a philosophy of art is of the highest. For the work of art in isolation from human beings has no discernible value whatsoever—animals, in spite of Pliny, are not affected by it—and once the human being is admitted to be one of the determinants, but only one, of the value of a work of art or artistry, then it must also be admitted that a given work of art may have a variety of values at one and the same time, though not of course in the same respect. For unless one is prepared to argue that all human beings are alike in their sensitivity to and appreciation of works of art, one must admit at least the possibility of one man's admiring one aspect of a picture or poem, or whatever the work of art may be, and another man another. Two people may admire another person but not admire the same traits in him. This is a commonplace. We cannot, with all the good will in the world, look at an African mask as an African would, or for that matter look at a statuette of dancing Siva as a Hindu would. Yet we can admire the beauty of such things, the artistic skill, the composition, or even the expression, to use an eighteenth-century term, whether we are members of the culture which produced them or not. In fact our not being members of the culture is a help toward giving us a perspective on them. If this were not true, we should not be able to appreciate Shakespeare or Chaucer or Dante, to say nothing of Vergil or Aeschylus or Homer. It is we who confer value on things. We value them and if no one values them, they have no value except in some metaphysical sense which we need not entertain seriously. To ask what is the value of that which no one values seems like asking what would be the color of ultraviolet rays if we could see them. For regardless of the metaphysical status of goodness, truth, and beauty, it is their place in human life which concerns us.

We have said that the arts arise through the satisfaction of human needs by intelligence. We have not said what human needs are, nor that the arts satisfy only the good ones, nor that the word "art" is a eulogistic term, nor that art always remains what it was in its origin. We are not prepared to deny the reality of time and change and hence will not minimize the implications of our being historical animals. To live in history is neither inevitably to grow better nor worse, but it is to change. The direction of change, insofar as human history is concerned, is in part determined by human beings: they create their institutions as the occasion demands according to their lights. But once a problem is solved, men will try to be guided by the solution, if they think it a good one, while other men, who think it a bad one, will either neglect its directives or oppose them. Their opposition or acceptance will be partly determined by intelligence, weighing and balancing, drawing possible results through thinking, and certainly as much by unconscious factors such as simple dislike of change or enthusiasm for it. The differences between human beings may be matters of degree, not of kind, but the extremes are polar opposites and there is no reconciling stupidity and wisdom, recalcitrancy and submissiveness. It is the tensions —and sometimes open conflicts—between people which make history and the number of ways in which people can oppose one another, though not infinite, is very great, so great that it is practically impossible to calculate the chances of total agreement about anything. Majority rule, it should be remembered, is hardly a consensus and the reason why we have to resort to majority rule is because there is no consensus possible. This applies not only to politics, but also to aesthetics. Disagreement about taste is not only something which has become incorporated into proverbs but is something which points to the contribution of the individual in giving value to works of art.

CHAPTER II

The Temporal Dimension

THAT MAN IS a historical animal is now generally admitted. But each man has his own individual history just as groups of men have theirs. This is about as self-evident as any opinion can be. But what is not self-evident at all is what is involved in being historical.

A ball which rolls from one side of a billiard table to another, a train which runs down a track and back again, the decomposition and recomposition of a chemical compound, all seem like reversible and repeatable events. Strictly speaking, they are not reversible, since the energy which is given off when the first act is played is never recovered to perform the second act.[1] But in any event, on the level of common sense uncorrected by theoretical analysis, the bolt which is turned to the right to lock a door can be turned back to the left to unlock it, and we have the same bolt and a reversal of its motion in both cases. But a fertilized ovum which grows in the womb, emerges as a baby at the end of nine months, grows into a man, decays into senility and finally dies, is a really and obviously irreversible process and also a unique one. Though the number of possible combinations of genes is finite, it is so large that we can say that the same individual never recurs and also that no one person can ever live the life of another, no matter how similar the two persons may be and no matter how similar their experiences through life. It has been pointed out by others that even identical twins do not have the same experiences, though their genes are the same, for one twin has the experience of the other and the other of the one.[2] Furthermore, the very dates at which individual people and events occur may make a profound difference in their lives, since the total environment in which a man lives is itself always changing. The mere fact of a steadily increasing population presents problems which have not arisen before and to live in a large crowded city is not identical with living, though with similar people, in a small town. Hence we may say that the first differentia of historical beings is that they are all individuals and that they live irreversible lives.

This being so, one can see why the things they make, the problems they perceive, the way they try to solve these problems, are in part a function of their individuality. This is a trait which they share with the higher animals, no two dogs or horses being quite the same in their behavior, however much they may resemble each other. There is no very good way of discovering how individual babies are, though the fact that each baby has what is called a personality of his own is generally granted, at least by his mother. The uniformity of infantile behavior may well be an illusion caused by our crude methods of testing, but even in the tests which have been given to babies they show a certain range of speed in reacting, of perspicuity of perception, and of apparent liking and disliking. Be that as it may, it does not take more than a year or two for each child to show his character, and this is so obvious that examples seem unnecessary. When the child goes to school, his adjustment to others, his aggressiveness, his aptitude for learning the things which are supposed to be essential, his docility, his agreeableness, his ease in making friends, and a score of other traits vary, as all parents and teachers know only too well. And though education is a device for producing uniformity in men and women, it has always failed to do so. Even the doodles of adults vary widely, some being confined in space, others sprawling all over the page; some being tight geometrical forms indefinitely repeated, others rambling zoomorphs; some being faces, others animals; some flowers and trees, others abstract designs. Doodles are made under no direction from without and, though of course they are not uncaused, their causes lie in the unconscious or the preconscious of the individual. In whatever it is that makes babies babies, they are obviously identical. In their response to loud noises, they are highly similar, as in their fear of being dropped. But since a loud cry is a signal for the mother to cuddle the child in her arms, who knows whether a child is not crying in the hope of the cuddling which will follow?

When an adult is asked to draw from a model and has been taught the proper method of doing so, even then no two drawings will be more than superficially alike. Each will have its style, and the hardest thing in the world is to make a person discard his style and adopt another's. This comes out clearly in speech. Speech is the most highly standardized form of expression. We have it drummed into us from babyhood on that there is a correct pronunciation, a correct intonation, a correct vocabulary, and a correct syntax. But that does not prevent each individual from having his own manner of speaking, his own accent, intonation, choice of words, degree of respect for the rules, however much he may try to conform to general practice. The ability to mimic another's voice is very rare, so rare that it is always regarded as something almost impossible. We can usually recognize a person whom we know by his voice even though it comes over the telephone and we do not see his face, and blind people have what seems to those who see an uncanny ability to recognize from speech alone one who is entering a room where they happen to be. Similar remarks could be made about handwriting and even typing, about manners of walking and standing, to say nothing of subtler things such as conversational style.

Individuality varies from man to man, it goes without saying. The spectrum of self-assertion runs from almost complete obliteration of personality to its violent and fierce obtrusion. It runs parallel to the spectrum of submission and rebellion. In the domain of the arts there are artists who are faithful to the rules and who apparently demand nothing better than to carry on the traditions of a school, a movement, or a master. This is why a historian of art can spot the general temporal location of a painting whose author is unknown, saying that it is Florentine *cinquecento* or nineteenth-century English or fifth-century B.C. Greek. He may not know who painted it, but he does know when and in what style it was painted. It is also why unscrupulous dealers can palm off an anonymous painting as the work of Botticelli or Luini or Vlaminck, artists who had a clear and easily recognizable style of their own and who also established or reinforced a fashion of painting. But there is no a priori certainty that a given artist will paint in the same way throughout his life, especially if he has a long life. As a matter of fact even when a painter dies young, witness Raphael, he may begin as the docile pupil of someone else, and usually does, since very few painters are entirely self-taught, and then will break away for himself and assert his own style. Early Raphaels look like Peruginos; later ones look unmistakably like Raphaels. And when one comes to a painter like Ingres who makes a determined effort to paint like an earlier painter, he soon begins to paint like himself. Ingres had an almost religious devotion to Raphael, but no one with an eye that can see would attribute even an early Ingres to his Italian master. It is true, of course, that the costumes in the paintings of the two men are quite different, but one has only to compare the Madonnas in the "Sistine Madonna" and in the imitation of it which appears in Ingres' "Vow of Louis XIII" to see how impossible it is for one man to absorb the style of another. Similar remarks would be true of composers and poets. Even when it was fashionable to write in heroic couplets, no one would have confused Pope with Akenside. If this is obvious, so much the better.

Not only are individual artists merely more or less like others, but periods and ages are composed of diverse and often conflicting purposes. Not everyone living in the first part of the nineteenth century was Romantic and Professor Lovejoy has shown that the very word "romantic" was so ambiguous that it has lost all discriminatory power.[3] Not everyone living in England from 1832 to 1900 was Victorian. Not everyone living today is Modern. We sometimes think that the diversity of schools and styles which characterizes our own time and which leads to the charge that we are confused and undisciplined is a peculiarity of the middle twentieth century. The confusion, as it is called, has always existed as far as the evidence goes, and in every historical period in the Occident there have been a variety of artistic and ideological tendencies, some of which we can find only in lost or suppressed works.[4] It is of course true that there have been times when artists were forced to be more submissive than was necessary at other times. For until the artist ceased to be an artisan, producing his works under orders which were often very detailed, he had to conform to certain rules or perish. No one could deny that the restrictions on religious painting issued at the last session of the Council of Trent had considerable influence.[5] But no one could deny either that the manner of artists remained an expression of their individualities. We, to be sure, or at least some of us, have put a high price on self-expression in the sense of self-assertion. But we often forget that to some people resignation, submission, docility is a way of achieving happiness. This has been granted in religious matters when men have said that salvation lay in complete submission to God, a program which in its extreme form was Quietism, a doctrine which had to be condemned by the Church.[6] It had to be condemned because it utterly nullified the individual's power of making decisions in moral as well as in aesthetic matters. One forgets that it takes as much will power for some persons to deny themselves as it does for others to assert themselves. A saint may appear to have no will of his own, but he has to have enough to refuse to lay out his own path and to follow that prescribed by higher authority. The saint may be rebellious in social or political affairs when he feels that there is a conflict between them and the will of God. Many a saint, both in the Orient as well as in the West, has had to deny the claims of his family to satisfy those which he believes to be divine. This was as true of Sakyamuni as of Saint Francis. In art one finds similar situations, especially since the end of the eighteenth century, when the individual self began to be exalted to a position above all authority, whether that of the Church, of the State, of the Family, or of other individuals.

This being so, one must think of history as a twisted rope of many little histories, histories of individuals, families, social groups, states, and larger conglomerates. One hesitates to use the word "growth" to describe this process, for it has taken on in some quarters a eulogistic connotation which we see no need to attribute to it. To us it indicates merely the following: a history, whether of an individual or a group, which is not simply a repetition of the past for, though there is a good bit of humdrum recurrence in any life, the past is carried along into the future in memory and tradition and, as it is carried along, it influences the present. It influences it by teaching us to shun certain things or to seek them; it becomes invested with an emotional cloak which may be agreeable or unpleasant, thus leading us sometimes to refuse to see what is physically before us or to turn it into a symbol of something which is very precious. We may say that the person whom we met yesterday is the same person whom we are seeing today, but it is that person covered with the pleasantness or disagreeableness of what we felt to be his character. And the same is true of every experience which we naïvely say is being repeated. In the nature of things no experience can be ever really repeated, for the simple reason that as an experience, as something experienced, it is dated and localized and each time we experience it again, it perforce takes on new color. We are not wearing crystal clear glasses through which we see the facts "as they are," i.e., as they would be if we were not there to see them, as they would be if they were utterly detached from all human interest. For scientific purposes we have invented a technique by means of which both the personal and the human equation can be disregarded. But in moral and aesthetic affairs this would be absurd. It would turn paintings to oil and pigment, sculpture to stone, poetry to sounds. I do not mean by this that there are simply individual differences in human perception, in the acuity of vision, for instance. I mean that a good part of perception is projected into what we perceive because of expectation, disliking and liking, admiration, fear, lust, horror, and all the other factors that are sometimes called our feelings.[7]

But in the second place, even when we speak of the repetition of the past, our accumulated experience naturally increases in bulk and, as it does so, the problem arises, if only on the unconscious level, of harmonizing the various increments. We soon become aware that there is a conflict within us, a conflict not only between what we like and dislike, but also between what we feel we ought to like and dislike. The process of growing, even in plants, is partly, though far from wholly, an interaction between what has happened so far and what is presented now. The seed begins to develop under what are called favorable conditions— favorable conditions being those under which it will develop normally, i.e., as most other seeds of its species develop—and then comes the day without water, without sunshine, or when the food supply takes a turn for the worse, when an animal steps upon it or a caterpillar begins to eat its leaves or a child picks it off near the roots. The plant can then die or struggle. There is as much drama in the life of a plant as in that of a human being, though the *agon* is stimulated by somewhat different causes, and the notion which certain Germans, such as Herder, had or seemed to have, that plants just "grow from within" is about as erroneous as any general idea can be. If what we say is true, then there is no repetition in growth except in the very abstract sense that each growing thing starts as a fertilized egg, matures, and dies. In short, growth is growth. New experiences —or it might be better to say new problems—are never identical with old ones, but simply resemble them more or less. We can and do divest them of their novelty in order to make them more similar than they are in first hand experience, for in this way we create a situation in which our intellects can operate more freely. We cannot handle novelty except by guesswork. We clearly cannot prepare ourselves for that which we have never experienced, however much we may preach the acceptance of everything with resignation. And so we purge the new of its novelty and maintain that we are merely repeating what we have already been through. But unfortunately it is the novelty of the new which frustrates us. And we wonder why. A few grains of salt in a cup of coffee may be thought of as trivial, insignificant, not worth bothering about. But who wants to drink it? One might as well say that since in every war people are killed, one form of warfare is the same as another. But that would be madness.

The process of intellectual purification is analogous to one aspect of the empirical method in the sciences. The scientist has a technique of simplifying the heterogeneity of raw experience and what he is really dealing with are materials purified for laboratory purposes. He can talk about molecules and atoms as if they fall into sharply defined classes, all of whose members are exactly alike. For Dalton an atom was only an elementary bit of matter with permanent weight, combining with other elementary bits of matter according to constant proportions. That was all he was interested in. He could not annihilate the other properties of atoms and had no interest in doing so. For if a man is working with pencil and paper, he thinks of things as if they were mathematical beings, and if he is in a laboratory, he sets up conditions which will eliminate diversity. He can concentrate his attention on one or two peculiarities of his subject matter and forget all the rest. The biologist can talk about *The Rose, The Cactus, The Scorpion, The Frog*—and even of *Homo sapiens*—though he is usually less general in his interests, and it goes without saying that he would give scientific names to his plants and animals as if each class were homogeneous. Unless he happens to be interested in individual differences, he will disregard them, and nowadays he can substitute the statistical norm for the perfect specimen. Most of us, however, are not scientists, but by the use of common nouns we act as if the scientific attitude were the normal everyday attitude. If the teacher we meet today in school is not the same teacher as the one we met yesterday, why is he called by the same name? If the dog with which we romped yesterday is not the same as the dog with which we are playing today, why call it a dog? Common nouns are supposed to name that which retains its identity through time and indeed the things they name do so as far as that is possible. One cannot think in proper nouns, for thought is always synthetic to begin with, analysis coming later. We are in search of identities and, that being our passion, we overlook diversity. If the child, as Aristotle says, calls all men "Father," that is because he is absorbed in what makes his father his father, and he projects pathetically enough those characters on other men. In fact, the tossing out of common nouns upon a world which is so bewilderingly various is a symptom of our hopes, not the automatic issue of our observations. We want to find *The Rose* and *The Frog* and we are confronted only with roses and frogs. We have learned through reading or oral instruction how to deal with *The Rose* and we expect to apply what we have learned to all roses. So the child with his pet dog may think that all dogs are identical with his dog and he learns, often to his sorrow, that they are not. Growth then, it seems, is the absorption of difference and what Professor Loewenberg has called the fallacy of generification [8] is our guide to what we hope for. It is a good guide in those fields over which we have complete mastery, where we can manipulate our data as we will, but it leads to mystification as often as to enlightenment when we happen to be people whose eyesight is sharp and whose sensitivity to the problematic is keen. Science is an art as much as painting or any of the other traditionally recognized arts, and its methods become an ideal as do those of poetry or architecture. The truth which it sometimes obtains is not a photographic representation of experience, but an organization of experience through intellectual ceremonies.

One of the great aids to forming a simple and stable world is habit. Any act which the human frame can accomplish may become habitual, whether it is useful or harmful. Acts which are harmful even on the biological level can, as we all know from having known alcoholics and rakes, become habitual, just as healthful ones can. There is no sense in urging a return to "the natural" or to the "instinctive" as a cure for civilization, for the obvious reason that it is human nature with which we have to deal and not the geological landscape. It is just as human to overindulge our appetites as to deny them their satisfactions. The Seven Deadly Sins did not enter the world with Christianity. The "noble savage" is as much given to sexual excesses as civilized men, to drunkenness, to the taking of drugs, as well as to all forms of self-discipline and self-torture. To this very day there are masses of people who in the name of God's command procreate children whom they cannot feed and others who live a life of extreme mortification in order not to do so. The Westerner is likely to be horrified when he sees the ascetics of India, almost naked, their hair growing wildly and matted, their muscles atrophied. He is likely to be equally horrified when he is accosted by a hundred beggars in the streets of Calcutta who clearly are near starvation and yet who permit sacred cows and monkeys to eat the food which they might be eating themselves. But the annals of Christianity provide an equal number of ascetics, men who beg for their food, who practice celibacy, who deny their wills, and who live by the decisions of their superiors. One can be horrified at all this and it is difficult, if possible, not to be horrified. But at the same time, given the religious beliefs of such people, the horror becomes unreasonable. I do not know whether the religious beliefs are the fruit of a desire for self-mortification or the self-mortification the fruit of the religious beliefs. But in any event the tradition is well-established and the men who approve of it find it just as reasonable as a life of self-indulgence, if not more so. Nothing would seem to be more natural than copulation, and yet most of us have a certain shame about it, perform it in secret, and dislike talking about it.[9] Tradition and habit have no roots in naturalness nor are they clues to goodness.

Once a habit is established, it drops out of consciousness and is carried out automatically. Few of us could tell anyone else how we manage to get the food on the end of our forks into our mouths without jabbing our cheeks or putting out an eye, how we manage to run up and down stairs without looking where we put our feet, how we persuade our fingers to touch the piano keys which our eyes tell us are indicated by the little black marks on a page of print. Such acts seem automatic, though in each case we know that they had to be learned and sometimes painfully and slowly. But the same holds good of speech. We never stop to think when speaking of where to put our tongue, of the rules of grammar, pronunciation, syntax, emphasis: we just speak. We write by hand as if writing were the most natural thing in the world, once we have learned. But similarly the artist paints, sings, dances, writes as if his artistry was second nature. If asked, he is likely to say, if he is truthful, that "the numbers came." But if he is given to correction and revision, he wakes up to the weakness of what others would call inspiration.

But even more interesting than this is the compulsive force which a habit takes on once it is acquired. This is most noticeable in bad habits. To break a bad habit requires not only the will to break it but the ability to break it. The most savage instances of this are alcoholism and addiction to drugs. The victim feels as if he were in the hands of a power greater than himself which forces him to drink or to take drugs. But the same is true of good habits. Once they have been instilled in a child he feels himself guilty when he has not followed their promptings. This sort of thing can be carried to excess too, as we see in clinical cases of cleanliness, excessive piety, excessive devotion to parents and children, excessive nicety of speech. The adjectives "extreme" and "excessive" would only be used by people who do not share or approve of the habits in question. Can devotion to parents and children or, for that matter, to God, ever be too great? Far be it from us to measure the limits of virtue, but zeal has always been recognized by the temperate as verging on morbidity. Even in the religious orders the superiors have to keep an eye on those members who carry their devotion "too far." But the victim of zeal, like the victim of drugs, feels himself impelled to make any sacrifice for the furtherance of his ideal.

Good habits are usually instilled in one through education in the broader sense of that term, the sense which classifies parents, brothers and sisters, and companions as teachers. The child is no sooner born than he is subjected to a routine which is none of his choosing—how could it be?—and no act, however intimately associated with his bodily life, is allowed to be carried out as he might wish if permitted to. A human child, unlike animal children, is helpless at birth and close to helplessness for some years after birth. If he is rebellious, he is forced into submission, not necessarily by corporal punishment, but by deprivation of privileges or by other ingenious means which his elders have devised to push him into conformity. I am not saying that the results are bad or even that the means used are bad. Nevertheless it would be foolish not to recognize that his pattern of living is not of his own designing. He is settled into a way of life which, once it becomes habitual, becomes also right. The rules of his parents and family and later of his social group, school, and church, are the correct rules and there must be no argument about their correctness. People who write books on ethics are inclined to elevate the customs of the tribe into the laws of a supernatural community. We know enough now to realize that the members of societies far different from our own feel as compelled to conform to the rules of their tribe as we do to those of ours. If all these conflicting rules do come from Heaven, one must conclude that Heaven either has not yet made up its mind which set of rules should become really universal or else has decided that morals must vary from place to place as they have obviously varied from time to time.

It cannot be denied that insofar as one is human, one has certain needs and that any society must permit them to be satisfied. We are informed by ethnologists that all societies have regulations about procreation, food, disposal of the dead, rearing of children, and communication.[10] But that is far from saying anything more than that every society feels compelled to regulate the satisfaction of all elemental desires. It does not mean that any two societies are somehow or other bound to draw up the same regulations. An ethnologist, to be sure, will give the name used in his own society to the acts regulated by the society in which he is interested. But such words as "family," "sibling," "marriage," "property," mean certain things in Western society and their meaning is almost definite. "Almost," since adopted children are considered to be members of a family just as biological children are and illegitimate biological children are not considered to be members of their half-brothers' family. The property of a corporation is not precisely what the property of an individual is. But these qualifications aside, the terms are univalent. We know what we mean by such a term as "incest," though whether one can commit incest with one's step-father or an adopted sister or brother, I do not know. Since incest-taboos seem to be one of those details which some ethnologists say are universal, if a society forbids a man to marry his mother's sister but allows him to marry his father's sister or even his own, is this an incest-taboo in our sense of the word? There have been cases in the Occident where a girl's uncle has married her and no law was violated. Cousins of varying degrees have been permitted to marry at least by statute, if not by canon law. We rationalize our incest-taboos by invoking the awful sequelae of inbreeding. But though the taboo if obeyed will indeed prevent inbreeding, and though the partners in the act may practice contraception and thus avoid any kind of breeding, we know perfectly well that contraception does not remove the sin of incest and that the people who set up the taboos had no ideas of Mendel's law. I imagine that marriage with one's father's sister, if she were young enough, would not seem so repulsive to us as marriage with one's own sister, nor does it seem any more horrible than marriage with one's mother's sister. The more complex rules of exogamy, if the ethnologists report them correctly, could also be called incest-taboos, if one were willing to extend the term a bit further. And before one is through with inflating the denotation of the word, almost any regulation of marriage or copulation will be called an incest-taboo.

There is probably no rule, whether ethical or aesthetic, which has not been violated by people who wished to violate it. But for the time being we are interested only in those people who feel compelled to submit to tradition or to social habit. My point is simply that men can be educated into observing any rule, however absurd it may seem to outsiders, and into feeling guilty if they fail to. To eat meat on Friday or pork at any time seems to be as revolting to some Catholics and Jews respectively as to lie or to steal. Such people will invoke conscience or some analogous faculty to justify their repulsion. It is only in very few places, such as England, where they will frankly say, when questioned, that they believe in doing what has always been done. Nor will these happy few see any point in pushing their investigations further. They are of course right. The taboos of any society are probably a crystallization of tradition and no one knows any longer, regardless of what he may claim to know, either their origin or their justification. We call that right which has always been called right and we call that wrong which has always been called wrong and we use the word "always" to mean "as far as we know." After all, even the Ten Commandments were not always known; the Bible gives us the circumstances of their issuance and the approximate date, *anno mundi*, of their deliverance. They were safe-guarded not only by punishment administered by the State but also by punishment from God. According to the Old Testament, the people to whom they were revealed were not excessively zealous in obeying them and this in spite of repeated disasters visited upon them by God because of their disobedience. But nevertheless, though few of us who have been brought up under their sway can honestly say that we have always been faithful to them, most of us can honestly say that we have felt guilty when we have disobeyed them. This is so whether we accept the theology of the people to whom they were first revealed or not.

It is indeed noticeable that even in those textbooks of ethics which aim at being nontheological, the burden is usually the justification of the traditional rules of good behavior. It is only the exceptional philosopher, someone like Nietzsche, who will make a thoroughgoing re-examination of our values. The philosopher may not be either a religious Jew or a Christian. He may pride himself on his freedom of thought. He may insist that he is trying to demonstrate his system of ethics on purely rational principles. But by the end of the book he has come out for the same virtues which all of us have always thought were virtues. He is strong for truthfulness, courage, loyalty, respect for the property of others, sexual restraint, if not chastity, and so on and on and on. He seldom discovers that theft and adultery and lying are admirable practices, that undetected homicide is laudable, that cowardice in the face of the enemy should be drummed into every soldier's heart. In short, he has accepted a certain set of values as obviously good and he writes his book to give his readers and, one suspects, himself reasons for believing in them. The same remarks could be made about aesthetics. I have yet to come upon a book in that field which rates comedy higher than tragedy, justifies pornography, and sets out to prove that ballades and rondeaux are nobler than iambic pentameter blank verse.

The point is that our education, like all education, is the acquisition of habits, habits of thinking, feeling, and perceiving. We do not form these habits by ourselves; they are given to us. Regardless of their source, once they are formed they are as compulsive as any other habits, and out of their performance will emerge the feeling of their intrinsic rightness. Since we are more interested in this study in art than in morals, let us take our exam-

ples from art. Why is it that in very early—one hesitates to say
primitive—painting the figures are usually in profile? Why is
Egyptian and early Greek sculpture usually frontal? Why did
Hellenistic sculptors develop contraposto and stick to it? Why did
mediaeval painters shift the visual point of view with each object
depicted in a single painting? Why did post-Renaissance painting
up to our own times cling to illusionism and linear perspective?
Why do most contemporary painters go in for abstract, nonfigurative, and action painting? Why is classical music always composed
in units of four bars? Why did most composers use the four voices
of bass, tenor, alto, and soprano, instead of three voices or five?
Why did architects for generations follow what they believed to
be the rules of Vitruvius? Dozens of such questions, each of which
indicates a custom which was taught as intrinsically right, based
upon some laws of nature, beyond the touch of individual caprice,
occur to one. Schopenhauer actually believed so strongly in the
essentiality of four voices in music that he devoted page after page
to showing that each was an expression of the will of one of the
natural kingdoms.[11] Every such rule has been broken and by being
broken has liberated some art from its guidance. None of them
is a rule of nature but of convention, to use the old Greek antithesis. But the rules of convention are almost as binding as those of
nature. They may arouse resentment in the hearts of recalcitrants
and they can be broken, whereas a genuine rule of nature cannot
be violated. For it is a description of what people actually do "on
the whole."

Our feeling that the rule establishes the right also creates values.
If I say "creates," I mean that no further source of value need be
sought. For goodness and beauty, to cite merely the moral and
aesthetic values, are little more than marks on paper if they are
not part and parcel of our feelings. The influence of these marks
may be widespread and indeed may sometimes determine our
feelings. But more often we give notional assent to what we read
and yet find it hard, if possible, to conform to it in our behavior.[12]
We read a critical essay and discover that the author admires

greatly some painter whom we dislike—let us say, Burne-Jones. Two typical situations then occur. First, if the author is someone whose opinions we prize, Clive Bell or Sir Herbert Read, we give a gasp of surprise and then switch our attention to what may possibly be the good points in Burne-Jones. For, we say to ourselves, neither of these men would praise Burne-Jones just to be naughty; they must be doing it out of a change of heart; they must have discovered something in this no longer fashionable painter which is more important aesthetically than we had realized. Can it be, for instance, that his ineptitude as a draftsman makes him resemble some of our contemporaries whose distortions are willful? Can it be that his limp and elongated anatomies are a continuation of that tradition established by Blake, the drawing of muscles without bones? We need not extend this series of hypotheses and shall stop here, for such questions are good enough samples of the kind of attitude which might be expressed by a reader such as we have imagined. But if on the other hand the critic were one, like the late Royal Cortissoz, given to ridiculing and dispraising all artists since, let us say, Manet, his praise of Burne-Jones would leave us either cold or contemptuous. We should see that his opinions were in line with the old school of criticism and we should either toss the essay aside with a sneer or wonder how in the world anyone could be such a survival from the cultural Dark Ages. In brief the probability is that we transfer our affection and admiration for a person to that which he loves and admires. But what is a value except the object of affection and admiration? What is the beautiful except that which someone feels to be beautiful, whether he can give any reasons for his feelings or not? [13]

The customary answer to this is that one can be mistaken about the values, that we may feel something to be beautiful which really is not beautiful, just as we may believe something to be good and yet discover that it is evil.

But, is there any such thing as a value which is not attached to something valued? This would seem like an absurd question were it not for a spurious Platonism which maintains that adjectives can be separated from that which they qualify and set up as independent beings. Thus not only truth, goodness, and beauty can be, it is said, considered in themselves apart from all true sentences, good acts, and beautiful objects, but presumably redness, roundness, awkwardness, grace, the grotesque, the tragic, and the comic and all other such qualities can be contemplated in themselves without any regard for what might be called their incorporation. This curious idea derives historically from Plato's *Symposium* where in the famous speech of Diotima, as reported by Socrates, a scale of beauty is outlined running from beautiful bodies to absolute beauty-in-itself. In our own times this notion has been expanded into a philosophical technique known as Phenomenology. It would be out of place here to enter into a polemic concerning the merits of this philosophic technique, but there are a few remarks which might be made by way of indicating our own point of view.

It is clear that if we call two things by the same name, they have something in common and that we can talk about that common property as if it existed by itself, detached from the objects in which we first became acquainted with it. If two pictures are landscapes or still lifes or portraits, we are not forced to discuss their dimensions or their dates or their place in the history of art when talking about them. Each genre will have some degree of homogeneity and we can talk about that. This is indisputable. So if we see two objects which are circular or red or heavy, we can talk about their shape or color or weight without bringing into the conversation their origin or their cost or any other of their properties. But first, how far up the ladder of abstraction is it profitable to ascend? And second, are not some of the characteristics of an object modified by their association with others, such as the color by the shape, the distance from one's eye, the presence of other colors nearby? Third, in aesthetics are we more concerned with what a work of art has in common with other works of art or with what differentiates it from all others? Fourth, is a work of art to be seen, heard, felt, in short, experienced, or simply talked about? Is a verbal description of a painting a satisfactory substitute for the painting itself? Would a plaster model of the Cathedral of Chartres be as good an object of study as the Cathedral itself? [14] Can we substitute the score of a musical composition for hearing the composition?

No one will deny that all pictures as pictures have a common property; otherwise we should not call them pictures, and so with all musical compositions, poems, buildings, and other works of art. In fact, all physical objects have something in common: that which makes them physical objects. But the chemist who is talking about carbon compounds and their peculiarities will find it a waste of time to discuss their size as they are found in trees and bushes and animals and minerals. The appearance of pure carbon in engagement rings will scarcely occupy his attention as a chemist and the cost of carbon as a fuel and its possible displacement by solar heat will never enter into his professional conversation. For the sentences found in a scientific treatise are answers to questions which have been put either by the man who framed the sentences or by someone else whom he believed to be an authority. Now I am not saying that there is any a priori way of determining what is relevant and what irrelevant to those sheafs of answers known as a science or a subject. But we do know practically that the cost of a diamond is irrelevant to the amount of carbon in a gram of sugar. Similarly the person who has put to himself certain questions about the arts will presumably know what kind of answers he wants. If he is interested in iconography, he will not at one and the same time believe that economic questions are important, whereas religious questions might be, and if he were interested in the history of taste, the economic question might be. A Christian will see nothing peculiar in the presence of a dove flying toward the Virgin Mary in pictures of the Annunciation, whereas a Buddhist who will accept the presence of an elephant serving a function similar to that of the dove may express some amazement at such a progenitor of the Savior.[15] If he is interested in what used to be called composition, he will not see the necessity of entering into details of iconography. Anyone can see for himself at what point classification becomes too abstract to provide an answer to his problem, if he understands precisely what his problem is. But this must not be taken to mean that no two questions can arise on the same level of generality. It must surely be evident that if one is interested in what all plays, called by their authors or by critics "tragedies," have in common, one can find out only by an actual survey of all such plays. But if one is interested in whether Shylock was a funny or a pathetic figure, the answer will not be found by first collecting all the plays in which a Jewish money-lender appears.

Second, just as a dove in an "Annunciation" will have a symbolic meaning which it would not have in a Chinese still-life of doves and peonies, or a Dutch genre painting, so many another characteristic of a picture will vary with the details associated with it. As in music a G on the piano may be either the dominant of the key of C or the tonic of the key of G, so a given spot of color may have been put where it is to balance another spot of a complementary color put somewhere else, and at the same time it may pull the eye toward itself because of its brightness, thus preventing the eye, for instance, from moving out of the frame into external space. The little babies which float overhead in some of the erotic eighteenth-century paintings, look like the *putti* of religious paintings of approximately the same period, but they are not the same at all. The false pediments which one sometimes sees over windows are not cross sections of hip-roofs nor does anyone think they are. Again, if Mozart in his *Jupiter Symphony* used the same theme as he used in the *Credo* of one of his Masses, is one expected to hear the *Credo* in the Symphony or to hear the third movement of the Symphony in the Mass or neither one nor the other? If the elements of a work of art can shift their significance, it makes little sense to analyze them out of the works in question and set up classes of colors, forms, symbols, and the like.

Third, no one has the power to dictate to others what should interest him in a work of art and I shall not be so presumptuous as to do so. But at the same time it seems reasonable that when we are reading or seeing a play, let us say *Hamlet*, we should not be asked to see in it what it has in common with other versions of the same story—most of which we have not read—nor what it has in common with other tragedies of the Elizabethan period, the whole of English drama, nor with all tragedies, Greek, Latin, French, German, Spanish, and Italian. For such a demand could not be satisfied by most of us anyway. The few historians of the drama who can see in a play echoes of previous plays and anticipations of still others have a legitimate interest and can often make comments on a play which are enlightening to the rest of us. Thus it is absurd to expect the mass of even intelligent readers to give up their enjoyment of a drama because they do not have the technical historical knowledge which a few scholars possess. The hundreds of playgoers who have seen and been deeply stirred by *Hamlet* may have found things in it which some scholars would find illegitimate, but nevertheless they are the kind of people for whom the play was written and to whom actors have addressed themselves. If such people were to see a series of tragedies which so closely resembled one another that the resemblance was noticeable, they would protest against their boredom or suffer meekly in silence. And if what is wanted in works of art is their resemblance to other works of art, why bother to look at more than one painting which for some reason or other is taken as typical of the class in general?

Fourth, as *pulcher* in Latin meant both beautiful and good, so did the Greek, *kalos*. It could be used of moral virtue as well as of visual beauty. It could be translated "admirable," "elegant," "fine," with no necessary reference to perceptual beauty. Because of this Diotima's scale of beauty was reasonable in Greek, as it is in English too, when a person reading it is willing to accept the slight shifts in meaning appearing in it. One can admire a beautiful body, a beautiful scientific demonstration, a beautiful act of courtesy, a beautiful character without assuming that one means the same thing by "beautiful" all the way through. If we translated the Greek by the word "admirable" there would be no problem whatsoever, for though one may admire a body for its visual features and a mathematical demonstration for elegance and a moral character for its virtue, what is common to them all is that they are all admired, even if for different reasons.

The truth of the matter probably is that we want a nice balance between originality and conformity to a traditional pattern, between the common and the unusual. If the work of art is sufficiently different from all others, one's reaction to it is bewilderment or downright anger, depending on one's temperament. Thus the originality of Gertrude Stein or of the Joyce of *Finnegans Wake*, of Cubist and Surrealist painting, of the music of the later Schönberg, when they were first encountered proved to be upsetting to many people, not to say insane. But in general there is little danger of any work of art becoming too original. For if the work is a painting, it will have to be on a more or less flat surface and in colored or black and white patches. This will already give it a certain resemblance to other paintings. The trouble is that it will also give the people who look at it the feeling that they can apply to it the same criteria that they would apply to the paintings with which they are familiar. This often leads to condemnation, for we frequently blame events for not fulfilling our expectations. In the long run most of us have to look for something in order to see anything. And for most of us also habit is our guide. Works of art—and this seems to be true especially of music and painting— are asked to stabilize a world of the familiar. Whatever the problems of the nonartistic world, they will never appear in the world of art and we shall feel secure and comfortable in it. We are then assured that time and change, the two great enemies of security and comfort, have been baffled. But here, as everywhere else, people differ in their tolerance of novelty. Probably every degree of tolerance could be illustrated, if one could make a statistical study of such matters. On one extreme would be found the "instinctive" lover of novelty, originality, or eccentricity; on the other the equally instinctive lover of tradition, of conformity, of normality.

In between would be the rest of us, clustered here and there at various points on the curve of distribution. This must not be taken to mean that what I have called the instinctive lovers of the novel love everything novel. A person may love pictorial novelty and hate musical novelty. Gertrude Stein was reported to me to have said that the English writer whom she most admired was Goldsmith, and I once knew a collector of Matisse who thought Schubert's *Unfinished Symphony* the greatest of musical compositions. But for that matter Cézanne admired Meissonier and Van Gogh copied Millet.

Fifth, most people interested in this subject would grant that, whatever else the aesthetic experience may be, it is a direct acquaintance with works of art, not a secondhand acquaintance with them through reading. Our reading will certainly influence our direct experience, will help determine what we shall observe in a work of art, and indirectly will help determine how we shall feel about it. Similarly, if we are honest, our experience of a work of art may be expected to influence what we shall think about it and of course what we shall think of other people's criticism of it. If this is granted, then it cannot be assumed that any two people taken at random will have the same experience and consequently feel and think identically about whatever is caused by a given experience. It must be granted that on the whole people may differ in their observations, in their feelings, and in their judgments of everything. There may be human beings other than identical twins who are so much alike in natural endowment that they see, feel, and judge everything in about the same way, but such cases must be extremely rare. For unless two people have the same past as well as the same natural endowment, they cannot be expected to have the same total experiences, including in the totality feelings of agreeableness and disagreeableness. But if this is so, then again we had best not climb the ladder of abstraction very far above the individual objects. For even if two men praise a work of art, it may be found that the psychological causes of their praise, as well as the reasons which they give for it, will differ.

Hence to abstract value from the act of valuation will lead to little more than scholastic quibbling.

We object then to abstracting from valuation something called
value and thinking of it as a separate and distinct entity. But we
also object to this on the ground that when one asks what is the
common property of all values which justifies our calling them
values, the answer is that they are valued, though the philosophers
of value do not put it so crudely. Suppose we ask what there is in
common among truth, goodness, and beauty, or, if one wishes to
extend the list, one may add health, wealth, and sanctity. The
true may be evil, ugly, deleterious to health and prosperity, and
certainly to sanctity. The good may be false, ugly, unhealthful,
bad for business and sanctity. Such conflicts are normal and well-
known. To escape from this unpleasant situation people who seek
harmony will introduce a scale of values, making some higher, as
they will say, than others. Thus it will be said, for instance, that
truth is the highest of all goals and that everything else must be
sacrificed to its attainment. But in that case, as in all analogous
cases, what is to be done about the other values? Are they all on a
plane below truth or are they on a series of levels leading up to
truth? If the former alternative is accepted, then goodness and
the others are all equally good or bad and there is no choice to
be made between, say, being good and being healthy or saintly or
beautiful. If this alternative is rejected, as it probably would be,
then we have the possibility of maintaining that the attainment
of one value will lead upward to the next above it until one has
reached the *summum bonum*. But since all this is discussed at
greater length below (Chapter IX), I shall leave the matter at
this point here.

Even if it were true that the values could be arranged on some
such scale and that the attainment of one led to the attainment
of the next above it, that would not prove that all the values had
any common property other than that of being goals on specifiable
occasions. Anyone who has ever climbed a mountain knows that
though the path leads upward, the stages in the path are very di-

verse. One may begin with a trail through a pine woods, then get above the timber line where only scrub trees and gravel are to be found, then find oneself in an area of rocks and boulders, and one finally emerges on a peak covered with snow. There is simply nothing common to the various stages in the ascent except that they all are stages in the ascent. Of course I realize that such discussions as this are worthless, for no one ever seeks truth or beauty or goodness *ueberhaupt*. People want to know whether a certain given sentence is true or not, whether a definite man or act is good or not, whether a certain woman or picture or poem is beautiful or not. No one need stop to ask whether all true sentences form a coherent system like a system of geometry, though, if asked, he would probably say they did. Nor does he ask why and in what sense of the word a woman and a poem can both be beautiful. He knows what it feels like to see a beautiful woman, though he would be hard put to it to define what it is that makes her beautiful. So a person can taste sweetness and sourness without knowing anything whatsoever about taste buds and their location in the mouth. The questions of definition and differentiae are questions which philosophers raise and which, like so many other philosophical questions, cannot be answered, it would seem, in a fashion satisfactory to all. To ask why something is valuable can mean little more concretely than why do people value it. But since the verb "to value" something may mean to like it, to approve of it, to think that others should like and approve of it, to prefer it to certain other things when asked to choose, to spend money to obtain it, to work hard to obtain it, to make genuine sacrifices to obtain it, to urge others to obtain it whether they like it or not, it is clearly a word which totters with ambiguities and is, one might think, of no explanatory use. For as soon as one does abstract the valuation from that which is valued and from the act of valuing, the thing abstracted is an empty formula. To say that the reason why something has value is that someone values it does clarify the problem by introducing the human valuing subject into it as one of its factors, but does nothing else.

This will also be true if one tries to abstract from artistry what its various forms have in common. Our own answer is that the arts are an unnatural way of satisfying our desires. I do not mean by unnatural anything bad; quite the contrary. I merely want to emphasize the fact that it is desires which are gratified by the arts, that they may be gratified by a variety of arts, though not equally well in the eyes of a given individual, and that it is neither the materials used nor the sense organs through which it is appreciated which differentiates one art from another.

CHAPTER III

The Arts and Society

ANY HUMAN BEING who is under orders, whether the orders be those of another individual or of a group, can obviously obey them or disobey them. He may obey them consciously in full knowledge of what he is doing; he may obey them willingly while disapproving of them, on the ground that the self-discipline of obedience is itself a good; or he may obey them without being aware of precisely what they involve or of what justification they may have. Anyone who has had military experience will recognize all three of these states. On the other hand an individual who refuses to obey orders may also do so for a variety of reasons and from a variety of causes. He may simply dislike being ordered about and the very fact that he feels the pressure of a superior may induce him to violate the orders which a superior has given him. He may also disapprove of the orders, though maintaining that he is usually willing to do what he is told to do: here he refuses to do what he believes to be wrong. Or he may be neither generally recalcitrant nor submissive, but on a given occasion reluctant to obey and unaware of the ground of his reluctance.

The orders which interest us in this study come from social groups. By the time a man has become conscious of aesthetic problems, his ways of thinking and of acting have been pretty well formed. Even the child who is drawing for his own amusement has been subjected to social influences of which he is not aware and of which students of aesthetics, as well as teachers of art, ought to be more aware.[1] He has become more or less conscious of the furnishings of his home, of the billboards on his street, of his neighborhood architecture, of the taste of his parents, of his schoolmates, and of his teachers. He may think he has invented his own style and manner of treatment, selected his own subject, his coloring, but he has already been submitted to a score of influences over which he has had no control and which have formed his manner without his having had anything to say about it. To call such influences orders is no doubt quixotic, but after all one yields to their authority; they have the sanction of the social group; in some cases one would lose face if one swerved away from their direction. They form a code of good behavior and it makes little difference for our purposes whether the behavior is moral or aesthetic. We have had the occasion to see many children's drawings and have yet to see one in which the people are naked. Is this because children are not interested in nakedness? Hardly. But by the time the child has reached the age at which his drawings will be seen by others, he has learned that people are clothed. The petrification of forms is found in children's work as in the work of adults and only the very recalcitrant child or the child who has become submissive to a recalcitrant teacher will be noticeably original. The observation of most authorities is to the effect that if the child begins to draw at an early age, his imagination will be relatively free from outside influences, but that as soon as he enters school his imagination is controlled and his drawings begin to resemble those of the general run of children of his age. Education is usually the death of individuality. In fact, that is what it is for. It has to impose an accepted way of doing things on human beings who have as yet no way of doing them.

Since the child as artist is not the typical artist, we have to accept the adult as the object of these remarks. Here we find that there are some painters, and our comments would apply to other artists, whose work can be spotted at one glance as, let us say, Italian Mannerist or nineteenth-century French Academic, whereas others look at once as the originators of something. One can see traces of Rubens in Fragonard and Delacroix and of Caravaggio in Velázquez and of Velázquez in Manet. And it may well be that, if we did not know the dates of these painters and could not recognize the modernity of the costumes worn by their models, we should locate Delacroix in the School of Rubens and Manet in the School of Velázquez. But on the other hand no one would think that Delacroix's "Greece Expiring on the Ruins of Missolonghi" or "Liberty Leading the People" was by Rubens. As for Manet, it is clear that if one were interested in schools, he could be put into the School of Goya ("Olympia" and the "Maja Desnuda"), of Giorgione (the "Déjeûner sur l'Herbe" and the "Fête Champêtre"), as well as of Velázquez. For that matter any French painter of the nineteenth and twentieth centuries with access to the Louvre would hardly be likely to avoid being influenced by someone of the past.

But more to the point is the belief of some that one ought to belong to a tradition, that what we call individuality and originality are not good things but perversities. Page after page of Ingres' *Pensées* emphasize his belief that to follow Nature is to copy Raphael, much as Alexander Pope thought that to follow Nature was to copy Vergil. And indeed the prestige of Raphael was very great through the seventeenth and eighteenth centuries. From Perugino through Raphael to Poussin (1594–1665), Lebrun (1619–1690), Drouais (1699–1767), David (1748–1825), Ingres (1780–1867), to Degas runs a style which is unmistakably passed on from one generation to the next. Yet each of these painters was also an inventor and, just as there is much more to Ingres than was given him by David, so there was much more to Degas than what he inherited from Ingres. The real traditionalists are those men who are satisfied with what has been produced in the past by some artist or group of artists and who therefore continue to reproduce it. That is why we can talk legitimately of schools and traditions. But it is also true, as has been frequently pointed out by historians, that originality is a modern phenomenon in the arts, dating approximately from the Italian Renaissance. The men of the fifteenth and sixteenth centuries were no doubt strong individuals, as both Gobineau and Burckhardt, to say nothing of Nietzsche, insisted, but even they were apprenticed at an early age to a master, worked on his paintings, and modified only slightly his style. Their originality came out in their lives beyond the walls of their workshops. The painters and sculptors of Asia never seem to have striven for self-expression in the sense of originality, but were content to copy a model which they and their society found good. In China even the brush strokes were formalized. And in the statues of the Buddha, as is well-known, all details including those of costume, hairdressing, the position of the hands and feet, were faithfully reproduced century after century. Indeed, if all that is important in a work of art is the finished product, why not copy a work of art which is good? If an original work of art differs from something recognized as perfect, it would seem foolish to praise it.

The weakness of this position is in the choice of an arbiter of perfection. At the present time, what painter is the perfect painter or, if one prefers, who approaches most closely to perfection? If it be replied that this is an age of confusion and that there is no generally accepted definition of the artist's purpose, we can move backward and ask whether in nineteenth-century France it was the *Ministre des Beaux-Arts* who defined it, if in the eighteenth century it was Roger de Piles or Du Fresnoy, if in the seventeenth century it was Bellori. The history of taste shows us clearly not merely that people have always differed in what they liked and admired, but that the artists of every period of which we have records were in a state of conflict with the critics who demanded of them something which they were not prepared to give.[2] Terms such as "naturalist" and "idealist," "Rubenist" and "Poussinist," "classicist" and "romanticist," though they mean opposing things, yet also name kinds of style which existed during one and the same period. The spokesmen for each of these styles named would pick out easily the artists whose work best exemplified it. If then the traditionalist wished to copy the perfect work of art of any period, he would first have to pick out the critic or group of critics whose judgment he was willing to make his own. He would also have to decide that the favorite painters of that critic represented perfection. When he came to get out his own paints and brushes he would have to choose, for example, between Rubens' "Rape of the Daughters of Leucippus" and Poussin's "Triumph of Neptune and Amphitrite," between Boucher's "Pastorale" and Chardin's "Le Toton," between Ingres' portrait of Bertin and Delacroix's portrait of Chopin, between Picasso's "Guernica" and Matisse's "Joie de Vivre." To put the question is to stifle it. It begins to look as if one were asking whether verse or prose were the more perfect form of writing, whether building in reinforced concrete or in wood were the more perfect form of building. The basis of traditionalism turns out to be worse than unstable.

Furthermore, a thing cannot just be perfect. It has to be a perfect example of something or other: in the case of works of art, of technical skill defined according to *The Rules*, of symbolic clarity, of originality, of spontaneous expression, words which in themselves are none too clear, of fidelity to a text, of fulfillment of the artist's purpose when known, of persuasively presenting the government's political aims, of moral edification, and so on and on almost *ad indefinitum*. Most aestheticians seem to believe that each kind of art, painting, sculpture, architecture, has a general aim, establishes a type or genus, and that each individual work of art in order to be perfect must exemplify the characteristics of the type. That is not the point of view of this book, but we can postpone discussion of that touchy subject for the time being. To say that Bernini's fountains in Rome are perfect examples of the Baroque, whatever that is, is surely not to say that they are perfect works of art which establish a model and archetype for fountains in general. (As for their being perfect examples of the Baroque, that is not astonishing since we derive our ideas of the Baroque in part from Bernini's fountains.) To say that Garnier's Opéra in Paris is a perfect specimen of Second Empire architecture is not also to say that all opera houses should try to resemble it. Yet if an architect were to design a fountain with the idea of reproducing in his own idiom what Bernini did, we could at least conclude that he had succeeded or failed in attaining his purpose. Fortunately we do not usually know what an artist intended when he produced his work of art, so that we can make up our own minds about its value for us. This requires a kind of courage which only the vulgar ordinarily have. I am not, however, setting up vulgar opinion as a standard of aesthetic excellence; I am setting it up as an example of intellectual independence.

Just as an artist operates under the influence of various dogmas, traditions, standards of right and wrong, over which he has little if any control, so the public, by which I mean the spectators, come to a work of art with preconceived ideas of which they have never had the opportunity even to be conscious. The most obvious instance of this is that a painting or a piece of sculpture must represent something and that its beauty or ugliness will be determined by the beauty or ugliness of its subject. The second of these preconceptions is not logically related to the first. It is true that with the exception of those cultures such as that of Islam or, on the whole, of Judaism, which discouraged the representation of animate beings,[3] most painting and sculpture did indeed represent recognizable objects. Even Islamic art did not avoid the representation of plants. Hence men of my generation grew up with the idea that the first question to be put to a painting was whether it really looked like the thing which it was supposed, *by us*, to represent. When then we came first upon the obvious distortions of Matisse and Picasso and their groups, and then upon abstract and nonfigurative paintings, we were puzzled and sometimes outraged, though we were willing to accept abstract music and architecture. We did not invent this principle for ourselves. A child of the early twentieth century took it for granted that when he sat down with crayons or pencil or water color, he was to draw a picture *of* something. He was given books with outline pictures in them *of* things which he was to color. He read books with illus-

trations in them of the incidents related in the books, and sometimes, as in Lewis Carroll or Dickens, these illustrations fixed forever the way in which the characters in the stories looked. The
child had no say in this matter whatsoever: how could he have
had any? He could, if he was a specially independent child, refuse
to believe that Alice dressed in that kind of dress and wore her
hair hanging down her back, or that the Duchess was quite such
a pudgy creature as Tenniel had made her out to be. But I imagine
that most children accepted them as right and proper and that
when they came upon other illustrations of their favorite classics,
refused to admit that the artists had succeeded in their tasks. But
when all is said and done, an illustrator like Arthur Rackham was
hardly a poorer painter than Tenniel. To the child, however, he
was a heretic.

We talk glibly about "society" as if we knew what it was and as
if that knowledge convinced us that it was all of a piece. But society in modern times, and probably wherever one had an urban
civilization, has been a collection of more or less harmonious
groups, groups which have been organized for religious, economic,
political, and even aesthetic aims.[4] Common interests may be the
raison d'être of a social group and when they are espoused by
several people, they may engender a hatred for groups whose interests are different and possibly irreconcilable with theirs. Anti-
vivisectionists never get on well with men engaged in medical research; Jews are used to being ridiculed, if not persecuted, by
Christians; Christians who believe in total immersion look with
scorn, if not hatred, on those who think that sprinkling suffices
to make baptism efficacious; Greek Catholics seem to be incapable
of accepting the supremacy of the Bishop of Rome; Jansenists
were effectively squelched by the Jesuits. There has always been
a battle between organized commerce and Christianity, a battle
in which there has been a sort of permanent armistice but no
peace. Pure scientists sneer at applied scientists and both sneer at
engineers. According to Sir Charles Snow, scientists and students
of the Humanities are so divided that each group has a culture

of its own.[5] Intellectuals have little use for whatever the name for nonintellectuals is. And the cries of horror and denunciation which are heard whenever there appears an innovation in the arts, such as cubism in painting, functionalism in architecture, the use of the twelve-tone scale in music, would make one believe that pictures, buildings, musical compositions are of a peculiarly important social significance. The most charitable of the critics stop at saying that the innovators are simply crazy; the less charitable call them wicked.

If the intrasocial conflicts were confined to the various interests in the large, commerce vs. religion, art vs. science, politics vs. ethics, the matter would be simple enough. If a businessman finds that his church expects him to sell all and follow Christ, he would at least understand where the issue was drawn. Or if a poet or painter or sculptor found that his originality was being stifled by the demands of patrons who are in league with the dealers, he too could see that he had to produce works which the public might want or which the dealers might be able to put over on the public. In this way he could get the money he needs to buy paint and canvas, stone and tools, pay the rent, and feed his wife and children. When a poet or novelist finds that publishers will not print his works, he has only to change his manner, hypocritical though that may be, and become a best seller, always assuming that such is his purpose in life. But all this points to conflicts within the various social groups. In a sense one could say that all painters form a single group and all poets another, but that usage would be too abstract. For the so-called academic painter, though he paints, does not have the same purposes as the nonacademic painter. The two of them neither define their art in the same terms nor do they admire what members of the complementary group produce. In fact, they usually dislike it intensely. But for that matter each subgroup is in turn broken up into still smaller groups. A Surrealist such as Dali is not an academic painter, though what he paints is representational, but at the same time he is not an abstract painter. He may paint pictures which in their detail look like the illustrations which Maxfield Parrish used to make for children's books, but an admirer of Dali would not be likely to be an admirer of Parrish. If that throws Dali into the ranks of the nonacademic painters, it does not at the same time classify him with Mark Tobey. And if Mark Tobey is thought of as the typical nonfigurative painter, are we to look at his canvases as if they were like those of Rothko? There is no need to expand this bit of rhetoric, for the truth of the matter is that we very rapidly reach the point where we realize that each artist stands on his own feet, even when he is a member of a school or tradition. He can be considered, if one wishes, exclusively as standing for such a school's tenets, but if so, his own peculiar contribution to the school is overlooked. Is this of no importance?

It is of no importance when one is thinking of a work of art as an incident in one's own experience. One can always isolate a physical object from its past, from the thousand other things which have made it what it is, and similarly one can read a book as if no one had written it for anyone to read but oneself, look at a picture as if one were the first person to see it and as if no one had painted it. Any work of art can, should one wish, be thought of as a spontaneous growth whose resemblance to other objects ought to be disregarded. So a child or a savage could be brought into the Louvre and he would then have this fresh experience, uninfluenced, as far as that is possible by any relevant past. What would he say of Mantegna's "Saint Sebastian," of El Greco's "Crucifixion," or of Ingres' "Turkish Bath"? For our purposes it is enough to ask whether this fresh and childlike experience is what we should seek in our meeting with works of art. There are those who would argue in the affirmative. But to do so involves a rejection of most of our life, of all of our past experiences, and in ten cases out of ten it deprives each work of art of any relevance to anything else. The child or savage could look at, say, a Chardin still life and recognize the loaf of bread or at Van Gogh's pair of boots and recognize them as boots. But the emotional aura of both pictures would evaporate, for no child and certainly no savage could possibly know what bread means in the life of a French peasant, of what it meant for a man living in the first half of the eighteenth century in France, the France of the Regency, of the Wars of Succession, of Nattier and of Boucher. And what of a twisted and worn pair of hobnailed boots, forming an arabesque as tight as the embrace of labor and poverty? But, I shall be told, all this is literature; it is not within the picture's frame. That is true. But why must we confine ourselves within the frame if we have memories, reading, in short, knowledge which we can bring to bear to illuminate what the frame encloses? Every man has to interpret works of art for himself and with his whole self, and each man differs from every other in the extent of his knowledge and the capacities of his heart. I am not saying that one has to go beyond the frame, for some people cannot do this; but I am flatly refusing to believe that ignorance is of any value whatsoever in the appreciation of art, even if it is disguised as simplicity of spirit.

While one must keep in mind the generating purpose of any social group, one should also remember that a group will not necessarily die when its original purpose has been achieved or found to be unattainable. The Knights Templar and the Sovereign Order of Malta illustrate how a social group may originate out of a desire to achieve a definable purpose and continue to exist when that purpose is obsolete. For once a purpose is incorporated into a body of men, it takes on a secondary purpose of self-perpetuation. The papal nobility no longer serves its original function and the obsolete uniforms of the Swiss Guards symbolize to the outside world the purely decorative purpose of those who wear them. The baronage of England includes men whose titles designate powers which their ancestors may once have exercised, but which their present holders would be jailed for attempting to exercise. How many academies exist today, and not only in Italy, membership in which is purely honorary? How many Doctors of Laws in America know anything about the laws? And for that matter, how many Bachelors of Arts could explain either what a bachelor or an art originally was? It is true that many societies continue to exist for the very reason that their aims are unattainable. No one would argue, I think, that the aims of any religious body had any chance of being achieved. No one would maintain that armies had ever kept the peace. Not even the internal police of a country can do that. Initiates to Phi Beta Kappa are told that those letters mean that "Philosophy is the Helmsman of Life," but few nowadays would ever think of turning to philosophy to lay out a course. And indeed if philosophy is simply linguistic analysis, as we are told, they are quite right to neglect it. Phi Beta Kappa is in fact a perfect example of a society's persisting when its original purpose is forgotten. And those societies whose purpose was the furtherance of the arts, such as the Royal Academy in London, the Académie des Beaux-Arts in France, and similar societies elsewhere, continue to exist merely to resist change and preserve the past. This is not strange. Few, if any, societies are willing to commit suicide. There is always a good reason for prolonging life even when life has become a burden to those who have to endure it. In social groups one can always summon up the desire for companionship, for talking over old times, sharing common memories, glorifying one's common heritage, boasting about one's ancestors, especially if they were greater than oneself, preserving ancient and worn out buildings as symbols of the past, putting pressure on those in power to satisfy one's demands, and finally just being a group separate from the rest of humanity, a group into which entrance is difficult and exit easy.

To make things more complicated, most people belong to several groups the purposes of which need not be harmonious. A scientist may believe in the conservation of energy and mass—though the conservation of the latter now seems less certain than it used to be—and at the same time believe in creation *ex nihilo*. "At the same time" should be perhaps emended to read "on some days" and "on others." But then psychologists have been known to argue that minds do not exist and that glandular secretions, muscle twitchings, incipient speech, take their place. Yet they will use in their ordinary language the same dualistic terms that the rest of us use. People did not cease to speak of sunrise and sunset after the general acceptance of the heliocentric system of astronomy. This seems like hypocrisy to some critics, since it seems to be self-contradictory. But behavior becomes contradictory only when it is translated into language, for only sentences contradict one another. Two acts may be in conflict, but so long as the agent is unaware of it, the conflict which others may see is inoperative. In aesthetics it has been urged by people like Ruskin that a work of art should be consistent in style, truth of this, that, and the other being held to be essential to beauty. It was a mistake to call this kind of consistency by the name of truth, for often, as in the work of the Baroque artists, its absence was precisely what produced an aesthetic effect of its own. By adopting Ruskin's theory, one found oneself rejecting as bad all art after the Gothic period. Such a position seems, at least to us, self-refuting. If you can toss out of the window all painting and sculpture after 1500 simply because its authors failed to read your books written 400 years after their death, you can go to any extreme in the justification of your point of view. It might be accepted as axiomatic that Truth did not wait for anyone in particular to be born before entering the world.

To expect a man to be consistent in the narrow sense of the word might be reasonable if everyone had a character, as Theophrastus used that term. The slanderer, however, does not always slander, the misanthrope is not always misanthropic, and even Achilles is not always Achilles, *pace* Horace and Alexander Pope. The painter who transforms a landscape into a painting is, while doing it, false to what he sees and only the portrait which is flattering is accepted as a good likeness by those who love the sitter. I imagine that even Bernini sat still once in a while, did not always fling scarves about, walk with arms indicating two points of the compass, or float in the air. A person is, as Royce used to say,[6] a group of purposes and he has only that unity which his purposes may have. Royce may have been more enamored of unity than we should be, but he recognized the common existence of men of many purposes. Since the days of Freud and his followers we have learned to accept a multiplicity of purposes as normal. A man's problem is to prevent one or more of them from hindering the fulfillment of the others. If this is hypocrisy, then hypocrisy is a virtue, for I can think of no purpose which can be accomplished without the co-operation of others. Leave all and follow me is to be sure a saintly program, the more so since unattainable this side of Paradise. Give all to love is equally futile, for how can one give anything to love if one has nothing to give? This brings up the question of artistic sincerity. Sincerity is a moral trait, not an aesthetic prerequisite, and all that is needed in communication is clarity. For if art is communication, it is the one form of communication that does not rely on evidence. A picture or a poem or a building is its own evidence and each spectator will have to interpret it for himself as far as he can. One hates to be taken in, I admit, and it would be a great shock to most of us to learn that Picasso was a Falangist in disguise and that his "Guernica" did not represent his real feelings. It would be the same kind of shock if we learned that Giotto had nothing but contempt for Saint Francis or that Haydn was an atheist. Yet we do not usually bother about the misdeeds of Fra Lippo Lippi when we look at his pictures nor of the meanness of Pope when reading *The Rape of the Lock*. When one is looking at a painting or listening to a piece of music, one cannot also keep in mind the character of their authors. In fact, most of the time their biographies are unknown to us and when they are known, they are known through interpretations of their lives written by others. I fail to see what light is thrown on Mozart's music by reading the obscene letters which he wrote to his cousin or why Van Gogh's paintings should become more beautiful when we learn of his self-mutilation. Van Gogh cut off his ear; he did not blind himself. And Mozart, as far as we know, confined his obscenity to his letters. What all this teaches us is that a work of art expresses one side of an artist's life, not his whole life. Instead of expressing his whole self, it conceals some of it. None of this prevents anyone from being deeply affected by a picture at which one is looking. Why should it?

The inner differences of a person may not necessarily be in conflict. The conflict may appear when each interest or purpose is put into words and written down for someone to read. But there is an obvious distinction to be made between those conflicts of which we are aware and those of which we are unconscious. The psychiatric problem is more likely to arise when a person finds that the satisfaction of one of his interests prevents, or at a minimum makes difficult, the satisfaction of another. But there are many purposes which, when put into words, would look as if they must present genuinely irreconcilable choices to an individual, but which in actuality exist side by side or in succession in apparent harmony. Fortunately tradition has established days of the week and clocks. Thus we can organize a schedule according to which certain desires will be gratified at certain times and forgotten at others. One can be religious, as we all know, on Sundays and holy days and feel no compunction about not being religious on other days. There is a kind of psychological insight in the trite slogans about business being business, about all being fair in love and war, about white lies, about the necessity of living, vulgar though they seem, for they indicate our established manner of overcoming potential conflicts. The individual may be a devoted husband and parent when home and a rake and spendthrift when away from home. The *Gestalt* will serve to justify his inconsistent behavior. So the painter may paint pot-boilers for a living and paint "for himself" when his belly is full. We are too often incapable of understanding a situation of this sort. We do not see how a man like Charles Swann, so sensitive, so appreciative of artistic subtleties, could ever fall in love with a woman like Odette. This, however, is not so unusual a case as to cause the astonishment which some readers of Proust have expressed. The sexual appetite, surely there ought to be no need to point out, is not a program like the desire to learn Greek. There happen to be certain desires which grip one and master one without any argument whatsoever. It is an assumption and one which seems to me, if not to everyone, contrary to fact that all our desires can be brought together to live in peace. The program is one of denial; two people do not live in peace simply because one of them is silenced or annihilated. Every ethical system has preached denial, except that of Nietzsche, and even Nietzsche denied man's love of submission. In matters of aesthetics the program is notorious. The choice of a style or even of a subject is talked about as if the artist first sat down in committee and decided what to choose. But I imagine that when a man becomes a painter, he does so because he is driven to paint things rather than write about them. He will at times submit himself to instruction and, if he is a certain kind of person, will accept the instruction given him and conform to it in his practice. But sometimes, and here the case of Picasso is relevant, he will shift his method and his subject and not only shift from period to period, doing one kind of painting in his youth, another in his manhood, and a third in his old age, but during any one period may paint different types of pictures. I recall no "blue" painting of Picasso done in recent years, but during his so-called Cubist period he was also painting non-Cubist pictures. This ought to seem reasonable enough since neither Picasso nor anyone else was ever all of a piece. What is important in his case to the philosopher of art is that he has been frank enough to exhibit all his various facets to the public instead of trying to conceal all but one.

Picasso is, to be sure, an exceptional artist and there are very few with either his talent or his frankness. But even he has been dominated by the social group with which he has been affiliated, the group of foreign painters enjoying the hospitality of France and living at a time when aesthetic rebellion was approved. He had no obligation to his adopted country and none to the country of his birth, though when the latter was attacked and brutalized, he commemorated it in his "Guernica," as Goya had done in his "Los Desastros." He accepted no responsibilities either to indi-

viduals or society as far as his art shows. For the famous Dove of
Peace is hardly payment of a debt. He came into prominence at
the end of the Bohemian Period when eccentricity was permitted
and in fact encouraged. One has only to compare him with Matisse to see how differently a man of French background, accepting France as his country in the fullest sense of acceptance, though
aesthetically having almost identical convictions, would behave.
This is not intended to be dispraise of either man for both deserve
our deepest appreciation. But no one can refuse to see the influence of social groups on each. The purposes of any group will
make demands upon the artist. Primary among these demands
will be the glorification of the group and satire of other groups. I
do not know whether Matisse's famous "Blue Nude" in the Cone
Collection (Baltimore Museum of Art) was a satire of all the Reclining Venuses which have been painted since the days of Giorgione or not, but its source must have been a revulsion against all
the academic female nudes which were being turned out by the
hundreds to whip up the appetites of aged satyrs, canvases which
now gather dust in obscure American barrooms or in the storage
vaults of provincial museums. To accept membership in a group
is seldom a deliberate choice. Most of us are born into them and
never leave them. But in a fluid society there is bound to be shift-
ing about, emigration out of the group into which one has been
born and immigration into some other. The shifts come about
without our being aware of what is happening to us. We enter a
school, usually chosen by our parents, and when we get there we
wake up to the fact that there are some people who do not share
our parents' ideas of what is good or bad, beautiful or ugly. But
then the moment comes for some of us when even the ideas of the
school become unacceptable. This may occur simply because we
resent the discipline imposed upon us to make us accept them.
For some reason or other, accident, random curiosity, talking with
friends, strolling into art galleries, we discover that unfamiliar and
strange ideas are abroad. We may be repelled by them, in which
case we strengthen our allegiance to our school. We may wish to

find out more about them, in which case the charm of the novel may begin to work upon us and to win us over. We may fall in love with them as if a religious conversion were taking place. We may simply discover that people whom we admire accept these new ideas and we transfer our admiration for such people to what they admire. But gradually, almost imperceptibly, we find ourselves allied to a new group of people and, if it is a question of art, we produce works of art which are similar in style to those of the members of our new group. At the present time we should be likely to have a manifesto before us setting forth the principles to which we adhere, principles which are obscure enough to satisfy numbers of people. For if principles are very clear, they give room for disagreement.

The ideals of the group will automatically be translated into an aesthetic doctrine. Thus we have had what are known as courtly art, proletarian art, folk art, religious art, commercial art, pornography, and purely aesthetic art. It will be observed that any given work of art, other things being equal, may be situated in any of these classes, according to the person interpreting it. Even a picture by Fra Angelico may become an economic commodity to a dealer in old pictures or to a collector in search of prestige.[7] We all know how a painting by Titian or Rubens or Courbet or pretty nearly anyone else turns into pornography under the eyes of Puritans. It will be pointed out that this has nothing to do with the picture's aesthetic value, which, I suppose, means its beauty. On the contrary, it has everything to do with it. Beauty can be so defined that it is to be found only in a certain type of picture, poem, building, what you will.[8] In that case we are arguing from definitions. I am, however, talking about what people find beautiful in reality, not about what I think they should find beautiful, what they cherish as something to be looked at, to be fondled, to be shown off with delight to their friends. Whatever else beauty may be, it is usually assumed to be good-in-itself and emotionally satisfying. It is a quality which is pleasant and indeed so pleasant that one cannot believe that it is not everlasting. The fact that a pic-

ture cost a lot of money may not endow it with beauty in the eyes
of the man who neither owns it nor is offering it for sale, but that
does not prove that it is unbeautiful in the eyes of him who does
own it or who is offering it for sale. We are too quick to ridicule
the collector to whom the rarity of a picture is what he cherishes
and we overlook the hard fact that he sees the rare picture as
something more lovable than the commonplace picture.[9] The
uniquely costly has a value which we are inclined to think of as
vulgar, but at the same time the sensuously unique is something
which we think to be the height of refinement. A rare color or
shape, a rare odor or taste, like any rare experience, is believed to
be better than the common type of the same order of experience.
But if one's main interest in life is making money and if one is
educated in a society in which the mark of social distinction is
wealth, what could be more natural than the investiture of sensi-
ble evidences of wealth with beauty? Unfortunately the men who
are out to make money seldom spend much time writing critical
essays, for their life's purpose is time-consuming. Consequently
their point of view is neglected and the transformation of costliness into an aesthetic value is denied. Yet those magazines of art
which are published for collectors and in the interest of dealers
never fail to emphasize the cost of works of art which they are
describing, the rise and fall of prices in the auction rooms, the
possibilities of making a fortune by buying pictures as an invest-
ment. The ideal of costliness is simply transferred to the realm of
aesthetics and what is costly becomes beautiful.

The notion that there is such a thing as a purely aesthetic art
can be easily seen to be nonsense. For to purge our minds of
everything except sensory data is an activity which is just as highly
specialized as devoting ourselves exclusively to business or religion
or love or politics. We attain a purely aesthetic attitude after long
practice; it is not by any means our starting point. A person un-
versed in the results of aesthetic controversy looks at a picture
without any of the preoccupations of the aesthetician. He will
have some, to be sure, namely those of the social groups with

which he has been associated and if they should be specialists in sensory data, so will he try to be. But in all probability when he sees a given picture for the first time, he sees it as big or small, as representational of something recognizable: people dressed or undressed, in contemporary or ancient costume, doing certain things or simply sitting for their portraits, against a background indoors or outdoors. He responds to the size, to the subject matter, to the color, to whatever action is taking place, as he might to the same thing if it were real and not in a picture. It is the response of a naïve person to a play, hissing the villain and applauding the hero. To emerge from this situation into one where he will overlook subject matter, signification, and see the picture only as a pattern of light and dark, masses, lines, colors, is something which may be desirable—though that is another matter—but is no more a starting point than the most detailed iconographical analysis is. Though it is an attitude in which much has been discarded rather than acquired, it is not for that reason any less the result of group interests. The Franciscan who has abandoned property, family, and the power of decision in order to follow Christ has reached a state of nakedness which is almost complete, but he has done so because of his education. His society is not that of the picture dealer nor the aesthetician nor the courtier, but all that is irrelevant. His submission to the will of God is something which he had to learn and the fact that he has learned to abandon worldly things does not imply that he has returned to a state of nature, to a more natural condition than the rest of us, or to one less conditioned by social demands. Quite the contrary. So the stripping of works of art of everything in them except sensory data is also conditioned by social demands. The program seems to have been invented by Baumgarten to provide a science for the senses which would be analogous to those set up for the reason (logic) and the will (ethics). But no one is committed either to the psychology behind this scheme or to its implications.

The social roots of the program come out more clearly when one knows its history. That history goes back at least to the aestheticism of Huysmans in France, Wilde in England (if not to Walter Pater), and to Huneker in the United States. Beautiful and intense sensations as the goal of life are all very well, but they are probably a substitute for love, devotion, courage, work, and all vital goods. Most of us get our pleasures as the end term in our daily occupations and we usually assume that we shall have some daily occupations. The purely aesthetic life is like the purely erotic life, or the purely commercial life, in both of which of course the hedonistic quality is important. But to love for the sake of pleasure is to forget that someone else is involved whom we must discard the moment she fails to satisfy us as intensely as is imaginable. For our relation to her is that of a man to a pleasure-making machine and when the machine wears out, or when one is simply bored with it, one abandons it for another. This sort of thing is what Ortega y Gasset called the dehumanization of art, for all human values which exist beyond the frontiers of the *jouisseur* are denied.

Allied with this is the tendency to find aesthetic values only in artistry rather than in the work of art. It is the manner which counts, not the matter. Now it would be absurd to overlook the beauty of workmanship and to attend to it is often a way out of narrow prejudice and censoriousness. In this respect the juggler is as great an artist as Pavlowa, the carver of peach stones as great a sculptor as Donatello. I am not denying the excellence of virtuosity, far from it. If all there is to art is artistry, then there is no reason to prefer one excellent artist to another. But the artistry does not go on like the movement of wind and clouds; it eventuates in a work of art, and it just happens to be the case that the work of art has values which the artistry does not have. It would of course be vastly different from what it is if the artistry had been less effective, but there is no compelling reason to force oneself into seeing nothing but the process and overlook the product. A good bit of Romanesque sculpture is awkwardly carved and almost any Italian carver of gravestones could do a better job. But the conception which is expressed in the Roman-

esque capital or tympanum is such that we can forget the
workmanship and concentrate on what it has achieved. One of
the reasons why men at the end of the nineteenth century were
so much more interested in artistry than in the work of art
was the hopeless sentimentality of the latter. The ideas of the
late Victorian novel, painting, and music were sickly and if one
lived in an Anglo-Saxon country one found their hypocrisy
repellant. This was far from being true on the Continent, but,
as it happened, the ideas of the Continental artists ran counter
to those which predominated in Great Britain and the United
States. The French, for instance, were not confined to the
produce of the Academicians; but a glance at the literature of
even the Edwardian period in England is enough to show why
rebellion set in. Yet the ideas of the so-called Decadents were
hardly more serious, though their workmanship was brilliant. One
had to be satisfied with that.

It requires little proof to show that a given work of art, even
as part of a single person's life, may have a variety of values. It
may turn out that a portrait of one's mother, let us say by Ingres,
is preserved by a man for purely sentimental reasons. The picture
is simply a remembrance of his mother; if it were of someone
else, he would not like it. But as he lives with it and the memory
of his mother fades, the painting becomes less a reminder of
someone than an object in its own right. He begins to see it
objectively, to see how it is painted. The drawing, the coloring,
the characterization, the perfect stability of the person represented, the expressiveness of the pose as well as of the face, all
take on an interest which they did not have at first. His interest
in these things will not be aroused automatically, but probably
through conversation with others. Then he discovers that the
portrait is "an Ingres," and he finds out too who Ingres was and
how highly he is esteemed by critics. His affection for the picture
grows but its motivation has changed. This, it may be said, is
an absurd and perhaps even wicked parody of the aesthetic
experience. Unfortunately all our experiences as they are lived

are mixtures and the names we give them, aesthetic, religious, commercial, and so on, mislead us into thinking that each facet can exist independently of the others. It is good of course to be able to make distinctions and to know precisely what one is talking about. But that in no way permits us to believe that there is an existential one-to-one correspondence between words and things. The distinctions are made after the fact and what they name may be so inextricably twisted together in existence that to separate them would be to exterminate them. The important factor in looking at paintings, reading poems, listening to music, is the fullness of the experience, not merely a series of fractional effects of its parts. To argue that we should reject four-fifths of an experience for the sake of the remaining one-fifth, is like telling a man that food has only taste and that its nutritive value is trivial.

CHAPTER IV

The Classification
of the Arts

THE PURPOSE of classifying things is to be able to talk about them in common terms. Once a generic character has been selected, it is believed quite rightly that one can then tell whether a presumed member of a class is a good or bad representative of it. Critics usually feel it to be their special task to say whether works of art are good or bad and they reach their goal by first laying down definitions of what given works of art ought to be. The word "ought" in this context, as in most contexts, is ambiguous. It may simply mean that if a given object is a member of the class A, then it will be found to have certain characteristics, x, y, z. If it turns out that it does not have these characteristics, then it is simply not a member of the class A. In this use of the word "ought," no praise attaches to a thing for having the characteristics in question, nor blame for not having them. If any praise or blame is involved, it should be given to the investigator, not to the object investigated. If one knows what a mammal, for instance, is supposed to be and comes upon a cow, one is pretty sure that she is a mammal; but one does not praise the cow for being a mammal. If on the contrary one comes upon a platypus, which is a mammal, according to most classifiers, but also lays eggs, one may not like its eccentricity, but one does not say that it ought not to lay eggs.

In the other sense of the word "ought," one assumes that a thing is trying to be something which it may or may not be trying to be. Thus if one could imagine that God in creating the platypus really wanted to create a normal mammal but had failed, one could say that He ought to have provided it with some way of carrying its eggs internally. But since one does not usually blame the Almighty for having produced the world as it is, one accepts the platypus as an egg-laying mammal and lets it go at that. It will be observed that in using the word "ought" in this way, one presumably knows ahead of time in what class a thing is claiming membership. If we say in ethics that a man ought to tell the truth, we may be supposed to know that, for instance, he wants to be trusted by his fellow men, or to obey tradition, or to be honored with a good reputation, or something of that sort. But if the person in question does not care whether he has gained the confidence of others or not, or what his reputation is, and accepts none of the definitions ordinarily accepted of the good man, then one may say that he ought to tell the truth, but one does not expect to be taken seriously by him. One may add that if all men did not tell the truth, then society would fall to pieces, but in that case one would be advancing a conception of the good society, membership in which could be acquired only by telling the truth. Yet again it might be replied that such a society has never existed and in all probability never will exist, and that a man would be a fool to plan his life for living in a dream world which was not of his dreaming.

In the arts we find, as I have said, both senses of the word used and seldom distinguished. One first surveys certain works of art which resemble one another to a high degree and calls them by a common noun: painting, sculpture, poetry, and so on. We shall omit for the time being what such resemblances consist in and content ourselves with saying that they are observable. We then come upon a work of art which has certain observable resemblances to the group under consideration but lacks some as well. Two decisions might then be made: 1) that it is not a member of the class as had been supposed; 2) that it is an imperfect member of it. But in general we seem to have a tendency to say that it ought to have the missing characteristics as well as those which it does have, the penalty being exclusion from the class in question. We say in effect, "This object may look like a painting in that it is painted, but it is not really a painting since I can find in it neither subject nor drawing nor composition nor plan. It claims to be a painting," we appear to be saying, "and it is only a would-be painting." Or again, "The words which we are reading look as if they were attempting to form a poem, but they are not arranged according to any recognizable meter or rhythm, and, needless to say, do not rhyme. Therefore, whatever else they are, they are not a poem."

Suppose now that the person who had produced the first example says that he had no intention of producing a painting in your sense of the word and that the second says that he does not feel bound to produce poems in accordance with your recipes. You may then reply that the artists in question ought not to call their works paintings and poems; but as a matter of fact it is not they but tradition which pastes on the labels. If the artists have any forensic sense, they will tell the critic to classify their works in any way he will, so long as he looks at them or reads them. Let him say something intelligible about them. Unhappily it is only too true that artists frequently want to rebel against the rules and at the same time to be praised by men who feel it their business to enforce them. The resemblance of a painting by Kline or Rothko to one by Renoir or Degas is at best superficial: they are in color and on flat surfaces. For either of them to pretend that they are developing the tradition into which Renoir and Degas fit, in spite of their differences, is unwarranted and unnecessary, and I doubt whether either of these painters would be so foolish as to say so. They are clearly producing a different kind of painting with a different kind of purpose, and the only reason why their canvases are called paintings is that this is the only word we have to call them by. We might call them visual patterns on a plane surface, but why use six words when one will do?

The class words which we use are seldom invented by us to suit groups of things which we are studying, but are obviously inherited by us from our predecessors. It would make for ease of comprehension if the world of things were not so complicated, if there were no intermediate forms of life, for instance, nothing so close to both animals and plants that one did not know where to fit it into the scheme of things. But as one looks over the world, one finds that diversification seems to be about as common as convergence. In biology alone, some genera, both animal and vegetable, show more diversity than others. The number of kinds —let us use that neutral term rather than species—of arthropods is astonishingly more numerous than the kinds of vertebrates.[1] But nevertheless there seems to be no reluctance on the part of Nature to let kinds become different and indeed, if that were not so, the world would be populated exclusively by unicellular organisms of one kind only. It is not, moreover, only in the non-human sphere that diversification is to be found. If we assume that the Indo-European languages are all derived from a common parent tongue, we have to grant that one language in a few thousand years has become scores of different languages and, if we include the dialects of each of these, the number runs into the hundreds. I suppose that in a sense one might say that Latin and French are the same language, but it would be in a very extended sense of the word "same." When we come to the arts, we find a similar diversification. Modern architecture looks like Greek architecture only when architects make a deliberate attempt to imitate it or insofar as the laws of statics determine that only certain shapes will stand up and carry loads. The drawings of the post-Renaissance masters do not look like the drawings on the walls of Egyptian tombs or Greek vase paintings. Oil painting does not look like fresco painting and the paintings of the different modern periods and schools are clearly distinguishable. I am not trying to argue that there is a historical law which forces artists to be different from one another; I am simply arguing that in the Occident diversification has occurred, though there have been times, as in the Neoclassic period, or in archaistic periods in general, when revivals of ancient forms became stylish. This does not happen to be so true in some places and times. For instance sculpture and architecture in the Far East have run closer to type than in the West, though it should not be forgotten that it is Western eyes which see it as more homogeneous.[2] In any event, where such diversification has occurred, it is absurd to think that the process is to be arrested by the command of a critic or group of critics. The result of diversification is merely that the old class terms have to be extended to cover the new items or new terms invented for them, as has been done in the case of *collages*, *mobiles*, and *constructions*.

An artist who has succeeded in making a work of art which perfectly exemplifies the demands of a traditional definition has done nothing more than that. If that was his purpose, then he has attained his purpose. He has been successful. But that does not mean that others should do as he has done or that critics should assume that his success is a goal for others to accept for themselves. I pick up a little dictionary and read that a dance is "a series of rhythmic movements of the body to the sound of instruments or the voice." Strictly speaking, a dance which was not accompanied by instrumental or vocal music would not be a dance. Yet no one could possibly be so stupid as to think that his bodily movements when unaccompanied really were being accompanied and yet at the same time he might maintain that the only name of an art which he could think of for his unaccompanied bodily rhythmic movements was "dancing." I imagine that such a person would feel that a critic who turned away from the performance on the ground that it was not *really* dancing was being grossly unfair. He would probably say that the critic, instead of niggling over terms, should have said something about whether his unaccompanied bodily movements were beautiful or ugly, interesting or dull, expressive or dumb, or something of that sort. But to assume a priori that a work of art claims membership in a class as a dictionary defines it and to think that membership in that class is a prerequisite to aesthetic value is entirely unjustified. One might as well look down on the anthropoid apes because they are not men or on roses because they are not apples. Why ask anything to be other than what it is, unless one has some reason to think that it is pretending to be something else? There are of course persuasive social arguments for maintaining a tradition, but such arguments are not compulsive. The artist who is inventive or dissatisfied for some reason or other with the traditional forms of his art will see no point in clinging to them even though by doing so his work of art would be more easily understood by the public. Why should he? He knows from the history of all the arts that innovations are always disliked at first and that in time they become accepted as normal.

The shallowness of the argument from class concepts appears when one looks at some of them. We have already spoken of Baumgarten's, but here may repeat that the fact that a picture is seen and a piece of music heard is of no more importance than that a written word is seen and a spoken word heard. The word does not change its meaning because of the medium through which that meaning is communicated. But out of the notion that the arts are in essence perceptual—and so is all experience in some sense of the word—came the inferences *a*) that anything nonperceptual in a work of art was illegitimate and *b*) that the arts could be classified according to the sense to which they were addressed. Thus if one had a story-picture, the story was illegitimate, being literature and not painting, and this in spite of the fact that all painting up to very recent times was illustration, comment, interpretation. The second consequence was that we had the arts classified as visual and auditory, and no attention to speak of was paid to olfactory, gustatory, and tactile arts. But smell, taste, and touch were thought of in Santayana's terms as lower senses, though they were quite as essential to life as the upper ones. But maybe their very utility made them suspect. Be that as it may, it was concluded that a painting must in the long run be thought of simply as a visual pattern of colors, shapes, lines, masses, along with their dynamic visual interrelations. It is undeniable that there is an art of producing visual patterns, but first, all paintings, though they contain visual patterns, are not only visual patterns, and second, there is no reason why a purely visual pattern should be any better or worse than a representation of solid objects, an illustration to a text, or what the eighteenth century called a historical painting, an allegorical painting, or a caricature. If one can be persuaded by the force of rhetoric that everything in a painting which is not purely visual is an illegitimate intrusion upon the canvas, then to be sure one will find such details bad. But before making the judgment, the premise on which it is based should be examined.

We use the word "to see" both in the sense of having visual experiences of colors, shapes, and movements and in the sense of understanding what is before us. This ambiguity goes back to ancient times in the vocabulary of the Greeks. "Do you see what I mean?" is a common enough question to illustrate this second usage and it involves nothing visual at all. When one looks and sees that the animal before one is a cat or dog, a flesh and blood cat or dog and not one made of wax or papier mâché, one has interpreted what one has before one and thus added something to the visual experience. What is added is what used to be called a judgment before logic ceased dealing with thinking. The overwhelming mass of visual works of art demand interpretation. They have what can only be called a meaning, though that poor word is so overburdened that it has become almost meaningless. Portraits, allegories, emblematic pictures, Surrealist pictures have meanings which are read out of their visual patterns. When we say, to take one of the simpler examples, that a portrait by Rembrandt or Holbein or Toulouse-Lautrec reveals the character of the sitter, we are going well beyond what is before our eyes and are reading the visual pattern as if it were a hieroglyph. A caricature, again, whether by Daumier or Herblock or some poor hack who has to produce some political comment every day, requires interpretation and once more is not simply so many lines and shapes. The frescoes of the Italian Renaissance artists, lives of saints, crucifixions, annunciations, descents from the cross, expulsions from Eden, have to be read, not merely looked at. The examples of pictures which are more than visual are so numerous that one has only to mention their existence in order to make one's point. As for Surrealist paintings, whether they be by Dali or Tanguy or Masson, their whole point is to evoke sentiment, thought, aspirations which we have repressed, and it is more than likely that the reason why they also evoke antagonism is that we are only too uneasy because of what they evoke in us. Criticism is often self-defense, throwing a veil over what we read into shapes and colors and pretending that it is not there. A glance at essays on "The Nude in Art" is convincing proof of this. If the critics who say that their sexual appetites are not even faintly stimulated by nudes are telling the truth, they had best consult a psychiatrist. The one argument against the nude in art which might be taken seriously is that it can become a substitute for the nude in life.

Music is probably the art closest to being purely sensory, for most listeners know so little about musical composition that they relax and enjoy the sounds which they hear and nothing else. Yet we know that at certain times musical figures and their interrelations were supposed to symbolize emotions or to express them or to arouse them. Some students of Bach, in particular Spitta and Schweitzer, claim to have found an intimate relation between the musical figures in the cantatas and oratorios and the text, so that it could be said that the figures meant what the text expressed in words. Wagner, as is well known, had themes to symbolize pretty nearly everything, fire, the Spirit of the Earth, the characters in his operas, both human (if they may be called human) and divine. And if the men who write program notes for concerts are honest in what they write, music can mean anything from "Fate knocking at the door," to the "restless reaching towards Eternity." Moreover, when one is listening to music, it is also possible and indeed normal to recall themes which keep recurring, which are in conflict with other themes, to hear developments which turn figures upside down and backward, as if the composer were juggling them, stringing them out in slower time only to break them off and then hurrying them up. Surely the drama of Beethoven's last quartettes is there and not merely imagined to be there. And of course there have always been known to be simple dance rhythms which actually are joyful, as well as slow movements of symphonies to which emotional terms have been applied by the composers themselves. There are undeniably people who can hear the development of a whole fugue as it grows and to whom there is both conflict and reconciliation in the *stretto* and conclusion. But clearly this is not simply sensory, though its source is of course sensation.

A second classification of the arts has been based on the materials which they use: colors, solids, sounds in sequence, words. The attempt has been made to emphasize the importance of bringing out the qualities of these materials in the work of art and never transcending the limits which they impose upon the imagination. Truth of material was one of Ruskin's slogans and it has remained a principle in the minds of some critics. Sculpture, according to this criterion, dealing with heavy materials, must look heavy and hence archaic sculpture is better than sculpture of, say, the Baroque period which defied the limitations of matter. The more a piece of sculpture could look like stone, for instance, the better it was. In this way Brancusi's eggs became better than Rodin's "Kiss" and the fantasies of Bernini became the worst of all possible sculpture. There is no question that the self-discipline involved in submitting oneself to one's material was admirable and my own generation grew up to prefer early Greek sculpture to that of the Hellenistic period.

Truth of material was often fused with a related idea, that since the word "sculpture" meant something carved, a piece of sculpture that had been modeled in clay and then cast in bronze was not really sculpture. It therefore had to be condemned. That one might retort, "Let's call it modelling and remain at peace," would never do. And when sculptors began making things out of wire and string and glass and lucite, or out of bits of clay thrown together on an armature and then cast so that sculpture turned into three-dimensional drawing, it was clear that the old rubrics would no longer apply and that if such things were to be called sculpture, then everything from Phidias to Maillol must be something else. One might have coarsely asked, "Well, what of it?" Is it essential to classify works of art? Could we not follow Croce and deny that there are any *genres?* Could we not just look at one of these three-dimensional drawings and see whether they were emotionally stirring, whether they might not perhaps be beautiful, whether they might not have "something to say"? Such an attitude was possible but very rare. On the whole the public was resentful, for it was confronted with the unfamiliar and hence frightened. And the practitioners of the new arts, for they were new regardless of what their makers claimed, were of no help. Their explanations of their programs, their manifestoes, were next to incomprehensible or downright nonsense.[3] Some of them, in fact probably the majority, insisted that there was nothing new in their program; they were simply doing what all great artists had always done; they were at one with Michelangelo, if they happened to approve of him, or with some anonymous sculptor of the Cyclades if they did not. Yet they never seemed to realize that if such claims were true, no explanations or apologias would have been necessary.

Allied to this approach of classifying the arts on the basis of their materials is that of Lessing with his differentiations between spatial and temporal arts. Poetry, it was said, cannot do what painting can do and painting cannot do what poetry can do. Hence each should be content to be itself, the one giving us instantaneous and immobile scenes, the other narrating episodes with beginning, middle, and end. There is no doubt that it takes time to read a poem or novel; one does not gulp it down all at once. But it also takes time to see a painting, unless it is simply an enormous patch of one color, like a dark room or the sky. How can anyone pretend to have seen a fresco by Giotto, Piero della Francesca, or Raphael, one of the religious or mythological paintings of Poussin, the allegories by Rubens in the Salle des Medicis in the Louvre, Géricault's "Radeau de la Méduse," Renoir's "Déjeûner des Canotiers," the "Embarkation from Cythera" by Watteau in one glance? All such paintings demand looking, searching, reading, letting the eye move from point to point, wandering about within the frame, in short, submission to the painting and design if they are going to be seen. If a painting is something out of time, if it is to make its effect instantaneously, then the best painting is simply a wash of one color over the entire surface of the canvas. And that is almost, if not quite, the point which we have reached in some of the paintings of Rothko. This is not to say, be it noted, that the precise color in a Rothko combined with a precise shape is incapable of stimulating the deepest aesthetic emotions. It obviously must have this capacity unless there are more hypocrites and snobs in the world than seems probable.

Lessing's argument was to the effect that the artist should recognize the limits of his art and not attempt to do the impossible, and in fact most critical theories which I have come across based on the classification of the arts do the same. But this also assumes that the important feature of a work of art is not its individuality but its conformity to generic traits. Everything which exists can be classified, for everything shares some qualities with other things. All science is founded on classifications when it tries to formulate general laws which are not simply rough statistical generalizations and even then the groups and populations and collections have to have common properties of some sort. For the purpose of knowing about things, for the purpose of saying something about things, for the purpose of applying common nouns to things, classification is indispensable. But for the purpose of appreciating things, of becoming acquainted with them as one would become acquainted with a human being, of responding to their beauty or ugliness or humor, such general or scientific knowledge is far from being necessary. The aesthetic situation, whatever else it may be, is a relation between an individual object and an individual human being. And though the human being brings to his experience of the object all that he knows and has lived through, and there is no reason why he should deny any of it, he is also confronted with something whose differences from everything else may be precisely that which moves him. Delight in recognizing the familiar in a new form is doubtless part of the aesthetic experience. There are without doubt many people who go through life in the hope that they will never come upon anything which they cannot label. They are like bird watchers or amateur botanists, cataloguers, identifiers. I fail to see why such people should be outlawed, but I also fail to see why their peculiar interest should become mandatory upon the rest of the human race. For some of us a work of art gains in interest if it seems to express a unique personality, an idea which is arresting because of its novelty, a revelation of something which we had never known of before. To such people it is the difference between *King Lear* and *The Chronicle History of King Leir*, if they know of it, which arouses their admiration, the differences between Racine's *Phèdre* and Euripides' *Hippolytus*, the difference between the "Resurrection" of Piero della Francesca and that of Grünewald which excites them. To them works of art resemble people in that we want to understand them and also to like them. The experience of seeing works of art in part is a quivering balance between scientific knowledge and direct apprehension. On the one hand there is generalization, on the other perception.

Now it will be observed that all such strictures are based on the principle that the artist is a submissive type or that he should try to be one. Let us assume that each art has a foreordained material in order to avoid forensic complications. But surely it is not obvious that submission to one's material is inherently better than victory over it. There also happens to be art which defies the limitations of matter. Baroque sculpture and architecture do precisely this, and sometimes with amazing success. I have written elsewhere [4] on how perfect is the congruence between Bernini's "St. Theresa" and the moment which is being represented in it, the artist overcoming the limitations of his material, the saint overcoming those of her body. The challenge which matter presented to the artist need not be refused. One can always accept it and meet it and conquer. Brancusi not only made ovoid lumps of matter which lay heavily upon the earth, but also the famous "Bird in Flight" in which the reflections of light on the highly polished brass played as important a role as the shape of the brass. Fountains when the water is turned on add movement to sculpture and, though one may not like the sculptures themselves in the fountains of Versailles, for instance, the moment they are splashed with the jets of water, they become transformed. I venture to say that a skyscraper would look intolerably heavy if its surfaces were not lightened by fenestration or inlaid glass and if the architect did not introduce lines which would lead the eye upwards. Half of the admiration which we feel for the Eiffel Tower must be attributable to its visual lightness as the lines swerve upward. It does not look as if bound to earth, squatting like the pyramids of Egypt, though its weight must be considerable. Does one admire the stoniness, the weight, the rectangularity of Perrault's façade of the Louvre, or the calm rhythm of the colonnade and pilasters, the openings, the play of light and shadow, the very antitheses of those qualities resident in the materials of which it is composed? One can as easily be moved by defiance as by submission, though it is equally absurd when elaborated into a generalized program. One cannot be in a state of rebellion to everything, it is true, but nevertheless if one is submissive to everything, one might just as well die.

Living is overcoming obstacles and so is thinking. There is no reason why the artist should be deprived of this satisfaction.

It is our thesis that there are no purposes inherent in materials, sensory qualities, or any other classificatory traits which determine the rightness and wrongness of what an artist has succeeded in doing. There is no reason why an art should not be both visual and auditory and verbal, witness, the drama; both spatial and temporal, witness Chinese painted scrolls or the movies or the ballet; visual and temporal, witness Calder's mobiles. There seems to be no reason to deny the human imagination its rights to create a universe of its own, as is done in literature, and, if a man can overcome the obstacles which matter sets up before him, so much the better. It is clear that there just happen to be some obstacles which in the nature of things cannot be overcome. One cannot build a building out of liquids nor expect a picture to dance automatically. But as long as what used to be called natural law is respected—and there is no way of not respecting it—the imagination cannot be prevented from doing whatever it wishes to do. Furthermore, in all likelihood when a possibility has been detected, someone will make it actual. When distortions were consciously introduced into paintings for the sake of design, design became superior to representation. It did not take long for painters to make designs in which there was no representation at all. They forgot that even in illustrations to well-known texts the element of design was present and distinguishable, but though two elements may be present and distinguishable in anything, that does not imply that in separation each would be of aesthetic interest. Representation without design, if such a thing were possible, would be close to formlessness; form without content is void of the very thing which would give it life and significance. It is as incomplete as a mathematical formula, useful as a pattern and possibly as a recipe but nothing else. Naum Gabo, for instance, in his *Realist Manifesto* of 1920 laid it down as a dogma that sculpture should be constructed as an engineer constructs his bridges and that the laws of statics should be the laws of Constructivism. But nevertheless he also realized that these laws must be made concrete in perceptual form. The spectator does not simply read the laws in the construction but sees the exemplification of the laws first. Here we are directed toward what we should observe by the artist's writings. But it must also be kept in mind that content may be contributed by the spectator as well as by the artist.

If the classifications mentioned are all unsatisfactory, what is to be done? It is the point of view of this book that the medium used by the artist is used for some human purpose or other, conscious or unconscious, and that this purpose is not primarily perceptual except where the artist wishes it to be. One can tell a story in words, in pictures, and in a limited way in the dance and in music. There are enough narrative ballets and program music to show that the last part of my sentence is not false. One can again express one's sense of humor in literature, in painting and drawing, in music, in the dance. One can express one's religious feelings in all these and in architecture and sculpture too. Whatever interests may be human can be satisfied through any art as far as one knows. It is true, I think, that there have been few attempts at what might be called fantastic architecture, but that may be because of the expense of building and the relative permanence of what is built. But there have been houses which were built not to serve some function as prescribed in the textbooks, but to serve a function as determined by the owners.[5] Gingerbread, Hudson River bracketed, *art nouveau*, Carpenter's Gothic, the works of Gaudi in Barcelona, octagon houses, may be criticized as in "bad taste," but how do they differ in essence from Frank Lloyd Wright's Kaufman house, "Falling Water"? They differ only in the reputation of their designers. There is no sense in building a house over a waterfall, if one means by sense anything other than pleasure. But what is the sense of building anything if it is not pleasant?

CHAPTER V

Functionalism

THE TASK of the aesthetician would be easier if one could assign a special function to each art so that the critic could tell whether or not it was being successfully performed. But since in the first place, no one has ever yet defined the limits of any art in a manner satisfactory to all, and in the second, a given work of art may successfully perform several functions, and in the third, an art as time goes on may change its function, how is the delimitation of function to be achieved? Our answer is simple enough, perhaps too simple to satisfy the philosophers. It is that we must first distinguish between the function of artistry and of the work of art; then admit that the function of the former is determined by the artist under the influence of tradition and of his social group, whereas the latter is determined similarly by the public. It is not determined by the material which the artist is using, nor by the sense organ supposed to be its target, nor by the class to which it is customarily assigned, nor by its spatial or temporal character, except insofar as these and other criteria are accepted by the artist, used by society, or carried along by tradition.

An Oriental sculptor makes a statue of the Buddha first, as a copy of an older statue and second, as an object of veneration.[1] But the Occidental who buys the statue of the Buddha buys it not to pray before nor because it reproduces an older statue, but to look at. An American Indian makes a basket to carry corn in; a New Yorker buys the basket as an ornament. Le Corbusier is the author, as everyone knows, of the famous phrase, "A house is a machine to live in," and he has been interpreted—wrongly—as meaning that a house has no other function. After all, a man who employs an architect wants a house which looks well, which "fits into the ground" on which it is situated, which conforms to certain standards of style, which will outlive him (at least this used to be true), which will symbolize his social status, and which will not cost more than 120 per cent of what he can afford. Many of these desires, a functionalist will say, are irrelevant to architecture. Nevertheless they help determine what a house will be. For that matter analogous things determine what a picture or a book or a play will be too. "Living" is a very wide term, for everything we do is part of our living, even though Diogenes of Sinope might consider some of our interests as contemptible. He himself was satisfied with a wine jar; a Cambodian peasant is satisfied with a platform on stilts thatched with palm or banana leaves. I have been told that the desire to have a house of a given style recalling the styles of former periods of foreign countries is to be condemned. But a man's longing for identification with the past or with the country of his ancestors is normal enough not to be tossed out of the window as trivial; it is an integral part of his living. Who knows why the American of today feels the need of a picture window which looks out on nothing but the traffic in the street or the walls of his neighbor's house? Who knows why American colleges ape the style of the late Middle Ages or early Renaissance or eighteenth-century Georgian? Such imitations can be sneered at, as every other desire of the human race can be sneered at, but conformity to the manners of the past, more or less remote, is never sneered at in other fields such as language or religion. In Guadet's *Eléments et principes de l'architecture*, which used to be the textbook of almost all architects, there is a chapter on the designing of theaters which is illuminating. He points out first that in France, whatever may be true of other countries, the audience is as much part of the show as what goes on on the stage. It is desirable, he says, that the procession of beautifully clothed women entering the auditorium be seen, and hence the architect should include a grand staircase with treads which are wide and which are well-lighted so that the audience with their jewels and evening gowns can be seen as they enter the building. He also points out that the staircase must be broken at certain intervals so that when the public is leaving the theater there will not be a tendency for the people in the rear of the procession to push against those ahead of them and send them stumbling down the stairs. In discussing Garnier's Opéra in Paris, Guadet describes the elaborate process of experimentation through which the carriage entrance was designed so as to permit the horses to move up the ramp in an orderly fashion, discharge their passengers, and leave before the following carriages could overtake them. Yet were one to define a theater as Le Corbusier defined a house, one would say that it was a machine in which to produce plays; that it is also a machine to make people comfortable while getting to their seats and seeing the play would be an afterthought. One might in this way define man as a machine for continuing the species and forget everything else.

Perhaps the most unfortunate statement of aesthetic function was the sentence which went back to the Ancients, that all art is an imitation of nature. No one can say with any confidence that he has understood this sentence, for it has been taken to mean that every work of art imitates the appearance of some natural object or act and also that every work of art reproduces the creative power of nature. Neither of these extreme formulas is true of all works of art. There is, to be sure, an art of reproducing the looks of natural objects, the best of which are illustrations to medical and other scientific books. There is also an art of reproducing natural processes which consists, as far as I understand the matter, of relaxing and painting, writing, singing automatically. The best examples of this second kind of imitation might be the painting of the late Jackson Pollock, the early writings of Gertrude Stein, and the singing of a child. The artistry consists in disciplining oneself to the point of rejecting all that one has learned. This is not so easy as it sounds. For one's training becomes an integral part of one's nature, ingrained by habit, and compulsive. One has only to try to write a page without regard for ordinary, that is traditional, grammar and syntax to appreciate the difficulty of abandoning one's past. I have seen parodies of Gertrude Stein and none of them read like Gertrude Stein, and I have seen at least one imitation of Pollock and it was equally ineffective. Whatever one may think of an art which is governed exclusively by the "unconscious," it is not easily acquired. The mind of an adult is too rigidly encased in habits to throw them off without a struggle. Moreover the unconscious, were it entirely in control of what we do, would lead us back into the arms of Nature and whatever was art would disappear. It always has partial control, but wherever there is artistry, there is some sort of discipline.

Whatever assignment of purpose is made to art by an artist may be disregarded by the spectator; whatever function is assigned by the spectator may be disregarded by the artist. If a spectator wishes, he may try to discover what the artist thought was his purpose and think of that alone when in the presence of the work of art. But who really knows what the purpose of any artist is? What did Homer believe to be the purpose of epic poetry, Shakespeare of the drama, Michelangelo of sculpture? Even when artists have left us manifestoes or, as in the case of Michelangelo, other autobiographical documents, however enlightening these may be, we are not in duty bound to deny ourselves and identify with them. Renoir may have thought that he was following the irregularity of nature in his paintings; we are not condemned to seeing only natural irregularity in them.[2] Manifestoes, moreover, are rationalizations; they do not and probably cannot reveal psychological causes except to a psychiatrist. What man really knows why he went into business instead of into the church or politics or one of the professions? The causes of human behavior involve a complex of biochemical factors, unconscious drives, social pressure, along with the emotional aura of certain occupations. But this is a field shrouded in darkness and, though a certain amount of light has been thrown upon it by the work of the Freudians and post-Freudians, they would be the first to admit that they have only begun to open the subject.[3] The kind of rationalization which one advances is itself determined by psychological causes of which we are usually unaware. A man may say that he has gone into medicine because his father was a successful physician and that he hoped to inherit his practice, but he does not know—or say— why he wants to follow in his father's footsteps. Another may say that he is going into business in order to make a lot of money, but does he really know why he wants to make money? A person may become a sculptor from an anal-erotic drive, from a desire to kill, to conceal his homosexuality, as an act of simple religious faith, or from other causes singly or in groups, but that might be true of any choice of a profession. Yet the sculptor in question would hardly give such causes as his reasons for choosing his art. If he did, he would probably not be a sculptor but a psychiatrist. Where a manifesto confines itself to indicating technical devices, this problem does not arise, for it will be merely a clear statement of the limitations which the artist has imposed upon himself. Thus the function of an art reduces to the question of the different sorts of techniques.

It may be thought a pedantic distinction to point out that the attitude of the artist is not that of the spectator, but it has to be made on historical grounds if on no others. We have preserved and cherished works of art from different cultures, ancient and modern, European and exotic, and it would be absurd to demand of those of us who look at a bit of African sculpture with pleasure to adopt the point of view of the savage for whom it may be an ancestor or a god. We cannot even look at a statue of Hermes or Aphrodite or Zeus as if they were substitutes for divinity. We simply do not believe in the divinity of these gods. They may be beautiful sculptures; we may be deeply moved by them; but in the nature of things we cannot treat them as the Greeks did. We assign to them functions of our own devising and the fact that it is we, rather than Phidias or Scopus or Praxiteles, is a matter of no importance to us. We know, moreover, that even when a statue is a good replica of a Praxiteles, it is no longer in the condition in which it was made, for in all probability it was originally painted. The eyes which Winckelmann thought were gazing off into Eternity had painted irises which, if they were restored, would make the images glaring horrors. Yet the mistake has been the source of great emotion. Again, some of the most beautiful architecture in the world is the relic of a civilization which has completely disappeared. We cannot, nor should we wish to, look at Angkor Wat as Jayavarman VII or his subjects looked at it. We may know from our reading that it was a symbol of the universe with Mount Meru in the center, with bodies of water surrounding it as the oceans surround the land, with four portals at the four points of the compass; but we do not believe that the universe is like that nor do we think that a temple need reproduce the pattern of the universe, nor that the Chief of State need sleep every night in the central tower with a Serpent-Queen, nor finally do we think that if an architectural complex has these characteristics, it would be more beautiful than if it did not. The situation can also be illustrated from literature. If it is true that Shylock was conceived as a comic character, as seems probable, that does not commit us to laughing at those of his speeches which strike us as pathetic.[4] If it is true that a temperance drama, such as *Ten Nights in a Bar-room*, was intended to be serious propaganda against alcoholism, that does not prevent us from seeing it as funny. The *Aeneid*, as far as I know, is no longer used as an oracle nor do we read it, when we do read it, as a panegyric of the house of Augustus Caesar. The epistolary novel may have been invented by Richardson as a manual of letter writing; no one wants to write letters of that type any longer, and if we read *Clarissa Harlowe* at all for pleasure, it is because of the story, the psychological analysis, and the usual purpose of entertainment. Who bothers any longer about the genetic theories of Zola when reading his books? About Tennyson's interest in evolution? About Stendhal's adherence to ideology? Only specialists in the history of literature and in the ideas incorporated in it. People still read such authors but have given a new function to their works. At a time when it was fashionable to look for "realism" in a book, books were judged by their fidelity to the realistic program. When functionalism became an architectural slogan, every building was thought of as a machine, more or less efficient. When fantasy is the rule, then the realistic novel will be said to have failed in its purpose or to have had the wrong purpose. For we always transfer the functions of what we believe to be art to all works of art. When we condemn a novel because it is indecent, we act as if we thought that all novels ought to be decent. And when we condemn one for preaching conventional morality, we argue as if it were the function of novels not to preach at all. There is an art of preaching and of preaching through fiction and, even when the homiletic purpose was farthest from an artist's intentions, some people find moral lessons in his work.[5] If general opinion counts for anything, it ought to prove that didacticism is no blemish on a work of art, for otherwise *Pilgrim's Progress*, the *Faery Queen*, *Paradise Lost*, the *Essay on Man*, to say nothing of Lucretius, Goethe, and even Bernard Shaw would be next to worthless.

Who has the power of assigning functions to the various arts? What legislative body or academy has been given the privilege of telling any artist, whether he be poet or painter or architect or sculptor or composer, what the purpose of his work must be? The artist himself, subject of course to the tradition which he has accepted, determines this in part, determines it at least as far as he himself is concerned, but unfortunately he is not the only person concerned. One has also the persons who are going to look at the picture or sculpture, live in the house, read the poem, or listen to the music, and there has seldom, if ever, been complete agreement between the two about the function of the work of art. It is simply not true that what I have called the spectator can look at a work of art in the same way as the man who made it does. The latter may have made it entirely to sell, thought of it as something he had to say regardless of who was listening, accepted a given view of what his art should be and tried patiently to realize that potentiality, been utterly innocent of any purpose except that of painting the scene before him or writing that particular poem or that particular sonata. It would be incredible that a spectator take the point of view of the artist, except in a purely intellectual fashion, saying to himself that the painter, for instance, was painting the façade of Rouen Cathedral at high noon and that it looked just right; reading a novel and saying, "This is the truth of that situation"; hearing a sonata and saying nothing whatsoever but nevertheless being carried away by it. I do not maintain that the spectator's reaction has precedence over the artist's intention nor that the artist's intention has precedence over the spectator's reaction. For looking, hearing, understanding are just not identical with painting, composing, and writing.

Nor am I denying that there are cultures and periods in our own culture in which artistic functions have been determined and maintained by tradition. Where one sees sculptures, made over the centuries, of almost indistinguishable form—indistinguishable to Western eyes—as in India, Siam, and Cambodia, one is forced to the conclusion that whatever else the statue may have as its purpose, one purpose is to resemble other statues made in the past. In Egypt certain forms were equally traditional. Frontality in statues in the round, profiles with modification of the eyes and shoulders for reliefs were the rule. Subjects too have been prescribed by patrons, both individual and collective, and by influential critics. Witness Boileau and Joshua Reynolds,[6] the last session of the Council of Trent, and all academies. In the eighteenth century certain musical forms were crystallized and it was possible to write manuals on the composition of, for instance, the fugue which were followed by all—except the masters.[7] Landscape painting was pretty well standardized according to species: the romantic, the picturesque, the pastoral, and so on, and rules could be laid down which the legislators at least thought were binding. Du Fresnoy's De arte graphica, translated by Dryden, had almost as much influence as Boileau's *Art poétique*, imitated by Pope in his *Essay on Criticism*, and itself an imitation of Horace. It is clear that such works cannot be written unless their authors believe that each kind of art has its own unique function. Ruskin's *Seven Lamps of Architecture* is a good example of the technique which such authorities use to prove their conclusions.

In view of Ruskin's influence in the nineteenth century, it may be well to point out on what assumptions it was based. The seven lamps are seven guides to aesthetic judgment. If followed, they are supposed to give one criteria for determining whether an architectural work is good or bad.

1. The Lamp of Sacrifice

It is perhaps unnecessary to point out that Ruskin's main interest in this book was religious. His emphasis was on art in the service of religion. The beauty of architecture was an offering to God, giving Him the best of our possessions as a witness of our adoration of His goodness and mercy. A beautiful church is a work of love and must be judged as such. Hence since the love which we express can be measured only by our intentions, a humble village church may express a spirit of sacrifice as great as that expressed in a magnificent cathedral. Bearing this in mind, we can better understand his saying, "Though it may not be necessarily in the interest of religion to admit the service of the arts, the arts will never flourish until they have been primarily devoted to that service—devoted, both by architect and employer; by the one in scrupulous, earnest, affectionate design; by the other in expenditure at least more frank, at least less calculating, than that which he would admit in the indulgence of his own private feelings." [8] Neither of these qualities can be seen by the unaided eye, for it is only figuratively that we can say that we see scrupulous, earnest, and affectionate design, nor can the measure of a man's expenditure be calculated by the market value of a building. For the designer may conceal his motives in his building and the Maecenas who pays for it may have so much money that cost is of no consequence to him. Ruskin's principle here is ethical. Regardless of what we may discover from looking at a building, both the architect and the employer know whether they have put the best which they possess into it.

Now the best, says Ruskin (p. 37), is indicated by the "apparent labor" which has been expended on a structure and the more the labor, the greater the beauty. The labor has a visual index then and it is that which will give us a clue to beauty. "All old work nearly has been hard work. It may be the hard work of children, of barbarians, of rustics; but it is always their utmost. Ours has as constantly the look of money's worth, of a stopping short wherever and whenever we can, of a lazy compliance with low conditions; never of a fair putting forth of our strength" (*Ibid.*). Apparently the slogan which preached the value of art which conceals art is not accepted by Ruskin; he wants an artist's labor to appear clearly before the onlooker. This does not mean that the puffing and blowing, all the little tricks by which one gets an effect, must show, for that kind of ostentation would have been disgusting to Ruskin. But there are indications of insincerity, of makeshift devices, of what he thought of as falsehood which we can all easily perceive and it is those which he condemns. "Do not let us boss our roofs with wretched, half-worked, blunt edged rosettes; do not let us flank our gates with rigid imitations of mediaeval statuary" (p. 38). Such things can certainly be perceived if we have sharp enough eyes and, if we do not, someone can point them out to us. One may not accept Ruskin's motivation in this passage, but it is worth observing that at the very outset of his book he assumes that the art which he is discussing, and by extension all the arts, can be judged only after a consideration of the artist's motives. The work of art is the outward symbol of an inner purpose and with all Ruskin's faults, he was willing to make allowances for individual capacities. He realized that artistry could not be isolated from the rest of a man's life but must be integrated into it as a whole. This was the polar antithesis of what has been called aestheticism. To waste labor was to him deceit in the eyes of men and an insincere sacrifice in those of God.

So strongly did he believe this that he deprecated leaving those parts of a building which could not be seen undecorated or unfinished. The backs of statues in niches, or in pediments, should be as complete as the fronts; string courses should not be terminated where they are no longer visible. Had he known more about Oriental art, he might have seen a dramatic example of this principle in the buried scenes of the Underworld at Borobudur, scenes which were, as far as anyone knows, deliberately buried though as finished as those which were visible. But if one must stop, Ruskin continues, then one must stop boldly, frankly admitting that one has no intention of continuing. One must use one's common sense and realize that intricacy of ornament cannot be seen from a certain distance, and having determined from what distance it can be seen, then the designer will finish his work with that in view. It is hard to understand how such a consideration comes under the rubric of sacrifice, for a man might think the sacrifice were greater if it were invisible. But as usual with Ruskin, he shifts his point of view from the artist to the spectator whenever it suits his purpose. An excess of ornament is wearisome to the spectator; he simply cannot take it in. One might conclude that from the artist's point of view the Lamp of Sacrifice has been burning brightly, but from the spectator's it has flickered and grown hazy. The situation unfortunately is critical. For if there is to be a meeting of minds in artistic matters, then the sacrifice should become visual for any enlightened mind to see.

2. The Lamp of Truth

This principle is perhaps the best-known of the seven and the one which was the most widely accepted. Here too we are involved in the ethics of artistry, and Ruskin is preaching against what he thinks of as deceit. Deceit first appears when one suggests a mode of structure or support other than the true one, "as in the pendants of late Gothic roofs" (p. 62). He is, however, willing to admit that there is a question of degree. Gilding in architecture is not deceit, for we know that it is not supposed to be gold, whereas in jewelry it is deceit. In architecture one need not exhibit the whole structure, for just as the human skin covers the muscular and skeletal anatomy, so the roof and walls of a building may conceal the supports. But in such cases we already know the truth; we know that the vaulting bears down on its supports, but in order to eliminate the feeling of distress which we would have if the stress were emphasized, we grant that it may be concealed, and that the building may be allowed to look as if it were soaring upward. "When the mind is informed beyond the possibility of mistake as to the true nature of things, the affecting it with a contrary impression, however distinct, is no dishonesty, but, on the contrary, a legitimate appeal to the imagination" (p. 64 f.). Ruskin admits that there is a "nice point of conscience" involved here and one wonders whether it is not his ineradicable love of Gothic which makes him excuse deceit and concealment in thirteenth-century cathedrals and condemn it in flamboyant architecture. Nice points of conscience are encountered everywhere and no one so far has been able to define their solutions. It would be convenient to have casebooks in aesthetic casuistry analogous to those which confessors use in moral matters, to the casebooks in law, and even to the Talmud, but unhappily none exist. Ruskin gives an architect permission to introduce flying buttresses (p. 67) because they are necessary. But when the flying buttress became in late Gothic an item of decoration and served no functional purpose, it was to be outlawed. Here he objects to something which is characteristic of the history of art: the retention of obsolete instruments as of interest in themselves. The flamboyant flying buttress was used, he points out (p. 68), where "it could be of no use, becoming a mere tie, not between the pier and wall, but between the wall and the top of the decorative pinnacle, thus attaching itself to the very point where its thrust, if any, could not be resisted" (*Ibid*). The question is whether anyone is deceived by such fanciful buttresses or whether they are not accepted as simply decorative items in the total scheme, showing the virtuosity of the builder. If they are to be condemned outright, then one should also condemn the pillars of many Egyptian temples because they derive from bundles of sticks tied together, or the vestigial beam-ends in Doric triglyphs, or for that matter the acanthus leaves in Corinthian capitals. Nothing enrages Ruskin more than this commonplace incident in the history of forms. The lantern of St. Ouen "where the pierced buttress having an ogee curve, looks about as much calculated to bear a thrust as a switch of willow; and the pinnacles, huge and richly decorated, have evidently no work to do whatsoever, but stand round the central tower, like four idle servants, as they are—heraldic supporters, that central tower being merely a hollow crown, which needs no more buttressing than a basket does. . . . It is one of the basest pieces of Gothic in Europe; its flamboyant traceries being of the last and most degraded forms; and its entire plan and decoration resembling, and deserving little more credit than, the burnt sugar ornaments of elaborate confectionery" (p. 69 f.). It does not occur to him that the architect who designed this may have known that no one would be deceived by it. The man whose tailor sews three buttons on his cuffs which button nothing whatsoever nowadays does not think he is deceiving anyone who looks at them and he is right. Forty or fifty years ago they did button the cuffs. Now they are there because it is customary to put them there. The broken wooden pediments which appear on doorways, mirrors, highboys, and even roadside signs are vestigial cross sections of a hip roof with the point bitten off. But no one thinks of them as such; their form has become presumably beautiful in itself in the eyes of people who like it. It is to be doubted whether anyone who has a Chippendale highboy surmounted by a broken pediment with an elaborate pine cone or other fantastic fruit in the hole even knows its historical source. Such things are links with the past forged most of the time in ignorance of what is being tied together and are also opportunities for technical ingenuity. The attention of the spectator shifts from function to appearance. It lights upon the look of the thing and, if the look is satisfactory, that is all that is demanded.

Similar restrictions were put upon the use of iron. For iron is now asked to do what clay, stone, and wood were doing. Ruskin in a moment of perspicuity prophesies that "the time is probably near when a new system of architectural laws will be developed, adapted entirely to metallic construction" (p. 70). That time has now come and we no longer pretend that our metals are stone or wood. Whether this is because architects have accepted Ruskin's truth of materials or not, I am not qualified to say, but their insistence upon utilizing to the full and, what is more, frankly the resources of the various metals, is obvious. Ruskin was willing to allow Brunelleschi his iron chain round the dome of Florence and the builders of Salisbury the iron binding of the central tower. The best he can do to justify this is to cite the example of iron nails in wooden structures, pretty weak since wooden pegs would be better. But in general he insists that metals may be used "as a *cement*, but not as a *support*." The moment iron is used to resist a lateral thrust or "to do what wooden beams would have done as well, that instant the building ceases, so far as such applications of metal extend, to be true architecture" (p. 74).

A second violation of truthfulness is painting surfaces to represent some material other than that of which they really consist or painting sculpture upon them. Marbleized wood or paper, *trompe-l'oeil* effects of any sort, lifelike polychrome statues, would probably all be examples of what he is condemning. He was willing to allow Michelangelo to paint architectural details into the ceiling of the Sistine Chapel, for there no one could be deceived. But the ceiling of Milan Cathedral with its painted fan tracery can deceive and is therefore to be condemned. Yet Ruskin was no more deceived by Milan than by the Sistine ceiling. He knew that the architectural detail in both was paint, not stone. And anyone interested in the material of which it was made could easily find out. It is not certain that whoever painted the fan tracery in Milan had any dishonest motive. He probably thought that it would be an agreeable way to finish it. One can understand that if a man buys a piece of wood painted to look like marble and pays the price of marble for it, he might legitimately complain. But there is nothing more wicked inherently in marbleized wood than in conjuring tricks. Feats of legerdemain deceive the onlookers and they enjoy being deceived. That is the reason why they like such tricks. They know that the rabbit must have been in the hat before it came out but they want to be under the illusion that it had not been there. To see the impossible being performed before one's eyes just happens to be something which the human race enjoys. I do not know how to rank the various forms of enjoyment and it may well be that such vestiges of primitive magic are at the bottom of the scale. But if we eliminate all traces of magic from art, there will be nothing left except material. To turn wood into marble, plaster into stone, a flat surface into relief, clay into flesh, these are stunts if you will. But they are artistry in themselves and cannot be appraised as if they were claiming to be another kind of artistry. If you try to appraise marbleized wood as if it were marble, then it is you who are deceiving yourself and not the artist who is deceiving you.

Even more Draconian is Ruskin's condemnation of all cast and machine made ornaments. It is "operative deceit"; it is all dishonest. "Exactly as a woman of feeling would not wear false jewels, so would a builder of honor disdain false ornaments. The use of them is just as downright and inexcusable a lie" (p. 97). But this could be extended to casts of statues and reproductions of paintings. It is true that such reproductions seldom are accurate, for our mechanical means of reproducing the color of paints are not perfect and a plaster cast does not reproduce the edges of the planes and the quality of the stone, bronze, or wood, of a piece of sculpture. If such reproductions are palmed off as originals, of course there is deception. Such deception is morally and economically unjust. But why should a man who cannot have an original of a painting or statue which he admires be reduced to going without a reproduction of it? As long as he does not confuse it with the original and make comments about it as if it were the original, what harm has been done? It is doubtful whether any woman who wears costume jewelry thinks she is deceiving anyone and certainly doubtful that anyone is deceived. One might as well argue that it is wrong for a woman to wear lipstick or rouge on the ground that someone might think her cheeks were really rosy rather than sallow and her lips red rather than a pale pink. Such deceptions are part of making life agreeable and that too is an art. Ruskin here starts with a narrow definition of the end of art which alone, he thinks, is legitimate, and then proceeds to rule out everything else. But what happens if one does not accept his definition?

3. The Lamp of Power

The discussion of this principle is introduced by a paragraph distinguishing between two sources of architectural excellence: that which is the veneration of natural forms and that which expresses man's domination over nature. Both of these give power to a building, the one the power of sublimity, the other that of beauty.

First in the requirements of the sublime is a certain magnitude. But size is not enough. It must be visible as a unit and in order to achieve this, the architect must have a single bounding line, whether it forms a pyramid or a vertical mass. The surface must be "wide, bold, and unbroken" (p. 140). The mind must have "space enough over which to range," and must be reminded, "however feebly, of the joy that it has in contemplating the flatness and sweep of great plains and broad seas" (Ibid.). Ruskin's recipes for attaining power, the use of the square and the circle, need not be examined here. What is of more interest is his throwing the emphasis now upon the observer. We must have the impression of power or sublimity. It is the look of the building now which counts. "The relative majesty of buildings depends more on the weight and vigor of their masses, than on any other attribute of light, of darkness, of color, not mere sum of any of these, but breadth of them; not broken light, nor scattered darkness, nor divided weight, but solid stone, broad sunshine, starless shade" (p. 181). He does not say that all buildings should be sublime or majestic, but he does rank sublimity and grandeur above all other qualities which a building might have. But again it is the impression which a building makes upon a spectator of which he is speaking, of the feeling of power which it stimulates, not the power which is felt by the builder himself as he builds.

If I emphasize this, it is because he is here frankly recognizing that art is much more than self-expression. It is the acceptance of certain moral qualities as guiding principles of the artist. If art is worship and demands sacrifice and obedience to truth, it ought also, he seems to feel, awaken in the spectator a feeling of awe at the majesty of nature. "An architect," he says (p. 184), "should live as little in cities as a painter. Send him to our hills, and let him study there what nature understands by a buttress, and what by a dome." Just what domes one would find in nature is problematic, but the leading idea is clear enough. Nature is the primary evidence of the Creator's art. To show our reverence for Him we should look for our own rules in His examples. If then we do this, we ought to produce buildings which like their natural models will be sublime and will be felt to be sublime. That mountains and cliffs were not admired before the eighteenth century except in China does not bother Ruskin.

4. The Lamp of Beauty

Ruskin here makes an assumption which might be questioned but, since he made it overtly, it must be accepted by us if only for clarity of exposition. That assumption is that the feeling for beauty is universal and instinctive (p. 187). He will, he says, only use as examples of beauty those which would be granted to be beautiful without dispute. This is all very well, but the problems of criticism arise when one comes upon examples of beauty upon which people do not agree. Generalizing from points of agreement induces one to overlook negative instances, and by overlooking them one overlooks the problems inherent in the situation.

Ruskin's argument here, like that dealing with sublimity, is not that one should copy natural objects in order to achieve beauty, but "that all beautiful lines are adaptations of those which are commonest in the external creation; that, in proportion to the richness of their association, the resemblance to natural work, as a type and help, must be more closely attempted, and more clearly seen; and that beyond a certain point, and that a very low one, man cannot advance in the invention of beauty, without directly imitating natural form" (p. 188). There are several terms in this quotation which are worth accentuating. First, the beautiful lines are *adaptations*; second, they are adaptations of the *commonest* lines in nature; third, there is a point below which man can invent beautiful forms. This would require some clear delimitation of adaptation as distinguished from copying, some specification of which lines are commonest in nature, some indication of just what the low point of adaptation is. The triglyph and cornice of the Doric temple are not imitative, he says (*Ibid.*), but "no one would call them beautiful." True enough, no one except a Chinese calligrapher would call three vertical lines beautiful, and he would do it only if the brush strokes showed a certain character which is admired in Chinese aesthetics. Be that as it may, the frieze of triglyphs is not obviously one triglyph, and uninteresting shapes in themselves when repeated in a border have often been thought beautiful. But this is a minor matter in all respects except one. That one is the appearance in our day of quasi-geometrical patterns in painting as well as in decoration and these according to amateurs of nonobjective art are beautiful. One other *caveat* should be entered here also: nature to Ruskin was the nature of the unaided eye in rural England. The forms seen under the microscope, both animal and vegetable, have in recent years also been used by artists and such forms as Arp's zoomorphs are now accepted as quite as beautiful as leaves and flowers.

His own examples are listed as follows: "The Romanesque arch is beautiful as an abstract line. Its type is always before us in that of the apparent vault of heaven, and the horizon of the earth. The cylindrical pillar is always beautiful, for God has so moulded the stem of every tree that it is pleasant to the eyes. The pointed arch is beautiful; it is the termination of every leaf that shakes in the summer wind, and its most fortunate associations are directly borrowed from the trefoiled grass of the field, or from the stars of its flowers. Farther than this, man's invention could not reach without frank imitation. His next step was to gather the flowers themselves, and wreathe them in his capitals" (p. 189). No mention is made in this place of crystals, e.g., snowflakes, and it is probable that he was thinking here exclusively of animate nature when he used the word nature. He is, however, so convinced of the truth of his principle that he is willing to say that forms "which are *not* taken from natural objects *must* be ugly" (p. 190, italics in text). This sounds pretty extreme, but as a matter of fact it turns out to be a *petitio principii*, since he believes it to be "out of the power of a man to conceive beauty without her [Nature's] aid." Clearly, if man cannot conceive beauty without the aid of nature and the aid in question is furnishing models for the beautiful, then in the long run all beautiful forms will be taken from nature. This is not argument; it is dogma. But it is a dogma which makes Ruskin a bit uneasy, and it was not long before he distinguished between the most natural forms and the least, the former being the most frequently seen, not the most frequently existent, be it noted. For this reason he condemns the Greek fret or *guilloche* because in nature it is found, he says, only in crystals of bismuth, which are not only unique, "but only attainable by an artificial process, the metal itself never being found pure" (p. 193). The Greek egg and dart molding, on the contrary, "is as beautiful as this is painful" (p. 194). The oval shape is clearly, as its name implies, a natural shape, but what of the dart?

Now one would imagine that if beauty is one of the Seven Lamps, then it would be good to have as much of it as possible. But, as so often happens when one is reading Ruskin, one comes suddenly upon an outburst of bad temper. It is all very well to have decorated house fronts, but when the same decorations are put on shop fronts, it becomes immoral. A shop should attract people by the quality of its wares and not by the beauty of its façade. This is surely reasonable. But what makes one think that if the front of a shop is attractive, the wares within must be cheap and tawdry? The same remark holds good for railway stations. Travelers by rail, we are informed, are not interested in beauty; they are in a hurry; they want to be off and going. But, one might reply, they sometimes have to wait, especially in France and England, to make connections with another train. Why should they at such times be deprived of the sight of something beautiful? After patiently reading such tantrums, one wakes up to another shift in the author's point of view. Beauty now becomes something we should all strive for, but it should be kept in its place. It is to be appraised relatively to that which it beautifies. And then it dawns upon one that Ruskin has forgotten all about the beauty of the building as a whole, of the mass, and is now thinking of beauty as applied ornament. His anger becomes such that he overlooks the orientation of his argument. For if the ornamentation of, let us say, a railway station is bad because no one has the time to look at it, an element of functionalism has entered the discussion. But then what happens to his previous counsel to finish decoration on the backs of sculpture and to carry out courses of decoration even into the corners where they will be invisible?

5. The Lamp of Life

Just as our contemporary architects have followed Ruskin, though often in ignorance of his guidance, in accepting truth of material, condemning false fronts, cornices, and fake materials, so they have followed him in rejecting applied ornament. The Lamp of Life also has cast its beams on architectural practice of the present day in our use of the word "organic" as a term of praise. We find Ruskin saying, "Things in other respects alike, as in their substance, or uses, or outward forms, are noble or ignoble in proportion to the fulness of the life which either they themselves enjoy, or of whose action they bear the evidence, as sea sands are made beautiful by the bearing the seal of the motion of the waters" (p. 270 f.). This, he continues, is specially true of buildings which in order to be dignified and pleasant must vividly express "the intellectual life which has been concerned in their production." The question, of course, immediately arises as to what are the marks of such vitality by which we may recognize it.

What Ruskin himself styled his "wretched rant" (p. 276, n. 52), prevents one from having a very clear idea of the distinction which he was making between dead and living architecture. One thinks at first that the former is simply that which imitates the past. And indeed in those architectural offices of the past in which the architect first looked up the proper style in a book of styles, the proper ornament in a book of ornaments, and turned out a replica of a French farmhouse or a Cotswold cottage for a house in America, the Palazzo Vecchio for an office building, the Baths of Caracalla for a railway station, little was invented by the architect on his own. But that is not Ruskin's point. On the contrary, he says, "It is no sign of deadness in a present art that it borrows or imitates, but only if it borrows without paying interest, or if it imitates without choice" (p. 277). The interest consists in modifications of the original, clear enough to be seen as changes but not so clear as to prevent recognition of their source. In short, Ruskin wants a real but slow modification of the traditional. There must be no sharp break with the past, nothing radical or revolutionary; but there must also be no slavish fidelity to the past. This sounds so much better than it really is that Ruskin has to throw up the sponge and confess that "while it is easy to enumerate the signs of life, it is impossible to define or communicate life" (p. 278). But if he wishes architects to take over these signs of life and incorporate them in their work, what is he doing but telling them to copy with a fidelity which he has just condemned? He admits that Raphael lifted whole figures from Perugino and Masaccio, that the architects who built the Romanesque churches incorporated into them classical capitals, but this was done *frankly* and with no attempt to conceal it. But after all the domestic architect of the early twentieth century was just as frank when he asked his patron whether he wanted a Queen Anne cottage or a French provincial manor. The reproduction of Marie Antoinette's Trianon which was built for Mme de Castellane on the Avenue du Bois de Boulogne made no attempt to conceal its origin but on the contrary flaunted it. How much change was required to give such buildings the quality of life?

At this point we must let Ruskin again speak for himself. Dealing with the history of Christian architecture he says (p. 283), "We have at first an imitation, almost savage in its rudeness, of a classical design; as the art advances, the design is modified by a mixture of Gothic grotesqueness, and the execution more complete, until a harmony is established between the two, in which balance they advance to new perfection. Now during the whole period in which the ground is being re-covered, there will be found in the living architecture marks, not to be mistaken, of intense impatience; a struggle toward something unattained, which causes all minor points of handling to be neglected; and a restless disdain of all qualities which appear either to confess contentment, or to require a time and care which might be better spent.

And, exactly as a good and earnest student of drawing will not lose time in ruling lines or finishing backgrounds about studies which, while they have answered his immediate purpose, he knows to be imperfect and inferior to what he will do hereafter,—so the vigor of a true school of early architecture, which is working under the influence of a high example or which is itself in a state of rapid development, is very curiously traceable, among signs, in the contempt of exact symmetry and measurement which in dead architecture are the most painful necessities." In brief then, vitality is shown by a lack of perfection, a rapidity of execution, and I imagine that this is the difference between a sketch and a finished painting where the latter is carefully rounded off, varnished, and polished. It is probably true that if we were to apply the adjective vital to either, it would be more appropriately to the former. This would be just, for living beings are seldom so well-balanced, so perfectly proportioned, as geometrical symmetry would require. To prove this one has only to trace a human face, a butterfly, or a leaf which looks symmetrically disposed about a vertical axis and then fold it along the axis. The two halves will never coincide precisely. It may also be the reason why modern imitations of Greek temples, such as the Madeleine in Paris, strike some people as "cold and lifeless." On the other hand, I have heard these very adjectives applied by Englishmen and Americans to French seventeenth-century tragedies which seem anything but either cold or lifeless to the audiences at the Théâtre Français. I recall my professors in college saying much the same thing about even Alexander Pope and other Augustans. An ear which cannot hear the subtleties of Racine's alexandrines may well find them mechanical rather than alive, and if he does not like mechanisms, may well find them distasteful. But this throws the decision back into the mind of the spectator.

It is true that some writers admired Gothic architecture because they thought it was irregular, like nature.[9] The truth was of course that they had never seen a finished Gothic cathedral and when it takes a century or more to complete a building, it is likely that modifications will be made in the original design or that some parts which were to have been included have been omitted. The two towers of Chartres are unlike each other, but were they originally planned to be that way?

Ruskin too has a yearning for slight irregularities and inequalities. As an example he cites the façade of the Cathedral of Pisa and enumerates the variations in its arcades and arches. And after citing the measurements, he says, "Now I call *that* Living Architecture" (p. 293). After similar remarks about St. Mark's in Venice, he then quotes a comment of the English architect Wood who thought it and the Ducal Palace next door extremely ugly. "Some persons," says Wood (p. 297), "are of opinion that irregularity is a necessary part of its excellence. I am decidedly of a contrary opinion, and am convinced that a regular design of the same sort would be far superior." This might have given Ruskin pause, but on the contrary he simply asserts that Wood, though "by no means unintelligent in his observations generally," here shows "the effect of a contracted knowledge and false taste" (p. 298). But a psychological effect caused by a material arrangement of details ought to appear in any normal human psyche, and if it fails to, the only reasonable conclusion is that its appearance is determined by something other than the object before one. Either the irregularity of Pisa and St. Mark's did not strike Wood as vital, in which case it is not the cause of the feeling of vitality; or Wood was not interested in vitality, in which case vitality is not inevitably one of the marks of great architecture.

Ruskin did not say that there was any recipe for achieving vitality. The workmen who built St. Mark's "built altogether from feeling . . . and it was because they did so, that there is this marvelous life, changefulness, and subtility running through their every arrangement; and that we reason upon the lovely building as we should upon some fair growth of the trees of the earth, that know not their own beauty" (p. 302). For this reason all good work is freehand work (p. 309), work in which the machine has had no part. It would be easy to point out that a chisel and mallet are machines and so are a plumb line, an adze, and a yard stick. But they are machines, it might be said, which permit more variation than an electric drill or saw or pneumatic chisel. These variations are of course errors if the aim is accuracy. But if the aim is evidence of handwork, then they become signs of vitality. The relativity of vitality to the instruments used is important, even if vitality is admittedly one's aim. For then one of the standards of aesthetic excellence is not any more irregularity than it is evidence of humanity. One wants to see the hand of a man in his work, not merely to know that it has been there. But Ruskin goes farther than that, for he is addicted to extreme inferences. He sees in what he calls vitality evidence of the workman's happiness (pp. 316 ff.) and joy. This is not only extreme but fallacious, for Ruskin is transferring his own feelings to the artist. For we must again point out that there is no reason to believe that the effect of a work of art upon a spectator is identical with, or even similar to, the feelings of an artist when he was in the process of making it. It may be the case and it may not. But to insist that it is always the case is as absurd as to maintain that the blue sky which fills us with joy is itself joyful.

6. The Lamp of Memory

Ruskin opens his discussion of this standard of excellence by comparing his feelings before a Swiss mountain landscape and what he imagined they would be before another landscape "in some aboriginal forest of the New Continent" (p. 323). A "sudden blankness and chill" came over him. "The flowers in an instant lost their light, the river its music; the hills became oppressively desolate; a heaviness in the boughs of the darkened forest showed how much of their former power had been dependent upon a life which was not theirs, how much of the glory of the imperishable, or continually renewed, creation is reflected from things more precious in their memories than it is in its renewing. Those ever-springing flowers and ever-flowing streams had been dyed by the deep colors of human endurance, valor, and virtue; and the crests of the sable hills that rose against the evening sky received a deeper worship, because their far shadows fell eastward over the iron wall of Joux, and the four-square keep of Granson" (p. 323). It is this remembrance of the past which architecture is specially equipped to preserve. The landscapes of America contain no record of the European past, and because of this the sight of them would be cold, lifeless, dark, depressing, and so on. Man desires a firm assurance of his link with what has gone before and the strongest of these links is found in architecture.

Architecture then should be built to last. We shall spare any possible reader Ruskin's long passage on the sanctity of the home, which to his way of thinking is the house, and his religious passion as he argues that impermanent housing is disrespect to God and morality. We are more inclined to build domestic architecture so that it may be altered to meet new sanitary possibilities, growth of family, and all the other problems which confront men as time moves on. He of course pays little attention to such matters and, moreover, to him it is the façade of the building which is of the most interest and importance. Light and air, interior space, adequate provision for sanitation and cooking do not concern him. A house is not an instrument. Hence he can pour out rhetorical passages on our debt to unborn generations, our yearning for the marks of history, our necessity to defeat transiency of things without once mentioning the use which a building is designed to meet. One is compelled to reply, our debt to the unborn is to be paid by giving them a decent dwelling, not in handing on to them an obsolete one; our yearning for the past had better be satisfied in literature than in living conditions; and rather than defeat the passage of time, we had better accept it and meet its challenge face to face. As a matter of cold fact, Ruskin himself can do little with the Lamp of Memory and spends more of his words singing the praises of tradition and castigating restoration. It would seem to me personally that the best way to apply this principle would be to continue doing what the average domestic architect of the United States does anyway: put up a colonial red brick dwelling and let its occupants dream of good King George III and Lord North, put up a Cape Cod cottage and let them dream of quahaugs and scallops.

7. *The Lamp of* Obedience

The opening of this chapter is a candid statement of what Ruskin's aims have been: to show how "every form of noble architecture is in some sort the embodiment of the Polity, Life, History, and Religious Faith of nations" (p. 361). This is indeed true. And Obedience is the crowning virtue of them all. To Obedience "Polity owes its stability, Life its happiness, Faith its acceptance, and Creation its continuance" (*Ibid.*). In a gloss of unusual sagacity he points out flatly that there is no such thing as liberty. This is sagacious in that he appreciates our dependence on our forebears, our contemporaries, our traditions, natural law, all of which determine our conduct and afford us our means of action. To this no one could properly object. It is simply the expression of sound common sense. The architect who is building with stone cannot do what he might do with adobe brick, and he who uses wood cannot do with it what he could do with concrete. But if this is common sense, we simply cannot be disobedient. As in our speech we have to accept with almost complete fidelity the customs of vocabulary and grammar if we wish to communicate, so clearly in building a house or skyscraper, we have to obey the laws of statics and whatever is expressed in the formulas of engineering. To disobey such laws is a manifest impossibility. What then can we disobey?

It turns out once again that we are to work within a tradition. Originality is deprecated, except insofar as it is an accident. Living just a generation before the most revolutionary changes were made in all the arts, Ruskin was shortsighted enough to exclaim, "We want no new school of architecture. Who wants a new style of painting or sculpture?" (p. 368). What is wanted is one general code of laws accepted and enforced from one end of the nation to the other. If this were to become the reality, then idleness, the source of all our troubles, would cease and happiness descend upon the land. There is little said under the rubric of Obedience which had not been said by him before.

Though Ruskin is always annoying with his preaching and denunciation, yet he has at least said one thing in the *Seven Lamps* which, we feel, should be taken with the greatest seriousness. And that is that the appreciation of a work of art is not made in a vacuum, but on the contrary in the total environment of a man's interests. Whatever his shortcomings, he at least saw that no work of art was just an aesthetic surface to be explored exclusively by the sensory organs. We may not feel impelled to see history in a building, to see a mountainous cliff in a skyscraper, to see happiness in a capital of leaves and flowers, but at any rate we are told that there is more to a building than a perceptual pattern. Everyone has always known this, but we have become intimidated by aestheticians who, to be charitable, have become sick and tired of the commonplace literal representations of natural objects. Ruskin never denied the beauty of some abstract forms, but he affirmed the presence in works of art of other qualities as well, and for that the man of today may be grateful. Remembering it, we can see the work of art as a whole and with our whole minds.

In the second place, there is a fusion here, as was inevitable, between moral and aesthetic values, meaning by aesthetic here the purely perceptual. If Ruskin had restrained his enthusiasm, it would be difficult to object to his ethics. Loyalty to material, obedience to tradition, love of nature, surely are not mean and base traits, however much he may have inflated his rhetoric to deal with them. But even if they are not the virtues which we specially admire, and if they are expressed in works of art, we might with a little good will grant that a man has a right to look for them and find them. And, what is more, if he does find them, he has a right to say so and to announce his appreciation of them. But, I will be told, we must distinguish between the ethical and the aesthetic. We have, it is true, two words here and they mean different things, but if what they mean is actually integrated in a work of art, why should we deny it? When Tolstoi says that a work of art which does not further brotherly love is ugly, that seems like a confusion. But is there any reason to assert that the same shudder of disgust which we feel in front of what we discover to be ugly cannot be stimulated by what we believe to be immoral? I am not saying that the differentia of evil is ugliness, but nevertheless the sight of evil may be ugly. And, for all I know, the sight of virtue may be beautiful. If this is possible, then it is also possible for a work of art to be immoral if it awakens feelings of moral ugliness in the spectator. And if it does, I cannot see why he should deny it. I am willing to confess that I find Ingres' "Bain Turc" disgusting, not because of any technical faults which I have been able to discover, but simply because I have the same feeling of revulsion before it which I would have before a pool of slimy water crawling with white worms. As far as I know, I have no objections to a crowd of naked women squirming about on the floor, if I am not forced to look at them. But all this may be a poor excuse on my part for a lack of manliness. I may in fact be trying to pacify a certain attraction which these bodies have for me and of which I thoroughly disapprove. Who can tell? If I see a bully torturing a child in the street, I am repelled also. A picture of such a scene might either please me, if I read into it a criticism of cruelty, or displease me, if I saw it as a glorification of cruelty. But it would be both very difficult and, I should imagine, foolish for me to look at the real scene and simply comment on its color, form, and design. I am not urging anyone to take an ethical attitude toward works of art, far from it. But since I believe that no painting is only a painting and no building only a building, but that all works of art have multiple facets, if one of these facets reflects moral values, that has to be taken into account.

Whatever one may say in dispraise of Ruskin, his basic idea was sound. The artist, he maintained, is a complete man, occupying a place in society, preoccupied by moral and religious problems, producing things for the enjoyment of others as well as for himself, things which moreover would inevitably be interpreted as something more than a source of sensory pleasure. When all is said and done, his general attitude toward the arts seems more congruent with experience than that of writers who would skim off colors and shapes and sounds and overlook the substance on which they rest. Yet it should never be forgotten that in spite of his extraordinary influence, he was still a man of the nineteenth century and did not foresee the radical changes which were to take place in philosophy, science, technology, as well as in the arts.

Great as has been the influence of such men, Aristotle, Horace, and their imitators, Boileau, Pope, Du Fresnoy, Guadet, and Fux, it is questionable whether it has ever been so effective on artists as on critics. For artists are more likely to be influenced by other artists than by theorists and critics. The followers of Raphael and Michelangelo, of Mozart and Beethoven and Wagner, of Brunelleschi and Bernini and Frank Lloyd Wright, of Richardson and Walpole and Faulkner, were in all probability more numerous than the dramatists who followed Aristotle, the painters who followed Bellori, the architects who followed Guadet, the composers who followed Clementi, and the novelists who today follow Edmund Wilson, Van Wyck Brooks, or René Wellek. This is surely not strange. One cannot believe that a man with an itch to write, paint, compose music, build, first reads books which criticize the works of the dead. Once such a man has begun his career, he will no doubt, if he has the time, read critical essays. But one can no more think that a painter, before beginning to paint, would first read Ruskin's *Modern Painters*, than one could believe that the painters of the Italian Renaissance tried to conform to what

Berenson was going to say about them 400 years after their death. Historically the work of art is always prior to the work of criticism. The critic would have nothing to criticize if this were not so, and the theorist would have no basis for his theories. The first Greek works on the arts were written centuries after the first works of art were made and the first serious treatise on the beautiful, by Plotinus, was not written until the third century A.D. Berenson's discovery of tactile values was made after examining the works of painters and not after receiving a revelation from the Muses or by deductive methods. Ruskin first studied Gothic architecture and what he thought was Gothic painting before writing his various critical essays. His Seven Lamps were universally illuminating simply because he said so and because he thought that the artists whom he admired were examples of excellence for all times and places. In fact in his case, the generation immediately following his violated every one of his rules and made a decisive break with the past which he thought was eternal. Common sense suffices to show that an aesthetician can describe only the works of art with which he is acquainted and theoretically he might be acquainted with all works of art up to his time. But obviously he cannot know the future and is merely shouting in vain when he pretends to dictate to the future. Critics would do well to wake up to the fact that the arts have a history and that in the Occident the history of the arts shows steady and unbroken change. This change will be found not only in the look of works of art but in the function which they perform also. There have been, of course, times when artists have tried to revive the past, but the Swiss Guards are not living in the sixteenth century simply because they wear uniforms designed by Michelangelo.

It is indubitably true that once one knows what function has been assigned to any work of art, whether the assignment has been made by the artist or by someone else, one can tell whether the function has been well-performed. But that does not condemn all humanity to liking or approving of the work of art simply because it has been a successful instrument. One may with a certain objectivity admire the skill with which the function has been performed, and that indeed is relevant to aesthetics. But I fail to see why our admiration for skill should entail our finding the instrument beautiful. We need not know how to express our sense of beauty in order to feel its power. No one can say truthfully why he finds a woman beautiful, though everyone will make the attempt. Nor does one first have to read a book on female beauty before being attracted to a woman. But we may also look at a landscape and be carried away by its beauty without being warranted in generalizing its character as the essential traits of all beautiful landscapes. As Delacroix said, there are *variétés du beau*. Romantic scenery, such as one finds in the canvases of Salvator Rosa, came in with the eighteenth century and the landscape without figures was to all intents and purposes a nineteenth-century invention.[10] Hence, though we may know the significance of the cryptic paintings of Tanguy or Mark Tobey or Masson or Kandinski and conclude that they have done what they set out to do, that in no way commits us to liking them or finding them anything more than "interesting." The interest may begin by being what is wrongly called purely intellectual, and it may of course grow into evoking in us admiration for a job well done and thence into a genuine liking for the artistry which has been so successful. So we may admire a perfect crime, could we find one, a perfectly successful advertising campaign, a perfectly successful skirmish of psychological warfare, perfectly successful social climbing, or any other perfectly successful bit of behavior, the end of which we find detestable. Hypocrites, liars, venal politicians, orators, financial wizards, sophists, may all be perfectly successful in reaching their ends, whatever those ends may be, and we may be forced against our distaste to admit that they have reached them admirably. The hypocrites have convinced the public that they were sincere; the liars have gained a reputation for naïve and candid truthfulness; the politicians have been elected over and over again; the orators have transported the public in wild enthusiasm; and the sophists have tangled up their adversaries in the spider webs of their arguments and then devoured them. Is one then compelled to like and approve of hypocrisy, mendacity, oratory, financial scheming, and sophistry?

It was Greenough's unfortunate admiration for the clipper ship, if I am not mistaken, which started the vogue for functionalism. Unfortunate, because simply as a spectacle the ship was a beautiful object when it glided over the sea speedily with all sails set. But the sight of the ship was no revelation of its functional success. The adaptation of instrument to end, whether in a tool or in animal anatomy, has always aroused the admiration of those who have known of it, just as the supposed interrelations of the parts of the solar system have convinced men that it must have been made by a God who shared their taste for instrumental efficiency. Most tools are successful: screw drivers, monkey wrenches, hammers, axes, buzz saws, telephones, and bulldozers. And when such tools become obsolete, men gather around to look at them in museums and they turn into *objets d'art*. The beauty of instrumentally obsolete instruments accounts for most of our household furnishings, our religious rituals, our college curricula. But it should be noted that we find such things beautiful because they *no longer* serve any useful purpose. Before they became obsolete, no one talked about their beauty. This principle, on which I have expatiated elsewhere,[11] has always sounded like a willful paradox to those who have heard of it. It seems to lower the rank of the beautiful and to make works of art trivial. Quite the contrary is the truth of the matter. From Aristotle down to our contemporaries, it has been pointed out that only that which is good-in-itself is worth striving for, and by definition, an instrument is good-for-something-else. If one has to know the purpose of an object before one can find it beautiful, how can a man find a woman beautiful just by looking at her? And what is the purpose of a landscape, of the sky, of flowers and butterflies, of a color? Even if it is believed on faith that everything has some purpose and that one can discover what it is and then be able to tell whether it has or has not performed its function well, the fact is that we find things beautiful long before we discover what their purposes are. In one sense of the word the function of a tree is to produce the seeds of other trees and thus insure the continuance of its species. It serves this purpose, as everyone knows, very badly, by which I simply mean very wastefully. But even if it did it well, would we not see that the tree was beautiful without thinking of its generative powers? The question is purely rhetorical. Like works of art, works of nature have not only their purposes in the biological or economic scheme of things, but purposes for which we and not nature fit them. Which purposes are we to choose before admiring them? We are back again at our starting point, namely that purposes or functions are given to things by us, and that we may all differ in what purpose we may assign to a given object.

CHAPTER VI

The Arrested Moment

ONE OF THE functions which is assumed by works of art, when they have become obsolete as instruments, is the freezing of time. This is not usually a function of which the artists are aware, though many of them seem to hope that they are working for posterity and that their works of art will have that quality which is sometimes called immortality. But whether an artist is aware of this or not makes little difference. One of the most potent forces in human desire is the defeat of time and change. Nor is it so unusual, as Goethe seemed to think, that man bids a moment, fair or not, to stay. And it is hard to see why the bidder should be turned over to the Devil.

The freezing of time is brought about in several ways. We retain the past in our language without deliberately meaning to, for as soon as a common noun is glued to a new object or event, that thing becomes fixed as a member of a permanent class and to it are attributed all the essential characteristics of the class. As a result of this inevitable but misleading procedure, no matter how much novelty is discoverable in the thing labeled, the novelty will be thought of as inessential or as deliberate perversion of tradition. The right way is then the traditional way and, though the traditional way can seldom be detected in the realm of history, it too has been congealed into a formula in the realm of ideas. One has simply to look up definitions of well-known animals and plants in a dictionary to see how much has to be left out if the definitions are to cover a large number of cases. The definition of the word *cow*, for instance, may include the colors of various cows, white, red, brown, and black, but obviously cannot include the description of any one particular cow which may be an Ayrshire out of a Guernsey dam. This is not the fault of definitions. They are not supposed to do more than give a reader the clue to identifying the thing which the word being defined names. Our comment is no more than an indication of their limitations. Any cow, then, will be covered by a good definition of the word *cow*, but no individual cow will be described by it except in so far as her traits are those of all cows. Thus a conception of what cows are and what they ought to be is fixed in our minds, but it is only a conception. If a cow turns up which has certain novel aspects of her own, then she is either not a cow or the novelty is not real or the definition bad.

Cows, like other works of God, seldom create a problem for philosophers of art. We accept them as they are and submit ourselves docilely to the natural order. But works of art are by definition made by man, and for some reason or other we want them too to maintain a fixity of nature which precludes novelty and change. When one considers the definitions of *painting, portrait, illustration, landscape, sonnet, ode,* and *epic, fugue, sonata, tone-poem, romantic* and *classic, poetry* and *prose,* the *comic* and the *tragic,* to say nothing of other class names of works of art and artistry, of movements, traditions, schools, one sees at once that we hope to transfer to the realm of human desires and their satisfaction the same immutable natures that we attribute to the nonhuman world. One cannot restrict communication to proper names. And the moment one ventures into the realm of universals (adjectives, relations, and common nouns) one runs the risk of violating the traditional definitions of the terms one uses. One sees a collage by Picasso and says, "What a beautiful—or ugly—picture!" Immediately the objection is raised that it cannot be a picture since a picture has to be a picture *of* something and, moreover, it has to be drawn or painted. The collage is labeled "Still Life," but there is no recognizable object in it and we are used to seeing jugs, tables, flowers, shells, dead game, and the like in still lifes. Therefore it is not a still life and we say that the label should be changed. Then we see that along with the pieces of paper which are glued to the board there are also certain areas which have been colored with paint. It is not even a collage, but partly collage and partly painting. And among the few recognizable scraps are one or two letters cut from a newspaper. But they do not spell anything. Bit by bit we are harassed into admitting that there is no word in common use which can be applied to this object. One is defeated. One's adversary, for there is always an adversary, walks off triumphant, having forced us to confess that we do not know what we are looking at.

Why has there been all this argument? Not simply in the interests of a stable vocabulary, for people likely to engage in this sort of dialogue know how language has grown and how it continues to grow. In part the trouble arises because of Picasso's violation of the traditional formulas and in part because of his introduction of such a degree of novelty into his work that the spectator cannot classify what he is seeing. To break through the limitations of tradition is a genuine threat to security. To be unable to understand, whatever meaning one gives to that term, is to be frustrated in the fulfillment of one of the characteristically human desires. But, one might ask, what is there to understand in a work of art?

If the work of art is of an art of communication, then one can expect to understand what is being communicated. One can communicate ideas, can transfer one's emotions to others, can raise doubts, can edify morally, or simply describe. The art of communicating ideas in its literary form is exposition and presumably when one understands an expository essay, one can paraphrase its ideas in declarative sentences, it being understood that the author will agree with what you have understood him to say. It is of course rare that this occurs, because most authors have a sufficient grasp of the language which they are using to deny the possibility of a paraphrase's being as good as the original. And if we assume that no two words are identical both in denotation and connotation, then such an author might be right. Synonyms are seldom exact. I open my dictionary at random and find that *decry* is given as a synonym for *depreciate* and when I turn to *decry*, I find that *disparage, derogate from, detract from, belittle*, and *minimize* are given as its synonyms and that the lexicographer has carefully distinguished the meaning of each of these synonyms from all the others and quite rightly too. So *witty, humorous, facetious, jocular*, and *jocose* are also given as synonyms and again care has been taken to distinguish their precise meanings. But this is an old story and needs no further comment here. On the other hand, though synonyms are seldom if ever exactly identical in meaning, the caution against using them is a bit pedantic, for we do all make abstracts and summaries of things which we have read and we use them in place of the originals. This in itself does not prove that we are right to do so, but it at least shows that a paraphrase may have pragmatic value.

As for the transfer of emotions, one usually does this by shouts, cries, laughter, gestures, facial expressions, but sometimes one attempts to do it in words. It is probably true, as Wordsworth said, and he surely must have known, that the emotion to be transferred must be recollected in tranquility, for when one is in the grip of an emotion, one can hardly be expected to write verse or paint pictures. To write or to paint is itself an experience surrounded by or bathed in emotion, but that emotion is hardly the one being transferred. I am not the first to point out that often some apparently insignificant detail of a situation will produce the emotional sting, whether it be the taste of a *madeleine* or the wood spurge's cup of three. I suspect that much of the emotional force of some of Utrillo's paintings comes from the little figure in black in the middle of the deserted street which appears in so many of them. Van Gogh's painting of a pair of boots with the worn hobnails showing, the thin trickle of blood on the scalp of Saint Stephen in Fouquet's portrait of Étienne Chevalier, the hands in Ingres' portrait of Bertin, are all good examples of what

the books call the pregnant detail. And if the emotion evoked by
the work of art is one felt also by the artist and then communicated to the spectator, it would be reasonable to attribute the
evocative power of the work to the detail in question.

But from the artist's point of view, what has been done is to
fix a moment of his past so that it will not disappear into vacuity.
His past, however, is never that of the spectator, nor could it be.
Yet a work of art can be so intimately absorbed into the life of
those who assume it to have been addressed to them, that the past
preserved in it becomes, as it were, their past too. This, one imagines, accounts for much of the power of Oriental sculpture. If
ever there was an art which is almost entirely foreign to Occidental ways of thinking and feeling, it is Indian and, in general,
southeast Asian art. We have nothing in Mediterranean Paganism, Judaism, or in Christianity which can help us understand a
dancing Śiva, a Buddha in meditation, or an Apsaras. Yet it seems
incredible that anyone could look at the sculptures in the caves of
Elephanta or the great heads on the towers of the Bayon at Angkor, and not be carried away by their sheer power. Both the simplicity and the size of these sculptures compel one to look at them
in silence and meditation. And bit by bit, they enter into one's
consciousness and fill it like a long poem or a slow piece of music.
One can judge such things only from one's own experience of
them, and all of us have a tendency to set up our experience as
typical of the whole human race. But on this basis, however shaky
it may be, one might erect a theory that it is not the pregnant detail at all which is most evocative of feeling, but the absence of
detail or, if one will, of the transformation of the entire work of
art into a single detail.

There seems, moreover, to be evidence that in one Asian country, Thailand, there is a desire to preserve the past by the scrupulous copying of a recognized masterpiece. Mr. A. B. Griswold in a
passage to which I have already referred (Chap. V, n. 1), tells us
that the Siamese "image-maker had no desire to be original: he was
always a copyist. It may be hard for us to believe that the master-

pieces are all copies no less than the stereotyped statuettes produced by the thousand for the general market; to us in the West
the difference between a genuine old master and a copy is im-
measurable, even if we have to get an expert to decide which it
is. In the art of the image-maker, on the contrary, copying is not
only the line of least resistance, it is (or was, until Western ideas
began to break the tradition) a necessity: an indicative reminder
is, by definition, a copy." In short, the image-maker resembles the
mediaeval scribe who preserved the literature of the past by copying it.

Since this idea seems so foreign to our ways of thinking, it
might be well to point out that it is more familiar than we seem
to realize. The Siamese have been criticized for their interest in
having a story retold in exactly the same words which were used
to tell it the first time they heard it. As one travels through the
Orient one sees incidents from the *Ramayana* painted on walls,
danced on the stage, and carved in reliefs. These images are not
ancient but have been frequently reproduced in modern times,
though the people who enjoy them know the stories by heart. But
after all certain literary masterpieces of the West, the plays of
Shakespeare for instance, are read over and over again, not merely
by successive generations, but by individuals who like to renew
their acquaintance with them. Gilbert and Sullivan operettas are
attended by Gilbert and Sullivan enthusiasts year in and year out.
The operas of Puccini, Verdi, and of course Wagner, are so often
produced that they crowd contemporary operas off the stage. The
public, we are told, prefers them. In fact in Bayreuth the annual
performances of the *Ring* remind one of the repeated performances of the *Passion Play* in Oberammergau and that in more
ways than one. Publishers continually publish books on painting
with the same illustrations in them of the frescoes of Giotto,
Piero della Francesca, and Michelangelo, and no proof is needed
that the purchasers of these volumes are not merely men and
women who have never seen the originals. The most striking example of the repetition of the familiar is religious ritual, which in

the minds of believers must be repeated *ipsissimis verbis* each time the services are given. And to insure the exactitude of the repetition, prayer books and missals are printed for the use of officiants and worshipers as well. In this way the passage of time is defeated and the past is preserved intact.

One should add to this Shakespeare's practice of lifting whole passages from North's *Plutarch* and Florio's *Montaigne,* modified only by the exigencies of blank verse. Well-known Latin tags, familiar quotations, the recasting of history and biography in fictional form resemble the petrified forms of architecture. Poetic diction, ceremonial speech, such as using the second person singular in addressing God, formulas of politeness as frozen as those in Japanese, are usually archaistic, as are the full-dress costumes of men, civilian, military, and academic. In these and similar matters we do not want the new to appear; we want the reassurance that the past is still with us, however illusory the reassurance may be. A work of art then may well be one of the instruments for achieving this end. The flight from time has always characterized Western civilization, even if we are not so aware of it as we are in the East. Art not only can freeze the present and carry along the past but also help in the avoidance of the future. The codification of laws which can actually do no more than congeal the status quo is used by courts to prevent any changes in the future, as if the future could actually be forced by the magic of words to repeat the past. The history of legal terms is enough to show that the courts of appeal act as if a concept verbalized in the time of Edward the Confessor could be applied to the present and future. Yet we have every reason to believe that this magic is performed by refusing to admit as real the obvious changes that have occured. A person suddenly realizing that he is not immortal will make a will supposed to be effective in carrying out his desires for three generations, if not forever. The document will not only prescribe his funeral rites but also, of course, the proper division of his property. Because of his present likes and dislikes, he will bequeath money to one member of his family and cut off another, tie up funds in trust for his grandchildren, dictate what should be done with his books, jewels, clothes, and family souvenirs, and thus try to prevent the accidents, which since they will be accidents cannot be foreseen, from happening. The older universities of this country have funds encumbered with absurd limitations which date from the seventeenth and eighteenth centuries, funds for scholarships for members of families now extinct, funds for books in subjects which are no longer of any interest, prizes for essays on subjects which no one studies any longer, and our contemporaries often fail to profit from their ancestors' mistakes. The present vogue for natural science, for instance, excellent in itself, is stifling work in the Humanities and turning the United States into a country of technicians. This is all in the name of self-preservation and no one would pretend that a nation should commit suicide. But it is sometimes forgotten that the basic metaphors and intellectual models used in the sciences come from the arts.[1] It is also forgotten that the dissatisfaction with the present which acts as a stimulus to scientific, as well as to social, progress is characteristic of the artist whose dreams of a more beautiful, more orderly, more intelligible world may be just as important in scientific as in aesthetic work.

There are, as we shall have occasion to repeat frequently in this study, always two extreme forms of temperament in any society, the submissive and the recalcitrant. And there is also always conflict between them. The submissive individual is only too happy to let things stand as they are and to do whatever he can to keep them as they are. His humility in the face of higher authority may be both saintly and stupid, saintly in its self-abnegation, stupid in its sloth. The recalcitrant individual finds no salvation in obedience and in his extreme form wants to change everything. The lasting security of a social group depends on the equilibrium between the two tendencies, for if the submissive souls have their way, a society will be unable to face the new problems which are bound to arise as long as there are neighbors beyond the social frontiers, or the possibilities of natural disasters, such as floods, droughts, earthquakes, fires, and overpopulation. But on the other hand, if one objects to everything and sets out to change it, clearly the result will be chaos and men will become unable to solve any problem whatsoever. For the solution of problems depends upon what one has learned from the past and, if the future repeats nothing whatsoever from the past, one is in a desperate situation.

The history of the arts illustrates this interaction between recalcitrancy and submission. If one takes the history of one art alone, painting, one sees clearly how a given painter, for instance, Duccio, preserves and also modifies the tradition out of which he emerged. Duccio retains much of Byzantinism, but he also, as everyone knows, introduces certain novelties. Giotto preserves much of Cimabue and yet modifies what he preserves. One can classify even Rembrandt as a Caravaggesco, but one also sees much more in his handling of light and dark than is in the sixteenth-century Italian. Monet, Seurat, Sisley, and Pissarro can, if one is enamored of classifications and schools, be lumped together as Impressionists, but the fact that the term Neoimpressionist had to be invented to label two of these painters is proof enough that they and their admirers recognized what they had added to the technique of their seniors. A single painter, moreover, unless he dies very young as Géricault did, inevitably grows and, though like Ingres he may think that he clings to the teachings of his master— in this case Raphael [2]—nevertheless in his old age does not paint as he did in his youth. This sort of thing can be illustrated in all the arts. Nor is it mysterious. No man is uniform. He is a sheaf of purposes which are sometimes in conflict with one another, though the conflict may be attenuated in some cases more than in others. It goes without saying that some people are not only self-satisfied but satisfied with the world around them, if they are ignorant of what lies beyond their immediate horizons. Ingres, for instance, was much more self-satisfied than Delacroix ever was, but since he was a man of the world and knew that there existed people unlike himself, he was at least dissatisfied with their existence and did his best to discourage them. He would have petrified painting in the condition of his own painting if he could have done so, but he realized his impotence fully and, like many another man in his situation, railed against the existence of variety and change. Unfortunately the appeasement which comes from venting one's anger in words seems to have little effect upon the course of history, for history does not listen.

There is of course a certain pathos in our desire to fix the past and thus retain it. We all no doubt have a strong nostalgia for whatever we think of as the happiest time of our life, and one can sympathize with this in spite of its futility. But what is of more interest is a survey of the possible reasons for our flight from time. Here we are in the realm of speculation, for no one really knows why human beings love the things they love and hate the things they hate, since no one knows why human beings are not more homogeneous. But one can see that just as reluctance to change in either an individual or a group makes for stability, so the equally irrational desire to change accustoms men to meeting new problems as they arise. Such problems are usually so pressing that they must be faced at all costs, if life is to continue. When a tidal wave, an earthquake, a hurricane descends upon a village, the villagers actually have but one choice: to escape. It is always theoretically possible to lie down and die and I am not denying that. But in general people will try to save their lives, even if after the passing of the disaster they go straight back to living as they did before. Now it is true that each day brings some new problem of small proportions to mankind. Each glance at the world about us shows us differences which are greater than the similarities. Each hour presents new irregularities, but we do not have to be conscious of them and happily our minds are skilled in overlooking them. Happily, since if we had to live in continuous novelty and to meet its challenge, we should go mad. The synthetic view of the world, which is able to overlook novelties and differences and see things as if they were obedient to general laws, our ability to disregard small deviations from the norm, is an essential of all rational thought. The arresting of time in the arts then is not

simply a refusal to face reality. It is the first step toward consoli-
dating experience and making science and philosophy possible.

How then is this accomplished?

First, by establishing the rules of artistry. From our vantage
point of 3000 years we can see that actually there have never been
any everlasting rules except those inherent in the materials which
are used. We have the requisite information now to comprehend
the changes which have been introduced into all the arts since
their origin and to reject the notion that they have always been
the same in method, in purpose, and in their effect on those to
whom they have been addressed. It should be obvious that frontal
Egyptian statues neither look the same as fifth-century Greek
statues, that the latter do not look like Hellenistic naturalistic
statues, that these do not resemble Romanesque statues, that
Romanesque statues do not resemble Gothic statues, and so on
down through the Renaissance to Lipshitz, Arp, Henry Moore,
Brancusi, and Naum Gabo. This will surely be granted. The same
is true of paintings, music, and buildings, to say nothing of literature. Yet each age of which we have critical writings stated the
artistic rules with precision, as if they were inviolable. Such writings are not copious for the earlier periods and sometimes we have
to guess what the rules must have been from the similarity of a
period's works of art. But nevertheless in every period there has
been a high enough degree of conformity to stylistic canons to
warrant the conclusion that most of its artists were agreed upon
their ends. Neither Aristotle nor Demetrius nor Longinus nor
Pliny nor Plotinus give any hint that they were legislating merely
for their own contemporaries. And the same is true of today's
critics.

Second, they fix the historical moment, intentionally or not, so
that men born at a later time will interpret it as given in the arts.
In this way we write the cultural history of early Egypt, Greece,
Alexandria, Rome, and the Middle Ages as these various cultures
appear in works of art. A book like Nilsson's famous *History of
Greek Religion* gets its evidence for the early period largely from the

Homeric epics. The gods thus are what they appear to be in the *Iliad* and *Odyssey*, supplemented by the Homeric hymns. When we come to the fifth and later centuries, we find in the sculptures of Phidias, Scopas, Polycleitus, and Praxiteles, mainly as described by Pausanias—for most of the original works have been lost—the Greek ideals of beauty. And many an essay has been written on the Greek sense of calm, of repose, of balance, of eternalism, of the *mens sana in corpore sano*, and so on, based on the appearances of such works of art.[3] Winckelmann is an amazing example of this type of writer, for he did not even seem able to distinguish between a statue of the time of Phidias and a Hellenistic work like the "Apollo Belvedere." The legend that the sightless eyes of the statues were sightless so as to show that they were gazing into eternity is only one of the more extravagant fantasies in this domain. Nor does it seem to have occurred to anyone before our own time that no one had ever seen any of the statues described since the days of Pausanias and that furthermore no one had ever seen even Roman copies of them *in situ.*[4] An hour in either the archaeological museum in Athens or in the Acropolis Museum would have sufficed to convince anyone with eyes to see that all the sculpture with only one or two exceptions is mutilated. But what I am saying of Greek sculpture can be said with unimportant modifications of Romanesque, Gothic, and Renaissance sculpture: in each case we derive the rules from practice and, insofar as the practice is uniform, we find uniform rules.

Third, art elevates a historical event into the realm of the timeless. Personages such as Socrates and Plato, Julius Caesar and Augustus, Alexander the Great and Antinoüs, have become types, determined by their supposed portraits.[5] We rewrite the trial and death of Socrates from Plato's *Apology* and *Crito*, though we have differing accounts of the man in two other works of art, the *Memorabilia* of Xenophon and the *Clouds* of Aristophanes, and all of the writings mentioned claim to be history. So in the early Renaissance events of the Old and New Testament history were removed from time to become inhabitants of an ideal timeless world: the Creation of Adam and Eve, the Temptation and Expulsion, Susanna and the Elders, the story of Tobit, the Annunciation, Visitation, Nativity, Adoration of the Magi and the Shepherds, the Baptism of Jesus, the Crucifixion, Resurrection, and so on. The way these events appeared in the paintings became the right way of presenting them. And what is the more interesting is that the Biblical texts upon which the paintings rest give but the scantiest details to guide the artist. The creation of Eve out of one of Adam's ribs might seem to present problems to the man who would visualize the process, but we now know what the event looked like because it has been painted in the same way so often. Any attempt of a sneering critic to make it seem absurd is bound to fail, for the dated and localized event has become a timeless emblem, not an illustration.

Fourth, art universalizes the particular. This is analogous to making the historical timeless. Just as historians of art speak of the Philosopher-type, so we can speak of the Saint Christopher-type, the Saint Sebastian-type, and the Christ-type. We know what each of these beings must have looked like for their looks have been fixed once and for all. Though the figures of Christ painted in the Renaissance and later do not resemble those in the early Byzantine mosaics, no painter would go back to the latter if asked to paint a Miracle at Cana or any of the other scenes in which Christ Himself is to appear. When Michelangelo overlooked the Second Commandment and dared to represent God Himself, he depicted Him as an old, but powerful, man with full and flowing beard, and elsewhere He even appeared crowned with the Triple Tiara. But still more extraordinary than this is the fact that when such books as Beverley's *History and Present State of Virginia* were illustrated, the Indians were modeled after the Baroque nude. Sir Kenneth Clark incidentally, in his book on *The Nude*, has justified my point. The nude is an idealized version of what the naked body *ought* to look like. It is, so to speak, an incorporated Platonic ideal.

Finally, the work of art by arresting time puts order, perceptual or conceptual, into experience. I imagine, though I do not know, that the conceptual order precedes the perceptual, for I fail to see how through the sense organs alone one could ever experience order. For as one's eyes turn from point to point, one sees variety not uniformity, variety of colors, of forms, of movement, and even when a group of objects have the same color or shape, the light which plays over them modifies it in subtle but noticeable ways. One suspects that just as a child asks, "How do you draw a man?" or a house, or a dog, or a horse, as if there were a standard way of doing so, so the adult first has an idea of how an object ought to look and then tries to put it down on paper. It ought to look as it does look in other men's drawings, seen from in front with the eye immovable. But the scientist does precisely the same thing with the material of his science, for, as is well-known and inevitable, he chooses the typical to talk about, not the deviant. And furthermore he produces the typical by a skillful laboratory technique of what one might call purification. Purification is best illustrated of course in chemistry, but it occurs wherever the intellect is at work. The physicists, who used to talk about bodies moving in free space, were purifying the bodies of which they had any acquaintance of their dissimilarities in order to have a pure subject of conversation. But similarly when one reads a book in zoology or botany, one finds that the author has imagined animals and plants free from any individual differences which can symbolize a concept, more true of the individual things subsumed under it than of any other concept but probably not true of any one of them in isolation. If this were not done, science would be a series of portraits of individual things and events.

So far it looks as if we had been talking of metaphysical constructions and indeed we have been approaching that as a limit. But actually the practice of an art is habitual for any artist and the looking at works of art is habitual for the spectator. In both cases a ritual has been developed. The artist from his training acquires a way of doing things which by definition has been repeated over and over again. If it is a question of subject matter, it will have become the *right* subject matter, and if it is merely a question of how one is to do something, the question involves the *right* way of doing it. But the spectator too becomes accustomed to looking for certain things in a work of art or in artistry and acquires the habit of looking for it. The artist is dissatisfied until he has accomplished what his habitual practices demand, and similarly the spectator is dissatisfied until he finds what he is looking for. All habit becomes compulsive, even if it is nothing more than the habit of drinking coffee for breakfast instead of tea or cold milk. And the same hostility is expressed by dissatisfied breakfasters as by dissatisfied critics and artists. Something is wrong. If a critic assumes that a painting ought to be a painting *of* something, he will disapprove, and often violently, of paintings which are nonobjective. If he assumes that everything represented ought to be in classical perspective, he will object if the view shifts within the frame. If he assumes that there ought to be a unity of design, he will object if he fails to find it. If he assumes that every color ought to be balanced by its complementary, again he will object if he comes upon paintings in which this is not the case. Right and wrong in artistry are names for what harmonizes with one's habits or with the traditions of the culture in which one is immersed. But this amounts to the same thing in the long run.

One can form habits not only of seeing and hearing, but also of thinking. One thinks in terms of categories, categories of space and time, of causality, purpose, origin, material, form, to list but the most common. There is no reason, for instance, why everything should have an origin, for, as some of the Ancients saw, matter at least is never created nor destroyed. Plato's Demiurge, for instance, found His matter at hand; He had only to organize it. Aristotle's entire cosmos was everlasting, without beginning or end. We have a tendency to ask what started or created or produced every type of thing. No one in his right mind would ask what was the origin of the cardinal numbers or what was the origin of gravitation. One could of course ask who first systematized arithmetic and who discovered the laws of gravitation, but that is clearly another sort of question. People addicted to looking for origins and sources will tend to universalize them and even try to find one origin for everything. That this is no more than a habit of mind is amply proved by the fact that some people are not possessed by it. Such is also true of artistic practices, not one of which can be shown to be genuinely universal. We have our standards of rightness which lead us to condemn works of art and artistry which are not in accord with them. The statues of Kwannon, for instance, in the Temple of Sansusangendo with their multiple arms are monstrous to be sure if we look at them as literal representations of women. But the Goddess of Mercy is not a woman; she is a goddess. And what would a Goddess of Mercy be if she did not have enough arms to embrace all suffering humanity? Similarly no man was ever so perfectly built as the Hermes of Praxiteles nor any woman so magnificent as the Venus of Melos. But again, these works were made in all probability according to a mathematical formula of what were believed to be perfect proportions, not according to the way any man or woman actually looked.

We have already—in Chapter II—expatiated upon habit and shall here simply recall that along with the drop of the habitual into unconsciousness comes the feeling that it is innate, though we know that all habits have to be acquired. It is this which makes people think that they are inspired when writing or painting or performing music. What else could they think? It all appears to be easy and effortless, and of course that is precisely the effect which long training is supposed to produce. The habitual becomes the instinctive, the automatic. It helps the artist appear to be untaught.[6] Let us also recall that as habits are acquired they take less and less time to perform. Their time span never reaches zero, but does approach it. The importance of this is that, combined with the compulsiveness and unconsciousness of the acts in question, artistry seems like a mysterious process initiated by genius or divine inspiration. And the arresting of time which is in the work of art is duplicated, so to speak, in the process of artistry.

Thus a tradition is established as the process is passed on from master to pupil, or from manual to reader. There seems to be no explaining how the values involved were initiated, nor is the question frequently raised.

To explain something is not to annihilate it or even to depreciate it, though all charms may fly at the mere touch of cold philosophy. Habit and ritual have a positive value which should be granted by any critic, no matter how enamored he may be of novelty and invention. For it is they which bind individuals together in society and give them a feeling of companionship. Since everyone acts in the same way, everyone feels kinship in the family of thinkers and doers. The fellowship of thought and action is something which must be valuable since so many people desire it. To be completely isolated, if that were possible, would probably be death. It is true that in all societies and at all times there have been artists who have sought hermitages and there are no doubt degrees of sociability among artists as among other men. But since the early days of Greek philosophy, thinkers seem to have formed schools in which by definition all the members thought in the same way and agreed upon their general principles. This must be one of the reasons why learned societies exist today. One wants to associate with one's fellow workers. I do not pretend to know why this should be so, for the annual meetings of most learned societies do not accomplish much in the way of co-operative work. Papers are read and listened to and discussed, and presumably both the readers of the papers and their audiences get some satisfaction out of the ritual. But painters and musicians and actors and architects have their societies too, not always run in the same way to be sure and sometimes very informal. Even the Impressionists met at a café and exhibited together, and they were the most individualistic of men. Their techniques were very dissimilar and it was only in their subject matter that they seemed to agree. If the feeling of belonging to a group is important, then one cannot deprecate the formation of group habits. Moreover habits stabilize social groups, from the little ones to the largest. Society with an initial capital has its laws and rules, some of which are obsolete and many of which are obsolescent, but all of which act as a sort of cement to bind the members together and to frustrate time.

Finally habit saves thought as well as time. To save time is not always of the greatest importance and a bit more leisure would do no harm to modern urban society. But we have come to believe that saving time is important whatever we may choose to do with the time saved. To save thought may also not be so important as we tend to believe. There is no great quantity of thought needed for living. One can live from day to day by following yesterday's pattern, and I imagine that the overwhelming majority of people do this. We may not all be like Immanuel Kant, the regularity of whose life was such that the Koenigsburgers are said to have set their watches by his daily walk. Still most people have an hour for rising and one for going to bed; have a set menu for breakfast and eat their meals at a set time; dress in a set way when going to work and in another when dining out or going to a movie; follow a set ceremonial pattern at worship when they are married; use the limited vocabulary of their social set; read the same papers and magazines; subscribe to the same book clubs, if they read books; and in general settle down to a well-ordered and utterly uncapricious life. All this is the negation of thinking. The philosopher may look down upon this, the critic may condemn it, the reformer may preach against it, but if any one of them thinks that the primary value of thought is pragmatic, he is mistaken. When there are real problems to be solved, thought obviously is needed. But most lives do not run into obstacles which habit cannot surmount. There are in fact manuals on how to do anything: cooking, speaking, bringing up children, engaging in the various arts, even behaving properly in company. Once one has absorbed the lessons, one is taken care of. It is true that if one ventures far abroad from one's neighborhood, whether geographical or mental, one may run into difficulties. But one need not be so adventurous. One can always confine oneself to the immediate environment, the village within the great city, seeing exactly the same people, patronizing the same shops, calling upon the same doctor and dentist, and attending the same church. Thinking is not merely useless in such a life; it is a positive nuisance.

Even when new problems do arise, intruding themselves upon one's peace, there is always the escape through submission. No force compels a man to see an exhibition of pictures which he knows he will not like or to read a book which is, as he will say, upsetting. He can always maintain that the frontiers of inevitable ignorance are close to his home and that to cross them would be sacrilege. The curiosity of the inventive thinkers has always been condemned by their fellowmen, whether in the Athens of Socrates or the New York of Cardinal Spellman. Well enough is to be let alone; sleeping dogs are to be allowed to sleep; such are the programs which keep the peace. And though keeping the peace may not be everyone's ideal, it is the ideal of enough people to make the lives of intellectual warriors unpleasant. Hence, though the primary purpose of thinking is the solution of problems, one is not obligated to solve problems or even to perceive their existence.

If any evidence other than one's own experience is needed for art's power of freezing time, one has only to think how forms become petrified and repeated even when their original purpose is forgotten. We have already illustrated this but here may add one or two more examples. In the cave temples of Ajanta [Plate 1], temples which were not built but carved out of the rock, beams and rafters were carved in them and the façades were made to resemble those of a constructed building, though the former support nothing and the latter just masks a hole. The flat roofs of the Mediterranean are found in the north and the peaked roofs of the north are found in the south. Poetic meters and stanzaic models are carried over from century to century, sometimes with laughable effects, as in "I am monarch of all I survey," an inappropriate dance rhythm if ever there was one. The five act tragedy and the four movement symphony, the eight bar song and the minuet, the three volume novel and the fourteen line sonnet, all are conventions whose main value is our familiarity with them. We find motifs in all the arts which have been carried along for centuries like vestigial organs and they have acquired a kind of sanctity. Sometimes the motifs were once symbolic, like the swastika or the various animal forms in Chinese decoration or the zigzags on American Indian baskets, but they are retained long after their symbolism has faded away. Recently sculptors began to imitate pencil and pen sketches in wire and string as if the visual appearance of pen and pencil sketches were beautiful in themselves and not a by-product of the instruments used to make them. I am not condemning this, nor anything else except illogical arguments, but it is worth knowing what is going on. One is reminded sometimes of the little vegetables made in marzipan which are given to children. No one is fooled by them except the childlike.

CHAPTER VII

Art and History

IN SPITE OF the fact that each work of art tries to fix a moment of time in the experience of the artist, or continues a tradition in the hope of defeating the passage of time, nevertheless no moment can be fixed permanently nor can any tradition continue without internal change. For in the first place, each work of art, if it is seen by someone, has to be interpreted. The interpreter projects into the work of art his own personal understanding, his anticipation of what ought to be in it and of what he ought to get out of it, and he will appraise it in his own terms. He does not invent these terms, to be sure, but in spite of that they have become accepted by him and integrated into his life, both emotional and intellectual. In the second place, traditions are carried along by real people and are manifested through the behavior of real people. Men contribute something to them and are not utterly passive. A set of ideas does not flow through an individual as water flows through a pipe. Even those ideas which are supposed to be the least subject to change, such as religious dogmas, regardless of what they are supposed to be, have a history which exhibits as much change as uniformity. Very little is said, for instance, about the Blessed Virgin in the New Testament. The story of the Annunciation itself occurs only in Luke (I:26–38); the Visitation in the same Gospel (I:39–56) only. She does not appear before the Cross in Matthew, Mark, nor in Luke. Nothing is said of either the Immaculate Conception or the Corporeal Assumption in any of the Gospels. Yet we know how, as the centuries have passed, Mary became one of the leading figures in Catholic dogma, until at present it is a matter of faith to believe in ideas which emerged long after the apostolic period had ended.

On a lowlier plane the "Apollo Belvedere" was considered the most beautiful of all works of Greek art 150 years ago by one of the most influential figures in modern criticism;[1] today it is more often ridiculed than praised. Until about 1780 there was no Hamlet-problem;[2] now everyone who writes on Shakespeare discusses it. The fortunes of both Shakespeare and Chaucer stubbornly resist all attempts to prove that great masterpieces and great writers retain an even career in criticism. Few of us have ever seen a play of the former uncut and in the eighteenth century the plays were rewritten in order to make them more palatable to the public. Though some of the dispraise of Chaucer was due to his English which some people had forgotten how to read, there is always the figure of Matthew Arnold, surely no insensitive critic, to refute the theory of his immortality. The marble of the "Apollo" except for its loss of color and the words of *Hamlet* are about as they always were; it is our interpretation of them which has changed. But similar remarks could be made about the tradition of artistry. What is asked of a picture or piece of sculpture, of poetry or of music, is not what was asked of them a century ago. The static order, the balance and harmony, the mechanical form, which were thought of as the aim of all artists, have given way to tensions, dynamic thrusts and retractions, to something called the vital and creative. The role of the Unconscious has been given more attention than would have been possible before Freud. Whether we know precisely what these terms mean or not, it is obvious that they do not mean what their antitheses mean. No painter of the middle nineteenth century would have utilized accidental effects deliberately; no sculptor would have cemented together a collection of children's toys, bits of hardware, *objets trouvés*, into a single mass and cast it in bronze; no composer would have cast dice to set a pattern for his compositions; no poet would have depended on his random associations for the emotional effect of his poems; no novelist would have avoided the balance of good and evil characters or —though this is less certain—omitted comic relief in a serious novel. In fact, most novels related the triumph of good over evil: that seems to have been the novelist's problem. I admit that my universal negative must be taken with a grain of salt, for artistry has never been absolutely uniform at any time. When I write "no," it should be interpreted as "no one to speak of," that is, the statistical "no." For there are always some artists who anticipate the future.

That human beings and everything that they do have a history is undeniable. History is admittedly irreversible; it has a direction. In this human beings differ from the animals, as far as we know, for it looks as if the ways in which the various kinds of animals live have been the same since they first appeared on earth. As we have said above, the birds' nests, the spiders' webs, the beehives, and the anthills are organized today as they were thousands of years ago. It is true that a bird can utilize for her nest bits of string and human hair which would not have been available if the creature did not live in the vicinity of human beings. It is also true that when an animal, like the mongoose, is introduced into a new country, it will adjust to the new environment rather than become extinct and eat foods which it might not have found in its original environment. But in 2500 years European man has changed in every respect except those rooted in his biological nature. He still produces children as his most ancient ancestors did, though once in a while a test tube may be invoked to supplement the tools of nature. Although his span of life has been lengthened greatly, one must grant that he still dies and that his body is disposed of. He still has children and rears them, but the rearing of the modern American child is totally different in all essential details from that of a child in fifth-century Athens. He learns to read and write, but what he reads and writes is not only different in language, but in purpose. I do not mean by this simply that *Winnie the Pooh* is not the *Iliad,* but that the reason why a Greek boy read the *Iliad* is not the reason why the twentieth-century American boy reads *Winnie the Pooh.* The reason why my generation read the Bible was religious, not aesthetic, and so the reason why the Athenian boy read the *Iliad* was because it was true, not simply beautiful. He believed in the historical reality of the heroes, just as my contemporaries believed in that of the patriarchs; moreover he believed in the reality of the gods as my contemporaries believed in the reality of Jehovah. If this were not so, Plato would not have been so severe a critic of the mythographers. It is as impossible for a later generation to turn into an earlier generation as it is for an old man to turn into a child, a moth into a caterpillar, or a plant into a seed. These are merely truisms, so obvious that few people even bother to think about their significance.

Not only is history irreversible, but every event in history is unique. History shows us no homogeneous classes of events. This may seem to be contradicted by wars, rebellions, assassinations, the rise of heroes, the shifts in dynasties, and all the other classes of things which are described by historians. But we have to have common nouns to name events and it would be only the most naïve of historians who would say that because the American Civil War was a civil war, it was identical with the French Revolution or the War of the Roses. Moving in the direction of classifications and general principles, the historian might become a sociologist, but the information which is wanted of an historian is what differentiates one historical event from another of the same general type. If we read a history of the Civil War, we do not expect to find in it general principles and pseudo laws, however interesting such information might be. We should expect the firing on Fort Sumter to appear somewhere in it, the formation of the Confederacy, the various battles, the relations between the Confederacy and the Union with foreign nations, the economic situations of both sides, the victories and defeats, Sherman's March to the Sea, none of which would appear, except as specimens of some class of events, if history were a compilation of what all civil wars had in common. In reality, all that they have in common is the fact that they are internecine struggles, group against group, and not even the groups are always similar. In other words, if one is writing history, rather than social science, one directs attention to the peculiarities of the events which one is describing. There is no law which compels a man who calls himself a historian to do this, for the names of professions are largely accidental. He can do anything he likes. But that the events in history are unique can hardly be denied, whatever their similarities.

But so are individual biographies. The lives of men resemble one another in certain respects and in an isolated community the resemblance may be very great. Just as twins, though biologically identical, have different experiences, so do all other men. Each of us differs from everyone else in our ability to absorb shocks, in our adventurousness, in our docility, in our interests, as well as in our genetic make-up. There is no need to deny this in order to preserve an imaginary homogeneity which might serve scientific purposes. Some people try desperately to be like others whom they admire and by whom they would like to be admired, and this must be granted. Others try desperately to be different from everybody else and this too must be granted. And since works of art are made by people, not by metaphysical or aesthetic principles, we may as well admit at the outset that they will reflect the differences of the people who make them. It has not required the publication of this study to convince people that even when two artists try to be alike, their differences show up before the observant eye. Luini was certainly influenced by Leonardo, but anyone with any powers of discrimination can see that a Luini is not a Leonardo. Maes followed the technique of Rembrandt and it may well be that some of his paintings have been attributed to Rembrandt. But nevertheless, the resemblance is not so close that on the whole a Maes cannot be distinguished from a painting by his master. Leonardo studied in the workshop of Verrocchio, Braque and Picasso both had a Cubist period, Seurat and Signac accepted the same methods of putting paint on canvas, Mary Cassatt was a pupil of Degas. Yet most students of art can tell who is who in this list. But this should require no demonstration when one thinks that no two people have exactly the same handwriting and most of us can identify a friend by his voice alone even when he is speaking over the telephone. Yet one might imagine that writing and speaking would be about as homogeneous within a group as possible, for we have lessons in both as we go through school. It is true that there are such things as an English and an American accent, but that does not mean that we cannot distinguish between the accents of two Englishmen or of two Americans. If what I say is plausible, then it might be expected that the focus of the critic's attention would be the individuality of the work of art and artistry rather than their lack of it.

One of the causes of cultural change is contact with other cultures. A community in a Kentucky mountain village may, as we are told, still speak seventeenth-century English, as the French Canadians have retained some of the vocabulary and pronunciation of seventeenth-century France. But one can be sure that as the mountaineers install radios and listen to them, their vocabulary and turns of phrase will change. So now that international communication has been facilitated, architecture and painting and music have become more international in style than they have been since the thirteenth century. The influence of the American novel in France is not attributable to any law of aesthetic evolution; it is attributable simply to the fact that Frenchmen are reading American novels. You cannot be influenced by what you do not know, except at second or third hand, though the mere acquaintance with something new does not suffice to put you under its influence. Matisse and Picasso could not have been influenced by African sculpture if they had never seen any, but again they were not influenced by other things which they had seen, such as academic painting.[3] Contact with different cultures then is not sufficient to cause a change, but it is a necessary cause. If Egypt was really as static and conservative in its arts as some of the books say, it was not because it lacked knowledge of other cultures. The influential cultures in all probability must have a certain prestige, as French culture did after the Thirty Years' War, but how a culture acquires and retains prestige I do not pretend to know. It is, for instance, admitted that "action-painting" at the present time is an international style and also that it originated in the United States. One can guess why American painters took to action-painting, as American novelists took to action-writing, but one can only guess. We are not an outstandingly meditative people; we have become more chauvinistic since World War II and more frightened of European art and civilization, and, if one may indulge in metaphysical slogans, we are more interested in doing than in being. Yet even if these conjectures are true, they do not answer the question of why the rest of the Occident and Japan among the Oriental cultures have adopted it too.

There have been values associated with change which have induced people to look favorably upon the new as inherently better than that to which they have become accustomed. Along with the nostalgia for the ancient past, the Golden Age, there developed a desire for the future as bringing into existence something better than what men possessed. This took several forms in antiquity. There was the cyclical theory of history according to which one might be on the upturn or the downgrade. But since Hesiod and others had maintained that the present was the worst of times, the cosmic cycle could bring about only an improvement in human affairs, a return eventually to the Golden Age. Then there was the account of man's history as given by Lucretius, according to which man had steadily progressed toward a better civilization through the use of his intelligence, once he had accidentally discovered fire. In the third place, there was the

Messianic dream of the early Christians, the dream of a Second Coming, which appears to have seemed close to realization in the early days of Christianity. Later it was postponed to the millennium, and after that date realization of its promise has become indefinitely postponed. In any event, the mixture of these hopes gave men as a mass something to look forward to, and in modern times, that is, after the Renaissance, it became more generally held that history through its own momentum would bring about the betterment of life on earth. The various theories of evolution, biological, economic, sociological, intellectual, even aesthetic, joined in making the word *progress*, which etymologically connoted nothing good, a model of hopefulness. As the material welfare of the Americans seemed to be steadily increasing, and since in part this was due to their willingness to abandon the old and try the new, it may well be that our prestige increased because of that alone. There is and always has been misery in the United States, but the general atmosphere up to very recent times has been one of faith in the future. Our technological successes produced dramatic changes in our ways of living and only sour-faced critics despise material comfort.

Moreover, one of our outstanding contributions to philosophy has been pragmatism and, in spite of what William James and John Dewey actually thought and indeed said, that set of vague ideas has been interpreted by Europe and Latin America as a philosophy of action rather than of thought. It is true that James spoke of the cash value of ideas as their truth and Dewey of thinking as problem-solving, and both phrases were said—by others—to indicate that one could profitably act without reflection. It is obvious that one cannot build a building nor choose a college nor do anything other than routine without taking thought. The most *terre-à-terre* behavior, unless again it is habitual, will be random thrashing about unless it is planned. But the breezy American does not look like a planner; he looks to the outsider like a happy-go-lucky fellow who is the darling of fortune. Some of us apparently believe this ourselves, in spite of all evidence to the contrary. It is perhaps the image which we should like to present to the world, what the psychologists used to call our ego-ideal. Regardless of the truth of the picture and the validity of the doctrine, it presumably has seemed to be a stage in progress toward the good.

But, as we have said, there has developed alongside of the theory of progressive amelioration, the theory of primitivism. This point of view is chronologically earlier than its opposite. And when one looks at contemporary forms of cultural primitivism, one sees how it too harmonizes with the picture which we have of our contemporary ideals. For since the middle of the eighteenth century the Noble Savage has lost ground to the Child, the unrestrained Unconscious, the Neurotic Genius, and the Folk. Dr. Lawrence Kubie in his lectures on *The Neurotic Distortion of the Creative Process* has shown how some artists have believed that the cure of their neuroses would entail the loss of their artistic powers. The return to the promptings of Jung's Collective Unconscious has been the program not only of painters but of poets as well, and this not merely in order to find significant subject matters, sexual urges, uncriticized activities, irrational and even nonsensical combinations of events, but also an appropriate technique. The drawings and paintings of children, who are supposed—wrongly—to be uninhibited, are regarded as works of art on a level with those of thoughtful adults, and some painters have tried to be more childlike than they really are. Critics have spoken of Klee and Miró as if they were the village innocents and have seen in their paintings the expression of the child who survives in all of us.[4] Folk art also has been elevated to a position of serious consideration as if it really were the production of the collective folk and therefore better than the work of intelligent individuals. This movement as a whole is a sheaf of ideas which has emerged out of cultural primitivism, yet is presented as progress.

Both sets of ideas attach to the temporal dimension a value, as if cultures could be appraised according to their date. The child is obviously prior to the man and for that reason alone may be thought of as superior to the man. The neurotic is the man who behaves "inappropriately," that is in rebellion against the criteria of decency, goodness, sociability, legality, or what you will, and since these rest upon standards which are not those of the savages from whom we are supposed to have evolved, they must be discarded and the neurotic restored to his ancient prerogatives. The folk, the peasant, like the savage, are survivors of earlier, if not primitive, times when men were fresh from the hands of the Creator, with none of the false sophistication of the urban dweller, the intellectual, the bourgeoisie, and consequently their ways of life are inherently finer than those of modern man. The tradition that the earliest period of history is the best is combined with the logically independent tradition that the best period is that which has none of the accretions of civilization and, though no one really knows what primitive man was like, we have to find a substitute for him in savages and children. Since the neurotic often acts with the irresponsibility of a child, he too becomes an exemplar of the good life. It is true that civilization does restrain the individual from carrying out all his wishes, and sometimes the restraints seem needless and perhaps even bad. But until someone can find a society which employs no restraints and in which the greatest number have the greatest happiness, the nostalgia for a past which never existed seems a bit absurd. One cannot change this by argument. It is too deeply rooted in our nature to be eradicated.

It would be almost impossible to dig out the motivation of this attitude, for it is pretty well buried in the depths of the minds which preach it. It may come from a genuine disgust with the pretentiousness of oversophistication, with the wastefulness of urban living, with the love of inessentials, superfluities, and luxuries which characterize civilized people. It is such disgust which drove Walt Whitman to the animals since,

They do not sweat and whine about their condition;
They do not lie awake in the dark and weep for their sins;
They do not make me sick discussing their duty to God;
Not one is dissatisfied—not one is demented with the mania of
    owning things;
Not one kneels to another, nor to his kind that lived thousands of
    years ago;
Not one is respectable or industrious over the whole earth.

But it may also come, as far as Occidentals are concerned, from the religious thesis that man's happiest time on earth was before the Fall of Adam. No one seems very sure of what the condition of Adam and Eve was and there exist conflicting views about it,[5] but no Christian Father was uncertain that man would have continued in that blessed state if only the Father of the Race had not sinned. A third source of the idea may well be simply dissatisfaction with life, the *taedium vitae*, and the inability to find any historical society in which it is better.

The probability is that there is no rational argument which would prove that the adjectives "first" and "subsequent" imply any value whatsoever. When looked at coolly, no date connotes any superiority to any other date. But regardless of that one must admit that dates do possess an emotional coefficient, however difficult it may be to justify it. When men look back to their childhood with longing, it is surely not because they have trustworthy evidence that it was any better than their manhood. It may be due to a desire to escape from the responsibilities of age, to find a substitute for suicide, to retreat into the womb, or to a dozen other psychological causes. But psychological causes are not reasons. The appraisal of the remote past, whether the past of an individual or of society as a whole, may well be simple nostalgia. Anyone who can recall his homesickness when first going away to school knows perfectly well that it was a genuine psychical sickness, not an argument. One just did not like the new environment. Any new environment presents problems of adjustment and problems of any sort are troubling. The homesick boy may have been as unhappy at home as he is in school; in fact his unhappiness may have been one of the reasons why he was sent away from home. But it was a familiar unhappiness. He may, furthermore, adjust to his school in a few short weeks and forget his homesickness. It is equally possible that the longing for primitive times may be only a symptom of an analogous sickness. At least in Hesiod's case we have reason to believe that he hated his own time, just as the early Christian Fathers hated theirs. But it does not require much argument to show that hatred of one time is no proof that any other time was better. Yet whether there is any evidential value of goodness or badness in hatred of this sort, still the alternative to chronological primitivism is death or futurism. The latter, however, demands a kind of hopefulness on the part of a person, a willingness to admit that reform is possible and that all is not lost. But here too we have little to go on. Reforms have been made, it is true, and if one overlooks their subsequent deterioration, one can fight for more and more reforms. That vague period called the "future" then is envisioned as the great possibility which men have only to work for to make it actual. Thus we can argue that if men really wanted peace instead of perpetual war, they would have it. But the implementation of the program is the problem. The anti-primitivist is the man who too often thinks that by some historical law amelioration will arrive, progress being the magic word which will command its advent. But history seems reluctant to obey any command.

This being so, dates do make a difference and one's feelings about the distant past and future will be turned into arguments for returning to the former and pushing on toward the latter. The former, however, is an impossibility. It is a longing, *Sehnsucht*, which will be satisfied by reconstructing in poetry or painting the Golden Age. The magic of living in an imaginary world will be a substitute for creating one, as the relic of a saint can act as a fetish and be venerated in place of the person with whom it is associated. The future is equally imaginary and exists at present only as an ideal. Yet it has proved to be a greater stimulus to realization than the past could possibly be. Men are incurably optimistic; it is their optimism which keeps them alive, optimism not in the sense that things are constantly growing better of their own accord, but in the sense that the best is attainable if only men will work doggedly for its attainment.[6] This in itself does not prove that what they work for is any better than what they have; it is, however, proof that they think it is better. To lay out a program for reform in which present evils are eliminated and no new evils introduced is the only method which we have of improving our lot, however childish though we may be in our conception of what improvement is. We can of course lie back and do nothing, like Quietists, but no Quietist could ever be an artist nor could he have any interest in the arts. For if everything is believed to be equally bad, then there is no sense in doing anything whatsoever and even the drawing of a sketch or the writing of a letter becomes a silly waste of energy. God, evolution, the laws of history, or something equally remote from human action will do the job for us if there is a job to be done.

Happily there are practically no limits to the human imagination. We can imagine impossibilities, such as mythological animals, centaurs, mermaids, giants, talking fish, fauns, nymphs, and tritons. We can imagine worlds in which all human desires are fulfilled and no man envious of another's goods. We may also project such dreams into the past or future and create in our imaginations Fortunate Islands in which we are all translated heroes. There have been men who have invented countries, like Islandia, drawn their maps, written their history, described their constitutions and economy, for no other reason visible to their readers than the sheer pleasure of depicting an imaginary country. Others, like Thomas More, have done this sort of thing with a reformer's purpose, hoping to illustrate concretely what a better world would be like. But frequently, just as a boy draws pictures of his ideal girl on his scratch pad or in the margins of his books or even satisfies his concupiscence by drawing obscene sketches, so the writer of Utopias may be simply satisfying his dreams of a better life by constructing in fantasy a better country. This is the art of the apocalypse, the completion of the daydream. If reason disillusions us, we negate reason. Only psychiatrists could explain why this is so, what good it does to the dreamer and what interest we have in listening to his dream, but that the good and the interest exist is undeniable.

If the human race did not have this temporal dimension, its works of art, like the artifacts of animals, would show no difference over the centuries. Like the spider's web, the bird's nest, the beehive and the anthill, painting, poetry, architecture would be today just what they were in the Neolithic Age. We would have become accustomed to living in caves and chipping arrowheads and the possibility of doing anything else would have been unheard of, not to say sacrilegious. But man does have a history and his arts have a history too. If the flight into the past and the drive into the future have been important stimuli to action, it must have been because these periods, however imaginary their descriptions, seemed better than the present. The seeming need not have been more than seeming and may have resulted simply from the recalcitrancy which is always found in every society. The refusal to accept what one has need not be followed by the creation of a substitute; it may be followed merely by inertia, sabotage, or grumbling, all of which are probably interconnected. But this reaction leaves no record. It is only the dreams which are recorded in literature and the other arts of which we know anything. And they show simply that dissatisfaction projects into the world of ideas at least two values, the value of primitive times, either collective or individual, and of its antithesis. This is the contribution of history to art.

1. Ajaṇṭe: Chaitya Cave No. 19, façade, general view

Reproduced with permission of Superintendent, Department of Archaeology of India.

2. Peasant Family by Louis Le Nain
   Reproduced with permission of Archives Photographiques, Paris.

3. The Fall of Icarus by P. Breughel
   Copyright A.C.L., Brussels.

4. Étienne Chevalier and Saint Stephen by Jean Fouquet

Reproduced with permission of the publisher, F. Bruckmann, Munich.

5. Saint Thomas Aquinas by Benozzo Gozzoli

Reproduced with permission of Archives Photographiques, Paris.

CHAPTER VIII

The Social Complex

BOTH PRIMITIVIST and antiprimitivist tend to think of "man" and "society" as units. Man as a whole is very heterogeneous in so far as those characteristics are concerned which influence aesthetic values, and so is society. It is questionable whether primitive men were any more alike than we are, though if they wandered about in small groups, it is possible that the members of the groups were fairly similar. To be so they would have to want the same sorts of things, to satisfy their wants in the same way, always to co-operate with one another, never to be jealous and try to hurt the object of their jealousy, and to divide whatever food they had in equal portions which seemed fair to all. Such a state of affairs may have been possible but, if so, primitive men were not much like their descendants. That may indeed be the reason why some moderns are primitivists. From the point of view of physiology, it is reasonable to suppose that they showed only those deviations from the norm which are to be expected, differences in height and weight, in rapidity of action, in pulse and breathing and metabolism, in perceptual acuity, and perhaps occasional congenital malformations of the heart and other organs. Such differences may seem trivial to philosophers who talk about man as a unit, but they are precisely what cause disagreements and conflict among people. If two men are out hunting and one does not see the game as clearly as his fellow, does not shoot his arrows accurately because of his poor

147

eyesight, has a slower rate of reacting, the two of them are not going to return in a happy frame of mind. And was it never possible that two men in the group should lust after the same woman and fight together in order to have her? Were there no lazy members of the little bands? Did all work at collecting food with the same zeal? If primitive man was as homogeneous as we are sometimes led to believe, one wonders how the present heterogeneity ever arose.

But society, at least in historic times, has always been composed of smaller societies, groups of men and women who work at different things, for instance. In some communities, as in the United States, we have the members of the armed services who live in a socialistic state of their own, with special privileges enjoyed by no one else in civilian life. The Catholic clergy and monastic orders are in a similar situation, insulated to a certain degree from competition with secular groups. Sometimes, as in Sparta, the division of labor was made according to race. If the Helots, as we are told, were remnants of conquered indigenous tribes, that would explain why they were separated from the upper classes to carry on the burdens of the society—much like the pariahs in India.[1] In Athens there were three classes of residents, the free Athenians, the slaves, and the *Metoikoi*, resident aliens. Each class had its own privileges and duties, and status was assigned according to whether one was free, slave, or alien. The Middle Ages with its feudal system needs no illustration; we all know how rank from sovereign to serf carried special rights and even its vestiges in Great Britain induced in the mass of the people a certain respect for what is left of special privilege. With us privilege goes with wealth or with ancestry or fame. This we may call the hierarchy of prestige. Even when it emerged from conditions which no longer obtain, it subsists with only minor criticism.

But there is also a hierarchy of power, both that power which is recognized by law and that which is exercised without benefit of legality. We all know that powerful industrialists and labor leaders can get what they want simply by exercising their un-legalized, if not illegal, power. The magic word "contacts" names some mysterious force which facilitates the life of such men. The force may lie in their ability to ruin a man's livelihood by boycotts, threats of boycott, strikes, combinations in restraint of trade, price fixing, and all the other melodramatic gestures which fill our newspapers. Many a college is frustrated by the influence of prospective donors, just as many another has found ways to lubricate the machinery of bequests and donations and grants. These lines are written at a time when industry fattens on govern-ment orders. These orders cannot be filled without technological skill. The technological skill can be found only in the universities and in a few laboratories supported by industry. The universities cannot provide it from normal income. The conclusion is obvious.

What has this to do with the philosophy of art? Its main effect is to reduce the arts—and the humanities as well—to a position of inferiority. They are on the defensive. Instead of its being taken for granted that music, painting, poetry, and drama should be supported with all the fervor with which the sciences and engineering are supported, arguments have to be elaborated to prove that they have their place in the curriculum. A great news-paper such as the *New York Times* will devote a whole section of its Sunday edition to business, another to finance, a third to travel, and put all painting on part of a page. By actual count 74 columns of the Book Review section on March 12, 1961 were given to book reviews, illustrations, letters from readers, and requests for information; 130 columns were given to advertising. And when one thinks of how the editor of a more venal paper would choose the books to be reviewed, one requires little more to demonstrate the influence of power on art. If an exhibition of painting is not so much news as a murder or a divorce, one can scarcely expect that all classes of society will be informed about the exhibition. In this way a start is made toward stratify-ing a society, assuming that it was unstratified to begin with. The truth is that it was stratified all along and that the editors of the various papers and magazines recognize the stratification and have to decide to which stratum they will address themselves. But it would be as false to think of that stratum as representative of the whole society as it would be to select the most backward or the most advanced as typical.

Even if society is stratified according to the division of labor, each class will have its own interests, not only economic but also aesthetic. For the arts often idealize the interests of a class and its ways of satisfying them. Portraits of sovereigns and members of the royal family, of warriors, of influential social leaders were not made in the same way as those of peasants. Most painters, with the startling exception of Louis Le Nain [Plate 2], portrayed peasants as comic figures, drinking and dancing, or as they were portrayed in the plays of Shakespeare. Or else, as in the paintings of Breughel the Elder, they might be represented as heavy bumbling louts. It took men like Daumier and Millet and Courbet to give us a peasant class which was serious, pathetic, or even noble. Whether this was attributable to the rise of socialism or not, I do not pretend to know, though in Courbet's case it may well have been.[2] In our own time painting and literature, if not the other arts, are clearly oriented toward satisfying the interests of the various social classes and not one only. We recognize folk art, as we falsely call it, the art of the great masses in the covers of the *Saturday Evening Post* and similar magazines, the art of the rich bourgeoisie in fashionable portraiture and the slick magazines, and the art of the intellectuals in the paintings and sculpture of the *avant-garde*. It would be folly to assume that the paintings of Mondriaan, for instance, or Kline or Rothko say much either to the main body of troops or the rear guard. Where there is no subject matter, there is little if anything for the great mass of people to grasp in a painting. This may be denied or condemned as snobbishness, but nevertheless one has only to go to a museum and listen to the comments of the visitors to realize its truth. One has only to go to a concert, moreover, to see that the thundering applause is given to Tchaikovsky, not to Bartók or Schönberg, not to speak of more recent contemporaries. As the government of the Soviet Union was reported as saying in regard to some symphony or other of Shostakovich, "The People should be able to whistle the music which it hears." Whether the report is correct or not, the sentiment is. Listening to atonal music is hard and the whistlers have not yet become sufficiently accustomed to it to whistle it. But Tchaikovsky himself when alive received all the abuse which Schönberg and Hindemith and Bartók received two generations later.[3] The violence of such abuse is perhaps proof enough that the works of art in question have a deep emotional effect. One does not have a tantrum before something which leaves one cold.

That there is a conflict of interest among the various social classes then can be easily proved. The conflict does not of course pertain to all interests, nor am I saying that it does. The laborer and the peasant may join with the banker and industrialist in worshiping God, or in national defense, or for that matter in politics. The rich gave as high a percentage of their sons to the Army and Navy as the poor did, even if the superior educational opportunities which are open to the rich placed their sons in positions demanding more intelligence. Where there is no evidence that one's economic position can be correlated with one's taste and in countries where there are many museums open to the public, it is to be expected that the peasant's or laborer's son will see as great paintings and sculptures as the millionaire's, though he will not be able to buy them. It is perhaps likely, though by no means certain, that as far as economic and religious interests are involved, members of a given class will stick together, but that does not imply that all laborers go to the same church, like the same music, play the same games, wear the same clothes, eat the same food, speak the same language, read the same books. The contrary of this is plainly demonstrated every day. But the same is as true of individuals as of classes. The fact that I prefer Bach to Gershwin does not commit me to preferring Rousseau to Camus or Frederick the Great to F. D. Roosevelt. We have

mentioned this type of difference within the individual before
and I shall not labor the point. It is, however, worth repeating
in passing, for there is too great a tendency to think of individuals
as well as of social classes as homogeneous.

Since certain social classes, the agricultural, the military, and
the ecclesiastical, for instance, have a longer history than some
of the others, they will acquire greater prestige. One of the
constant criticisms of Courbet's "Stone Crushers" was that it was
socialistic propaganda. If he had painted two peasants somewhat
in the manner of Léopold Robert, his picture would have been
praised as an idyll. Some of the distaste for Courbet, if not all,
was the feeling that he was rubbing salt into the wounds of the
bourgeoisie. These wounds were of course self-inflicted; they were
feelings of guilt. If a painter of today were to paint pictures of
an auto-da-fé, he would be treated in much the same manner
in a Catholic country. Why dig up unpleasantness? Why always
show the seamy side of history? Why can't we all be friends? [4]
People have never been friends on a grand scale, for that would
be impossible, since friendship like love is selective. If people have
not always been friends, maybe there is something about human
nature which stands in the way. That something may be the
ineradicable difference between people, a difference which runs
from their anatomical structure to their likes and dislikes. Not
enough is known of human nature to permit one to explain such
differences. They may reside ultimately in physiology, for all one
knows, but it is safe to temper that judgment with some thought
of educational and other environmental influences. Until we
know why there are differences of taste in erotic matters, which
one would assume to be all equally appealing, we had best
suspend decision about such differences in aesthetic matters.
Gentlemen may prefer blondes, but surely some men, and some
gentlemen too, must prefer brunettes, or else whole nations would
have died out by now.

Not only does one admire a social class because of its historical
antiquity, but also because of its necessity for society's survival.

Since the Industrial Revolution we have become used to thinking
of the interdependence of people, the reliance of one class upon
the others, as normal. We are more aware than our great-grand-
parents were of the contributions of all classes to civilization.
This occurred earlier in the United States than in Europe, for
we had no tradition of a leisure class. But by now the sentiment
seems to be fairly general that everyone works and should work.
The privilege of enjoying the arts is no longer reserved for a
select few, and it is customary for municipalities to take the place
of patrons, much as the national government does in France. The
threat of "leveling" which used to be predicted as inevitable has
turned out to be unrealized and no one could honestly say that
the municipal art museums in the United States show a lower
grade of paintings and other objects of art than were formerly
shown in the collections of the eighteenth-century virtuosi; that
the symphony orchestras play worse programs than were formerly
played in the nineteenth century or at the royal opera houses;
or that even the radio always plays trash. The fact is that such
institutions follow the trend of the times and, should there be
a reversion to "story-paintings," to program music, to highly
decorated architecture, the abstractions which have crowded out
the story-pictures would be put in the vaults and the Gérômes
and Alma-Tademas and Landseers would emerge from darkness
into the light of day. There are already murmurings against
action-painting and abstractions emanating even from the intellectuals. And no one would be rash enough to say that our interest
in the Baroque and Rococo is attributable solely to their sensory
beauty. After a period of functionalism in architecture, we begin
to find the leaders of taste turning to Gaudí. Even the Museum
of Modern Art found some interest in Art Nouveau. Fantasy is
staging a comeback in almost every field, including that most
stodgy of fields, men's clothing. How far this may go only a
prophet could tell. But one thing seems very plausible: that,
having recognized the necessity of work, we also recognize that
of play. Now that all of us have more leisure than anybody but

the very rich ever had before, we also want the amusements of the leisure class. In the long run those amusements come from fantasy. We have probably had enough of reason, of hard common sense, of the useful.

What is the antecedent of "we"?

It can only be all of us, if we are to talk sense, and all of us who live in the twentieth century are just as complex as society is. We are each, to cite Royce again, a sheaf of purposes which we hope to make harmonious. We know now that we too exist in strata, that our consciousness is an affair of layers. Psychoanalysis has shown us that much of our past has been suppressed and suppressed because we do not want to remember it. If we wish to suppress something, it must be because it would conflict with what we want to keep in the foreground of consciousness. This is not the place, nor have I the competence, to discuss the reasons for suppression, but one can accept a fact without being held responsible for accounting for it. Hence whether we suppress experiences because they conflict with our ego-ideal, because they are censured by society, because we want to punish ourselves, or for some other reason, we do know that some things are suppressed. And being suppressed, they lie hidden and act as a brake upon the realization of some of our desires. The most obvious of these are sexual, sexual in the literal sense of that word, but we also suppress at times our sense of humor, our desire for self-aggrandizement, our desire for telling the bitter truth. Since almost all of our desires require other people for their satisfaction, it is probably always the other people, more or less consolidated in social groups, who lead to suppression. It seems likely that every man is an anarchist at heart, seeing no reason why each and every wish should not be gratified, but only subterfuge will permit him to live as an anarchist.

Suppression, however, is not the only source of complexity. Individuals may and usually do have a variety of interests. No man is anything in particular for twenty-four hours a day. If he were, he would be a broken-down neurotic, if not worse. The businessman has a hobby; reads books, listens to music, and perhaps even plays an instrument; goes to church and perhaps holds a place in the vestry; belongs to associations of various sorts which are not directly connected with his business; and, though he may assign different hours of the day and different days of the week to the satisfaction of these interests, that does not imply that they are not in possible conflict with one another. Setting up a calender is a *modus vivendi*, a way of letting various interests be gratified, not of eliminating their variety. But a man cannot act as if he were compartmented, or as if his interests were entirely separate things which could be let out of their cages for a run now and then. Their association with one another is bound to count for something. A banker who is also a mycologist, an industrialist who is also an ornithologist, a politician who is also a collector of contemporary paintings, these are not simple homogeneous people. And in modern urban society the possibility of having various interests and also of satisfying them is very great. One cannot, moreover, do two things at the same time and there is always the possibility that when one is doing one of them, the others will interfere. We are warned from childhood that we must make the great decision of what we want to be, as if one could be only one thing. But those of us who have had military experience have learned how to turn off one self and turn on another as occasion demands. This, I admit, is an extreme case and would not exist if military service were not compulsory. But after all we have the careers of Ives, the composer, Wallace Stevens and William Carlos Williams, the poets, to show that diversity of talents did not disappear with the Italian Renaissance.

The demand for harmony of purpose is, it goes without saying, pretty widely felt. We are taught that we must organize ourselves, that choice is rejection, that character is uniformity of behavior, that we must hitch our wagon to a star and at the same time keep our feet on the ground. But such lessons would not be preached if we carried out their precepts normally. The point is that we are not uniform and that we do try to move in several directions at the same time, that we are not organized. We look back to Leonardo da Vinci as if his width of interest were something abnormal, whereas it was really his ability to satisfy so many of them successfully which was abnormal. It is probably true that a man like Michelangelo who could practice architecture, paint enormous frescoes, carve marble, write sonnets, and even design uniforms, is not someone whom one meets every day. But that may be simply that the possession of manifold interests was less frowned upon in the sixteenth century than it is now. Such a man today would not be thought of as serious. He would not be given the opportunity to express his incipient talents. Why the idea developed that an individual must have a consistent character, which in the long run leads to a regrettable narrow-mindedness, I do not know, but I suspect that it is not unconnected with the belief in individual conscience. For if the most important thing in life is one's relation to God and if that relation is direct and not mediated by a church or a clergy, a heavy burden is put upon the individual soul to discover just what the relationship consists in, how it is to be exteriorized, and what is to be sacrificed to its exteriorization. There is literally, not figuratively, nothing to guide one to the proper path. Hence what is called harmony of interests frequently amounts to nothing more than repression of interests. We know how the Puritans scorned many of the arts and we know that one of the reasons was their power to distract the mind from the all-important religious goal. For the same reason one was taught to look down upon the satisfaction of our sexuality, of our desire to play, of our hunger for beauty. This asceticism resembled Greek cynicism with the difference that God was substituted for Nature.

When men decide to conform to socially imposed standards, and indeed it would be hard to find any others, then clearly all individuality tends to atrophy. People are always torn between their desire for self-assertion and for self-discipline. In most societies self-discipline wins out. For a social group by its very nature holds together by the willingness of its members to conform. One cannot reject everything, for by the time that one is aware of the problem, one's mind has already been formed by others and oriented in a given direction. One has at least a language which will in part determine how one will think. One has been punished for disobeying the social code and no one likes punishment unless unusually masochistic. I am not minimizing the pleasure which we take in self-mortification, the love of martyrdom, and it is always possible that some good comes of it. But again one does not annihilate that self who submits to the rule of others. It is always there in the shadows ready to pop out of them if only in disguise. In spite of all the laws and regulations, both secular and religious, both terrestrial and celestial, no one can deny that we still have malefactors. The jails are not empty. And though it is always more peaceful to follow the law in civil life, in business, in religion, and in art, where one knows the law, it is not only the criminal who is recalcitrant. But what self is the rebellious person expressing? Is he expressing his religious self, his political self, his ethical self, his erotic self, his ethnological self, or what? The psychomachy is not always a duel. It sometimes resembles a rough and tumble fight within a gang of hostile forces. And it is only by specious generalization and abstraction that they can be lined up as the forces of good and of evil.

The conscientious objector illustrates this. We may assume, for the sake of argument, that he has decided that the taking of life is always wrong. He therefore must infer that he should not join the Army even though he will violate the law. In doing so he will run into the objections of his social group, and he will normally want the respect of its members. His parents believe that one should obey the law whether one approves of it or not, for disobedience of the law leads to anarchy. He is also in love and had thought of marrying. Even if his beloved is willing to marry him, he has to think first of whether his wife would be done an injustice by marrying a man who will be put in prison, and second whether he will seem to be avoiding conscription by confronting the Draft Board with the problem of drafting a man with a dependent. He is, moreover, not at all sure of the grounds on which his conscientious objections are based. Does he really believe that life should never be taken or is he simply too cowardly to face the prospect of battle? He has read enough psychology to know that sometimes principles conceal genuine motivation to make one's acts more agreeable. In short, he is in a turmoil of emotion and reason and, as he will say, he just doesn't know what he should do. If the principle of the sanctity of life is an expression of "the good," then every temptation to throw in his lot with the Army is evil. If, on the contrary, obedience to the law is always right, then he should answer the call to military service. Can he do that and also marry? If he marries before being drafted, he may be evading the law. If he is drafted and then marries, he is doing an injustice to his wife. The debate will be interminable. For when there are more than two adversaries, there is no either-or.

The diversities within the individual may seem to be exaggerated by me, for after all they are all enclosed, as it were, within the one body. But unfortunately for the lover of unity, there are corporeal diversities within the group's corporeal make-up as well as within its psychical make-up. The studies of Professor Roger J. Williams show such an extraordinary range of differences in such features as anatomy, chemical composition, enzymic patterns, endocrine activities, and so on that one wonders why anyone should have thought that all human beings could be put in the same class.[5] If such things have a significant influence on a man's likes and dislikes, his artistic ability, his sexual pattern, his aggressiveness and docility, and it is obvious that they do, then individual differences are not merely curiosities of nature, like two-headed calves and three-footed geese. The very concept of normality requires reconsideration, for we have in the past spoken of the arithmetical mean or the statistical mode as the normal, as if anyone with a little good will could approach it as closely as society demands. We have also talked as if this were desirable. It would be desirable, to be sure, if our goal were unanimity and conformity, but it would also be desirable that everybody speak a universal language. The desirable and the possible, as we all understand, are hardly the same thing and a philosophy of art, like a philosophy of morals, would do better first to plot the possible and only afterward the desirable. It is all very well to identify normality with social adjustment, but to what social group should one adjust? The grosser crimes and misdemeanors rarely present any temptation to the general run of mankind. Few of us feel the need of murdering, stealing, and bearing false witness. Even these require at times neater definitions than the mere labels provide. A person who would not dream of entering a house and stealing will not find it hard to evade the customs when re-entering the country, mainly perhaps because his group does not look down upon that sort of theft. Petty thefts are committed every day by the most respectable citizens: students and professors stealing books from college libraries and stationery from hotels, souvenirs, as they will be called, and should anyone reprove them for this, the reproof will be laughed off. But it would be absurd to extend the list of such infractions of the law in a country where oaths taken before God in His temples are violated daily and then solemnly repeated after six weeks residence in Nevada.

There is then the likelihood that both self-assertion and self-denial are deeply rooted characters which can never be extirpated. They can be concealed and disguised and permitted to express themselves in socially approved ways. Decency of speech, for instance, may be a standard for the drawing room and not for the smoking car or men's gymnasium. Conjugal fidelity may be exacted of women but not of men. Observance of oaths may be insisted upon in trials but not in christening ceremonies. In time of war men will be ordered to slaughter other men, whereas in times of peace they will be punished for doing so. The state is permitted by law and custom to do what no subject nor citizen can lawfully do. The standards involved in all this have a history, though its earlier stages are lost, and the standards also vary from region to region. But the important feature of them all is that they are imposed upon the individual by society or by social groups and are not invented by any individual. We all, I suspect, fundamentally believe that the satisfaction of our personal desires is self-justified. When one is hungry, one wants to eat—for that is what hunger is on the psychical side—and when one wants to eat, one sees no reason why one should not be fed. We learn from Paul Radin [6] that in primitive societies "the idea of withholding food from anyone for any reason whatsoever, no matter what the status of the individual, what crime against the community he may have committed or how unwilling to work he may be, is . . . simply unthinkable. It would be tantamount to denying his existence." Some of us would take the point of view that he who won't work won't eat, though we do feed our criminals in jail and before those sentenced to capital punishment are executed, we feed them whatever meal they request. No one objects to this, as far as I know, or, if someone does, his objections are not heard. But hunger is only one of the impulses to action which we control through social sanctions. No baby has any innate desire to keep quiet when he is in pain, to control the elimination of urine and feces, to sleep at night and be awake in the daytime. It is almost foolish to point this out. We all know perfectly well that we are trained to conform to the standards of others from infancy on, for the only standard which is inborn in us is to do what we want to do when we want to do it. Nothing is gained by overlooking this. To recognize it is not to deny the importance of education or, if one prefer, conformity to social standards. Societies differ in what they will permit all their members to do, in what they will permit various age groups to do, and in what they will permit the two sexes to do, and they consequently differ in what they forbid as well.

There is no general law which describes the aims of all human beings even within a single social group, for if recalcitrancy and submission are always likely to be present and to manifest themselves, one can talk about the ideals of an individual but not of a single ideal for all. Where there seems to be a single ideal, one has substituted custom or statute for individual purposes. But there would be no need for laws and rules if everyone wanted the same sort of thing and would co-operate in its attainment. There would be a coincidence of law and behavior. In art schools this is almost realized, though even here the contribution of individual temperament, of personality and character is not to be discounted. The role played by ideals in behavior is undeniably of the greatest importance, for no one in all probability is so mercurial, and so lucky, that he can satisfy all his wishes as they arise. We set up ideals for ourselves and we also accept some which are given to us by tradition and reading and schooling. And it will be observed that when groups of individuals break away from the rest of society to "live their own lives," they set up customs at once which they expect the whole group to observe. They must be unconventional in the same way, if it is only the way of growing untidy beards, wearing blue jeans, and hanging a defiant medal round their necks. But how could it be otherwise, if they are objecting to the same conventions? If one disapproves of monogamy, one has to be polygamous. If one disapproves of sobriety, one has to be intemperate. If one disapproves of traditional syntax, one can only be ungrammatical. The choices open to defiance are strictly limited by what one is defying. And thus rebellion is often enslavement to another set of rules. A nonfigurative painter has to eliminate from his paintings any resemblance to recognizable objects. And if one wishes to write nonsense, one must beware of sense. This was amusingly illustrated by that form of art known in Surrealist circles as the "Exquisite Corpse." Lest any vestige of individual reason control artistry, a group was set to work on a single work of art, each contributing his share in ignorance of what the others had done. Thus there could be no logical link between the parts and reason was defeated.

CHAPTER IX

Ideals and Values

IDEALS THEN ACT as guides to behavior. They are whatever goals a man is trying to reach. We need not discuss their status, whether they are Platonic ideas residing in a world of their own, whether they are purely material twitchings and strainings, whether they come from a divine or terrestrial source, or any other questions of that sort. We are simply stating the fact that men sometimes act in order to reach some end which they think, regardless of what others may think, is worth reaching.

A value is not merely the satisfaction of an interest, but the apparent realization of an ideal. I say "apparent" deliberately, for nothing is more common than to be disillusioned when one has reached the goal for which one has been striving. There may be some men who are satisfied at all times and on all occasions, whose program of life consists in living from moment to moment. These individuals may indeed be the happiest of mortals since they never entertain the possibility of possessing anything other than what they have. If plants and animals are lacking in self-consciousness, they would be exemplars of such happiness. But they do not seem to be typical of human beings. For, as we have pointed out above, they have no history, but once established in a mode of life, they persistently cling to it. But surely no one will deny that human beings are distinguished from other animate creatures by their ability to form plans for the future which will be different from their traditional ways of living. It is such plans which I am calling ideals.

One thing is certain. An ideal in the context of this study must be present to consciousness. I am not speaking of patterns of behavior embedded in habit which might be said to operate as ideals. One can speak figuratively of a man's daily schedule as an ideal if one wishes, but it is an ideal which is always realized and therefore cannot serve as a guide to action. It may well have begun as a plan laid out ahead of time to guide one's action, as a protocol or *aide-mémoire*, but as it sinks into habit and becomes compulsive and unconscious, it is no longer an ideal in the same sense as a newly formed plan is. There is no doubt an instrumental value in such patterns of behavior, but they are no better than the patterns of involuntary acts, such as digestion, pulse, and breathing, which one performs because they are an integral part and necessary condition of living. What I am referring to is plans which need not be carried out but which one would like to carry out for some reason or other. The so-called "ego-ideal" of psychiatry may never be fulfilled and usually is not fulfilled. But though each man's plan may differ from every other man's, all men will probably have one or several in succession. The child who wants to be a fireman or a policeman or an astronaut may very well turn into the most prosaic of mortals, and his childhood ideals may linger on in his memory to be laughed at later or to be regretted. Regardless of the importance to society in general of such ideals, they have their importance to the person who forms them and one has the impression, when they are being entertained, that their realization would be happiness.

This may well explain why an artist is so often disappointed at the outcome of his work. Just as the perfect circle is never found on paper, so the perfect picture or story or poem or sonata is never found on canvas or in sounds or words. It is a platitude that one's intentions are never satisfactorily realized. Carrying them out may be an intense pleasure, but once finis is written, the brushes are cleaned and dried, the last note has died away, one sees that the result was not exactly what one had planned. The same is true of the one art which we all practice, conversation. To make one's meaning clear seems to be an impossibility and nothing is more ironical than a conversation between philosophers trying to convey to one another what they have on their minds. The Platonic dialogues seldom come to any conclusion and that may have been what Plato was trying to demonstrate. This makes one think that the German Romantics were right when they said that striving was more important than attainment, though there is an element of sour grapes in the saying. It is doubtful whether anyone would strive for anything if he was convinced that he would always fail to reach his goal. But no one actually is convinced of this. The next time or the time after the next will see success. The moment when the artist accepts the inevitability of failure is the moment when he breathes his last as an artist.

We have given two examples of the use of ideals in art, primitivism vs. anti-primitivism, individualism vs. traditionalism. When primitivism is drummed into people, they will preach a return to primitive life, as they conceive it to have been, and when artists belong to that sect, they will strive to realize in their art the qualities of the primitive.

Individualism, as I am using the term, idealizes the differences of each man and preaches both the right and the duty to express his own personality. The traditionalist, on the contrary, argues that every man, whether he likes it or not, belongs to a tradition and that whatever he does in the way of artistry is influenced by a tradition. Consequently he for his part preaches fidelity to the tradition and the artist's need to "belong" to something greater than himself. The facts in both cases are correctly stated. Every man is an individual, more or less integrated, and, as we have insisted, genetically, anatomically as well as mentally, no two men are exactly alike. But also no man is entirely cut off from his ancestors genetically—for from whom did he get his genes?—and resembles all other men to some degree and has been educated by others whom he cannot shake off. But the facts are not an ideal.

They turn into an ideal when a person maintains that he ought to be as centrifugal as possible, emphasize his differences, be himself rather than a copy or reflection of his fellows, or on the contrary that he ought to be aware of his origins, both biological and cultural, and devote his art to perpetuating them.

We know that we are both tied to the past and different from it; that, though we speak our mother tongue, it changes as the years go on; that our environment itself changes while still retaining much that has already existed; and that both rebellion and submission vary from man to man. How far a man can change his congenital equipment is an unsolved problem, for we simply do not know how closely we are bound to our native endowment nor to what extent the education which we receive can change it. The wisest course to follow is to recognize the inevitability of both tendencies and the variation in men's ability to resist them. We find in the history of all the arts both fidelity to tradition and innovation, as we have pointed out above. Neither can be imposed on all men, for even when the state with all its power tries to force artists to conform to an official pattern, it fails. But regardless of that, a submissive artist, when he expresses his submission in his art, will give traditionalism as the reason for what he produces. And similarly the critic who admires traditionalism, will praise it when he sees it appearing in artistic form. Likewise those of us who are individualists, will look for originality in works of art and praise it when we find it and, if we are artists, we shall write manifestoes saying that we want to be original and not "slavish copyists." But such reasons are not in any sense of the word an explanation of the psychological—or other—causes at work. At best they are rationalizations.

The distinction between reasons and causes is important. In the nature of things we cannot be aware of the causes of our behavior, many of which are well below the level of consciousness and others of which cannot rise to consciousness. We may be aware of the psychological fact that we are hungry, but few men are so skilled in physiology that they know why the feeling of hunger arises when the walls of the stomach contract. We know when we are sexually stimulated, when we are angry, when we are restless or bored or hopeful or despondent, but none of us, unless we are trained endocrinologists or psychologists or specialists of some other sort in the causes of feelings, have the slightest conception of the mechanism by which such feelings are aroused. It is true, for instance, that any unfamiliar experience is likely to be unpleasant, but its unpleasantness will vary from man to man. Yet it is probable that no man will say that the reason why he dislikes a dish or a foreigner or atonal music is because he has never run into them before. On the contrary, he will say that bird's nest soup is disgusting, the foreigner obviously inferior, atonal music formless. If he is a trifle more sophisticated, he will say that the ingredients of bird's nest soup are unwholesome, that a man ought to stick to his own people, and that the diatonic scale is rooted in the natural series of overtones and *therefore* the only correct basis for musical composition. But the feeling of unpleasantness is prior to all this rationalization; it is the datum which the rationalization attempts to justify. To substitute the reasons for the causes would be like arguing that the Law of Gravitation is the cause of the planetary motions or that the change in the color of a piece of litmus paper is the cause of acidity or alkalinity. This is not to say that we cannot act from reasons in the sense that we cannot modify our reactions by our awareness that certain principles are or are not being exemplified in a picture, poem, or piece of music. But just as in morals, we may see the better and do the worse, and also refrain from doing the worse because we know the better, so in art we can see something attractive and disapprove of it or be repelled by something and yet learn to understand it.[1] One may of course understand why a work of art was made as it is and yet not like it, but at least one's annoyance is sometimes mitigated by understanding.

To become aware that we are liking something of which we ought to disapprove is familiar enough in the field of ethics and is in fact one of the basic moral problems. We strive to harmonize

what we want to do and what we ought to do. But the desire is
rooted in us and the principle which we hope to harmonize with
it is given to us by others. This need not make it the less powerful
as a corrective to our behavior, though just how an acquired principle corrects our behavior is somewhat mysterious. In part, I suppose, we accept the principle and follow it because we have been
punished as children for refusing it. We are punished for incor-
rect speech and manners and acts in general from babyhood,
sometimes severely enough to make us wish to conform. It is true
that conformity is easier for some individuals than it is for others,
but it is doubtful whether anyone is congenitally adapted to accepting all the rules which have been elaborated over the centuries. If such a person exists or has existed, he would have no will
of his own beyond the will to do whatever he is told. Most of us
have to grow into such docility or be beaten into it or gently persuaded into it. For even the traditional version of the Lord's
Prayer, whether textually correct or not, includes a plea that we
be not led into temptation. If most of us were not prone to yield
to temptation, it would be inexplicable that such a plea would
have been included in the prayer. But this is not peculiar to
morals, unless consideration for the feelings of others, social
amenities, and good taste in art are part of morals. In school we
are usually told to read books which at first sight are boring. Most
of us feel that Caesar's *Commentaries, Silas Marner,* Burke's
speech on *Conciliation,* to name three classics which were inflicted
on the boys of my generation, are needlessly tiresome. It is probably true that Caesar is a good start if one is to learn how to read
Latin, just as Czerny's *Fingerfertigkeit* is a good start toward
learning to play the piano. But most of us, even if we can be convinced of the necessity of such exercises, find them no more interesting than other painful duties. They are among the tiresome
things which adults put upon us, we know not why. But visits to
art galleries filled with Italian primitives, pictures of the same old
martyrdoms and crucifixions, awkwardly drawn in spite of their
piety, endless rows of Roman sculptures, all stiff and pompous,

cases filled with Greek vases of a few traditional shapes and ugly color, this may indeed be an impetus to a love of art, but it takes on aesthetic interest only after a few sermons on why it has aesthetic interest. If my views seem exaggerated, one has only to eavesdrop on a gallery tour and listen to what the docents tell the youngsters. They may of course arouse an intellectual interest in the works of art on which they are lecturing, and they probably do, but one seldom sees a spontaneous interest expressed by any of the pupils. They will build up an interest after such tours and that cannot be denied, but here the aesthetic feeling is posterior to the conviction that one ought to experience it. The lecture confers an aesthetic ideal upon the listeners, awakens interest, and may suggest understanding. In short the pupil acquires reasons for approving of the works of art and the hope is that his approbation may lead to liking.

Such ideals have to do with artistry, the way in which the artist has constructed his work of art. They may have to do with the subject matter, with the life of the artist, his reasons for making that particular work of art, with the historical setting in which the work of art was made, with the people who commissioned it and why, with the total context in which the work of art is located. But such details are selected out of a score or more of possible subjects of conversation. One hears gallery talks in which design alone is emphasized, pyramidal composition, balance and rhythm of masses and lines, color harmonies and contrasts, tensions, thrusts, unity and variety. But one hears others in which supposed psychological facts are brought out, the artist's feelings, aspirations, repressions, thoughts, all expressed, it would seem, in his work of art. Each side of the complex datum, the work of art, is accentuated, as if it were the unique and proper focus of attention. Yet all these sides are there and there is no dogma which can tell us which is the most significant.

If one takes pictures alone as fair samples of all works of art, it is obvious that there are at least nine different aspects which may be talked about. Most pictures up to recent times represented

actual physical objects which have been called their subject matter. But the term "subject matter" means at least two things, as it
has been used. It may mean first, the physical objects themselves
or second, that for which they stand. For instance, in a Crucifixion one will see the body of a man hanging on a cross, usually,
though not always by any means, with three women at the foot of
the instrument of torture. If the subject matter is just a crucified
man and three women, then the critic will probably talk about
how the four people are drawn and grouped. But if he is thinking
of the subject matter as the Crucifixion, then he will talk about
the artist's conception of that historical event. In early Crucifixions, the eyes of Christ were open and the head was not hanging
on one side. For, it is said, the early Christians could not accept
the idea that God, whether incarnate or not, had really died.[2] (I
take no responsibility for this explanation.) Again, few paintings
have been so much discussed as those of the Annunciation. Here
too there are usually represented a woman, Mary, and a young
angel, Gabriel, though the famous "Annunciation" of Antonello
da Messina has no angel in it. But Annunciations also frequently
have other figures present and the Virgin is now represented as a
royal personage, now as a peasant. If the subject matter is simply
the human and superhuman figures, then what the critic will emphasize is not the meaning of the scene. But if it is the event itself,
then every artist will have his own interpretation of it, an interpretation which the critic will elicit from the pose of the figures,
the costumes, the setting, the attendant figures, and so on.

But no paintings, except certain still lifes, are merely subject
matter. Third, the artist is supposed to have "something to say."
That this is possible is proved by caricatures and portraits, where
the facial expressions and bodily stance of the sitters carry the
message of the artist. If we call this message the artist's interpretation of his subject matter, we shall not be doing an injustice to
his art. If Christ is represented on the Cross with His eyes open, it
might well mean that the self-sacrifice was deliberate, which of
course dogma says it was. It might simply be an affirmation of the

belief that the Redeemer was both alive in His godlike nature and dead in His human nature. The number of things which it might mean is undoubtedly very great—how great we do not pretend to know—and the artist himself might not be too clear in his mind about which of them he was expressing. If Giovanni di Paolo puts an Expulsion from Eden in the background of an Annunciation, it may be because he thought that just as the Expulsion was the penalty for the original sin of mankind, so the Annunciation was compensation for it. How clearly he realized this, no one could say, but that it is suggested to the modern spectator of the picture is undeniable. The only danger into which the critic runs when he makes this sort of comment is that of substituting his own mind for that of the painter. He has no right to say that what he reads out of a work of art is what the artist intended to put into it. The artist may simply have been following orders and the elements in his picture may have been dictated to him by the man or group who commissioned it.

We know that many details in a painting are symbolic, fourth, both in the sense of being unconsciously revealed symbols of the artist's suppressions and fifth, in the sense of being part of the traditional vocabulary. The gods of antiquity with their attributes, the saints of Christianity with theirs, are in essence no different from pictographs. They are symbols which require interpretation, though it goes without saying that we make our interpretations of them so rapidly that we are unaware of the process. To read a word is to interpret a visual symbol, to translate it into its intellectual meaning. Similarly when we see a picture of an old man in ancient clothing holding two large keys, we know at once that the figure stands for Saint Peter. In the same way when one sees a little naked boy with a bow and arrows, one knows at once that he stands for Cupid. Such symbols have been accepted over the years and no questions about their meaning ever arise in the minds of Occidentals. They form a sort of sign-language, like the arrows which indicate directions, the red and green lights which signal to us to stop or go. But such symbols also vary in their in-

telligibility. The meaning of some has been lost and the whole field
of iconology has been developed to discover what it may have been.
The earlier representations of Cupid, for instance, were very different from those which we today think of as normal. He began
by being a young man, old enough by the end of the classical
period to fall in love himself and marry Psyche. But such a Cupid
nowadays would have to be labeled, as the figures on Greek vases
were so often labeled.

Unconscious symbols are more difficult to read, though in the
early days of Freudian psychology it was assumed that there was a
lexicon in which the meanings of all the symbols of dream and
fantasy could be looked up. Its place now seems to have been
taken by Jung's archetypes.[3] Freud himself recognized that each
unconscious symbol must be interpreted in terms of the sym-
bolist's own life and indeed when one thinks of what people have
read out of music or painting or poetry or any other work of art,
one realizes how the meanings are in part—though by no means
entirely—contributed by the spectator or auditor. But that is true
even of words, for a large part of communication is devoted to
clarifying what one is saying. I realize that this is no problem
when day-by-day topics are being discussed, but as soon as one
ventures an opinion of a critical nature, one finds that one is in
great danger of being misunderstood. Since critics habitually think
it their duty to say whether they like or dislike, approve or disapprove of the work of art about which they are talking, they soon
find themselves involved in sorting out the various meanings
which even ordinary terms of praise and blame have taken on.
Nor would they be called upon to express their feelings about such
matters if they had no reason to believe that other people did not
share them. T. S. Eliot in his early essays spent most of his time
showing his readers that the works of art which were traditionally
praised did not deserve the praise which they had received. Later
he wrote essays to show that some of the works of art which had
not been praised should have been. This was the more amusing in
his case since he believed in the value of tradition. Why then

break a tradition or reorient it? The answer would be found, I suppose, by first deciding whether one was appealing to critical tradition or to artistic tradition. In his early essay on *Hamlet* he attacked critical tradition which had thought of that play as one of its author's undoubted masterpieces. But in his lectures on *The Use and Misuse of Poetry* he seemed, whatever the reality may have been, to be defending artistic tradition. If critics over the years have agreed that a given work of art is great, one would feel humiliated to believe it little. On the other hand, it can be shown that even when critics have been agreed on the greatness of a given work of art, it is not always for the same reasons. To value highly the *Aeneid* because of its epic grandeur is not the same as valuing it highly because of its magical powers, as in the *sortes Vergilianae*. The symbols involved in a poem often change their value as well as their meaning, and it is doubtful whether any schoolboy working his way through the *Aeneid* can read it as a Roman would have read it. To a Roman it was history as well as poetry. We simply cannot take it as such.

But I have digressed from the topic of unconscious symbolism. Whether one accepts Jung's archetypes or not, one is forced to admit that to some minds a given symbol will have an emotional coefficient which may vary from the repulsive to the admirable. A great many people dislike, and some are repelled by, snakes, toads, and other reptiles and amphibians. A great many others like and are attracted by birds, flowers, and trees. It would be ridiculous to try to prove the obvious and I shall not attempt to do so. We all know this and we also know that when someone likes what we dislike, we wonder how it is possible. If the emotional coefficient of all symbols were pervasive of the human race, disagreement on such matters would be as impossible as it is for human beings to live on raw grass or to breathe under water. There would then be general, in fact universal, agreement in matters of taste. But this clearly is not the case. Just as taste varies in so important a sphere as sexual attraction, so does it in what looks like less important fields. We are told that we can be educated into changing our taste and that may be true. But why we should submit to such a modification of our feelings is another question. It might lead to uniformity of opinion which some hold as a great ideal. But we should first try to find out why opinion is not and never has been uniform.

The interpretation of unconscious symbols has often led to a reconstruction of the artist's life. Miss Spurgeon's classical study of Shakespeare's imagery was used by her to demonstrate his interest in weather, birds, domestic matters, food, sickness, sports and games, and personified emotions.[4] With Marlowe, she found, metaphors from classical learning lead, the celestial bodies and animals came next, whereas in Shakespeare nature and animals lead and classical learning has fourth place. In Marlowe images drawn from personification are more numerous than those drawn from daily life, whereas in Shakespeare images drawn from daily life are twice as many as those based on personifications. There was no attempt on her part to perform any psychoanalytic interpretations here but simply to set up criteria for studying the interests of Shakespeare and possibly distinguishing between the genuine and apocryphal works. Norman O. Brown, however, in his *Life against Death* uses the symbolism of various authors to penetrate deeper into their psyches. From Luther's metaphors he derives his anal-eroticism, as he does for Swift as well.[5] But we have a warning against such interpretations in the work of Dr. Lawrence S. Kubie who in his *Neurotic Distortion of the Creative Process* points out that, "Where *conscious* processes predominate at one end of the spectrum, rigidity is imposed by the fact that conscious symbolic functions are anchored by their precise and literal relationships to specific conceptual and perceptual units. Where unconscious processes predominate at the other end of the spectrum there is an even more rigid anchorage, but in this instance to unreality: that is, to those unacceptable conflicts, objects, aims, and impulses which have been rendered inaccessible both to conscious introspection and to the corrective influence of experience, and which are represented by their own special symbols in impenetrable and fixed disguises. As long as their roots remain unconscious, the symbolic representative will remain unmodifiable. This is what renders them rigid." [6] To be genuinely creative in art is to make use of flexible imagery and this can be done only by the co-operation of the pre-conscious. Since few critics have ever been able to analyze their authors professionally, to say nothing of ever having had any clinical experience whatsoever, the function of an artist's symbolism in his own life is always a matter of conjecture.

Moreover, what an artist tries to conceal is as important as what he overtly reveals. If one believes that only in the Collective Unconscious will be found the universal values of which one is in search, then of course the ostensible meaning of a symbol is not so important as its hidden meaning. I have seen doodles made by Hitler which represented, or suggested, high towers, plumed helmets, mountain peaks, and other so-called phallic symbols. I have also seen doodles on the walls of men's urinals which represented male genitalia without disguise, accompanied by verbal invitations to sodomy, *fellatio*, and other deviant practices. The *graffiti* in Pompeii are good examples of this sort of thing. Such symbols running from the literal to the figurative may tell us something about the people who used them: they are afraid to be themselves openly. They are right to be afraid, for revelation of their repressed desires would be disastrous. But as far as our present interests are concerned, two things should be noted. First, we cannot overlook man's desire for telling others about himself whether overtly or not nor, second, the emotional reaction of the person to whom the revelation is made. Are we to suppose that because mountains were not highly praised before the eighteenth century that 1) they were not phallic symbols before that time, or 2) that people were less repressed sexually in earlier periods, or 3) that people disliked phallic symbols before that time—or a combination of all three possibilities? The situation is almost hopelessly complicated, for apparently one may like or dislike something without knowing why, so that one cannot say that a symbol is not sexual because someone dislikes it, though all people ought to like it given its biological importance. There is, moreover, such a thing as mendacity. And finally it is always possible to dislike that which one has learned to disapprove of.

Hence the value of a work of art, as far as symbolism is involved, is more likely to be the value from the artist's point of view. If our psychological theory is correct, then we can see what the work of art "meant" to the artist. But this does not give us any clue to what value it will have for a spectator. The "Excremental Vision" of a Swift will have one value for Swift and another for his readers. One can enjoy the song of a bird or the sound of running water or the sight of the stars in heaven without any knowledge of ornithology, flumenology, or astronomy. Such knowledge may well enrich our sensory experience and I am not pleading for the impoverishment of our lives. If one knew what the bird was saying in his song, one might well be shocked, for all I know. Nor do I believe that we unconsciously associate ourselves with the bird as he reveals whatever it is that he is revealing. There is a level of aesthetic enjoyment which does not penetrate beneath the surface of things. And so long as one does not maintain that there is nothing below the surface, one is on safe ground. For the approach to any work of art is bound to be through the sensory surface and the first attraction to it will be on that level. The error consists in denying to others the right to go further and in dogmatically asserting that only the surface is of aesthetic interest. For if that were true, then all poetry would be sound and nothing more and all painting nothing but colors and shapes. Unfortunately that thesis too has been propounded by some critics.

This brings up the sixth focus of criticism, design. By design I mean that order which all works of art exhibit. I should call it form, had not that word taken on a discouraging variety of meanings. Now design too may be produced unconsciously as well as deliberately. It may have been deliberate in the early stages of an artist's career and later dropped into his unconscious, or what would be better called his habitual way of doing things. The child who learns to speak is taught to correct his pronunciation and syntax in accordance with rules which have been given to him by others. So the painter and writer as students of their arts learn how to paint and compose and write. That is, someone else gives them a method which he believes for reasons which do not concern us here to be the right method. Once learned, that method ceases to be deliberate and becomes habitual. Nevertheless the works have design in them which is imposed on the raw material with which the artist is working.

The order of which we are speaking is seldom inextricably united to the matter which is being ordered. A moment's reflection will show how at certain times accurate representation or realism was the target of the artist and the focus of the critic's attention. If the design of the work of art did not reproduce the design of that which was represented, the work of art was condemned. But then it was realized that some things which might be represented were ugly or uninteresting or trivial or otherwise displeasing, and consequently the design had to be that of beautiful objects. But, as Sir Kenneth Clark has shown in his book *The Nude*, the beautiful in art is always a modification of the real; it is an ideal form selected, arranged, distorted in short, to make the object represented more beautiful than it is. In the case of the human body, it has been elongated, flattened, rounded, proportioned according to supposed perfect numerical relationships.[7] In all cases the artist is forced to select certain features and eliminate others. A standard design or form is at length developed and that becomes the criterion of correct design. In landscape it was decreed that there be a foreground, middle ground, and background, though it is obvious that no natural scene is ever so divided except by convention. By the seventeenth century a complete vocabulary was developed for expressing the emotions in gestures, a vocabulary which in the eighteenth, if not earlier, was transferred to the dance. And later, at the time of Lavater, Gall, and Spurzheim, artists were given a convention by which they might express character by cranial and facial conformations. Similar conventions were adopted for lighting and for cast shadows. And there were also the rules of perspective and, as everyone knows, Italian painters played with perspective as a good-in-itself, enjoying foreshortening, representing complicated shapes in various lights, and painting their scenes as if there were one observer frozen at a single spot in front of them. To complicate matters, standards of order taken from geometry and statics were then introduced and such criteria as balance, harmony, rhythm, were utilized to judge pictures, poems, musical compositions, and architecture. In architecture and sculpture such criteria may have made sense, since the works of art were not supposed to collapse when once erected, but they were once removed from the facts of other works of art. In our own time the paradigm of order has become the organic. Works of art are asked to exhibit a vital dynamism, not a mechanical equilibrium. But this is little more than a shift in the basic metaphors on which all theoretical considerations are founded.

To speak of the balance of a flat visual design is to introduce a concept which is literal in statics into something in which it can be only figurative. The paintings of Raphael, for instance, are frequently constructed about a vertical axis in bilateral symmetry. According to the theory of Lipps, we would feel ourselves unbalanced if this were not so and our lack of equilibrium would make us uncomfortable; hence we should dislike the picture in question. In fact the old schools of art instruction went so far as to insist that if a shape of a certain size were placed at a certain distance from the vertical axis, shapes on the other side must, if not equal to it in size, be placed at that distance which would produce balance on a pair of scales. Thus a weight of a pound can be balanced by a weight of half a pound placed twice as far from the fulcrum. There may now be some justification for such a rule in a visual design on a flat surface, for we have become accustomed to it for so long that we might indeed feel uncomfortable if it were not obeyed. But on the other hand, there are plenty of designs in Japanese art in which the balance is occult, to use the term given to it by Dr. Denman Ross,[8] and we do not feel uncomfortable when we look at them. Hence there seems to be nothing inherently valuable in this principle. It must be accepted simply as another of those rules which became sanctified by usage rather than by natural law.

Organic form too is metaphorical when applied to works of art which have no temporal dimension. The term "organic" is as vague as most terms used in aesthetic criticism and sometimes it means nothing more than the reproduction of organic shapes, such as those of microscopic organisms; sometimes the use of the internal organs of the body: liver, kidneys, the heart; sometimes an emphasis on something known as growth. One can understand how a work of art, like a narrative or a drama or a piece of music, can grow in a literal sense of the word, but surely when a picture or statue or building is said to be organic in this sense, the meaning becomes metaphorical. The metaphor may be a good one, in that the eye, for instance, seems to light on a particular spot of the design and be carried upward and across and in various directions as the painter has desired. But on the other hand the mere fact that a design is zoomorphic, like an amoeba or paramecium or blob of jelly, is no proof that it symbolizes growth, vital dynamism, creativity, or anything antimechanical whatsoever. D'Arcy Thompson has shown us that in all organic structures there is an effect of mechanical forces.

But if one has been captivated by the biological as opposed to the mechanical, then a suggestion of life, however stimulated, will induce a feeling of satisfaction and the critic will announce to his readers that the work of art in question is dynamic, vital, creative, as if these words in themselves were terms of value. Bad things, however, grow and live and create, as well as good things do and it is only by decree that we prefer suggestions of vitality to suggestions of mechanism. We shall have more to say of this below, but here may note that the order which is produced by the artist is order, whatever its roots may be. And if we are looking for form in a work of art, we may find it both in machines and in organisms. We do want forms which can be easily spotted, geo-metrical shapes of the simplicity of circles, squares, triangles, as well as organic shapes of easily grasped outlines. But whatever the design, it will have to be produced by elimination and selection. There is no other way to do it. If one should try to count all the details which are held together in even the simplest geometrical shapes, the rounded pebble and the heart-shaped lilac leaf, they would be too great for any eye to apprehend. We do not hear all the tones and overtones produced by any air waves as they vibrate and we do not see all that is to be seen in a piece of bark. In the first place, our sensory organs are selective, and in the second, we have to look in order to see and we look for what we expect to be there. The more fundamental question for the aesthetician is why we look for certain things and not for others.

A seventh focus of the critic's attention has been technique or artistry. It has been fashionable for some years now to decry tech-nique in favor of spontaneity. That may be the reason why the works of art of children, peasants, savages, and the untaught have become specially favored. For, regardless of fact, such people are supposed to be free of convention and the rules of the schools. Nothing could be farther from the truth than this assumption, for savages are highly ritualized in their artistry as in their social rela-tions; children, like Sunday painters, have definite ideas of what they are trying to do; and peasants are the most conventional of men. We all know that the Sunday painters achieve their charm by their technical inadequacies, for if one repainted their pictures according to the rules, they would lose most of their picturesque-ness. We admire Henri Rousseau because of his romantic imagi-nation and his insensitivity to what is rational. Gypsies do not lie sleeping on sofas in the wilderness, however amusing it may be to see one doing so in a painting. But it is precisely the amusing, the totally unexpected quality of what one finds in the modern primi-tives which capitivates us and makes us apply to their works such adjectives as childlike, naïve, innocent, fresh, and spontaneous. The cult of the childlike is modern and no doubt responds to some need which we feel for escaping maturity. But the justification of such adjectives lies in us, not in the pictures themselves. There was really nothing naïve in Henri Rousseau, any more than there is in Grandma Moses or John Kane. These painters have been wide awake and conscious of their aims. Their technique is not that of the academies and the reason why we admire it, when we admit that it exists, is the reason why we are sick of tradition. Most of us would prefer to look at a child's water color than at an Ary Scheffer, an Alma-Tadema, or a Cabanel. But would we prefer one to a Winslow Homer, a Courbet, or a Degas?

There seems to be no good reason for depreciating technique. Artistry is an answer to the challenge of matter, an overcoming of its limitations, and even virtuosity, however trivial its goal, is something which it is not disgraceful to admire. I suppose that coloratura singing is about as purposeless as any artistry could be, in the sense that it is no more than doing something very difficult, as are acrobatics, rhymed and metrical verse, fencing, mountain climbing, ballroom dancing, and most conversation. The person who engages in such exercises is showing that he can surmount difficulties, and it would be absurd to justify his attempt by looking for some more profound significance in it, if by profound one means something of biological utility. Virtuosity is an extension of the drive to conquer the environment, not merely to adjust to it. There is no need to conquer it in order to live. One can always remain at the point where one has just enough food to eat, enough sexual satisfaction, and enough sleep. But though this would be a possibility, it has never been a reality in our civilization. Men, at least in the Occident, have always wanted more than the necessary and by getting it have created their culture. At the same time they have always met the criticism that civilization was superfluous and have been urged to return to something more primitive. But this criticism in itself is praise of civilization, for it indicates precisely that which differentiates man from the beasts. I realize also that people have existed who preferred the beasts to men. Such a preference, however, is unfortunate, except in the sense that it too indicates a desire for the unattainable and thus constitutes the best of ideals. There is little reason to strive for what one already has.

The value of artistry exists of course, like all other values, in two areas, that of the artist himself and that of the spectator. To overcome the limitations of matter and make it do what one demands of it is certainly a great satisfaction, analogous to the control of the body. And it is also a great satisfaction to watch another doing this, a vicarious satisfaction, to be sure, but none the less important. To Aristotle and some other Greeks observation was better than participation: the spectator at the games was better than the athletes. This is not supposed to be our own point of view, but nevertheless the "sidewalk superintendents" also have their day and many a man has stopped work to watch another manipulate a crane or bulldozer. This is not very different from watching a dancer or listening to a pianist, except that both the dancer and the pianist may be realizing something more emotionally exciting than lifting heavy weights and scooping out roots and boulders. That, however, simply adds another value to what one is observing. It would not be revolutionary to maintain that it is better to hear a fine piece of music well-played than a poor piece of music well-played. One would imagine, for instance, that the "Chromatic Fantasy and Fugue" well-played would give one greater pleasure than one of Liszt's operatic transcriptions well-played, though the technical difficulties are about equal. All I am saying here, however, is that overcoming the technical difficulties of Liszt's bravura compositions is not to be despised as mere technique, because technique is not in itself something trivial. One may retort that there is no sense in wasting one's efforts on trivialities, but the retort is beside the point. Technical excellence is in itself a focus of values and always has been. And when a critic is talking about it, he should not be scolded for not talking about something else. A good bottle of Mouton-Rothschild is not to be dispraised because it is not a fresh egg.

What a man chooses to do in the arts will always be used by

some critics, eighth, as an index to his psychology. And in recent times we have become more interested in what a man's actions reveal about his soul than we are in the actions as an end in themselves. This may be due to our increasing sense of individual differences. Freud's study of Leonardo da Vinci is relevant. Such a study tells us more about Leonardo than it does about his paintings, it will be said, but as a matter of fact it integrates the paintings into the life of their author or, if preferred, it extends the life of the painter into his works of art. Art is a part of life and the apparent break between what one does as an artist and what one does as a man can be mended when one knows enough psychology. The artist's life is his art and his appearances in the drawing room may be simply a relief from his work. His work as an artist is done in a world, so to speak, of his own creating. A novelist may be perceptive and sensitive before his typewriter and obtuse and without insight in society. But his social life is no more his real life, to be explained through his artistic life, than the reverse. People often change in different situations and their lives are therefore as multiple as the situations in which they live. Nonartistic experiences flow into artistic work and art flows back into nonartistic activities. How could it be otherwise? Even if a man deliberately tries to eliminate from his art everything which he does outside of his studio, that attempt itself will be symptomatic of the kind of man he is and will affect his paintings or writings or music. He may be hiding from himself; he may be revealing things which he dares not reveal ordinarily; he may be escaping from the problems which beset him when he is at home. There are scores of possibilities here. But the kind of things which he is trying to hide from, to conceal, to escape from, are important as indexes to his total character. The critic's error consists in maintaining that a psychological reconstruction of a man's total character on the basis of what his art reveals is a judgment of the value of his art to anyone else or could be used as a basis for such judgment. That it is possible, and indeed usual, to judge works of art in ignorance of what they do for the artist, of what repressions they express, of his sincerity or hypocrisy, of his motivation, of his hates and loves, is obvious. For in most cases we know next to nothing of the men whose works we most admire. No one thought any the worse of the Homeric epics when it was believed that they were collections of anonymous folk ballads. And even to those who believe that they were written by Homer himself, they give us but the faintest clue to who Homer was, what kind of man he was, why he wrote them. And yet our ignorance of Homer's biography has not obscured the epics or lowered them in our estimation. We know a little bit more about Shakespeare than we do of Homer, but to all intents and purposes we are enclosed within each play and poem as we see or read them. The invocation to light in *Paradise Lost* gains added pathos when we know that it was written by a blind man, but it is not necessary to know that in order to be deeply moved by the passage. The autobiography of Benvenuto Cellini contains in all probability exaggerations and bragging and hence would not do as strict history. Yet no one has ever said that it was not an enjoyable book. Even John Stuart Mill's autobiography, though certainly more straightforward and true to fact than Cellini's, is not read with a view to going beyond it for indications of what he has omitted. No work of art can fail to indicate something of the kind of man who made it and, if it is interpreted as biographical material, an added interest, and sometimes added understanding, has been acquired. There is no obligation of interpreting any work of art in this manner and much foolishness has been perpetrated by biographical critics. But the fact remains that it is impossible to talk about anything in complete isolation from everything else, for the simple reason that it would cease to exist if so cut off.

In point of fact, when a man says that he is simply looking at a work of art in isolation from its maker, the cultural environment, the historical antecedents, and so on, he is doing no more than looking at it in exclusive relation to himself, as if it had swum into his ken from outer space. I admit that the important part of what is known as the aesthetic experience is the impact which a work of art makes upon a human being. But this does not imply that one not only chops off the work of art from everything past and present which made it what it is, but also chops off oneself from one's own past and present. The man who thinks he can accomplish this miracle is deluded and is, moreover, attempting something useless if it could be achieved. Just reading a plain English sentence is interpreting it in the light of what one has learned. After all one cannot look at a sentence in an unknown foreign language and understand it by simply gazing.

Similar remarks may be made about the critic who uses works of art, ninth, as indications of social and cultural states. It would be absurd to say that social reference is all that exists in a work of art, but it would be equally absurd to deny that such reference is there. Certain qualifications again must be made. To separate works of art from their "times," as they are called, and speak about them as if they were influenced by their times or expressed their times, is as fallacious as to lop them off from their authors' lives. A time is as much made by its works of art as by its economic structure, its political constitution, its military adventures, its religious beliefs, its social stratification. To make this clear demands a word or two on causation.

1) Causes can be assigned only to classes of things or to individual events insofar as they are representative of classes. Thus one can discuss the cause of yellow fever, of rainfall, of population growth, of death, but there will always be a margin of doubt between the cause of this man's contracting yellow fever on this particular date and of yellow fever in general, of the rain which fell yesterday at 3 P.M. along the coast of Cape Cod and rainfall in general, of the growth of population in general and of the growth of the population in the United States between 1930 and 1940, of death and the death of Herbert Smith on May 22, 1898. What one wants to know is why a given person contracted yellow fever at a specific time and the answer is not merely that he had been bitten by an anopheles mosquito which had bitten someone suffering from yellow fever twelve days earlier. It is true that if

the general cause of yellow fever is not known, the cause of the specific and individual case of it cannot be known, but to know the general cause is not sufficient to inform us of the specific cause. When Herbert Smith, Jr., asks why his father died on May 22, 1898, he does not want to be told that it was because his heart stopped beating. Apply this now to our immediate interest. We may discover why painters paint and why sculptors sculpture and why poets write poetry, but that does not tell us why Michelangelo painted the Sistine ceiling when and as he did or why Renoir painted the "Déjeûner des Canotiers" when he did, why Shakespeare wrote *The Tempest,* or T. S. Eliot *The Cocktail Party.* We know why ships sink, but that does not tell us why the Titanic or the Lusitania sank, and I assume that what one wants to know is at least that the former hit an iceberg and that the latter was hit by a German torpedo. Both sinkings were cases of sinking, to be sure, but that is not all they were. Both Michelangelo and Renoir were painters, but each also was very different from the other and a lot more than just painters.[9]

2) No event that happens outside a laboratory in uncontrolled conditions is a pure sample of anything and, whatever else causation may be, it occurs in an environment peculiar to itself. In a laboratory a falling body may fall through a vacuum, but outside the laboratory it falls through air or water or some other medium. In aesthetic matters works of art are produced in a cultural atmosphere which includes religion, science, economics, psychological factors and everything else which happens to interest both the artist and the spectator. These factors help determine the effects of any cause. It is true that anopheles mosquitoes transmit the bacillus of yellow fever, but it takes twelve days or so for the bacillus to incubate in the insect host; it will not incubate at certain low temperatures and at high altitudes; and it will not affect a man who happens to be immune. So Leonardo may have painted the "Mona Lisa" because of his suppressed incestuous love of his mother, but the converse is not true. By which I mean that not everyone suffering from an incestuous love of his mother paints a

"Mona Lisa." One of the reasons why Michelangelo painted the frescoes in the Sistine Chapel is that he was commissioned to do so by the pope. But if the pope had commissioned Raphael to do so, the frescoes would have been different from what they are, even if their subject matter had been the same. This would seem to be obvious.

3) Though the number of these determining conditions is not infinite, it is so large that many of them are unknown and, since they are so numerous, the probability of their all occurring together is very slight. We may say that the reason why the frescoes are as they are is that they were painted by Michelangelo who had been commissioned by the pope, and that would be true, if not very informative. But the probability of two events occurring together is, other things being equal, the product of the probability of the independent events which must concur. If then we could calculate the probability of the pope's being just the pope he was and the probability of Michelangelo's being just the man he was, the probability of the two would be the product of these fractions of probability. But when one tries to think of the fraction of probability of the birth and survival of any one man times the probability of his being elected pope, multiplied by the probability of another man's being Michelangelo and commissioned by the pope to paint the frescoes, one sees that the denominator is so huge that it seems to indicate an impossibility or a miracle. And when one thinks of two men being just what they are and of the probability of their meeting, leaving it at that, one begins to realize that *on the basis of probability alone,* the creation of any specific work of art at a specific time and place is to all intents and purposes inexplicable.

4) Causes are normally thought of as occurring prior to their effects. One first has to swallow a dose of poison if it is to kill one. One first has to plant a seed before the germination will take place. This will be granted by everyone who is not a general teleologist. Hence whatever the cause of the production of works of art may be, it will have to exist prior to the work of art. But the

times, the social structure, the cultural atmosphere, and so on, do not exist prior to that which they are said to effectuate, but on the contrary they all exist together. It would be ridiculous to say that Renaissance art was caused by the "spirit" of the Renaissance, for that spirit did not exist until Renaissance artists and scientists and philosophers and statesmen and bankers and warriors began to operate. Remove the Medici and the Florentine Academy from the later fifteenth century and what would be left of the Renaissance in Florence? But in the same way remove Dickens and Thackeray and their fellows in all the arts, as well as the British statesmen and industrialists and philosophers from the middle of the nineteenth century and what would become of the Victorian Age? The names of the *Zeitgeist* and ages are good enough shorthand expressions for certain chronological periods, but they are in no sense of the word explanatory.

5) When we think of causation, we picture it as a cause acting upon a patient and changing it. Aspirin, for instance, is taken to reduce fevers. Since we are more interested in the effect of the drug on the feverish patient than the effect of the patient's body on the drug, we overlook the fact that something has to happen to the aspirin before it becomes effective. A biochemist would of course be as much interested in what happens to the drug as in what happens to the fever. Analogously what I am writing here is written because I have read books and articles which try to explain works of art by the age in which they were produced. But if there is a reaction on the part of the patient to the causes influencing it, then it is inevitable that an artist will affect his age as his age affects him. In my case I have the hope, feeble though it be, that what I write will influence whatever readers I may have. To the best of my knowledge this has not happened in the past. But at least in one case an article of mine has influenced a colleague to try to refute it in three chapters of a little book. Both he and I are in our small way parts of our age. We are not a great part, but at least I can say that one of my writings has had a definite effect on at least one reader and, though it has not made him

change his mind, it has induced him to continue the discussion. One launches an idea and then someone picks it up, either supports it or tries to refute it. One has only to look at any exhibition of contemporary painting or sculpture to see how works of art are influenced by earlier works of art. The fashion of nonfigurative painting at present did not arise because we are living in a nonfigurative age, but because of Cubism which, at the time of its origin, was in no sense expressive of anything other than the aesthetic ideals of Picasso, Braque, Juan Gris, and their imitators. Why younger men began to imitate them is another question. But it will not be answered by any appeal to the spirit of the times since the nonfigurative spirit came later. To invoke such spirits simply rephrases the question in declarative form.

The arts then are all parts of the ages in which they are practiced and help historians to describe the character of their age. Causality is not involved in this except in the most general way. That is, we might be able to explain why England has had so many great poets and so few great painters, though I should be skeptical about the success of such an attempt; but we shall never be able to explain successfully why a specific work of art was produced precisely as it was produced by the man who produced it at the time when it was produced.

All nine of the foci of criticism, and the enumeration is not exhaustive, exist together, fused into a single work of art, but in the nature of things are not usually seen together. For few critics know enough to look for all of these things and to speak of them informatively. The public memory is weak, moreover, and the interests of one set of critics are easily forgotten by their successors. Levels of meaning, for instance, have drawn the attention of literary critics in recent years almost to the exclusion of everything else, and few people seem to know that they were distinguished as early as Clement of Alexandria. The hieroglyphic paintings of the Renaissance had very little interest for critics after the seventeenth century—indeed after the sixteenth, and it is thanks to the members and former members of the Warburg Institute that such an interest has been revived. Now that these scholars have published iconological works, iconology has become the fashion and some critics overlook everything else which is to be found in a painting. But after all, no iconologist of the first generation that I know of has ever maintained that the only interest of a painting lay in its iconography. Similarly when A. O. Lovejoy first began finding philosophic and other ideas in poetry, his works were so interesting that a number of his juniors began to adopt his method and carry out his program for themselves. Now we have a whole school of intellectual historians and a journal devoted to the publication of their articles. The result has been that unfriendly critics have maintained that a poem is no better nor worse for incorporating, let us say, a philosophic idea than it would be if it did not. That of course is true. But no one, and least of all Professor Lovejoy, ever said that it was. I should think personally that anything which makes a poem more interesting is all to the good. But there happen to be human beings who distrust the intellect and like to think of poets as irrational and inspired animals, like Plato's Ion the Rhapsode.

If then there are fashions in criticism and changes in the emphasis which critics put on the various aspects of a work of art, it may be useful to say something of how this comes about. We can do no more than suggest an answer to this question, but the suggestion may be useful.

CHAPTER X

The Orientation of the Critic's Eye

IF VALUES are the satisfaction of wishes or the realization of ideals, then each of the foci of criticism should stand for some ideal which either the artist or the critic is attempting to realize. I have listed only nine of these, limiting myself to this number, not because it is exhaustive but because these nine seem to be the most usually found in aesthetic matters. I have been maintaining then that 1) artists wish to see clearly the world about them and to fix it in recognizable form and that critics look for such vision in works of art. To be able to clarify the world of perception is both a useful and a pleasant process, since our vision is often obscure both literally and figuratively. Clarity of vision, even in the figurative sense, is an aid to understanding. It may make things more intelligible if nothing more. That is why after all there has to be visual illustration in a scientific text as well as in works of the imagination. Descriptions in literature are not so rare that anyone need be astonished at this. Even in music we have descriptive passages, ranging from incidental bits such as the storm in Beethoven's *Sixth Symphony* to the elaborate details of Strauss's tone poems. What will be illustrated and clarified has varied. In paintings it will be found running the gamut from the *trompe-l'œil* still lifes of some of the classic painters to Harnett's dollar bills and scraps of printed paper. But there is more to the matter than this. In Loyola's *Spiritual Exercises* he urges his readers to visualize the sufferings of Christ so as to render them more real and a good anticipation of this is found in the *Revelationes* of Saint Birgitta. Realistic or illusionistic painting, then, has been put to various uses and, regardless of current fashions, there is little sense in decrying it.

2) In the second place, all men, except the stupid, have ideas about things which they wish to express and there happen to be others who want to listen to them. These ideas may simply consist in saying, "This is the way it was," or may, on the contrary, be satirical, eulogistic, deprecatory. They may be calls to action, exhortations. The various paintings of such scenes as the Slaughter of the Innocents, the Flight into Egypt, or the Adoration of the Magi, on the one hand, or victories, surrenders, triumphs, apotheoses of secular incidents on the other, are more than representations. They invite us to pity, to self-satisfaction, to pride in our nation, to contempt for evil, or simply to laughter. Greenough's famous statue of Washington "said" that Washington was a lawgiver above all, not merely a general. Elgar's "Pomp and Circumstance" is a musical satire as Ravel's "La Valse" is, though the latter may also have political overtones. The Gothic revival in architecture, insofar as it was a revival, was a definite attempt to get away from the Neoclassic, and presumably pagan, churches of the eighteenth and early nineteenth centuries to what was believed to be the more religious architecture of the Middle Ages. In the early days of the modern dance, ballets were composed on political themes, such as Joos's "Green Table" and even such a dance as "Shore-leave" was not without satirical reference.

3) That we also like to present our thoughts and fantasies through symbols, again, is an ideal, the more so since we have learned that some ideas cannot be expressed adequately in literal language. The obscurity of contemporary poetry and painting may at times be willful and the artists may desire simply to bewilder their public. But there are jokers in every pack and the

mere fact that a spectator fails to read a picture correctly, does not prove that the picture symbolizes nothing. We may look at action painting, for instance, as *doing*, not as that which has been done, much as a Chinese sees a good bit of the interest of calligraphy in the boldness or timidity or serenity or what not of the brush strokes.

4) The use of unconscious symbols was practiced in the belief that they were of more universal interest than the conscious and possibly idiosyncratic symbols of the individual. If the theory of archetypes is true, then anyone anywhere can read them and, what is more, be stirred by them. There is nothing in the desire to find a universally intelligible art which needs belittlement, even if it cannot be satisfied. But if there are symbols which all mankind can apprehend, though one may not be able to translate them into words, that is all to the good. The uneasy balance between legibility and obscurity may be the very thing which makes such symbols powerful. If one knew in reading the Oedipus trilogy that what Oedipus did is what we should all like to do but dare not do because of social reprobation, then it is likely that we should think of the drama as scandalous. But as long as it can speak to our unconscious, we can accept it and be purged of pity and fear. Once more we have no way of knowing how serious the artists are who utilize the archetypes and the so-called Freudian symbols deliberately, but it is good tactics to credit others with as much sincerity as we have ourselves and it must be admitted that, if it is desirable to make works of art which mankind as a whole can appreciate, this ideal is hardly an unworthy one.

5) The desire to enter into another's life and share his experiences is once more an ideal which many men have shared and when it is a question of the great men of art and history in general, this desire is the more understandable. Other people obviously are what count most in our lives and if we do not succeed in understanding their behavior, the world is even more puzzling than it normally is. No practical good perhaps will come

from understanding Pétain or Benedict Arnold, for they will never reappear, and we can do nothing about the dead. Still one would like to know why they behaved as they did, what moved them to acts which seem inexplicable to some of us. This ideal of understanding our fellowmen is complemented by the desire which many of us have had to be understood ourselves. There are not so many autobiographies as biographies, but yet the number is impressive. Some desire to explain oneself to others must have motivated Saint Augustine, Rousseau, and Cardinal Newman, to say nothing of the hundreds of other men who have unlocked the doors to their souls and thrown them open to the public. Those of us who live on a lower plane take it for granted that our lives need no apologia. We assume that we are understood except in minor matters, but that we want to be understood is undeniable. One can call this exhibitionism, as one can call the desire to understand others voyeurism, but there are more charitable explanations of both. To a large extent our lives depend on communication with our fellows and communication depends in part on sympathy. The words which we use to pass on to others our deepest experiences are never so clear as they should be, and there is always a residuum of what we should like to have said which is never said. If then the biographical critic can illuminate the motives of a Shakespeare or a Racine, so much the better.

6) The discovery of design in our experiences, like the ordering of our experiences, is again a step toward clarification. It clarifies things for ourselves as well as for those to whom we are addressing ourselves. The search for order is the search of the scientist as well as of the artist and in both cases order may be imposed upon a subject matter as well as uncovered in it. We see only bits of the universe and have to use them as pieces of a larger pattern, but the larger pattern has to be imagined by us and is not given to us from without. The novelist we may imagine as a man looking at a life or a group of interacting lives and trying to find some meaning in them, meaning in the sense of some reason why the

characters behave as they do, some explanation of their disasters or successes, should there be any successes. Out of his ruminations may come the idea of a curve rising and falling as in Balzac's *César Birotteau* or one which as in *South Wind* would seem like steady decline to some and steady rise to others. For these geometrical metaphors suggest only the most superficial aspects of a novel. But we know also that sometimes a writer will impose a design upon his story, as in the variations on the theme of the triangle or the kick at the end of a short story by O. Henry. But in any event, the desire to organize experience in terms of a dominant pattern is there. The pattern may now be derived from geometry, now from one of the natural sciences, as in Zola, now from theology—when vice is punished and virtue rewarded. And even when the artist is merely taking over from tradition the design which he deliberately imposes on his experiences, the spectator need not care for he may find the organization enlightening. The fact that the usual nineteenth-century novel, like the nineteenth-century play, utilized a balance of good and evil, age and youth, poor and rich, the laughable and the serious, was surely not always present to the consciousness of the public which found some satisfaction in living in a world in which things came out as they thought they should come out. So customary was this design that the repertory theaters maintained crews of actors who could play each type of role, heroes and heroines, juvenile leads, heavies, character actors, and clowns. In such works of art the value as the ideal could not be missed, for, as in flattering portraiture, the artist produced a world better than that in which his public lived from day to day.

7) I can offer no well-grounded hypothesis to explain our admiration for artistry as an end in itself. We do find, it is true, that the material world, "the Other," is an adversary to be conquered and much of our energy is spent in conquering it. The arts exist in their origin to bring about such a victory and everything which we learn is a skirmish in the battle over Nature. The only spectators who are always spectators are, as Bacon said,

God and the angels.[1] The rest of us have to participate in the interchange of natural and human forces. We can therefore understand our own efforts to win out in this struggle and feel a certain pleasure in our success. But this does not explain the pleasure which we feel in another man's success. Do we look upon the artist as our servant? Is our pleasure in his good workmanship the pleasure of a master whose servant has done a good job? Or is this just another case of vicarious self-satisfaction? Is this the reverse of that experience by which we shudder at another's misfortunes? One fears to answer that question since after all there is such a thing as jealousy. Maybe in the long run our admiration for artistry is our admiration for an ideal in the process of realization.

8) The one value which cannot by its very nature be an ideal of the artist is the expression of unconscious symbols. If the theory of Jung is correct, there is nothing else which an artist can do anyway. The archetypes well up from the Collective Unconscious willy-nilly and one is simply the medium through which they are passed on to others. They are, says Jung,[2] "autonomous factors," "living subjects," and presumably we have no control over them. When one is writing, one has to use words and, though the words may be chosen deliberately to convey a certain idea, the choice is always partly determined by forces of which we are unconscious. Dr. Kubie would locate these forces in the preconscious, a zone between the individual's unconscious and his conscious. But regardless of their location, words are in the last analysis metaphors and no one can be sure of why one metaphor seems juster than another, since none, in view of figurativeness, is strictly accurate. Hence we may as well submit to whatever laws of psychology exist, for rebellion would be futile.

9) The discovery of the archetypes or unconscious symbols or of the artist's strategy, as Kenneth Burke would call it, may be an ideal of the critic, if not of the artist. Depth psychology is a modern science and has proved enlightening to all except those

who need it most. It has seemed to some of us the surest clue
to the puzzle of human nature. Until it has become better established as a science, no outsider will feel that he can use its
results with the confidence which he gives to physics and chemistry. But in the half century or so of its existence it has given
us all some reason to believe that no one can conceal himself
from all scrutiny. The moral effect of this should prove to be of
the greatest value. For even if we are not so presumptuous as to
pardon those whose behavior we understand, the understanding
in itself is something which we all desire. The search for such
understanding is of course abused, but not all curiosity is idle.
For one of our principal goals is understanding and it would
certainly prove more satisfactory for critics to discover the real
Shakespeare, for instance, in his plays and poems than to reveal
to the world their appraisal of those works of art.

Since no man can know everything knowable and since no man
can talk of more than one thing at a time, the question arises
of why men talk of certain things at one time and of others at
another. Is there any way of finding out what orients the critic's
eye, attracting him now to design, now to symbolism, now to
biographical indexes, now to technical excellence? To answer this,
as far as individual critics are concerned, would be practically,
though not theoretically, impossible. For we do not know enough
about even the most famous critics to answer such questions.
Berenson, for instance, was more interested in the effect of paintings on him than in their iconography, but do we really know
why? Panofsky is more interested in deciphering the iconography
of paintings and translating it into ideas, but again it would be
absurd to explain this as due to the decline of Impressionism and
the rise of iconology. It is true that in a general sense we can
spot certain fashions in criticism and correlate them with certain
regnant ideas, just as we can correlate certain aesthetic programs
with popular nonaesthetic movements in science, politics, and
religion. Such correlation is not proof in any sense of that word.
For though we can say from the vantage point of two millennia

that the early centuries after the birth of Christ were dominated by religious problems, we forget that there were many people, and not the least influential, who were not interested in religion at all. We can judge the past only in the light of what remains of it, and frequently what remains of a past epoch is only what has not been deliberately destroyed. As far as one's own time is concerned, in spite of the speed of communication and the availability of books and articles, every man has his own interests and some are reluctant to spread them. Aesthetic movements, moreover, reach different countries at different times. Dada, for instance, is dead in Europe, but is being born in the United States in music. So, long after the waning of Zola's popularity in France, Dreiser began practicing the same technique in America.

It may very well turn out that historians of the future will think of the spread of existentialism in some of its forms as the characteristic feature of the middle twentieth century. But if one reads the philosophic journals in this country, one finds much more space given to ethics and to logic than to existentialism. Moreover when a field of study captures the imagination of scholars, they soon form groups which specialize in it, and before long they publish a journal given over entirely to it. At that point men who are not professionally interested in it seem to find it difficult to read the specialized journals. The symbolic logician, for instance, will tell you that he cannot be bothered reading articles on aesthetics or religion or politics, and the aesthetician will shrink from reading articles on logic. If one reads *The Journal of Aesthetics*, one is not impressed with the spread of existentialism, and analogous remarks could be made about the contents of other learned journals. This seems normal enough and nothing to excite either approval or disapproval. It took well over 300 years for Christianity to become the official religion of the Roman Empire and there were practicing Pagans until much later. In fact, as is well-known, Christianity gained power by absorbing many of the divinities of Paganism and giving them new names. Furthermore, what one will call Christianity will depend upon one's tolerance for difference. Are Arianism, Gnosticism, and the various doctrines later called heresies Christian? The more one studies the matter, the more convinced one becomes that Christianity is simply the religion which someone calls Christian. But this too is to be expected.

The term "regnant ideas" must be taken with a grain of salt. No field of inquiry has ever been pervasive of a European culture or a time or a society. The present moment is one in which physics, especially nuclear physics, has great prestige, and many undergraduates are being urged to become physicists, though more for political than for scientific reasons. Civilization is threatened with extinction because of the release of atomic energy, and the feeling seems to be that if everyone finds out how to produce weapons utilizing this energy, no one will dare to use it for exterminating his fellows. At the same time museums are flourishing and paintings have become a means of making fortunes—at least for the dealers. Just as people who think that the world is coming to an end will sell all their goods, though they should know that they will have nothing to spend the proceeds on, so with a kind of desperate excitement, men buy pictures for unprecedented sums though there will be no one to look at them, nor will the pictures themselves escape the holocaust. The middle classes, moreover, are busily acquiring real estate in housing developments, as if they and possibly their children would live to enjoy life in them and every city in the land spreads out its tentacles into the surrounding countryside, until a person looking down on the ground from an airplane has the impression that cities now touch one another. From Portland, Maine to Richmond, Virginia, if not farther, there spreads the Megalopolis, to use Jean Gottmann's phrase, and daily more little houses and shopping centers crystallize along the strings of the roads. There is of course justification for calling this the "Age of Anxiety," but the general population does not seem to share Auden's feelings on the subject. If they did, the birth rate would go down instead of up, the collecting of works of art would cease, and no one would care whether he lived in a new house on the edge of Suburbia or not. If by some chance, or by a rare use of reason, we are not exterminated, the historians of the future may well call our time the "Age of Confidence."

With these qualifications, then, we may say what are the nonaesthetic ideas which achieve an ingression into artistry and criticism. The most important of these in both the Orient and the Occident is religion. Not only are the religious themes illustrated in the arts, as is obvious, but the way they shall be illustrated is determined by religious and theological ideas. To return to our example of the Crucifixion, if Christ was not represented on the Cross until several centuries had passed, it may have been attributable to a theological mystery. Theologically Christ had to die if man was to be saved. He had to be dead for three days. But if Christ and God the Father are one, then Christ's death would leave the world without God and that was unthinkable. To represent a mystery visually is as difficult as it is to express it verbally. But a verbal expression is not so impressive as a visual representation and the number of people who can see things but cannot read them is always greater than the number of literates. To become habituated to seeing the dead Christ might propagate the idea that the world had been left God-less for three days. But once the mystery of the Trinity was accepted by all and the dangers of Arianism avoided, then the scandal and the stumbling block were also avoided.[3]

To take another example, the earliest representations of the Blessed Virgin show her as the Mother of God, holding her divine progeny on her knee. But as the Litany of the Blessed Virgin was elaborated and spread about the Christian world, and the verses of the Song of Songs were used to address her, painters represented her as the Closed Garden, the Ivory Tower, the Queen of Heaven with the crescent moon at her feet, and even the various black Virgins, such as the one at Chartres, were justified by the verse, "I am black but comely." The Byzantine Theotokos was transmogrified into the Second Eve holding the

Second Adam, who in some cases reaches for the apple which is held out to him by the Virgin Mother. And as the theory that the Old Testament prefigured the New gained popularity, one finds reflections of it in pictures of the Annunciation and the Crucifixion as well, the Sacrifice of Isaac occurring in the background of the latter, the Expulsion from Eden in the former. To read such pictures demands a knowledge of the two Testaments as interpreted by the Fathers and the Doctors. One's eye unaided by religious doctrine is helpless. But for that matter the representations of Christ Himself are modified by changing conceptions of His role in history. He may be the terrible judge of Michelangelo, the Good Shepherd, the miracle worker, the heavenly child, the sacrificial scapegoat. Emphasis will be placed either on His humanity or His divinity, according to the beliefs of the artist or the demands of his patron.

It has been pointed out by others that the nineteenth century was the age of the landscape. There may be several reasons for this, running from the Wordsworthian cult of Nature to the agnosticism of materialistic science. As late as the first quarter of our own century, it was common to see vestiges of divine goodness in the rural scene, in much the same way as Saint Bonaventura saw them in his *Mind's Road to God*. But the peculiarity of many nineteenth-century landscapes was their lack of human beings. They were just scenery. This also may have been due to the artist's notion that scenery was beautiful in itself and was not more beautiful when peopled with men and women, peasants, herdsmen, picnickers, nymphs and fauns. But it may also have been due to a growing sentiment of man's unimportance. Just as some economists believed that reform was always ineffectual since the laws of economics were as immutable and as omnicompetent as those of physics, so artists may well have felt that man as the plaything of economic law was of less importance than the stage on which he acted. It is to be noted that the latter half of the nineteenth century saw the first thesis of pessimism that had ever been pronounced in the West, not only in the

metaphysics of Schopenhauer and Hartmann, but in the poems
of Leopardi and James Thomson, the novels of Thomas Hardy
and Gissing, and the plays of Strindberg. Christian painting
reached an all time low and it was not until the coming of such
men as Puvis de Chavannes and Maurice Denis that a fresh
beginning was made toward renovating it. It is true that the
Nazarenes in Germany preceded these men, but their paintings
had all the sickliness of Ary Scheffer and fully justified Nietzsche's
comment that Christianity was the religion of slaves. Every
painter has his own beliefs and ideals, but it would have been
strange if the nineteenth-century artist had not been affected
by the spread of religious skepticism. The number of religious
themes in the works of Courbet, Cézanne, Monet, Manet, Degas,
Pissarro, and the Postimpressionists, to say nothing of our contemporaries, is insignificant compared to the purely secular. And
though there existed alongside them such painters as Holman
Hunt, Watts, and the Pre-Raphaelites, Scheffer and Bouguereau
—not to mention Henner with his innumerable Magdalens—
these men were not the innovators whom we are likely to consider as representative of their time. Their works are usually rated
nowadays as only a step or two higher than those of the Quartier
Saint-Sulpice. Men had to wait until our own time for a renas-
cence of religious art and even now it is far from pervasive.

Political programs also have not been without influence in the
history of the arts. The glorification of princes has always been
a favorite aim, together with the commemoration of national
victories. But it is one thing to see the symbol of a country in
a prince and another to see it in a people. The nation as "the
people" is probably a contribution of the French Revolution and
in this bit of iconographic history Delacroix's "Liberty Leading
the People" is of outstanding interest. Just as the style of Louis-
Philippe was "Roi des Français," so Napoleon's before him was
"Empereur des Français." Neither was King of France. This shift
of accent was indicative of a shift in mood. The Demos now
became the center and before long the national symbols, John

Bull, Uncle Sam, Marianne, came from the middle classes and replaced the older feudal symbols. In the tenth century Alcuin could ridicule the idea that the voice of the people was the voice of God, but by the nineteenth century it was not only not ridiculous, but sacred dogma. There are very few painters before Daumier and Millet who portrayed the lower classes seriously and sympathetically, Breughel, Louis Le Nain, whom we have already mentioned, and occasionally Goya being the most important. Power has no doubt always resided in the purse, but one waited for Karl Marx to see this stated as a cardinal principle of politics. When Proudhon came out with his famous slogan, "Property is theft," he struck a note which jangled harshly in the ears of society's leaders. If one has any doubts about what Millet, for instance, meant to some of the more sensitive men of the nineteenth century, one has but to read the letters of Van Gogh.

There was, of course, as far as nineteenth-century artists were concerned, a streak of cultural primitivism in all this idealization of the peasant. He and by extension the working man were more natural than the man of the upper classes, less given to luxury and superfluous enjoyments. They replaced the "noble savage," who also was able to do without things, to subsist on the strictly necessary, closer to that mysterious thing known as "reality." The peasant was a sort of latter-day Diogenes. As long as people thought that labor was a punishment for the sin of Adam, that economic prosperity was the reward of virtue, no one was going to waste any sympathy on the poor. One might give them alms, for almsgiving was a step toward the acquisition of merit. But one did it more for one's own good than for that of one's beneficiaries. Rank had for centuries been a mark of divine favor. But when one began to suspect that it was not God but Mammon who reduced the poor to their level in the social hierarchy, sentiment changed. Perhaps the most significant symptom of the change is found in the cant phrase, "the Dignity of Labor." If people could be made to believe that labor was dignified, they might also be induced to represent it in a dignified manner. How hard it was for this change of mind to be brought about is shown by the reception given to Courbet's "Stone Crushers." [4]

One of the most influential of the forces changing artistry was in physics, psychology, and anthropology. The physics of light we know was a powerful influence on the technique, if not the subject matter, of a man like Monet. That what we see is illuminated surfaces and not solid objects appears to have been the guiding idea in his painting.[5] Anyone can see its effect in such series as "Rouen Cathedral," the "Haystacks," the "Poplars," and finally the "Water Lilies." If painting is essentially a visual art, which though doubtful is a popular belief, it is reasonable for the painter to eschew everything but the visual surface. The all-importance of sensory impressions appeared not only in painting, but also in music, as in many of the works of Debussy, and as for philosophy, phenomenalism and Comte's positivism had their heyday at this time. That all knowledge is a mosaic of sensory data was accepted by almost all who had become tired of absolute idealism and, even in the writings of such men as the American New Realists, R. B. Perry, E. B. Holt, W. P. Montague and their colleagues, the basic nature of sensory data was taken for granted. What they refused to take for granted was that there was any perceiving mind to enjoy the data. This tendency, though modified, has persisted into our own time and it might with reason be maintained that paintings such as those of Jackson Pollock, where all reference to objective reality has vanished, are as purely visual as is possible.

I say purely visual since colors in themselves are not inherently the colors of anything. When one sees blue, one does not necessarily see the sky or the sea or the eyes of a blonde or cornflowers or any other blue thing. And since all colors, when put on a canvas, seldom occupy the whole field of vision, they must have some shape, but that shape need not be the shape of any recognizable object. It is true that some of Pollock's canvases call to mind the swirling of water and of thin clouds, but such an association of ideas is far from universal or inevitable. On the other hand it is possible, though not as yet demonstrated, that the majority of people have emotional associations with certain colors, such that blue might be depressing and pink cheerful.[6] Yet since all colors on a canvas are usually combined with other colors, whatever the emotional effect may be, it must be that not of any single color but that of the combination. The whole thesis can be no more than a rough statistical generalization and a reading of Van Gogh's letters in which he sets forth his notion of the emotional, indeed the moral, significance of colors makes one wonder how anyone could believe all his fellows to be affected in the same way by a malachite green or a lemon yellow. There have been people who have said that major keys are gay and happy and minor keys sad and depressing. But such people have overlooked the demonstrable fact that many of the folk tunes, dances for instance, are in the minor keys and certainly not depressing.

In recent times the psychological theory which has most impressed artists is that which derives from Freud. When one reads the criticisms of the sculptor, Jacob Epstein, one sees that at least in England, and as a matter of fact it would also hold of the United States, there was a real need of liberating people from the fear of expressing sexual emotions. Epstein lived well into our own time and yet the average critic kept harping on the supposed indecency of his works. The indecency consisted in the absence of fig leaves and loin cloths. When men are willing to print such impassioned objections to seeing what everyone knows is beneath the fig leaf, it can only be concluded that they have a pathological fear of sexuality, or perhaps I should say of their pathological interest in the sexual organs. The psychoanalysts, whatever the faulty details of their various theories, at least freed some of us from this morbid condition and there has never, to the best of my knowledge, been such a flood of sexually oriented works of art produced in civilized times. The Ancients with their phallic symbols were open and above board and, until theologians began to preach against it, they had no inhibitions against representing men as men and women as women. In our own time artists have in a few cases, such as that of Miró, stated the facts openly, but on the whole their sexual references have been hints contained in what they believed to be "Freudian symbols." Critics, however, have gone well beyond this, have looked for and of course found sexual symbolism almost everywhere.[7] Much of this has been done by letting one's undisciplined imagination roam at will and it requires no great study or effort to see genitalia in any straight or curved shape. This seems to be an extension of the sniggering habits of school boys, but on the other hand it is also part of our satisfaction in defying the restrictions of a century of prudery.

Along with this has come the belief, found most clearly in Surrealism, that truth will be discovered by releasing our unconscious from the chains of reason. Such terms are loaded with emotion and should be clarified. For sometimes the word "reason" is used as an equivalent for "social approval" and sometimes for objective realism. There is a grain of common sense in granting society the right to censor our speech and control our behavior. One cannot rebel against everything. But it is also true that the arts have yielded to the pressure of the rebels rather than to that of the submissive. To read the arguments over the key in which Mozart wrote the opening of his so-called "Dissonant Quartette" (K.465), usually said to be in C-major, is to realize how passionate critics can become when they detect something which violates the traditional rules.[8] Such innovations are mild compared to a complete surrender to automatic writing and painting, but nevertheless they are a step in that direction. The present vogue for what looks like automatic painting, painting which emerges from whatever happens to occur to the painter while he is painting, paintings in which accidents are left as they happen and the painter is proud to admit that he was not aware of what he was up to, shows that automatic painting can be as emotionally satisfying as disciplined painting. One cannot believe that all men are snobs and hypocrites, and if one cannot enter an exhibition of contemporary painting and sculpture and find a single piece of representational art, one has to grant that the day of the "unconscious" has arrived. This does not imply that it will last forever. In the long run, the history of every art is the history of fashions. The history of fashions is to some extent propelled by fatigue with the old and a desire for the novel. But such fashions do not last very long and the vogue of nonobjective painting and sculpture has already passed its zenith. One can say that with some confidence in that such artistry has already become routine.

One of the troubles, as is always the case, is that the people who write books and essays on art are seldom of the generation of the artists about whom they are writing. To them an art is what it was in their youth and they are reluctant to admit change as a reality. Laments for the past, for the good old days— usually undated—are nothing new. The slightest knowledge of cultural history would suffice to show that cultural change is inevitable. Within a cloistered society such as the Church one may find a minimum of change, but even there a historian could point out that dogma as well as its interpretation has grown. The very heart of Catholic liturgy, the Mass, is not what it was in its beginning, as is shown by the vestiges of the Greek in which it was originally celebrated. The United States Constitution which was supposed to be frozen as of 1789 has, as everyone knows, not only been changed by amendments, but also by the decisions of the Supreme Court. All culture is bound to be modified as new problems confront the human race. If an artist can be thought of as a serious interpreter of life, and I do not say that this would be true of all artists, then he should be encouraged, rather than forbidden, to meet life's problems as other men do. What would one think of the critic who said that the transmutation of the elements was wicked because an element by its very nature must be immutable? This may have been reasonable before 1900. But since the days of the Curies, Rutherford, and Soddy, it is nonsense.

If the unconscious operates in accordance with its own laws, those laws will establish a rational order, as they did in psychoanalysis. It is irrational for an adult to act as a child, "inappropriately" as the psychiatrists say. But the irrationality of such behavior consists not in acting in an inexplicable fashion but in acting in an extremely unusual fashion. It is abnormal in the sense of not being modal. But that simply means that few if any people know what the reason for the abnormal behavior is. It is not irrational as a logical fallacy or a mathematical error is. So in the art of painting, if it is assumed that painting is the art of reproducing ordinary objects as they appear to the normal eye, then one can logically infer that any deviation from objective realism is irrational. But not even the most dogmatic Realist or Naturalist, not even Courbet or Zola, ever succeeded in creating a world which was a complete reproduction of the objective world. In fact Zola himself pointed out that art was nature as seen through a temperament. The *trompe-l'œil* painters almost re-created the world, but they too had to see objective reality through their own eyes and not through some standard eye which was that of the mythical being, Humanity. Though the birds may have pecked at the grapes of Apelles, they soon found out that their pecking was wasted effort. And even Pygmalion had to invoke the help of the gods before he could actually embrace his Galatea. Most painters, even when they clung to the doctrine of objective realism, modified their models to make them more beautiful (or ugly) in accordance with their own standards of beauty.

But it is obvious that whatever is put into a painting, and by extension into any other work of art, will have to be composed of parts first seen. But what is seen is determined as much by psychological laws as by physical. One of those laws expresses the conditions under which attention is oriented. Another expresses the influence of the observer's emotional set, his liking and disliking for certain objects. A third states the influence of expectation: one looks for things before one sees them and what one looks for is what one expects to see. But all this is modified by the materials in which an artist is working. One simply cannot with the pigments at one's disposal reproduce all the tiny shades of color gradation which a scrutinizing eye will observe. E. H. Gombrich in his *Art and Illusion* has clarified this matter definitively and what he has to say is harmonious with what contemporary students of perception have discovered in the laboratory. If someone is asked what he is seeing, he will reply, "A tree," "A bird," "A cloud," and not "A colored shape." That is, he will contribute what he believes to be before him to what his eyes report. But the minute he does that, he has to decide where he is going to stop. For such words as "tree," "bird," and "cloud," are not the names of visual perceptions but of things. And though they do well enough in ordinary conversation, they are not very explicit. He knows that no bird is just a bird. It is also an ornithological specimen, a biochemical specimen, a combination of atoms and molecules, and with all that a symbol whose meaning has been determined for him by all that he has learned in life. If one sees Picasso's famous dove, one cannot just say that it is a bird. And if one sees Aldus' printer's mark, one cannot just say that it is a dolphin twisted round an anchor. No reclining nude is just an anatomical specimen. For artists, like critics, see with their whole mind, not merely with their eyes.

Beyond the range of scientific ideas lies that of political and national allegiances. A few years ago there was a hue and cry for urban poetry, along with this went another for the American Scene. In Russia, we are told, the artist is ordered to make works of art for the proletariat, and all nonobjective art, even if only so far from Realism as Cubism, is denounced as an appeal to capitalistic and bourgeois taste. As early as 1860, Henry Ward Beecher condemned Renaissance Italian art as undemocratic. And not too long ago Congressmen denounced a traveling exhibition of American painting as Un-American. Emerson in his well-known oration on the American Scholar wanted to free his fellow countrymen from their enslavement to Europe and by the end of the nineteenth century composers were being nationalistic, as they thought, by introducing folk tunes into their compositions. Regardless of the historical absurdity of most of these fancies, the call to artists to express the political and national ideals was not unheeded. But no culture in the Occident has ever been fenced in and, though we may talk about the American language, as distinguished from English, American is at best a dialect of English. The fact that we drop the *u* in such words as *color* and *honor* and have slang expressions which would not be understood in Great Britain does not constitute our speech as a separate language in the sense that Norwegian is separate from Swedish, to say nothing of Spanish being separate from Portuguese. What one calls a separate language depends on one's definition of a language. But the differences between English and American are exaggerated by the nationalistic spirit of people who dislike the speech of others. There is nothing to dislike in either English or American, but there are plenty of Americans who dislike the English for reasons which have little to do with their speech, and similarly plenty of Englishmen who dislike Americans for analogous reasons. One can easily transfer one's dislike for a person to his speech, his clothes, his sports, his arts, and his religion. Thomas Craven in his book on *Modern Art* took out his dislike of the French by attacks on what he called the School of Paris. And Léon Daudet saw in every work of art which he disliked the hand of the International Jew. If Chagall is a Jewish painter because he has painted rabbis and ghetto life in Russia, then what of Rembrandt? For that matter, what of all the hundreds of painters who have illustrated the New Testament? One might as well say that Landseer, since he painted dogs, was canine and Alma-Tadema Greek. We now know how monkeys paint and have no reason to think that the man who likes to paint like a monkey is simian. The pallid drawings of Flaxman were the poorest imitations of Greek vase paintings and no one would say that *Lakmé* was more than the most remote approach to Indian music. The point, of course, is that most artists deal with those subjects which surround them, either really or in their imaginations. It is one thing to talk about national subject matters and another to talk about national artistry. But even here there has been much exaggeration. No one any longer denies the influence of Scythian designs on Chinese design, but also no one asserts that they cannot be distinguished. The degree of isolation of a culture depends on the degree of communication between it and other cultures. As one descends from China, for instance, into northern Thailand, one sees sculptures which echo Chinese sculpture both in decoration and in subject, but the farther south one goes, the less the resemblance. If there were such a thing as a Chinese or Siamese spirit, it would express itself wherever Chinese and Thais were to be found. But that is contrary to fact.

In such ways the critic's attention is directed to a variety of possible targets. It is always possible to find in any work of art or in any artist's style indications of all the things which we have mentioned and of others as well. What a critic will look for will depend upon his preconceptions of what he ought to find, and these preconceptions naturally will depend on his total education. Standardization of both subjects and manners is no cause for surprise—most living is ritualized. But the adult might be expected first to realize that he is not the "human race" and second, that all the elements of a culture are mutable. One can scarcely object to a man's painting or writing as he thinks fit and not as some critic thinks fit. The artist has to pay the price of his independence nevertheless. That price is usually abuse, which may extend from mild expressions of dislike to downright slander. That critics think it their duty to transform their likes and dislikes into principles of approbation and disapprobation is normal. We all do it. To see one's ideas as peculiar to oneself is rarely achieved. Men hunger for the universal and unchanging. They seem inevitably to believe that their taste, their family's taste, their neighborhood's taste, and what they imagine to be their country's taste is the world's taste and always has been. I suppose that just as some Christians believed that Adam and Eve spoke Hebrew, so the Chinese believed that the first men to inhabit the world spoke Chinese. In the mythology of every people is the idea that their country is the center of the universe. And it is, for them. When the Bodhisattva was about to be born and descend from the Tushita Heaven, he had to decide just where his descent would take place. Of course it occurred in the center of the world, India.

Surely one might expect our contemporaries to have outgrown these childish notions. We know enough about the history of criticism to see that critics from time to time shift their point of view and look for different things. For that matter we also know enough to see that at any given time a group of critics will take various points of view. Though men like Clive Bell and Roger Fry formed schools of criticism, they were surrounded by other men who disagreed with them entirely. For instance, Charles Marriott (*Outlook,* 21 February 1920) writing about Epstein's "Christ" could say, "At this time of day neither Mr. Epstein's nor any other artist's ideas of the Redeemer are of the least interest to anybody. They are, in the true sense of the word, impertinent. Above a certain level of importance, all historical figures are true in proportion as they are traditional, and any attempt to 'reinterpret' them makes them relatively untrue. . . . But, apart from the folly and impertinence of all such reinterpretations, Mr. Epstein has made another mistake: an artistic mistake. Reinterpretation, or even interpretation, of the subject is not the business of sculpture. . . . The business of the sculptor is to interpret not the subject but the material; to make the stone or bronze or whatever it may be more like the subject than anybody has made it before by the nice recognition and skillful handling of its properties. This applies to every kind of art." [9] One week before this J. Middleton Murry in the *Nation* had said, "Epstein's 'Christ' is a man, austere, ascetic, emaciated, having no form or comeliness. He is a man of sorrows and acquainted with grief. There is pain, bodily agony, not merely in the gesture with which he points to the torn flesh of his out-spread hand, but in the poise of his proud unseeing head. If he has risen from the dead, he rose as a man, by virtue of a tense and concentrated effort of the human will. . . . What Epstein had to express was the nature of the man who knew every second of his agony and disillusion. The man of reality swoons under the pain, gives up the ghost; but art can envisage a man who remains fully a man under sufferings intolerable. This is a Christ-Prometheus." [10]

Most people would, I think, agree that both Marriott and Murry were men sensitive to whatever it is that art communicates. Murry has given an interpretation of the "Christ" which he believes to have been the sculptor's—and since Epstein published it with approval, he could not have been far wrong. But Marriott not only says nothing about what the figure symbolizes, but denies that it has a right to symbolize anything. I confess that I am far from certain about the meaning of making stone more like the subject than anybody has ever made it before, especially since in this case no one has the remotest idea of what the subject looked like. But even if one understands this cryptic phrase, it is obvious that what one critic denies, the other affirms. These two opinions cannot be reconciled, for they negate each other. One can only conclude either that one of the opinions is wrong and the other right, or that each critic is looking for something which he believes ought to be present whether it be there or not. Marriott was disappointed at what he found and he found exactly what Murry was delighted and deeply moved to have found.

There is no Supreme Court to tell critics what they ought to look for. It had become stylish after the publication of Clive Bell's *Art* to look for "significant form" and significant form was the form which gave rise to an "aesthetic emotion." Unfortunately the only definition which he gave of this kind of emotion was that it arose from looking at significant form. His book was an important item in the rise of modern art, for it justified, or tried to, the distortions which the Fauves and later Postimpressionists had introduced into their representations of human bodies. To have called people's attention to this was a valuable contribution to the appreciation of the visual arts. But unfortunately it also gave people the impression that anything else which might be present was illegitimately there. The verdict was to be sure unwarranted. It was judgment based upon the use of words. Etymologically, as we have pointed out above, the word "aesthetic" suggests that the values of works of art must reside exclusively in the perceptual surface. Anything other than the purely perceptual which might be apprehended in a work of art would therefore not be aesthetic. The skeptical reader might then reply, "What of it?" He might take the point of view that more than one value was to be found in most pictures, sculptures, poems, buildings, and pieces of music. To contemplate a painting as a focus of concentrated ideas might be thought of as one of the values of the painting. To see one as a religious effigy, a magical tool, a moral argument, is not aesthetic in Bell's use of that term, but then one must invent another term to cover all the values which are fused together in a single work of art. To refuse to do this is like refusing to see in a mountain anything more than its mineral possibilities or in a tree anything more than its cubic feet of lumber. But both a mountain and a tree are much more than that and are valued for more than that. So, though a painting may have significant form, it may also have other significance and it is only by fiat that one can rule that other out of court.

This raises the question of just how values are related to human life as a whole and we shall now turn to that.

CHAPTER XI

The Hierarchy of Values

WE HAVE DESCRIBED the role of values as that of ideals which guide our action. They are that which we hope to attain, the personal reward of our struggles and the compensation for our disappointments. As such they are seldom achieved in real life. They are, to refer again to Fichte, what ought to be, not what is. At the same time there is such a thing as finding something valuable. The thing may be either an object or an act. I see no way, as I have said, of substantiating the existence of values which no one finds valuable. Those which, like justice, are rarely actualized and which are usually taken seriously only when one is oneself involved, have nevertheless been valued at some time or other by some real person. The valuation may exist only in a book or in legislation and never found in practice. But in spite of that someone must once have envisioned it as a good and at least hoped that the day would dawn on which it would be sought by all men.

One of the great difficulties in discussions of this sort is that we use too general terms to name our values. Even the criminal would agree that he thinks justice ought to prevail; he would maintain that the sentence passed on him was not just. In ethics it is specific acts, dated and localized, which are in question, not the abstract principles upon which most opinion is uniform. A Nietzsche may have the courage to say openly that he does not accept the usual virtues, which he believes to have their origin in the Will of Slaves, but he is a very rare exception to my generalization. It is understandable why this should be so. The names which we give to our values are all question-begging; by their very nature they include an appraisal of the things they name. We all approve of the virtues and disapprove of the vices, but we differ on whether a given act actually is virtuous or vicious. It is here that moral casuistry enters the debate and for its part it asks whether or not a given act should or should not have been performed. The perfect tense of the verb is important, for before an act is performed one can never prophesy what its effects will be and the effects have to be taken into consideration in appraising it. And when motives also enter, who really understands his motives? Though it would be an error to say that all acts are *actes gratuits*, there is always a gratuitous element in every act: one wants to do it or does not want to do it. We can theoretically generalize about the kinds of act which we have wanted to do in the past, but when we are confronted with a new problem, we usually discover that there is just enough novelty in it to make our generalizations fall short of covering it.

The same holds good of artistry. We have a vague idea of what we want to make, but the process of making it modifies our plans. Accidents happen; new ideas come to us; our friends comment upon what we are doing; the thing does not seem to be turning out as we had anticipated. Or, from the spectator's point of view, we have a mass of memories which orient our eyes and then come upon a picture which conflicts with them. How can we reconcile the new with the old?

A distinction must of course be made between those ideals which we have been told to make our own and those which we do make our own. In view of the indisputable fact that men have changed their values as time has gone on and have succeeded in imposing new values on society in the form of custom or statute, there is nothing to be gained by maintaining that some things valued are real values and others simply the values of a single individual or small dissenting groups. The triumph of governance is achieved when a society as a whole accepts as its ideal the values of the governor. This has never happened as far as the record shows, for there has always been debate and conflict in all societies. The history of regal power in England is a clear example of this and one can see from John Lackland down through Henry VIII abridgement of power in law and continuance of power in practice. Oaths sworn by the kings were not observed and at times papal dispensations were given to free a man from the consequences of his oaths. The King did not want to swear falsely and hence had to salve his conscience by a papal dispensation. Yet his act was in effect a violation of his oath. Can an oath be unsworn? Again, I doubt very much that an infant exposed by his Greek father would have esteemed his parent's act very highly if he had had the ability to speak. And similarly there must be very few criminals condemned to death who believe sincerely in capital punishment. They themselves may have taken the life of someone else and thought their act excusable, but no one has the right to take theirs. The criminal, however, like the infant, has no power to make his desires felt by others and he is marched off to the electric chair or gas chamber whether he likes it or not. The State in his case commits an act which it punishes when an individual commits it.

Through the establishment of public schools, supported and controlled by the State, we have found a method of making our values fairly general. The school boy has little to say about how he should behave, about what is right and wrong, beautiful or ugly. He no longer has much to say about what subjects interest him. His teachers in co-operation with his schoolmates see to it that he accepts the *mores* of the school and any rebellion on his part will be severely punished by one or the other. If after his punishment he still believes that he is right and the rest of his little society wrong, he will accept his punishment and continue on the reprehensible road which he has laid out for himself.[1] Conformity is something upon which all groups insist and it takes years for a group already established to admit the ingression into its customs of new customs. The immigrant into the United States had to choose between remaining a perpetual outsider or accepting what was called Americanization. His children, because of the influence of the public schools, almost automatically became Americanized, refused to speak the language of their parents, were ashamed of their manners, clothes, and above all, food, and when they grew up had little hesitation in changing their names into something resembling Anglo-Saxon names. Ironically enough, there was a countermovement to all this. It took but another generation for Yiddish phrases, Italian cookery, Negro music, originally despised as alien to the "American way of life," to become integrated into the way in which Americans lived. Whether this was because of sending thousands of young Americans abroad during the two wars, thus weakening their provincialism, or because of the independent spirit of certain individuals, no one seems to know at present.

Unfortunately there is no longer any way of discovering what values a man would find for himself if he were not indoctrinated in childhood. But we do know that whenever a man has wanted to go his own way, he has done so regardless of social reprobation, corporal punishment, suffering, and poverty. This has been particularly true of artists. Innovations in the arts have never been received with enthusiasm by critics in general. For innovations are always a puzzle. Where people received Beethoven's early quartettes with equanimity, the later ones are sometimes still attacked by traditionalists. The *Eroica*, now received as one of his undoubted masterpieces, got what the newspaper critics call a mixed reception when first played.[2] The *scherzo* which seems to have bewildered listeners, now seems to be heard as if it evoked no problems. The use of the twelve tone row has not yet won unanimous approval by any means, but one can see that it is gaining ground and will one of these days be as acceptable as the ordinary harmonic system. Nonobjective painting and sculpture still meet with ridicule and abuse, but they too are taking their places on the walls of museums as in private houses. When such innovations gain general acceptance, they incorporate values which seem reasonable and in time no one to speak of—though those of whom we do not speak nevertheless exist—objects to them as insane, immoral, or insincere.[3] Hence, though we do not know what values, if any, are inherent in human nature, we do know that there is no single embodiment of them all which has been really universal. If this seems exaggerated, I invite a scrutiny of the history of the novel, of the ballet, and of the drama for impressive examples of fundamental changes in artistry. If artistry is a means of communication, then we may conclude that a new language has been invented in several of the arts, a language so new that practitioners of these arts who died a century ago would not be able to understand what was being said to them, were they to be resurrected today. This may seem incredible, but would Diderot, or even Baudelaire, be able to understand Dubuffet?

The question of justifying any new language is answered in the following ways. 1) What one has to say cannot be expressed in the standard vocabulary. We see this in physics when the scientist tries to put into words the nature of quanta. The debate over whether they are waves or particles, for instance, may arise simply from the attempt to find something in the macroscopic world which would be analogous to what is in the microscopic world. It turns out that the analogy is inept. 2) The program of the speaker is radically new; he is trying to communicate something which has never been communicated before. Thus we find Karel Appel saying, "What is happening I cannot foresee; it is a surprise. . . . I never try to make a painting, but a chunk of life. It is a scream; it is a night; it is like a child; it is a tiger behind bars." Or again, we learn of Dubuffet that "he has been searching not only for the sources of creative inspiration, but for visible signs to express the very sources of life." [4] Neither of these purposes was, as far as anyone knows, the usual purposes of earlier artists. I am far from sure of what such language means concretely, but can nevertheless see that it means something very different from the programs of either the Impressionists or the first generation of Postimpressionists. They were not what one might call ejaculatory painters nor were they searching for the very sources of life. A new pictorial language would clearly be needed to express or communicate these new ideals. 3) All forms of communication, even ordinary language, change as time goes on, whether from boredom with the old or from a frantic desire to destroy what one has come to hate. We have been intimidated into feeling, if not believing, that our civilization is rotten. We no longer feel comfortable in the world, having been told that it is pregnant with the seeds of death. Since 1914 we have seen civilized men embark on campaigns of slaughter which have few parallels in the past. These campaigns have been made possible by scientific advances, but one cannot blame the desire to exterminate our fellowmen on science. It is the use which we have made of technology that is the nightmare and who really knows why we have been willing to succumb to the temptations afforded by our weapons? In any event, literature and painting alike have tried to create a world of horror and because of that desire have had to use new means of artistry.

Whatever man's congenital valuations might be, were they able to make themselves felt, it is true that in the arts our primary satisfaction arises from looking, seeing, hearing, reading. No one can justly deny that the first contact with a picture, poem, or musical composition stimulates what we have called liking or disliking. That minimal appreciation of a work of art is the first step toward fuller appreciation and understanding. If you like a work of art when first seeing it, you may not and usually will not know what there is to like in it, but at least you do not turn away from it in disgust. But individuals once more differ in their reaction to what is novel and it is probably true that the familiar is more likeable than the strange. Parents soon learn that their children are happier following a routine than being forced to adjust to novelty. The habitual is the norm; so much is a tautology. The habitual, as we have tried to show, is by its very nature felt to be the necessary, the right, and the good. This feeling does not stop with childhood. Otherwise would orators fortify their opinions with quotations from the Sages? But at the same time there is such a thing as boredom and some of us reach the point sooner or later at which we say that the old saws are no longer adequate to express our ideas and feelings, regardless of their truth. Whether Gilbert was right in saying that men are born little Liberals or little Conservatives, I do not know, but the tendency to acceptance or rejection of the novel appears at a very early age. The child of parents who are not incorporated into the group may become defiant of custom before the child of traditionalistic parentage. He may, but that is not certain.[5] For the desire to be like everyone else is so strong in some people that they will make any sacrifice to conformity: family, friends, and God himself. It is perhaps wiser simply to grant that we do not know how recalcitrancy and submissiveness arise.

One thing is indubitable: you cannot like or dislike something because someone tells you that you ought to. The critic may advance arguments showing you that everybody always has admired a certain picture or poem or piece of music, that it exhibits all the marks of technical skill, that it expresses something which all men want expressed, and talk himself blue in the face pointing out all the excellences of the object in question. But the pupil may still look him in the eyes and reply that he finds it boring, dull, ugly, repulsive, and meaningless. The critic's sermons are not, however, futile, for if he succeeds in interesting his pupil in the work of art in question, that interest itself may be productive of liking. We say to ourselves, "If T. S. Eliot says that it is all right to like Kipling, we need no longer be ashamed of liking him," or, "If Marcel Proust admired George Eliot, there must be more to her than I have found for myself." [6] It would be pleasant if everyone made up his own mind about everything, but that is a pleasure which we shall never have. For one's mind is taken in hand right after birth, as we have repeatedly said, by people in authority and before one can speak one's mind, it is no longer one's own.

Whatever else one may say about the act of valuation, one can at least see that it is always determined by the psychology of the individual, for that term includes his relation to the various social groups with which he is identified. It is important to realize that *groups* is in the plural. There is no way of living in isolation from other men and we unconsciously absorb the values of the men with whom we are associated or else we rebel against them. Usually our rebellion unites us to another and dissenting group, for we must have a language and a set of principles, as we shall call them, by means of which we can articulate our acceptance or rebellion. If we are timid, we may keep our lips sealed, but the moment always comes when we talk to ourselves and confess the truth. Pretense cannot be kept up twenty-four hours a day—twelve are enough to bring one to the breaking point. Our dreams at least will give us away. And many of us in college, studiously taking note of our teachers' opinions, have used them only for the purpose of passing examinations. In class we believe one thing; in the dormitory or fraternity house or club we believe another. If truth is the highest of values, then a good bit of teaching is an incentive to lying. I still recall, though no longer with bitterness, those dreary hours when as an undergraduate I listened to lectures on Tennyson and Scott and Pope and was told that they were among the great masters of English litera- ture. At the time I thought them about as tiresome as human beings could be and vastly preferred Fielding, Shelley, and Blake. It was only much later that I was able to read my teachers' favorites afresh and find in them for myself the kind of satisfac- tion of which I was in search. If I had become a Professor of English Literature and had given courses in the nineteenth cen- tury, I should in all probability have followed the lead of my teachers and reserved my honest opinions for myself, assuming of course that by that time I should have had any real opinions.

My contemporaries who were interested in literature were discovering such writers as Samuel Butler and later Shaw and Wells.
The irreverence of such men was what delighted us, not the
purity of their style or the plausibility of their ideas. But the
ability to be irreverent when one has to attend compulsory chapel,
not to mention other niceties of etiquette, was very precious and,
if we could not be irreverent outwardly, we could at least live in
a fictitious world of audacity and impoliteness.

We thus had at least two sets of values, as far as literature was
concerned, that of the classroom and that of the parlor. These
values were in a state of conflict. We were not so stupid as to
deny the excellences which our professors found in the classics.
We could see that they were there, for we had on the whole
good teachers. But they were the excellences of artistry and we
could give them our approval without feeling their sting. As students of English literature we could admit the influence of the
Waverley Novels, for instance, Scott's ability to draw lifelike peasants, Saxons of course, and his narrative gifts. But the point was
that such skill was not that of which we felt in need. We wanted
a sort of sauciness, a gesture of defiance at tradition which we
identified with independence of spirit. The conflict between Saxon
and Norman, the heroic deeds of crusaders, the beautiful Rebeccas
and Rowenas, all that might be well done, but what was the use
of doing it? Unfortunately we found little enough in contemporary literature to replace it. We knew that H. G. Wells
and Galsworthy were neither Thackeray nor Swift. It was not
until we discovered the Russians that we realized how flimsy were
the characters of even the greatest English novelists, how thin
and transparent. But that is irrelevant here. As we grew older we
saw something of greater relevance. That was that the values
which are sincerely admired and appreciated need not be those
of Humanity with an initial capital. If our mothers admired
Margaret Deland and Maeterlinck, we had to admit that mothers
too must have their day in court and that in all probability
lavender and old lace were a necessary relief from the drudgery

of running a house and bringing up children. We might not need such soporifics, but others might. And similarly, when people whom we admired, for instance, in the Army read Robert Service and the *Barrack Room Ballads*, we could hardly condemn them because they were not reading Jules Laforgue and Rimbaud. In fact the great gap between the generation of students who took their degrees on the eve of World War I and their teachers was that between men who still believed in eternal values and men who saw the relativity of values to valuation.

A social group in its origin is a number of people trying to achieve a given purpose, if only that of staying alive. When the purpose has been achieved or found unattainable, the group does not usually go out of existence but remains as something self-justified. That need not, however, trouble us here. In the achievement of a purpose, as Royce was the first to see, loyalty is necessary and loyalty demands self-abnegation to a certain extent. That point is determined by the limitations of one's goal. Eating, for instance, has value and one has to give a certain amount of time to procuring food, having it cooked, and eating it, to say nothing of storing it, cleaning up the dishes, disposing of garbage, paying for the fuel which cooks it. But nevertheless no one, however gluttonous, spends all of his energy in food collecting and consumption. The enterprise is limited in its lateral spread and in modern urban societies does not demand all of our time. To leap into a nobler sphere, religion and the furtherance of our religious ideals also demand loyalty. With the exceptions of feasts and fasts, it has little if anything to do with eating. No one would say that the normal man need let his food requirements interfere with his religious practices or his religious practices interfere with his food requirements.[7] The two sets of values are practically without contact, though religious values are more pervasive than gastronomic. Recreation includes another set of values which in the United States have taken on great importance. But except for the observance of the Sabbath, which has become mitigated in recent decades, and the danger to health of gluttony, the three sets of values are mutually independent. One can be sincerely religious, eat sufficiently as well, and indulge in sports without any conflict arising. Some people also belong to the reading public and the reading of books may not necessarily be recreation in the sense that games are. Religion has interfered with the choice of books and no doubt still does and sometimes one has become so absorbed in a book that one has skipped a meal. But in general one can enjoy reading, sport, and food, as well as fulfill one's religious duties without morbid conflict. It would be absurd to say that religious values, piety and saintliness, are to be found at the dinner table or on the golf course or in literature. I suppose that the novels of Dostoevski and perhaps Graham Greene might be called religious novels, but reading them is neither an act of piety nor the practice of saintliness, for it is one thing to do something and another to read about doing it.

Hence it would seem likely that one need not have a consistent set of values, if by "consistent" one means values which are sought in all one's interests. The satisfaction of one set of interests may, but need not, prevent the satisfaction of another. Moreover even in a single field, that of the arts, there is no reason that I have heard of for looking for the same values in, let us say, music and painting. The two arts are different and may have different ends. Why should one not like both Picasso and Gounod? Or dislike them both? Or like one and not the other? If one admires Giotto, must one also admire Guido d'Arezzo? It is true that the values which one finds in Giotto, his broad simplicity, his gravity, his nobility of movement, might induce one not to admire some tempestuous composer like Berlioz, but if one has a sympathy for the Romantic movement and because of one's sympathy understands the ideals of the men who participated in it, I can see why one might appreciate both. For a good part of appreciation is understanding. If Berlioz had been a painter, he would have probably painted in the manner of Delacroix, but that is far from certain. William Blake may have written the *Songs of Innocence*, but there is nothing childlike in his illustrations to the Book of

Job. When Liszt played for himself, he played the preludes and fugues of Bach.

One cannot in spite of all this maintain that there is a Peaceable Kingdom of Values. If one lists the usual values as truth, beauty, goodness, health, wealth, and saintliness, which most of us would agree were all values, one can easily see that the attainment of some of them is prerequisite to the attainment of some of the others, and that if some of them are pursued as the greatest or highest of values, others will never be attained. The identification, for instance, of truth and beauty, popularized by one interpretation of John Keats, is far from justifiable. To make all forms of beauty forms of truth is to change the meaning of the word "truth" radically. If one means by truth consistency with fact, then most literature and all painting, except possibly *trompe-l'œil*, is untrue. For remove the contribution of fantasy from literature and painting and what is left? What is true in Michelangelo's frescoes? The anatomy? The themes? The color? To raise the question is to answer it. They are Michelangelo's interpretations of the story of mankind and if we include his "Last Judgment" in the series, it runs from the beginning of human life to the end. But what are the Sybils doing here? What is true about the athletes? What sense does it make to include any of the ancient philosophers in the "Last Judgment"? Why should Charon be there? One is ashamed to continue, for it is obvious that such questions are irrelevant. I do not know exactly how many people find these paintings beautiful nowadays, but surely enough do to permit us to say that a great many find them magnificently beautiful.

A beautiful painting or piece of music might make one morally better and up to recent times it was taken for granted that the arts had moral edification as their goal. But again it is only by an extension of the word "good" that one can call looking at a portrait or a landscape moral improvement. I am willing to admit that visual pleasure is a good, but I doubt whether such pleasures are those of ethics. There have been plenty of hedonistic ethicists and they are not the feeblest thinkers either. But even hedonists have usually been forced to discriminate between "higher" and "lower" pleasures and between pleasures which are followed by pain and those which are lasting, between pleasures which do not deprive others of pleasure and those which do, and so on, until one reaches the point where one clearly sees that it is not merely pleasure which is the good. Furthermore the reason why so many critics have fulminated against certain paintings and novels is that they are immoral, not ugly. Reclining nudes have been painted which are admitted to be both indubitably beautiful and for that very reason immoral. In this manner one might say that Matisse's famous "Blue Nude" was one of the most moral pictures in existence. I doubt whether most people would say that Boucher's nudes were ugly, yet what Puritan would find them good? It is true, of course, that much depends on what one means by moral and immoral and a man like Tolstoi seemed to find all beauty immoral. For beauty is a gratification of the senses for the most part and there have been many ethicists who condemned all sensory pleasure.

It might even be argued that the enjoyment of most works of art, regardless of their subject matter, was immoral. Lyric poetry, stage comedies, the ballet, almost all music, have nothing to say which is clear and they induce in those who enjoy them a kind of reverie which is the negation of the serious business of life. It is not hard to find condemnations of novel reading as an escape from life and the same arguments could be applied to looking at pictures, listening to and playing music. It could be said that such enjoyments are a waste of time which could be better employed in earning one's living and in helping those who need help. One might be stirred to the depths by the music of Bach and Beethoven, by Mozart's *Requiem*, by the lament of Dido in Purcell's *Dido and Aeneas*, but the moralist might reply that the depth of an emotion is no substitute for brotherly love. The lamp would be still unlit and the loins ungirt, the moral sense distracted from its purpose. For an artist to express himself, assuming that one knows what this sacred phrase concretely means, may be all to the good, but might a man not better express himself in doing the world's work? Poets may be the unacknowledged legislators of the world, but who executes their laws? Let them lay down their pens and enter politics. The arts might construct a substitute world and thus gratify noble intentions not where they would have any effect on real life but solely in the realm of fantasy. I have never been quite sure of what Matthew Arnold meant by deep seriousness, the lack of which led him to depreciate Chaucer, but does even deeply serious poetry eventuate in deeply serious action? One can scarcely deny that the world has always been in need of moral improvement, or that the sermons of the last 2000 years have no appreciable effect in meeting this need. Most sermons are written with the idea that they express divine, not simply human, law and are listened to in the House of God. If they are futile under such conditions, why should one expect that even morally uplifting poetry, painting, and music should be any more successful? In fact, one could well maintain that the enjoyment of works of art is a block to action. And if that is so, then the conflict between beauty and goodness is radical.

It was an argument of this sort which inspired such playwrights as Brieux and Bernard Shaw and which nowadays has led left wing critics to plead for works of art which would speed up the dictatorship of the proletariat. Art whose purpose is simply enjoyment is said to be play, something to amuse the leisure class but hardly suited to earnest men and women. But for that matter, when Aristotle says that tragedy purges us of pity and fear, he also is trying to justify an art by its moral effect. When at the end of his *Politics* he points out what kind of music is fitted for children's ears and what for adults, he again is using a moral criterion of aesthetic value. The case of Plato's restrictions on poetry, as laid down in the *Republic*, are too well-known to require any exposition here, but once more it is clear that he ranks morality more highly than artistry. In the long run most people, whether they realize it or not, are Platonists in this respect. They usually agree that art can influence action, wherefore they believe in some form of censorship which will prevent undesirable action from ensuing. That the premise in this argument is true to fact may be doubted.[8] And yet if there is not some truth in it, most education is a waste of time. For even where education consists merely in passing on rules of conduct, as in the learning of languages, of laboratory techniques, of logic, it is assumed that the words of the teacher and the exposition of textbooks will not be vain. It should not be overlooked, however, that in this case practice—exercises—usually supplement the verbal instruction. It is doubtful that a man could learn to write a grammatical sentence simply by reading about what a grammatical sentence is. And since there must always be some incentive to carrying out the prescriptions of a text, it is more doubtful that incentive would be stimulated rather than dampened by reading all the complicated rules which the books lay down. But if practice is needed, then reading is only half the battle. And one could conclude that no man was made better or worse by contemplating or enjoying any work of art. In schools the practice is initiated by the teacher; in daily life one has to be one's own teacher. Does one imagine that a story of crime unaided by outside forces would induce a man to commit the crime narrated? The answers given to this question vary with the prejudices of the respondent. Who really knows why some men are good and some bad?

If our values could be arranged in a hierarchical order such that those at the apex of the pyramid would be higher in some intelligible sense agreed upon by all, the problem would be simpler. Most people would agree that wealth is lower, as they would put it, than saintliness, beauty, or goodness. In short, they would say, it is better, absolutely better, to be good than rich. But such people forget that the base of a pyramid is that on which the altitude rests. If you are really poor, so poor that you do not know where your next meal is coming from, you will be hard put to it to get an education and you will be the victim of superstition and gossip. Truth, in the sense of scientific and philosophic truth, will escape you and the credulity of the poor is a function of their lack of education.[9] In the second place, such poverty is hardly a source of health, for in order to be healthy you obviously, at a minimum, have to eat wholesome food and take exercise. But even a wholesome loaf of bread costs more than the really poor can afford and one need but stand in line in a supermarket to observe what the moderately poor purchase in the way of food to realize how a bit more education might change things—or might eliminate the excuse for not changing things. When unhealthful living conditions bring on disease, the poor man is at the mercy of charity and, though our doctors and hospitals are amazingly charitable, patients in dispensaries and wards not only wait hours before being attended to but are so driven to impatience that some prefer to go back to work and earn a little money. The public libraries are at the disposal of all who want to use them; art museums are open six or seven hours a day, though usually the poor cannot spare the time from work to visit them; and in the summer there are often open-air band concerts which will introduce them to music. But even if the art museums are open after working hours, a man who had little understanding of painting would derive next to nothing from wandering through them. A skeptic has but to watch the crowds shuffling through the galleries on a Sunday afternoon to be convinced of this. But at least, someone will say, a pauper can always be saintly, follow the Franciscan life and accept the decree of God who has made it easy for him to live without possessions. That of course is true, but it is a question whether the saintliness which is unavoidable is saintliness in the religious sense of that term. Is a man who prefers fish to meat fasting on Fridays?

The conclusion is that a reasonable amount of money is needed for the attainment of any of the other values and from then on the construction of the hierarchy is almost automatic. Economic values are seen to bring about health; health will bring about intelligence; intelligence will lead to truth, truth to goodness, goodness to beauty, and the beauty of goodness to holiness.

This is all very well, but it happens to be factually false. It seems to be a fact of human behavior that the pursuit of any ideal or value is self-stimulating; like Schopenhauer's "will to live," once satisfied it does not subside but demands more satisfaction. Just as the drug addict thinks that one more dose will end the matter and takes it only to find that there is no terminal dose, so the man who thinks he wants just a modicum of wealth finds that there is no modicum. This is such a commonplace in American life that one hesitates to insist on it. Most of our millionaires have so much more money than they need, that they have to give it away. How many men stop making money when they have made enough to live on in comfort? But the same is true of every other pursuit. One may start a sport for recreation, but soon one becomes so absorbed in it that it takes over completely. The gambler at the races or the card table or roulette wheel is not there to make money; he is there to have a good time. He knows —or could find out—that if the game is fair, he cannot win by continuing to play. The man in pursuit of health becomes a hypochondriac and the lover of beauty becomes a feverish collector. The good and saintly man deprives himself of all the other values in his search for goodness and holiness. And, what is more, he believes that such a sacrifice is essential if his ends are to be reached. The problem which every man has to face is that of whether his values are terminal or instrumental. But at the moment when some good is being sought, that good is terminal. If a man is dying of thirst, he wants a glass of water; and the fact that his life is or is not worth living does not bother him. He wants the water in order to save his life, but the saving of his life is assumed by him, though not consciously, to be inherently good. To make life worth-while becomes a secondary problem.

The notion of higher and lower values can be decided only by first distinguishing between that which is a cause or condition and that of which it is the cause or condition. It has often been said, for instance, that just living is of no value, that only the good life, in some undefined sense of the word "good," is of value. But since no value can be acquired unless one is alive, and in the opinion of this book alive and able to pursue ends other than that of existence, one must conclude that life is more important than any other value. I am not denying that sheer vitality is a good and I recognize the deep pleasure of feeling thoroughly alive. But that is a matter which need not be discussed and for our present purposes we shall be satisfied if we can convince people that the dead have no satisfactions. If now we could actually arrange our ideals so that the lower levels would be in increasing importance as necessities for bringing into existence the other values, the hierarchy could be easily understood. But that unhappily is not the case. For a moment's reflection suffices to show that the causal chain described above, running from wealth to holiness is false, not only because one value swallows all the others, but also because some values are exclusive of others. But it is also true that the terms which we have used, wealth, goodness, beauty, and holiness, are too vague to be of much use. Every value exists in a context and the terms indicated are lifted out of context and have thus lost their relevance. This is a weakness of all philosophic arguments. As an example we might take Plato's "ladder of beauty" as given in the speech of Diotima in the *Symposium*.

In that speech, it will be recalled, one begins the ascent toward absolute beauty by enjoying the beauty of human bodies. One falls in love with a person because of corporeal beauty and one need not be able to define corporeal beauty in order to recognize it and love it. The experience of corporeal love is common enough to require no description. And though all men think the body of their beloved to be beautiful, each man may love a different and special kind of beauty. Nevertheless all are beautiful. The next step is the realization of this common beauty. But this can be done only if all the bodies are beautiful in the same way and the only thing they need have in common is their ability to arouse love. Let us suppose, basing our supposition on Greek sculpture, that all Greek men and women who were beautiful looked alike.

We could then conclude that one body would be as lovable and beautiful as another and that one could and indeed should love them all. But could one say that one was in love with "corporeal beauty," an abstraction, or with corporeal beauties? Whatever else corporeal beauty is, it is visible, not a mathematical concept, insofar as it is capable of arousing the erotic sentiments. But we are next told that we must prefer the beauty of souls to that of bodies. But the beauty of souls has nothing in common with corporeal beauty except a name. One may love someone for his intelligence, his wisdom, his sensitivity, and we may desire his company and friendship. But that is far from being identical with the attraction of bodily beauty. Socrates himself, we may imagine, had a beautiful soul, but admittedly his body was grotesque. One would certainly be a fool not to prefer the company of Socrates to that of Alcibiades, but if one were attracted to masculine beauty, the one would not annihilate the other. I am not saying that one should not discipline one's self to the point of preferring psychical to corporeal beauty. But I am saying that the use of the same term to name both forms of excellence does not in any way prove that they are identical or have similar properties. And when one moves up to the beauty of laws, "to beautiful observances, from observance to beautiful learning, and from learning at last to that particular study which is concerned with the beautiful itself and that alone; so that in the end he comes to know the very essence of beauty," [10] one becomes bewildered at the ambiguities which have piled up and wonders why Plato used one word to cover them all. For though it is a commonplace in articles on aesthetics to speak of beautiful mathematical demonstrations and beautiful surgical operations—and one might add for one's self beautiful micro-organisms, landscapes, and ideas—no one would suggest that all these beauties are associated with erotic feelings or could emerge from them.[11] That we call them all beautiful does not prove that they all have any common property, for we could cite plenty of words which have shifted their meanings. Sentences written as late as the eighteenth century using such words as philosophy, history, democratic, for instance, would be misread by a twentieth-century reader who read into them the current meanings of these words. There is very little if anything of what we call philosophical in what the eighteenth century called natural philosophy and no history to speak of in what it called historical painting. Democracy then meant mob rule. One need only to consult the Oxford Dictionary to see how words have proliferated in meaning and, though sometimes there are vestiges of ancient meanings in the words as they are now used, sometimes there is no similarity whatsoever. Who, citing the Hippocratic sentence, "Art is long but life is fleeting," realizes that "art" meant "medicine"?

But analogous remarks could be made about the names of the other values. A good drink is not good in the sense that a good man is good, nor is a good book good in the same sense that a good deed is good. And for that matter value itself is as much of an abstraction as the names of the various values. The very concept, moreover, of higher and lower in the sense of better and worse is subject to objection. There might be a scale of preferences according to which certain kinds of things would always be preferred to certain others, such that, let us say, of ten kinds of things, one kind would always be preferred under all circumstances, one kind never preferred, and in between eight kinds which would be preferred in decreasing order. In some such fashion A. P. Brogan once made out a list of vices which were to be ranked in order of wickedness.[12] We do indeed say that there are some things which we would never do: "We could not live with ourselves if we did them." Aside from the fact that most people seem able to live with themselves under any conditions, I fail to see how any act whatsoever can be performed in a vacuum. We live in a social plenum and even the Church, which believes in the sanctity of life, has also believed that the lives of heretics were far from sacred and that warfare was not always to be condemned. This is inconsistent only if one abstracts "life" from the circumstances in which it is lived and the type of people who live it. One can even take the three theological virtues of faith, hope, and charity, and realize that what is involved is faith in the true religion, not in everything; hope for salvation, not for everything; charity to all except the enemies of the Church. This may sound cynical, but it is merely observation. There was very little charity on the part of Mary Tudor toward Protestants and just about an equal amount on the part of Elizabeth I toward Catholics. Both ladies may have erred, but both had good precedents for what they ordered in the history of organized religion.

It seems therefore a bit superficial to rank the arts in order of greatness, as if under all circumstances tragedy was greater than comedy, or epic poetry greater than lyric, sculpture greater than painting, or painting greater than sculpture, in those unending controversies which disgrace the history of criticism. Such hierarchical arrangements will work in the armed services or the ecclesiastic organization, where as one goes up the hierarchy one attains more and more power over more and more inferior ranks. Power is something concrete which can be measured: one knows just what the power of a colonel is as compared with that of a major general. But there is no power in this sense of the word in art. Wagner, it is true, held that opera was the highest art since it combined music, poetry, drama, visual beauty, and, I suppose he might have added dancing. But this in itself gives no rank to the various arts which are fused in opera. One might again rank the arts on the basis of their popularity, those which are most popular being at the top, and it is at least theoretically possible to collect statistics showing how all the others would then rank. But this is clearly useless, since if opera were more popular than hillbilly tunes, it would also turn out that some operas were not so popular as others, and some in fact might prove to be less popular than some hillbilly tunes. Most lovers of music would rank the *B Minor Mass* above twist music, but if they were organizing a dance, which would they prefer? If the obvious answer is granted, then the circumstances in which a work of art is enjoyed have to be considered when it is being appraised. That throws the problem back to ranking circumstances themselves. Religious ritual might be said to be more important than balls. Let us admit that the Bach *Mass* could actually be performed as part of liturgy. We still have to grant that there are occasions on which it is not only permissible but desirable to dance. This is not universally believed, I realize, but, aside from some Puritans, the consensus would be in favor of the diversity of enjoyments. Since everything which human beings do is done in a complex of other human beings, purposes, and restricting possibilities, it is wiser to judge the value of a work of art from the point of view of its fitness for the occasion, the satisfaction it gives those who are supposed to enjoy it, and its adequacy to the restricting conditions. No one, for instance, thinks that a symphony arranged for piano duet is a satisfactory substitute for the symphony itself. And yet it is an excellent method for learning a composition and a good bit of fun to play, if not to listen to. It is not, of course, the same piece of music, but no one thinks it is if he stops to think at all.

There is one more comment which should be made on the ranking of the arts. If the arts are classified according to the sense organ to which they have been said to be addressed and if some senses are lower than others, as Santayana believed, then painting and music are the higher arts. But to what sense is literature or architecture addressed, and what are we to make of historical painting, portraiture, and allegory? Are they purely anything? Is "pure poetry" simply sound? But does not that definition confine us to the early writings of Gertrude Stein as a standard? The fact is that all works of art have many aspects and none is purely anything. A work of art, like a person, is an individual thing and not merely a sample of a class. Its values then may be multiple and will emerge as the attention and interest of the spectator shift. The multivalence of works of art and artistry must now be discussed.

CHAPTER XII

Multivalence

MARCEL DUCHAMP, in a statement published by Kepes, points out that "the creative act is not performed by the artist alone; the spectator brings the work in contact with the external world by deciphering and interpreting its inner qualifications and thus adds his contribution to the creative act. This becomes even more obvious when posterity gives its final verdict and sometimes rehabilitates forgotten artists." [1] Aside from the fact that posterity never gives a final verdict, this position is coincidental with that which we have taken and since it has been assumed by an eminent and influential painter, it has added significance. The deciphering and interpreting indicate that the artist is or may be talking to someone not himself and that what he is saying is not univalent. As words have different connotations as they swim into the consciousness of various listeners, so do paintings and other works of art. The differences during any one period may not be very great but they are differences nevertheless. And when a man is deciphering and interpreting works of a much earlier period or of an exotic culture, they may be so great that the artists who made them would reject them. It is this which gives rise to multivalence from the spectator's point of view.

Anything whatsoever, and not merely works of art, which is valued may possess several values, though the books like to locate one kind of value in each kind of thing. We are told, for instance, that money has value only as a medium of exchange, but in spite of that some people value it for its own sake, for its value as conferring prestige, for the ability it gives them to be generous, and for the power which accrues to them through possessing it. But besides all this, numismatists value it for historical reasons and aestheticians for aesthetic. Men, again, value their genealogy, not merely because they may think that they inherit their ancestors' good qualities, but also because it is better to belong to an old family than to a new one, though no family could possibly be older than any other. Regardless of our own merits, we enjoy the idea that our forefathers have been famous or can at least be discovered, for then we can play moon to their sun. Patriotism as well is valued as a virtue good-in-itself, but it is also an instrument for loyal service in war and peace. The sweetness of dying for one's country has been a bit attenuated in the last two wars, but nevertheless the fact that one has enlisted in the armed services is a badge of virtue. As for works of art, they have been valued as beautiful, as moral instruments, as religious emblems, as economic goods, as symbols of social status. This is a platitude, but like all platitudes, worth taking seriously. Some of these values are said to be illegitimate, but if a value is that which a person values, then the technique of determining what is illegitimate and what legitimate must first be clarified.

In some cases the so-called natural end of an act is considered to be its sole legitimate end. It has been said that eating exists in order to preserve life and sexual intercourse for procreation, language for communication and the various crafts for producing useful articles, medicine for curing diseases and architecture for building buildings. Such statements seem true enough but they tell only part of the story. For eating also is pleasant and always has been and even in the most purely intellectual and religious circles, banquets and feasts have a place on the program. There are of course some ascetics who object to our enjoying a good meal and who think that all food should be appraised only on the basis of its dietary value. But aside from such truncated souls, the rest of us acknowledge the desirability of eating food which has an agreeable taste, looks well, does not have a disgusting odor, and does not feel like raw dough or ashes in the mouth. Anyone who has ever seen a meal as it is served in Japan knows that the very color of food has been carefully planned, and yet we do not eat color nor does one color have more nutritive value than another. As far as copulation is concerned, one has the *Kama-Sutra* to inform one about its nonprocreative value, if a textbook is needed. Language does indeed serve to communicate our ideas, but it also has some inherent beauty which is normally enjoyed, and the use of language itself—witness the existence of writers— satisfies a need for self-expression and has been used by some lucky mortals as a means of earning their living. There is no activity in which human beings engage which does not have both utility and inherent value, for someone may use an object for an end which neither nature nor custom has foreseen, and the original purpose of an act or object may become obsolete and yet the act or object retain value.

An excellent example of the argument from natural purposes is found in Tertullian's book on the theater.[2] "We were not given eyes," he says, "for concupiscence nor the tongue for slander nor the ears for listening to slander nor the gullet for the sin of gluttony nor the belly to be the partner of gluttony nor the genitals for shameless excesses nor the hands for violence nor the feet for vagrancy; nor was the spirit put into the body to become a planner of treachery, fraud, or iniquity. That is not my idea at all. For if God who demands innocence hates all malignity and malice, there can be no doubt that whatever He created was not created to eventuate in deeds which He damns, even if those very deeds are done by the organs which He created, since this is the entire reason for damnation: the perverse use of the created by His creatures." On the other hand, Emerson was able to say, "If eyes were made for seeing, then beauty is its own excuse for being." Emerson's idea could be applied to all the functions which Tertullian lists and one can only relax and decide that God made us not only to achieve the useful ends resident in our organs, but also to enjoy their use. If man is an unnatural animal, and he is according to some philosophers, then we must not attempt to criticize him as if he were a natural animal. It is human nature which concerns the moralist.

The fact then that something came into existence as an instrument does not imply that it cannot remain in existence as something good-in-itself, nor does the fact that something was first made without any thought of utility imply that it will not some time or other be put to use, for example Hero's steam engine. Our houses are full of obsolete instruments which have been preserved as *objets-d'art*, running from open fires to plants which bloom and bear no fruit. The Greek tragedy may have begun as a religious ceremony, but by the time of Euripides it was much more than that, and today no one believes that even *The Bacchae* loses all value because we no longer believe in Dionysos. The retention of obsolete instruments is no stranger than the compulsiveness of habit and should be accepted as normal rather than perverse. Are we to say that because musical compositions once called sonatas were suites of dances, Beethoven's sonatas are to be condemned because no one—other than Isadora Duncan —ever danced to them? Once again, let us repeat that what special value is resident in anything, object or act, is determined by the person who values it, not by nonhuman nature nor by the consensus nor by its supposed original purpose. If that were not true, then the arts for one thing would have had no history and almost everyone who has ever existed since primitive times would have been in error, to say nothing of sin. But the arts do have a history and my assumption is that where human desires are concerned, everyone cannot be wrong. We may all be mistaken in matters of fact, but hardly in matters of policy. A man knows what he wants at the moment of wanting it; later he may discover that he has made a mistake. But that mistake is not his assertion that he wanted a given thing at a given moment.

Objections to this will be directed toward my apparent confusion between instrumental and terminal, sometimes called inherent or final, values. It was Aristotle, as might be guessed, who first pointed out in a preserved document that some things are good for the attainment of other things and that some are good because they are that for which the instruments exist. The distinction is roughly that between means and ends. The clash in opinion is over whether a means may also be an end and an end a means to some further end. My thesis in this book is that any means may be valued as an end in itself and any end may be used as a means. It seems to me obvious that, just as a professional soldier may enjoy fighting without any thought of its end, so an artist frequently is more interested in the act of painting or writing or what not than in what he shall have produced. The value of just creating something is not trivial. One is too often acquainted with the letdown following the process of artistry to deny this. From Lessing down to our own time, men have emphasized that the good is in the doing rather than in what is done. Most amateur artists, whether they produce works of art or spend their time playing musical instruments, acting in plays, singing, know that what they do is of no importance to anyone else, but that does not mean that it is of no greater importance to themselves than it is to others. There are in the United States at this moment probably thousands of amateur painters, some in art schools, some working in isolation, whose work will never be seen outside of their immediate environment. Few of them have any illusions about the greatness of their canvases and, if asked to justify them, would simply say that they enjoyed painting. To build up a sense of design is both pleasant as an occupation and a help to the appreciation of other men's paintings. The two ends may get mixed together and usually are. Nine times out of ten one does not know precisely why he does anything. Can a scientist really tell why he is a physicist or chemist or biologist rather than a mathematician or historian? He may be able to tell you how he was influenced by his teachers to take up his specialty, but what has that to do with his present continuance of his work? It is said that when Bach was asked why he composed music, he replied, "For the glory of God and a pleasant occupation." And that was no doubt as full an answer as anyone could give to such a question. I realize that nowadays it is the style for artists to write manifestoes and self-analyses, apologias which explain nothing. In the long run a person becomes interested in something or other, he really does not know why, and his interest is sufficient excuse for his indulgence in it. If one takes an abstract enough position, one can always find some noble reason for whatever one does. But such reasons are seldom those which were operative when we started on our careers.

Like all good Americans I have before me on my desk a telephone. A telephone is an instrument for talking over distances too great for the voice to carry. There are occasions on which I use it to convey information and to ask questions, but there are other occasions on which I use it for the sheer pleasure of talking to a friend. To convey information may be useful, but to talk to a friend for the pleasure of hearing his voice and exchanging, as we say, the time of day, is just pleasure. Aside from the probability of interrupting a person who is working, closing the line to someone who might want to tell me that my house is on fire or something equally urgent, what evil is there in using this means as an end? I shall also admit that a telephone conversation is not so satisfactory as a tête-à-tête. But if one is talking to a friend or to a member of one's family who lives at a great distance, it allows one to annihiliate space for a few minutes. A man of my generation, who can remember the first telephone which was installed in his house as a child, still feels an elation at leaping across hundreds of miles and suddenly hearing a voice which vivifies for him a person to whom he is attached. One could write a letter of course and perhaps even get an answer, but no letter can be a satisfactory substitute for a voice. Telephoning begins to take on the color of some romantic adventure and, though nothing in the conversation is of ultimate importance, the illusion of immediate contact between persons is what one is seeking. Thus something which is supposed to have only instrumental value acquires terminal value as well.

But suppose I had been born in the telephonic age. There would be no great likelihood of my feeling any special excitement in talking from Baltimore to Berkeley or from Istanbul to Paris. That would be a matter of course, as emotionally neutral as a simple "Good-morning," to cite Jules Laforgue. Most of my associates are now my juniors and to them what I put into long distance telephoning would seem nonsensical. Are they right or am I right? If valuation is made by human beings and not by some supernatural agent, we are both right. If a man cannot distinguish between red and green because he is color-blind, he is not in error when he says that he sees no difference between them. It always seems strange to people that others do not resemble them in their tastes. This is understandable since the only person whom one is directly acquainted with is one's self. Our knowledge of other people depends on what they tell us, and we are never quite sure of what they mean when they are talking about their likes and dislikes. It seems incredible to us that some Africans should think steatopygous women beautiful, that Mexicans should like to eat maguey worms, or that the Chinese should take their little birds on walks. Some of us remain incredulous when such exotic tastes are announced and others call this perversity or foolishness. So in the same way, *parler pour ne rien dire* seems unworthy of an adult. On which principle we could condemn the works of Lear and Lewis Carroll.

Both artistry and works of art may have both kinds of value, depending on their appraiser. The artist who is immersed in his artistry will seldom be worried about the end product of what he is making and the spectator who is lost in contemplation of a picture may not be thinking of anything other than its moral effect. But the reverse may also be the case, and indeed when an artist has finished his picture, he may then look at it as if he were a spectator and tear it up. There is no law which compels anyone to take any attitude whatsoever; one shifts one's point of

view with freedom. It would be normal for an artist to ask himself whether he has succeeded in accomplishing what he wanted
to accomplish, though he would hardly be "objective" in answering the question. And it would be normal also for the critic
to tell the artist that what he has accomplished is not what he
ought to have wanted to accomplish. Some critics will go to the
trouble to ask an artist what his aim was; others will simply lay
down the law and tell him what it should have been. When the
Fauves began to exhibit in 1905, there were few enough critics
who made any attempt to do the former; they knew somehow
or other that the paintings violated all "the correct rules of
representation," which was obvious, and that this was an artistic
sin, which was not obvious at all. When one sees an exhibition
of paintings made by competent artists, and no one could say
that Matisse, Derain, Vlaminck and their companions were in-
competent, paintings which do not conform to the traditional
rules, one could also decide that they had had no intention of
conforming to them. The next problem was what principles were
guiding their artistry. It should have been sufficient to look at the
paintings and see. But so compulsive is the force of habit, that
the critics could see nothing more than a violation of the rules.
At that point a verbal program was called for,[3] and though the
verbal program was much less clear than the evidence of the
paintings, it became the critics' guide. The most reasonable reply
of an artist to the question, "What were you trying to do in this
painting?" is, "To paint this painting." For just as one cannot
express in words the character, the peculiar quality, the feel of
any individual experience, so one cannot succeed in completely
describing a work of art. The most important lesson for the critic
is to learn the limits of speech. The more submissive the artist
is to tradition, the easier it is for the critic to point out what
he has achieved; the more rebellious, the more difficult.

As far as instrumental value is concerned, it is determined by
success. If a plan of action succeeds in achieving that for which
it was laid down, it is good. The value of the end is irrelevant. A

plan for a perfect crime is good if it comes off, and no matter how reprehensible the end, the means as means may be judged without reference to that. I accentuate this for the simple reason that from the artist's point of view, performing the act itself may be his main purpose. For instance, a great many people today are pacifists and see nothing praiseworthy in war. But that does not prevent them from appreciating the strategy and tactics of a successful general. To force the enemy to surrender is the aim; if one's strategy succeeds in reaching this aim, then it is good. The appraisal of ends themselves is quite a different story. Some things, for all I know, may be inherently evil. Cruelty, slander, hypocrisy, cowardice are for my part examples of downright badness, regardless of their effects. But the man who is cruel will either deny that he has been cruel or will coldly say that the person to whom he has been cruel deserved it. The probable truth is that such maleficence is committed rashly, in a state of passion, without much thought to what is being done. Even the hypocrite and the coward do not recognize their hypocrisy and cowardice at the moment when they are being hypocritical and cowardly. The basest of acts, like burning heretics at the stake, can be defended on the noblest principles. And one often does something which one thinks is kind only to find that it has been humiliating to its beneficiary. Artistry starts from the artist, not from the critic, and the appraisal of the work of art is posterior to the artistry by the very nature of the case.

Just as the means may be good and the end bad, so the end may be good and the means bad. If William Blake's boneless anatomies were to be judged by the traditional standards, they would be condemned as amateurish. But when the moment came in which people began to look for what the eighteenth century called expression rather than drawing, Blake became a master. The emotional power of his designs is undoubtedly very great and one can see how in his preliminary sketches he was more interested in the general movement of his lines and masses than in correct anatomical drawing. He came before his time, critics might say, though it was in part thanks to him that the times changed. At any rate when the dynamic aspects of a picture became the primary target of the critic, Blake came into his own. His clumsy and bungling sketches are there to show us how unsure of himself he was. In fact, even in his poetry he hesitated, crossed out words and phrases, reinserted them, and finally dropped his pen. To compare his manuscripts with those of Mozart, another type of artist, is to see at once the difference between a man who knew what he wanted to say before he set pen to paper and the man who gropes toward his goal as if he did not know where he was going. Blake's art grew out of his artistry; Mozart's artistry out of his sureness of purpose. But Mozart also had accepted a ritual within which he worked in obedience on the whole to its commands; Blake was an innovator.

At this point in our argument it may be well to introduce a few examples of the kind of ambiguity which gives rise to multiple interpretations and hence to multivalence. We have first the obvious cases of historical personages and events: was George Washington a patriot or a traitor to his king? At the time of the Revolution, the English undoubtedly thought of him as a traitor, but later they erected a statue to him in Trafalgar Square. Was the American Civil War a rebellion or a struggle for states' rights? It was a rebellion in 1860 but its centenary is being celebrated at present with Federal funds. Gluck's *The Pilgrims to Mecca* treats insanity as comic; could we emulate this treatment nowadays? In Genoa there is a statue to a Saint Josaphat; Josaphat was originally the Bodhisattva. Did the transformation of this Indian into a Christian saint give him the power of working miracles or are the miracles performed by him not really his? Panofsky in his *Renaissance and Renascences* (p. 68) points out how Niccolò Pisano turned Dionysos supported by a satyr into Simeon witnessing the Presentation of the Infant Christ at the Temple, a nude Heracles into a personification of Christian fortitude, and a Phaedra into the Blessed Virgin. If symbols have inherent meanings, how was this possible? Bach in his *Cantata 11*

(Oratorium) uses the "Agnus Dei" from the *B Minor Mass* with entirely different words. The second movement of Beethoven's *Ghost Trio* (Op. 70, no. 1) was originally composed as instrumental music for *Macbeth*. The opening of his *Fifth Symphony* and the *Piano Concerto in G Major* are identical; do they mean the same thing? Auden uses Breughel's "Fall of Icarus" [Plate 3] to suggest that the world goes on its way regardless of the tragedies which may be happening, but it is also likely that if the picture has any moral at all, it is that of the *Narrenschiff* in which Sebastian Brant says that if Icarus and Phaeton had only listened to their fathers, they would not have met their death.[4] There are scores of such ambiguities which are inherent not in the symbols themselves but in the minds of the men who think about them.

If this is so, then multivalence is inevitable. Critics can interpret works of art only in terms of a code which they already know. Turning to Slonimsky's *Lexicon of Musical Invective*, we find that Beethoven's *Second Symphony* was *ein Krasses Ungeheuer*; the *Third*, "infinitely too lengthy"; the transition to the last movement of the *Fifth*, *n'appartient pas à l'art que j'ai l'habitude de considérer comme la musique* (Oulibicheff in 1857); the *Sixth* was enough to make one look and weep as the composer's genius is thrown into the claws of a chimaera; most of the *Eighth* was "eccentric without being amusing, and laborious without effect"; the last movement of the *Ninth* was an "incomprehensible union of strange harmonies." We may feel superior to the blockheads who said these things, but we do not approach music with their preconceptions. They were not much more stupid than some of our contemporaries who write of contemporary painting, poetry, and music. And what is even more curious is that the critic who has lost his heart to contemporary art can see no good whatsoever in traditional art. It is true that the difference between Varèse and John Cage on the one hand and Mozart, Beethoven, and Brahms on the other is great enough to make one believe that there are two kinds of music, just as the difference between Pollock, Rothko, and Kline (or Klee, Miró, and Mondriaan) and Courbet,

Manet, and Toulouse-Lautrec have established two kinds of painting. But for the Modernist to condemn traditional art is like saying that Latin is worse than French, and for the Traditionalist to condemn modern art is like someone who would say that French is bad Latin. No one can read Latin who knows only French and no one can read French who knows only Latin. But it requires only a minimum of common sense to say that they are two different languages. If the differences between two kinds of painting are as great as they seem—and what is painting if it is not seen?—then it is obvious that you cannot write as if Klee, for instance, was trying to do what Delacroix did and failed. All musical composers will handle sounds and all painters will handle colors, but that is too small a similarity to define a single art.

Sooner or later critical judgments of good and bad in art will be based on what a critic likes. Liking is both spontaneous and individual. It is not, as we have repeatedly pointed out, the result of reasoning. For we all know that though there may be no reason to disapprove of a work of art, we may not really like it. There just happen to be dull and uninteresting writers, painters, and composers, but their degree of dullness and lack of interest will be determined by us as individuals, and if a critic honestly dislikes a given work of art, there is no reason why he should not say so. Unfortunately this has been stigmatized as impressionistic criticism and I admit that the impressions of commonplace people are also commonplace and no better than one's own. But an examination of even the anti-Impressionists will show that they too have to be seduced by works of art before they will begin taking them seriously. T. S. Eliot, for instance, in his brochure on Dante, seems to take this for granted when he pleads with his readers to read Dante whether they understand him or not, since after a while the light will dawn and appreciation will come. But what is this appreciation other than a sentiment or an emotion stimulated in this case by understanding? I doubt that Mr. Eliot would identify the ability to translate Dante literally and to recognize all his references to contemporary life, the philosophy of Saint Thomas

Aquinas, the symbolism of the Victorines, and whatever else is usually relegated to explanatory footnotes with the sting of poetry. He is probably as weary as the rest of us of the objective correlatives of emotion, nor has he maintained, to the best of my knowledge, that simply to see the correlative and not feel the emotion sufficed.[5]

I admit that it is not enough to say that the strange is always bad and that familiarity will be enough to sooth the hostility of critics when confronting the unfamiliar. The strange is always a threat to us. By its very nature it puzzles us. It upsets our balance. We do not know how to deal with it. This is not a trivial matter. For part of our life is understanding things, in fact it is the major part. Consequently when we are confronted by something novel, the understanding of which is proportionate to its familiarity, we shall usually either reject it or try to find out what in the world the man who made it was trying to do. In that way what I have called approbation may set in. It will be found, for instance, that the same dynamics which we observe in nonobjective painting is enjoyed in looking at an open fire in a fireplace, falling leaves, the wake of a ship, rain drops moving down a window pane, a fall of snow, the swirling of water in a stony brook, the movement of clouds, the dance of willow leaves, and a dozen or more everyday sights. When you watch a fire, you do not have to think of the forests which have been despoiled for the logs, of the savage cooking and warming himself in the shelter of Laugerie-Basse, of the theory of the four elements, the temperature of Hell, cremation, the ubiquity of oxidation, or of anything else of that sort in order to enjoy it. All you have to do is look. And similarly, one might think, when one looks at a whirl of colors on a canvas, looking would suffice to induce a feeling of pleasure. But tradition has insisted that there must be a recognizable source of a painting in Nature: even in Picasso's most tormented canvases there are identifiable objects. There is to be sure a difference between the sight of a burning fire and a picture of the same color and dynamics: the fire moves. But that aside, we miss what we are looking for and what we are looking for has been determined not by us alone, but by us as influenced by society. The society in question may be merely the authors of a group of books on art appreciation. That is of no importance. They are not we.

The sanctity of the past cannot be doubted. We never speak ill of the dead. Since most of our higher education is given over to historical study, whatever congenital tendencies we may have to reverence the past are reinforced by our schooling. The appeal to national, religious, political tradition is as common as the appeal to aesthetic tradition and every innovation in all fields is criticized first as fidelity or infidelity to what has always been. To go back to the Bible in religion and to accept nothing which is not in it has not been unusual in religious history. But the Bible itself has to be interpreted and interpretations change as textual criticism and archaeological discoveries bring new information to bear on the text. A man going back to the Bible in 1800 would find in it things which the man of 1960 would not find. No one reading the Bible seriously today can fail to take cognizance of the E and J differences. If he is interested in Christianity, he must give some thought, if not much, to the harmony of the Gospels and perhaps to the Dead Sea Scrolls. But all of us do not have a scholar's equipment with which to interpret this book. That will not prevent our reading it and interpreting it in the light of what we do know, unless we have sufficient humility and confidence in our pastors to let them do the interpreting for us. Why should we not rather simply admit that we are not interested in how the past interpreted the Bible and are content with present day interpretations? Why should we not go further and merely say that, as far as religion is concerned, philosophy and science can supplant theology? Some people have indeed taken this road, but only a few. On the whole men have wanted a link with the past, have wanted to feel themselves emerging from the past with only the slightest change. They have wanted to resemble their fathers and grandfathers and great-grandfathers. They have wanted not merely scientific knowledge of their origins but the power to identify themselves with them. I fail to see how this could be disputed in view of the sacrifices which men have made to defeat the passage of time and to live as if they were one with their ancestors.

This is as true of the arts as of religion or politics. We can understand things only in the light of what we already know and what we know, if I may be permitted the truism, is what we have been taught. Thus books are written on French painting of the nineteenth century which begin with Delacroix and Géricault and proceed down through Courbet, Cézanne, the Impressionists, the Postimpressionists, the Cubists, Futurists, and Abstractionists with the purpose of showing how everything evolves from what has already existed. There is of course nothing else from which it could evolve. But the thesis seems to be that contemporary art is potentially present in Delacroix, as a chicken in the egg. It is true that if you cut out a square foot from a Delacroix, you will have a nonobjective painting, and, if you are not frightened of *boutades,* you could say that whereas painting in Ingres was colored drawing, in DeKoning it is color without drawing. The details of such a story are of no interest to us however; what is of interest is the need which our contemporaries have of proving that the art which they practice or admire has its roots in the past. That seems to give it an added value. It is rare to find a man like Klee who frankly says that he wants to be born anew, to forget Europe, to paint as if he had never seen a painting before.[6] But others will see in what Klee actually painted nothing new but a revival of primitive art and the art of childhood. Two attitudes are possible here, that which praises Klee because he is primitive and childlike, and that which dispraises him for the same reason. In point of fact he is neither, for the savage does not have to try to be primitive: he is primitive; and the child does not have to be childlike: he is childlike. There are thus at least two values in a picture by Klee, that found by a person who is looking at it without any remembrance of its antecedents, and that which is found by someone who knows Klee's theories.

These differences cannot be eradicated by decree. There just happens to be a difference in what a person looking at Picasso's arrangement of Delacroix's "Algerian Women" with a memory of the original will find in it and what a person who does not know the original will find in it. No one can compel the latter to keep away from the Picasso. Why is the Picasso not enough? Should one also keep in the back of one's mind the Bach original when listening to a Busoni arrangement of it or Vivaldi when listening to Bach? But this will lead to the demand that we know the entire history of each art before enjoying any work of art. If one does know the origin historically, not psychologically, of a work of art, an added value may be found in it. But the experience of hearing Bach through Busoni or of seeing Delacroix through Picasso is different from the simpler experiences, and not necessarily more valuable. Some of us happen to be historically-minded and know enough to see the whole tradition in its outcome. But this is not universal by any means, nor is it right to demand it. The value of such historical knowledge and feeling exists, but it does not become a substitute for the value of a first approach to a work of art.

The past is carried along in a work of art into the present just as it is in an individual's memory, retained and modified. And we conclude that to see this satisfies a need, not the only need to be sure, but one need, that some of us have for not feeling cut off from our origins and left floating like a log of wood. As in all such matters the intensity of the feeling must vary from person to person. Just as some individuals feel lost if they are not identified with a group of their fellows, or with an environment, a bit of landscape or even a street, so others feel that they are lost if they are not in sight of emblems of their past, be they only a family crest or a name. It is all very well to talk about individualism, but the achievement of a self or of individuality demands a strength of character which few of us possess. Complete independence is impossible in any event and it is clear that some of us need more indications of our dependence than others do. A writer who constantly refers to previous writers who he thinks are in agreement with him does not fortify the logic of his argument. Quotations, for instance, are in the long run nothing more than *argumenta ad hominem*, evidence at best of a man's modesty, at worst ostentatious erudition. But somehow or other we seem to feel that if we can pull out of our files a quotation from Cicero, Horace, or Seneca, from Plato or Aristotle or Marcus Aurelius, which will say what we are struggling to say, our words gain in truth. It is as if we were saying, "I am not advancing anything original; this is what the best minds of the past have always believed, the wisdom of the ages." In reality such quotations become more effective if they are yanked out of context. When left in context, they usually turn out to be irrelevant.

Our power to persuade ourselves that change is illusory is so great that we can take over works of art from exotic and even savage cultures and maintain that they have the same values as those of our own culture. This makes them universal. An African fetish nevertheless was not made for modern Occidentals. To look at a Congolese mask as if it were made by Matisse and had no religious nor magical overtones is an investing of the object with a value which it could not have had for its maker and divesting it of those which it did have. It is like attending Mass for the beauty of the liturgy. The mask or idol may, and frequently does, have plastic qualities which are finer than the works of Praxiteles or Scopas, but that does not imply that its maker was searching only for those qualities when he carved it. Some years ago it was stylish to use Chinese mandarin robes as piano scarves and today it is stylish to decorate our rooms with Japanese flower arrangements. No matter how inherently beautiful such things may be, a mandarin robe is not a piano scarf in the country of its origin and all our talk about heaven branches and earth branches, the Yin and the Yang and all the rest, does not transform us into Japanese. We have given such things a new value of our own and it is an impossibility for us to leap out of our own culture and dive into another. We can pretend to be Congolese, ancient Greeks, American Indians or Elizabethan Englishmen, but we are about as successful in our efforts as a child wearing its parents' clothes who thinks he looks grown-up. It is all make-believe. The point is, let me say once again, that works of art are multivalent for the simple reason that value is imparted to them by people, not by God.

It is multivalence which keeps works of art alive. For if people changed and works of art remained the same, antiquity would be identical with death. But as time goes on we see new values being attached to old objects. The furniture of our grandfathers, made in the Victorian period, which our fathers found hideous, has become quaint. Serious dramas have become comic. The comic has become serious. *The Castle of Otranto* does not horrify us; it amuses us. *Don Quixote* is no longer a satire on romances of chivalry but a symbol of practical idealism. Our sports are by and large exercises in combat of which the serious purpose has been lost. No one learns to fence with the idea of ever having to fight a duel, nor does one think of chess as a war between two tribes, the Red and the Black. To abstract the rituals of either religion or argument or warfare from their original contexts is normal and *homo ludens* is an invariable companion of *homo sapiens*. It would be folly either to condemn or to advocate this. It just happens to be a factor of cultural history which we have to accept. But it is a factor which explains the survival of much in art's history. Nothing in the past is so dead that it cannot be resuscitated. But a revival is never an exact resuscitation of that which once was alive. The plea is sometimes heard that we should become again as little children and see things with a completely fresh eye. But we can only be ourselves, living at a definite time and in a definite place. We can see things only through our education and experience modified by our congenital endowment. All our hopes of escaping are vain and it is the part of maturity to realize and accept this. But the power of realizing and accepting the facts of life varies also, as psychologists have pointed out, and it is doubtful whether anyone will be persuaded to move in this direction by a book.

We have laid such emphasis upon the contribution of society to our tastes that the individual himself may seem to have been forgotten. We shall now turn to that.

CHAPTER XIII

The Contribution
of the Individual

WE HAVE already indicated in general terms two variations in individuality which would modify works of art and the appreciation of works of art: recalcitrancy and submission. We have pointed out that even identical twins, though biologically the same, may differ psychologically and that their difference may be of importance in their relation to art. We shall now indicate further differences which should be taken into account, basing our opinions on the researches of Roger J. Williams in his *Biochemical Individuality*. These are congenital traits and, unlike recalcitrancy and submission, cannot be eliminated by education, though they may be modified by food.[1] We all know, for instance, that there are variations in perceptual acuity, some of which can be corrected by eyeglasses and hearing-aids, but there are others which so far have never been eradicated but have to be accepted as permanent. The most surprising of these is the reaction to phenylthiocarbamide which to 65 per cent of people tastes bitter, to 7 per cent tastes salty or sweet, and which to 21 per cent is tasteless. I have no report on what it tastes like to the remaining 7 per cent, but since taste in this sense of the word has little relevance to our special problem, we need not inquire.

Professor Williams' findings are of more immediate interest.

He points out (p. 37 f.) that in Anson's *Atlas*, an atlas of human anatomy, "the variations in the extensor muscle of the index finger" occupy two full pages. "The accessory muscles to the middle finger, to the ring finger, and other accessory muscles of several forms are present in some patterns and absent in others. The result is that there are depicted eleven different patterns, each distinctive. In the same source book, there are presented eight different patterns of the extensor tendons on the back of the hand. If the patterns of the nerves were depicted as the patterns of facial nerves are, we would doubtless find many variations in this area too. *The hand* is far from an assembly-line product."

The implications of these differences as far as the arts are involved are obvious. Handwriting, manual skill, ability to play either the violin or piano, may be conditioned by the kind of hands with which one is born. We need no scientific researches to realize that handwriting is individual; when banks utilize this difference in cashing checks, even the hardheaded businessman takes it seriously. But the difference in drawing a line which is found in the lines of Paul Klee and Matisse, for instance, is a difference of aesthetic importance. Klee's line was as much his as the brush strokes of a Chinese calligrapher are his. His famous paragraph called "Taking a Walk with a Line" and illustrated by him, shows the wavering, indecisive character of an improvisation; it has a sort of somnambulistic quality in perfect harmony with the kind of result which he apparently wanted to produce. In contrast with this, Matisse's line is bold and firm and sweeps down and around the page like a hawk. Knowing nothing of the anatomy of either Klee or Matisse, I cannot say with confidence that these differences are due to their manual conformations. But the point is that such individuality could have its source in the hand itself. But it is also possible, though far from certain, that a man might be more happy looking at the work of a hand like his own than in seeing the handwork of a different pattern. Such adjectives as those which I have used, "wavering," "indecisive," "somnambulistic," have subjective overtones. They name effects which Klee's line makes on one observer, but in the field of aesthetics the observer's emotional reactions are relevant.

Second, Professor Williams says (p. 89 f.) that "it seems probable . . . that individual normal males . . . vary through wide limits (probably tenfold or more) in their production of both androgens and estrogens. If we classify individual men roughly as *low, intermediate,* and *high* producers of each of the two types of hormones, we find that an individual may belong to one of nine groupings. . . . Exactly the same classifications could apply to women."

Again, we have no reliable data on the endocrine patterns of either famous artists or critics. Their biographies never do more than guess at sexual differentiations on the psychological level. But surely if our sexual tendencies count for anything in influencing our tastes, and if they are linked to physiology as seems more than probable, then it would be absurd to maintain that a person with a high androgen output would produce the same kind of works of art as one with a high estrogen output. I am only too willing to admit that we classify men and women on the basis of their gross superficial anatomy and not on that of their endocrine physiology. But this may be the reason for our crude handling of sexual problems and of the artistic activity of unusual people. Instead of two kinds of people, we have at least nine. If their behavior in recognizable areas varies, it may also vary in those areas which we do not ordinarily associate with sex. We already know that sexuality manifests itself in religion, for instance, a field which might be thought of as entirely remote from procreation. Why is it unlikely that it should also appear in art where sexual motivations are frequently overt and not concealed at all?

As a matter of scientific fact we know that no two individuals, except identical twins, are ever genetically alike. "We can be sure," says Professor Medawar, "that, identical twins apart, each human being alive today differs genetically from any other human being; moreover, he is probably different from any other human being who has ever lived or is likely to live in thousands of years to come. The potential variation of human beings is enormously greater than their actual variation; to put it another way, the ratio of possible men to actual men is overwhelmingly large." [2] By "possible men" Professor Medawar means obviously possible kinds of men, not possible numbers of men and among these possible kinds there may well be some whose aptitude for both making and appreciating works of art will be very small and others whose aptitude will be very great. There will be some whose aesthetic imaginations will be different from those with which we are familiar and others who will let well enough alone and make no innovations. As far as anyone's genetic constitution is concerned, it will all depend on who marries whom and we have no means of predicting that.[3] But aside from a few cases of apparent inherited aesthetic aptitude, such as the Bach family and that of Peale, we have no reliable evidence that such abilities are passed on from parents to offspring. One reason why the evidence is not reliable is that no trait, no matter how congenital, can manifest itself in a vacuum. All men want to eat, but if there is no food they starve. The mute inglorious Miltons might very well have been talkative and famous had they lived in a city like London. Indeed that was probably the point of Gray when he wrote the line. No geneticist has as yet discovered a Miltonic gene, but there is no evidence that anyone picked at random out of the population contemporary with Milton could have been trained to write *Paradise Lost*. Who would have trained him? Haydn gave a few lessons to Beethoven, but he did not simply produce another Haydn in the process. Until we know more about the etiology of artistic skill or interest, we can only conclude that the potentially gifted are genetically different from all other men, just as the potentially ungifted are, and that the congenital differences of both populations may make significant differences in both artistic ability and critical orientation. To put the matter in its simplest form, the common sense observation of differences in taste is paralleled by the scientific evidence of constitutional individuality. The fact that you cannot graft the skin of one man upon the body of another is no proof in itself that the first man will prefer music to painting, but it does prove that individuality of some sort is ineradicable.

Let me add parenthetically that even if such phenomena as bodily structure could be correlated with aesthetic preferences, scrawny people preferring line drawings to oil painting, and fat people the reverse, this discovery would be no more evidence of differences in taste than the evidence of common sense. It would be an interesting fact, of course, and, if it were proved, artists whose patrons are thin would do well to offer them line drawings for sale rather than oil paintings. But the patron coming into the studio or sales room would himself make his taste evident before he was measured or sized up by the artist or dealer. Aesthetic problems occur on the level of common sense, not on the level of science. It would, I imagine, be folly to tell a scrawny man that he ought not to buy a Rubens, but rather a Giacometti sculpture, because ectomorphs have to like line rather than mass.

We can leave the matter here and point out that three situations arise when a work of art is produced. First, the artist may be making his work for no one other than himself. If he is satisfied, he will say that no one else need be considered. Second, he may be making his work under commission, in which case he has to consider the taste of his patron and what results will be a compromise between what he approves of and what his patron wants, unless the two happen to share the same tastes. Third, the critic may wander about, so to speak, in the history of art and write about works of art of the past or those made by artists whom he does not know, and write about them. In the long run and on a very abstract plane the differences in taste between two people will come down to a preference for the familiar or for the novel, and the history of any art will be the result of the interaction between these two. I have said frequently in this book that these two tendencies can be called submission and recalcitrancy, but since there are so many possibilities of novelty and so many things to which one can be submissive, or the contrary, that the submissive or traditionalistic critic may find in a novel work of art something which recalls the past and seems to develop out of it. When Clive Bell wrote of significant form, he did it to arouse a sympathetic interest in those painters whom Roger Fry had called Postimpressionists. But he also tried to point out that almost everything from the most primitive to the most advanced might have significant form. It was in other words a trait of all great art. But art which did not have significant form he declared to be not great, no matter how much it was admired by others. This technique was analogous to that used by other critics, whether they looked for dynamic symmetry, tactile values, illusionism, romantic frenzy, or childlike innocence. In short, they knew ahead of time what works of art they thought to be great and then found some common trait observable in all of them. But if they were determined a priori that works of art must be great because of some one trait which is not self-evident, this was inevitable. It led, however, to the rejection of great numbers of works of art and of styles as bad which large numbers of intelligent men had thought were good. To Ruskin, for instance, everything after Raphael—or perhaps even Giotto—was bad. To Cardinal Bellori, Caravaggio and, one supposes, the works of the Caravaggeschi were bad. To Ingres the colorists were bad and to Delacroix the Ingristes were bad. To the Poussinists the Rubensists were bad and to the Rubensists the Poussinists were bad. The Baroque became respectable in the appraisal of Wölfflin and when the Baroque came into its own, so did the metaphysical poets. This is common knowledge.

Now no one denies that sometimes large numbers of people disagree even about factual propositions. But sooner or later the scientific community seems to be able to accept certain statements as demonstrated. Thus everyone today in the field of biology accepts the theory of evolution; disagreement arises over the *modus operandi*. But in time it is likely that that too will be demonstrated by acceptable scientific techniques. Individual differences will come into play only when it is a matter of either performing conclusive experiments, making adequate deductions from demonstrated premises, or simply understanding what one's colleagues

have proved. But in the field of art, one can theoretically prove
whether a picture has tactile values or not, whether a musical composition includes consecutive fifths, enters the tonic through a
leading tone, or has a number of measures which is a multiple of
four. So one can tell whether in a novel the characters are true to
type, assuming that one knows what the type is, whether the
motivation is plausible, whether every incident carries the plot
forward. But to approve or disapprove of the existence of these
and analogous traits is quite another matter. If I am repelled by
Ibsen's symbolism, for instance, my repulsion can be determined
as a fact; but I can be criticized for being repelled. I need not
know why I dislike symbolism; all I need know is that I do dislike
it. I also know that a number of other people do not dislike it, and
I fail to see that it makes any sense to say that I am either wrong
or right in reacting to it as I do. I can, however, see that the sym-
bolistic technique is part and parcel of Ibsen's style and that his
having the Master Builder killed by the tower which he has built
contains a suggestion of irony in it which apparently impresses
people as a deep philosophic truth. This can be phrased as, "Love
is the Great Destroyer," or "Each Man strives towards his own
Death," or some other universal proposition which runs counter
to common opinion. But suppose I dislike such generalities and
rationalize my dislike by saying that they are usually false, trite,
or irrelevant to artistry? They may not be false; they will be trite
only within the literary experience of certain people; and the purposes of art are assigned by artists and critics, all of whom are individuals. But the point is not what they actually are, but how
they seem to me at the time when I feel my dislike for them.

This dislike can be explained only as an individual trait. For if
we survey the field objectively, we come out with the result that
some people admire Ibsen and some don't, that such and such
kinds of people do and other kinds don't, or that people at a certain time or in a certain place did and others did not. I have not
made such a survey. But I can see that the individual differences
here need not be rooted in genetic make-up or endocrine patterns,

though they may be for all I know. If one approached Ibsen after having read D'Annunzio, for instance, the symbolism would seem part of the normal technique of literature. I do not know why some people evaded plain statements of fact and why others enjoyed such evasions. Ever since Wordsworth's "Peter Bell" the tendency to see everything "implied," as the saying goes, in every detail of experience has grown, and though the Post-Kantian metaphysics on which this was based is now abandoned in philosophical circles, it is still influential in artistic. One of its effects has been a dwindling public for painting and poetry, for there are still enough human beings left who prefer calling a spade a spade to find allusive works of art and compacted metaphors meaningless. The distaste of such people for symbolism is of course not entirely rooted in their physiological make-up, for their education has a large role to play in the formation of taste. It seems fairly certain that one such influence came from the work of the Freudians, which convinced men that one does not always say what one means even when talking fact. To go behind the ostensible meaning of words and sentences to their significance in the life of the man who says or writes them is by no means to be dispraised. But on the other hand each reader or spectator cannot make an individual analysis of the mind of the artist who interests him, and the passage from the overt to the hidden meaning is far from safe. Even ordinary conversation is in part allusive and gestures, facial expressions and tones of voice have their part to play in determining the meaning of most sentences. But here too people vary in their sensitivity to such things, just as they vary in their ability to catch a joke.

Though education is of the greatest influence in determining taste, it is not something apart from individuality but acts upon the innate endowment of the pupil. One absorbs one's education; one does not stand aloof from it, unmodified by all that it confers upon one's ways of thinking. We cannot arrest the growth of a baby immediately after birth and make an inventory of his aptitudes and disabilities. But as far as the two most important features of character are concerned, recalcitrancy and submissiveness, they begin to appear soon after birth. The baby's mother puts him on a feeding schedule or will go in for "permissive feeding" as the case may be. He will either be given toilet training or not. His food will be selected by his mother from whatever items are available. His hours of sleep and waking, his toys, his isolation from the other members of his family or his presence among them at all times, his clothes, all are and must be determined by others. He may protest or he may give in, and everyone knows that some babies are more susceptible to training than others. If he has brothers and sisters, they too will begin to influence him. They will play with him or not, will take him out in his carriage or not, will talk to him or not, will tell him stories or not. He will develop habits of eating, of talking, of general behavior, again depending upon the dictates of others. At the age of five or six, he will go to school or have a governess or tutor, and by this time his character will have revealed itself. His taste in literature will be oriented by his teachers if only through the books and poems which they require him to read. His speech will be corrected, both his vocabulary and his accent. The frontiers of his intellectual life will be marked out by his superiors and by the scholastic tradition in which his textbooks are written. The pictures which he sees will be those on the walls of his classrooms, the halls of the school building, and his home. If he has drawing lessons, he will be given a technique by the art teacher. In fact, in the ordinary school he will have little chance to make his personal taste, if any, known, though in the more progressive schools his freedom will be greater. But even there the way in which he uses his freedom will be surveyed by his elders and criticized by his contemporaries. Any parent knows that a child is induced to want to dress, speak, eat, amuse himself as his fellows do, and, if he happens not to care, he will soon be shown the error of his ways. Thus at a very early age a child either follows or rebels against social standards. He will not usually, if rebellious, rebel against everything, and, if he is submissive, there will also be limits to his amiability. For his

first conflict is that which comes from the differences between
his family and his school and it is rare to find that the standards of
both are identical. The child then is forced to make a choice and
where he accepts one set of standards, he must obviously reject
the other.

As one matures, one either slumps into complete acquiescence
or discovers that one has aims of one's own. Let us assume that a
boy decides that he has a vocation for painting. As Malraux says
somewhere, he will begin by copying the paintings of some artist
whom he admires and only later find his own subject matter. He
will either go to an art school or study under a professional artist.
In both cases he will be taught. He will not be discovering for himself how to achieve whatever purposes he may have. If he is interested in writing, he will read and cannot escape the influence of
his authors. In the United States he will probably go to college
and there will take courses in English literature. He will listen to
older men telling the classes what they think of the classic authors
from Chaucer down to T. S. Eliot. He may not, and probably will
not, slavishly accept all the standards of his teachers, but if he
wants to write himself, he will usually be interested enough in
literature to listen. A dialogue will ensue between his own opinions and those to which he has been listening. And frequently the
same kind of dialogue will take place between himself and his
friends, some holding to one point of view, some to another. Here
too his respect for one professor and contempt for another will
modify his willingness to accept what they respectively say. In
my own day courses in literature stopped at the point where authors were still alive. A living author was not a classic, and we were
told that we must await the judgment of posterity before pro-
nouncing upon their greatness or littleness. Why posterity would
be any wiser than we was never explained to us. The result was
that those of us who had a deep passion for literature immediately
decided that our teachers were old fogies who were simply passing
on what their teachers had told them and were incapable of judging for themselves. There seemed to be little sense in writing for

people as yet unborn, since we could have no idea of what they would be like, what they would want to read, and what their problems would be. As it turned out, we were right. For we left college on the eve of World War I and by the time it was over, pretty nearly everything in Western European culture had changed. But regardless of that, we all acquired a baggage of reading which built up for us what the psychologists used to call a copious apperceptive mass.

Though the term is old-fashioned, what it names is still with us. To begin with, it determines what will be familiar and what strange. I remember talking to a young Italian in the Boboli Gardens who was an art student. He told me flatly that there was no such thing as French painting. Italian painting alone existed. But what chance would a man who had never been in a museum other than the Pitti and the Uffizi have of seeing even the great seventeenth-century French painters, to say nothing of Ingres, Delacroix, Géricault, Courbet and their progeniture? To him painting was Italian painting. When one talks with a young man of that background, one realizes why it was necessary for Marinetti and his group to revolt. Had this boy been shown a Monet, it would have been so unfamiliar that he would not have known what to think about it and would probably have made the same kind of comments as those of the French critics of the '70's made.

To continue, our apperceptive mass will give us directions for looking and listening. How could a man brought up on the paintings in the Royal Academy shows see what is in an Impressionist painting? One sees this sort of thing clearly in the "Discourses" of Sir Joshua Reynolds.[4] Reynolds simply could not perceive the beauty of the Italian and Flemish primitives, even of the Ghent altarpiece. The art in them was so different from the art which he practiced and taught that it seemed crude and barbarous to him. To look at each picture with a fresh eye may be desirable, but how is one going to do it?

To take examples from another field, it is next to impossible for a modern philosopher to accept the premises of Locke, Berkeley, and Hume, since we have learned from psychology that the so-called sense data are far from being primitive but are precipitated out of our total experience by the help of our anticipations. Again, when one reads Proust, his psychological analyses which seemed so persuasive in 1920 now seem superficial, and they seem superficial because of what we have learned of psychodynamics. Can anyone take seriously the phrenological descriptions of George Eliot and Balzac? And yet neither was exactly a fool. For generations novels dealt seriously only with members of the upper classes, and we have already indicated briefly why. It was not until the Goncourts and Zola began to take the lower classes seriously that we could have novels in which they did not merely furnish comic relief. No wonder the critics found it hard to swallow George Moore's *Esther Waters* and Dreiser's early novels. Rank throughout the Middle Ages, *dignitas,* was intimately bound up with a man's moral importance. Rank had to disappear before people could accept the equality of man, at least in theory. Now that it has disappeared, except in social status, things have been turned topsy-turvy and one gets the impression that only the lowly are worth writing about. The revival of Henry James recently may be a revulsion against this dogma.

For that matter we are dependent on others for something to rebel against. One cannot just rebel; one has to have an opponent. The Imagists rebelled against deep thoughts, the *vers libristes* against strict meter, the Naturalists against ideal beauty, the Cubists against literal representation, the Futurists against static composition, the Surrealists against rationality, the Ash Can School against the mythologies and drawing room refinements, Delacroix against Ingres, Berlioz against Rossini, Wagner against all Italian opera, Le Corbusier against the Beaux-arts, and so it has always gone. Courbet, the most loquacious of the rebels, retained the technique of the academies; he rebelled only against its subjects. Cézanne rebelled against its technique and retained the academic subject matter. The contemporary American novelist rebels against the polite vocabulary of gentility. The contemporary

American painter rebels against conscious control of his brush in favor of "action painting." Paul Klee rebelled against maturity and tried to retreat into childhood. Debussy rebelled against the diatonic scale; Schönberg against the traditional rules of composition. If anyone asks why these revolts were staged, he would have as hard a time answering the question as if he were asked why they were successful. There is nothing in the times which makes twelve tone music better than music written according to the traditional rules of harmony. It was Schönberg in revolt against academicism who made the change and if he succeeded, as he undoubtedly did, in forming a school, that again was simply because other younger composers found his innovations to their taste. Whatever may be true of the "Great Man theory" of political and social history, it alone is apposite to cultural history. I am not using the word "great" in any eulogistic sense; I am using it simply to denote the man who introduces a change which is successful.

Normally the artist produces goods for a consumer, the public. There have been times when this was frankly admitted by the artist. Throughout the Middle Ages and part of the Renaissance, artists took commissions and tried to fill them as if they were carpenters, tailors, or cobblers. Haydn worked for the Esterhazys as a servant. Constable changed his skies, reduced the height of his pictures, chose dimensions for his canvases to meet the demands of those who either had ordered them or were likely to buy them. At the present moment, for that matter, if a publisher asks an author to write him a book, he tells him what sort of book he wants and is no more obligated to publish it, if it does not suit, than any customer in a dry goods store is obligated to pay for goods which do not suit. An architect has to submit his plans to his patron and, unless he is a skillful debater, will modify them to meet his patron's criticisms. The notion of the isolated artist turning out works of art for no one but himself is not only a modern notion but almost a contemporary one. At most, it applies to painters or to those artists who are financially independent. There have been artists in our times who have not worried about a public. A composer like Ives, for instance, wrote largely for himself and seldom if ever heard his most important pieces played. Since he also had a profession on the side which supported him, the financial pressure which others might feel did not bother him. But in general, even if an artist produces things, as he would say, for himself alone, he does not shrink from publishing, exhibiting, or selling what he makes. It is true that the public is much more docile than it used to be, much more humble, much more willing to wait and see what the artist will produce even when an order has been placed for a specific work of art. But nevertheless, if an artist does not turn out works of art which please some public, he will starve to death, unless he has an income of his own or a grant from some foundation.

The importance of this is that most works of art are addressed to someone other than the artist who made them. They are like letters which are written to others than oneself. If they are not, they become modes of exhibitionism. There is a paradox in the writing of diaries, very much like the paradox of doodling. No one is supposed to read one's diary; it is sometimes kept under lock and key; no one other than its author is going to read it except by chance. Why then write it? The complete journal of Amiel, for instance, contains Amiel's most secret thoughts, thoughts so secret that when it was first published, it could be printed only in excerpts. Pepys's diary, as everyone knows, was written in a cipher. If I say that this is similar to doodling, it does not mean that it is random and trivial scribbling, not at all. My point is simply that as the doodle is not supposed to communicate anything to anyone else and yet is objectified on paper, so the diary is self-communication too and is also objectified. When one reads a diary like Gide's or Julian Green's, one knows ahead of time that it was deliberately written for publication. Green has of course shown a certain reticence in what he has published and has said that "the whole story" has not been told. Why say this unless there is an intention on the writer's part to tell it later, to let it be printed after one's death? A dozen motives will suggest themselves, but one thing is certain: the unpublished parts must be self-communication during their author's lifetime. Now all of us daydream, think in solitude, meditate, but we do not necessarily commit our reveries and meditations to paper. As soon as that is done, there is always the obvious possibility that someone else will see them. When that happens, the exhibition is complete.

All writing, like all painting and all musical composition, is bound to be autobiographical. But the amount which is revealed depends in part on the skill of the reader or spectator. I have heard a professor of literature interpret the tiniest details in Melville's novels as evidence of his sexual life. I have heard the same lecturer point out that *Huckleberry Finn* is a revelation of Mark Twain's suppressed homosexuality. If there is anything sound in such interpretations, then there is a kind of exhibitionism in all art, even when the artist draws the mantle of Noah tight around him or drapes himself in it from head to foot. Most of us are too naïve to see through the drapery, but there are enough people who are curious to know every last detail of an artist's life to make such interpretations popular. But every time we open our mouths to talk, we are exhibiting ourselves, if only as slippery hypocrites, unwilling to say what we really mean. To talk is to use a medium of communication which our interlocutors will understand. It is the acceptance of a standard of clarity which they and their forebears have developed. We modify but do not invent our language. And this with appropriate changes is true of all artistry. The man who is going to see the picture or hear the sonata is expected to be able to grasp their sense. And the more sincere our works of art, the more revealing they will be. I recognize that there is a scale of clarity running from the most hermetic and unintelligible, which is a form of narcissism, to the most crystal-clear, which can be understood by all normal and educated people. But even the most elegant mathematical demonstration, self-denying in its surrender to communal standards of speech, is a balance between insistent individuality of the speaker and the demands made upon him by his public.

Just how original a man may be permitted to be is nothing that can be settled by statute. As in all cases where there is an uneasy equilibrium between polar antitheses, one muddles along and no formula seems able to set down the proper conditions under which an individual will be allowed to operate. It is easy enough to say that one should not be so original as to be eccentric nor so conformist as to disappear into the general mass, but what precisely does that mean? The amount of tolerance which a critic may have will depend upon his knowledge of history, of psychology, and his plain human sympathy. We know that artists who have seemed so abnormal while alive that they were to all intents and purposes lunatic, later have been accepted not only with forbearance but with enthusiasm. William Blake is a case in point. What recognized critic during his lifetime saw what he had to contribute to the aesthetic community? As far as his artistic skill was concerned, it is probable that if he had wished to conform to academic standards, he could have done so. Why then was he in revolt? What incentive did he have to swim against the current? Why did he not resign himself to obscurity and cease to rail against Reynolds and the Royal Academy? What was that spirit of prophesy which both tortured him and led him on to more and more tortures from the public? The usual answer is his need for self-expression.

It is interesting that at least as late as Spinoza no ethicist ever thought that the individual self had problems which could not be solved by obedience to general rules. The moral casuists knew better than that, but they had to confine their knowledge to practice in the confessional. Nor did they feel that a man had any duty to himself which would bring him into conflict with custom, Nature, or the Law of God. "To thine own self be true" was said at the beginning of the seventeenth century and put in the mouth of a man not always famous for his wisdom. It was taken for granted that ethics was a set of rules binding on all men without distinc-

tion of individuality. Men were merged in mankind and the human essence was the thing which counted. It is a commonplace
of the history of art that we do not have the slightest idea who
made the great works of art of the Middle Ages; with the exception of one or two architects, the artists are all anonymous.
But anonymity ceased with the Romantic movement and soon
difference, individuality, personality, originality took on the same
values that conformity, traditionalism, obedience had had before.
But not even the most fervent adherent to the practice of self-
expression thought that one could express himself in all respects.
The self expresses itself in reason, in its emotions, in its perceptions, in its hopes and aspirations. To devote oneself to irrationality is possible; to love what one's fellows hate and hate what
they love is also possible. It is possible to want what the law and
custom forbid and to look for what other men do not see. But to
do all this at one and the same time is impossible if one's plan
includes conveying one's ideas, emotions, perceptions, and aspirations to others. When Dada began, the public could not make
head nor tail of it. But to prove their irrationality, the Dadaists
had to use the elements of common speech in an irrational manner, just as the criminal to show his disrespect for private property
or life has to steal and murder. If I am going to be deliberately
irrational, I have to know the laws of logic; otherwise I might slip
into making sense. And to show my contempt for the laws of
painting, again I have to know what they are lest I obey them un-
wittingly. A child cannot be said to be indecent, if he has not
learned the rules of decency and many a youngster has used forbidden words simply because he is ignorant of their traditional
meaning.

Hence to express a self, one must first have a self. I am not
maintaining that the baby is not congenitally different from all
other babies, but that as we grow older we find ourselves in a state
of conflict which we hope to resolve by making our purposes harmonious. One cannot help wondering whether this is not also the
problem of the artist who thinks that he is expressing an already

existing self, whereas in reality he is building a self through his art. If that hypothesis is worth serious consideration, then the diary and the doodle could be objective proof either of what a man starts with or of his growth. They stand as a sort of examination of conscience, the need of which is fairly good evidence of self-ignorance. But similarly the painter who, after finishing a picture, says, "This is the way I see it," is talking about himself, not about the visual object. He did not know how he saw it until he had painted his picture. He may have known how others thought he should see it and he usually does. But what he wants is an overt revelation not only to these others but to himself as well of his own personal vision. The external world as a potential field of experience along with our fellow men presents a challenge to us. We do not know what we think of them until we have expressed our thoughts. But once the expression is uttered, then we are committed to it. The words or images have floated out from us into space and into the minds of other people. They have become our responsibility and we have to defend them as an integral part of ourselves. If we are still ignorant of what they are, we can be confronted with them. The fact that as we grow older we see things differently, feel differently about them, learn new things and hence change our ideas, is ample proof that we do not have a psychic lump within us which is "The Self" in some transcendent manner. That permanent self is our congenital constitution which differentiates us as psychophysical organisms from all others. But to all intents and purposes it is a blank, a mere potency, until it encounters the material world and other men. The discipline which we impose upon it builds up what most of us call our selves and when we ordinarily talk about self-expression, it is the results of that discipline of which we are speaking. Our bodies, again, are all composed of certain chemicals and in that respect are all alike. But that does not prevent us all from behaving in ways which are more or less different and it is our behavior, rather than our biochemical make-up, which is involved in self-expression. Hence to be true to ourselves, insofar as that indicates a program, is to select a sheaf of purposes which are not in a state of conflict and doggedly pursue them. The self in that case is not something which already exists but which we hope may exist at some future date.

It is indeed something which may never exist. For as we go on living, new problems arise, some of which will frustrate us or at least slow us up. And again we either surrender and do nothing about it or continue stubbornly to pull things together and work out some *modus vivendi*. Habit takes care of many of our problems and we may simply go along repeating the old formulas and refusing to admit their inadequacies. Or, if we are deeply interested in building a character for ourselves, we will revert to philosophy, science, religion, and the arts for possible solutions to our difficulties. But as one thinks about all the obstacles to the fulfillment of our aspirations, one realizes that the search may turn out to be fruitless. At this point the conclusion of Lessing in his famous epigram about the search for truth being better than its discovery, the metaphysics of Fichte which put the greatest value on striving, the decision of even R. L. Stevenson in his little essay, "El Dorado," that we do not want the road to end, or possibly even that of Schopenhauer, that the whole enterprise is evil and illusion, may be accepted. To use the old division of our interests into intellectual, moral, and aesthetic, we may achieve intellectual harmony but neither ethical nor aesthetic; and so with the others. Usually, however, the same solution will be applied to all our pursuits and, if we resign ourselves in intellectual frustration, we shall do the same in moral and aesthetic matters. But that is far from universal. A painter like Constable was an innovator in his painting, but hardly in religion and ethics. On the other hand, Delacroix was frequently on the popular side of the barricades and Courbet always was. Few sculptors were ever so inventive as Donatello, but we have no evidence of which I am aware that he was not a traditionalist in religion. Leonardo on the contrary was as inventive in philosophy, science, and engineering as he was in painting. It was indeed his restless search for satisfactory solutions to all problems which individuates him: all problems were his problems.

The work of art is the only index which we have of an artist's self when he has left no journals, letters, or autobiography. Even when he has left such confessions, they are not always trust-worthy, for they tell us more of what he was trying to do than of what he did. But when we look at a work of art and try to find in it the self who made it, we inevitably transfer its effect upon us to the artist's intentions. In the case of Alberti and Piero della Fran-cesca we have good evidence of their aesthetic programs. But what a mass of inharmonious, if not contradictory, judgments have been made about Piero's "Resurrection"! [5] Aside from fanciful re-creations of this picture by critics, it should be pointed out that the general scheme is one which had been used by others before Piero and that the outstanding novelty is the facial expression of the risen Christ. It is almost impossible, it would seem, not to see in that face a man who had just emerged from Hell. But this is fancy also. We may misinterpret the picture, but we cannot miss its individuality. No one had ever painted the risen Christ like this before Piero and no one ever has since. The fresco is a com-bination of tradition and innovation, the very balance between the old and new of which we have been speaking.

I emphasize this because it also illustrates how innovation al-ways occurs in a context of ritual. Nothing else is possible if an artist is addressing himself to other people. To show Christ arising out of a Roman sarcophagus is not authorized by anything in the Gospels, but it had become customary by the fifteenth century. There is nothing biblical in His holding aloft the labarum, but that too had become traditional. But there was nothing whatso-ever in the tradition on which a painter could base his ideas of what Christ's face looked like after the Crucifixion and the three days in Hell. Here an artist was free to do as he wished. If the sarcophagus and the labarum had been omitted, the spectator might not have known what he was looking at. They were part of the language in which to express the idea. The contribution of the

individual may of course be either in artistry or in what is communicated by the artistry or in both. Michelangelo in his frescoes
on the Sistine ceiling took over, as he had to, the biblical material,
but presented it in a relatively novel manner, by which I do not
mean merely his nudities, his athletes, his putti. I mean such
things as appear in the scene of the creation of Adam where the
finger of God is enough to show what is occurring. Yet in the
Temptation we have the traditional Tree and the serpent coiled
round it with the two figures of Adam and Eve on each side, a
conception which was commonplace by the sixteenth century. It
is only in our own times that we find complete revolt against all
tradition, both technical and substantial. The result is that we
require utter re-education in order to respond to the canvases,
poems, and music which we are now offered. This may be all to
the good, for all I know, and I am far from objecting to it. I am
simply pointing to the facts and saying that no man educated in
the history of art, fed on the pictorial classics, knows what to say
before a Rothko, a Kline, or a Pollock. He will feel of course a certain bewilderment, but, unless he is incorrigibly reactionary, he
will not conclude that he was supposed to be bewildered.

The individual then is congenitally different from all other
men in his bodily constitution and for that reason will react individually to whatever the world confronts him with. His education, however standardized, will affect him in ways which are not
identical with the ways in which it affects others, though he may
make an effort to suppress his peculiarities for the sake of peace.
Yet, if he is an artist, his individuality will be bound to emerge
into view and he may use his art to intensify either his likeness to
others or his difference from them. But since the pressure of all
social groups is in the direction of conformity there will be very
few artists who cannot be classified in schools. One reason for
this, it must be granted, is that we no longer have the works of
the most eccentric artists; they are inevitably rejected and hence
lost. Yet a few names remain in the histories of art: Piero di
Cosimo, Magnasco, Blake, Odilon Redon among them. But what

is of perhaps more significance is the lack of individuality of critics. On the whole they have assumed that each type of art—and they seem to be able to define the types—has its own standard of excellence, regardless of the fact that no work of art is univalent. One of the most popular of these standards is form. We shall now turn to that.

CHAPTER XIV

Form as a Standard

IN THE SEARCH for something which will differentiate aesthetic value from all other, critics have come up with the concept of form. Every other feature of a work of art could be relegated to a special science. For if one eliminated subject matter, which might belong to history or literature, the purely perceptual which was clearly a problem of psychology, the "meaning," message, or lesson which could be ethical, religious, political, or something similar, the biographical references which would again be part of history, the so-called social significance and reflections of intellectual history which might be referred to philosophy, then what would be left? Since of two paintings of the same subject, one may be great and the other small, one beautiful and the other ugly, one full of anachronisms and the other faithful to historical record, along with various other differences, it does not look as if subject matter were of essential importance in a work of art. The purely perceptual, though a favorite focus of the aesthetic movement of the '90's, skimmed off the works of art everything which might interest a man beyond the age of childhood: after all, one cannot spend one's life just looking at colors, listening to sounds, and feeling textures, unless one wishes to emulate Des Esseintes. The meaning of works of art became boring probably because didacticism itself was too frequently confined to platitudes. If one were interested in biography, it was simpler to read a straightforward account of a man's life than to dig it out of covert

references in his works of art. Historical reflections were too ambiguous, since any moment in history has so many aspects that
they grow confused when seen through a picture or piece of music
or poem, and no one really looked at a painting because it reflected the courtly life of the Medicis or the bourgeois mercan-
tilism of the Dutch. All such aspects are likely to be present in
any work of art. But aestheticians, and following them critics,
needed a speciality of their own. The subject of aesthetics had
been invented to fill a gap in our information. We have, if I may
simplify the problem, a sense of beauty; we must of course find
out what satisfies it and how. Since all works of art have some
form, and since no other science or discipline studies form in itself, why should it not be the center of the critic's attention?

The argument then seems to have run: if that which differentiates art from everything else which men make or do is form, then
one must look for the formal elements in a work of art and, when
one has found them, judgment may be pronounced. The adjective
"formless" became a term of the greatest dispraise and one would
have imagined that the presence of form would be in itself the discovery of beauty. Unhappily form in itself did not seem to suffice.
For some forms, however defined, seemed trivial or even ugly. In
Clive Bell, as it will be recalled, it was only "significant form"
which would do. For others, geometrical patterns were more important. For still others, form had to be something called organic.
But in each case one had to distinguish further between those
examples of the kind of form which the critic found satisfactory
and those which he found unsatisfactory. This being so, it was
not the presence of form alone which conferred value on a work of
art, but the presence of one kind of form. This did not prevent
arguments that the formless was bad, as far as logic was concerned.
Nor was there anything wrong about studying form to the exclusion of everything else, if such a study interested anyone.

The trouble arose from the hopeless vagueness of the basic concept. It is the purpose of this chapter to dispel the obscurity as
far as possible.

In the first place, the formless is usually that form for which we have no name. A picture which is divided vertically by a line on both sides of which things are symmetrically distributed has a visual form which is easy to grasp, much as a series of notes which are related by some simple ratio, such as tonic, subdominant, dominant, leading tone, and tonic is easily spotted. I imagine that no painter ever painted such simple symmetrical arrangements as Raphael. Everything is balanced by something else and no spectator is puzzled. When one comes to a man like Rubens, the composition is a bit more complicated, for instead of balancing things about a central axis, he often used an S-like curve and disposed his details about that. He also of course introduced a good bit of motion into his paintings, whereas Raphael seems to have been more interested in keeping things stable. An analogy in music would be that which is featured in elementary books on composition, where it is said that the difference between harmony and counterpoint is that the former proceeds chord by chord "vertically," the latter by running voices "horizontally." This is to be sure misleading and at best only a figure of speech, but it has no pretentions to being anything more than a suggestion. To take another kind of example, if a coin is thrown into the air ten times and comes down heads each time, or tails, or one head, one tail, one head, one tail, five times, or in some other easily spotted order, we are tempted to say that the series of throws has a form. But if it comes down a head, two tails, three heads, one tail, three heads, we are likely to say that the order is random and the series formless. But now if we name this series by some name, merely indicating the prescribed throws, and if on the second ten throws the same series occurs, and on the third, fourth, fifth as well, we should say that the repeated series had an order, though we should not be able to explain why the series should have come out as they did. In short the repetition of the formless turns into a form, the elements of which might not be recognized as formal, but the relation between which composes a form.

A further complication appears when one realizes that sometimes a form is introduced into works of art, or, more accurately perhaps, is the unpremeditated guide to one's artistry. Composition, as it used to be taught in art schools, was always intentional. One was taught design in terms of symmetry, balance, rhythm, harmony, and one built up patterns on paper into which one poured one's materials, as liquid plaster is poured into a mold, or the human figures fitted into a pediment, the ones in the center upright, those in the angles lying down or crouching. Colors had to be balanced by their complementaries; a large mass on one side of the vertical axis must be balanced either by one of the same size at the same distance from the axis or by one of half its size at twice the distance. One was taught how to keep the spectator's eye within the canvas and how forces which would lead the eye off into space beyond the frame must be counterbalanced by forces which would pull it back again. Anyone can take a picture of the classical type, overlay it with a piece of tracing paper, and work out the design or form for oneself. In fact, books on art appreciation are full of such schemata. Analyses of musical compositions proceed in much the same way and the reading of the old-fashioned program notes of a symphony will furnish a pretty good example of what I am driving at.[1] Such forms are much like the recipes given in cookbooks or ceremonial rituals within which an artist can retain a high degree of originality but which nevertheless provide a structure which is familiar to the spectator. He is never lost, never in doubt about what to do or look for, always on more or less well-known territory. Unintentional form may be produced either by habit or by psychological impulses over which the artist is not aware of having any control. In the former case the artist is working as an ordinary man speaks; he obeys the rules of grammar and syntax automatically, that is, through habit. In the latter, his interests, his personal mode of expression, his repulsions and attractions, determine the way in which he will express himself or organize his thoughts and feelings. There are various degrees of awareness on the part of artists. We know, for instance, that Piero della Francesca, at least most of the time, was a careful and deliberate designer. We also can imagine that the early Renaissance painters with their persistent symmetries began by building up their compositions through their delight in perspective, which gave them the idea of a central point or focus of attention toward which all lines converged. If that point was situated in the middle of the horizon, symmetry followed as a matter of course. This technique soon became second nature with painters. They designed, so to speak, by heart. One can hardly say the same about the Baroque painters. The elaborate arabesques of Rubens seem almost to have been improvised for each canvas and when we come to the more recent painters, men like Matisse and Picasso, we find that almost every painting is unique in design. After their day and in the work of the Action painters, the form seems to be dictated by psychological impulses on the spur of the moment, impulses beyond their control. Yet this in no sense of the word implies that their works are formless. Even a blot of ink has the form of a blot.

Traditionally it is the simple geometrical forms in painting and sculpture which are thought of as identical with form itself. Triangles, circles, rectangles, squares, these are recognizable at first glance; one does not have to search for them. The interlocking curves of Rubens' beautiful double portrait of himself and wife in Munich are not more difficult to see. Such forms are transferred to literature as balance, symmetry, opposition and such, though the meaning of the terms is of course figurative. Good does not really balance evil, or man balance woman, as two weights balance each other on a scale. For that matter, even in painting the balance is figurative, for the space and masses in a painting are not real space and real masses. If the theory of *Einfuehlung* is true, then such balance or opposition may be due to incipient movements of our bodies and in that sense the figurative meaning of the comment is diminished. The nineteenth-century novel, like the plays written for the repertory companies, displayed the same sort of form, where hero and heroine, villain and villainess, character actors, juveniles, and so on, seem to have been chosen to give the same kind of structure to a play, and by extension to a novel, as we find in Renaissance Italian painting. This is seen as early at least as the plays of Shakespeare. If this is the kind of form of which the critic is in search, he could do no better than look for it in such dramas as *King Lear, Othello,* or *The Merchant of Venice.* But the well-made play, as it came to be called, followed the same recipe. I do not know whether the standard repertory company was organized to act the plays which happened to be written or whether the plays were written to employ all the actors in the companies. Similarly I do not know whether the nineteenth-century novel was written because of the influence of the plays or whether the answer is not much more obvious: such an organization had grown to seem natural and inevitable. But that there was a stock form for such works of art is as true as that there was a stock form for historical painting, portraiture, still life, and landscape. In any event we have here a form derived from statics and imposed on the subject matter with which the artist was dealing.

But there was another kind of form which was not so ritualized and which might be said to be internal to the subject. When a novelist imagines a group of characters interacting with one another, he can start out by giving his readers some idea of what they are like. He can then ask himself what would happen if one of them did something which would, it is hoped, be true to character. This act or gesture would then serve as cause to other incidents which would then be detailed and they in turn would have a causal influence and their effects would be set down. Here the plot would not be worked out beforehand, as it apparently was by such writers as Maupassant and O. Henry, Scribe and Dumas *fils,* but would grow out of the characters. A novel such as *Madame Bovary* develops as Emma's degeneration develops, though Flaubert did know ahead of time what was going to happen. Nevertheless he was successful in concealing this from his readers who have the illusion that what takes place occurs because of what has just preceded it. On the whole the modern novel, when it does not derive from Proust, proceeds in the same way. The writer has to have some theory of human behavior, it goes without saying, but unlike Zola, he does not necessarily tell his readers what it is. On the contrary, he introduces his readers to his characters and then relates what effect they have on one another. He may believe in something called destiny or fate or the hand of God or economic determinism or optimistic evolution or universal erotic motivation or even the gratuitous act. But on the whole he has abandoned the old mechanical plots. He acts like a biographer who simply traces the course of his subject's life and tries to clarify it.

I have made an exception of Proust and his followers since as a group they have been willing to accept inconsistency of character. This has been the most interesting innovation in fictional psychology. It is in one sense of the word a denial that human behavior is explicable. It is an admission that the human psyche is logically absurd. Appetites and drives have taken the place of reasons with the result that the novelist's world seems truer to life and for that very reason inexplicable. Swann is the prototype of such characters and now that we have accepted wholeheartedly the *intermittences du coeur*, we tend to grow impatient when we can predict just what any character in a novel will do before the book is ended. We now know too much of psychodynamics, of the influence of repressions, of irrationality, to mention only two or three of the bits of information which have changed our minds about the human race, to give assent to novels such as *The Virginians* and, if we can still read with easy consent *Vanity Fair*, it is because we overlook its mechanics. One can switch one's point of view with the greatest facility and, though we may find a novel as a whole absurd, we can still find certain scenes in it so captivating that we forget its absurdities. If this were not so, no one could read the Brontë sisters, Walter Scott, or much of Dickens, and would be left to spend his time with George Gissing. Fortunately one enters the world of art leaving his baggage of doctrine at the door. One does not have to believe in vicarious atonement to see the beauty in Rubens'

"Descent from the Cross," in Antwerp, or in the Lamb of God to be deeply stirred by Van Eyck's altarpiece in Ghent. Coleridge's willing suspension of disbelief—to which we should add a suspension of belief as well—is the great preservative of all works of art. How many people standing lost before Raphael's portrait of Castiglione know anything about the man portrayed in it? For years no one had the slightest idea who was the original of Titian's famous portrait of the "young Englishman" in Florence. Suppose for the sake of argument that the young Englishman was really Ippolito Riminaldi. Does the portrait become the more beautiful now that a name has been assigned to it? I am not, be it noted, saying that our enjoyment of these two portraits would not be greater if we did know more about their sitters. It might be greater or it might be less. Knowing them well, we might find the portraits poor likenesses. As things stand, our imagination is released to go on its own course. Our ignorance turns the portraits into paintings which need have no reference to any real people. Historical accuracy then becomes irrelevant.

There are some works of art whose form is determined by something which is external to them. I am thinking primarily of allegories. What happens in *Pilgrim's Progress* is determined by Bunyan's notion of how we achieve salvation. As far as the doctrine itself is concerned, it could be expressed as clearly, or perhaps more clearly, in an essay. But Bunyan's vivid imagination allowed him to see each step in the process concretely, to personify the various obstacles to salvation, and to invent a landscape in which the drama might take place. Yet an allegorical element may be read out of any work of art simply by translating the concrete details back into abstractions. A man's face may be a symbol of malice, ignorance, hopefulness or of any of the other human attitudes and emotions, and the face of nature may be treated similarly. There is hardly an event in human history which has not been used to point a moral, whether it be an event in the history of nations or of individuals. We come pretty close to committing the pathetic fallacy when we do this, but a generation which has turned to the symbolism of bones and waterless deserts had better not cast the first stone.

The pursuit of form, whether by the artist before his subject or the critic before the work of art, is in search of intelligibility. Intelligibility is found when one can attach an event or an object which puzzles one to something which one already understands. This involves of course having some idea of what system of relations the unintelligible must be attached to. In conversation we usually know beforehand what this system is. For we assume that our vis-à-vis is using the ordinary language of the tribe. We do not expect him to infuse new and strange meanings into his vocabulary. When a word or phrase is used which fails to fit in with our assumptions about their normal meaning, we ask him what *he* means by it. In the case of language there is, as we all know, a fund of symbols upon whose meaning we are all more or less agreed and as long as we do not stray far from the usual topics of conversation, we can communicate without constantly asking questions. But in the case of works of art, this is not true. When a man stands in front of a picture and asks, "What is it supposed to be?" or "What is it a picture of?" he is clearly assuming that it is supposed to be something other than a little universe whose frontiers are the frame and that it represents some object or other. Without that assumption, his question is purposeless. One does not look at an apple tree and ask what it is supposed to be or what it represents unless it is suddenly found growing at the intersection of Fifth Avenue and Forty-second Street or on the altar of a church or in some other abnormal place. The adjective "abnormal" gives us the clue to why the question is asked. When someone reads an obscure poem and asks what it means, he is assuming that it ought to mean something other than what it says. And when he looks at an assemblage of *objets trouvés* cast in bronze, and says, "Do you think he's sincere?" or, "I don't know how to judge it," or, "The man's crazy," he assumes that one ought to be able to understand works of art as one understands other forms of communication and the possibility that they are not media of communication does not occur to him. Or, in the second place, he assumes that one ought to be able to judge a work of art, presumably as good or bad, and that one ought to know by what standards it should be judged. One knows the points of a dog or a horse, of a Japanese arrangement of flowers or a realistic novel, because they are either agreed upon by convention or custom, and one can look and see if they are present in the case before one or not. The desire to praise and blame seems to be congenital and we have learned to appease it by accepting the standards of others, not by finding any of our own. That one can observe without praising and blaming may be possible for some philosophers who have reached a kind of intellectual apathy, but it is not common to the human race as a whole. And finally, as far as our examples go, people expect works of art to be made by normal, sane people and not by those who are demented.

Sometimes the form of a work of art is determined by unconscious forces. Indeed the unconscious must always play some part in artistry. The kind of painstaking work which has been done by Kenneth Burke on what he has called the strategy of writers is surely not supposed to persuade us that the writers in question were aware of their strategy. Artists are not usually generals planning battles, except in a metaphorical sense. And yet, as he has shown, each man has his own strategy as he has his own style of speech or handwriting. Just as Dr. Spurgeon showed how Shakespeare used certain images persistently and avoided others, so Mr. Burke has shown how every writer whom he has studied reveals his interest in certain aspects of nature and human nature to the exclusion of others. A book is a self-portrait if you know how to read it. It will be said, and of course has been said, that a writer does not intend to write a self-portrait when he writes a novel. Nothing could be truer. But we do lots of things which are unintentional and yet which have intentions of their own. The French philosopher, Brunschvicg, once said that the way a man buys a ticket at a railway station is a revelation of his character and we might add that nothing is so revealing as a person's idiom. To take but one stock example, the use of an unusual vocabulary both creates an atmosphere for the reader and also a personality for the psychological critic. This is an affair of manners which have become part and parcel of the agent. To be subservient to some arbiter of good taste is no sure sign of anything more than a desire to be polite, but it is at least that. It is always possible that a courteous person is courteous from respect for the man or woman he is dealing with; it is also possible that he is a hypocrite. A well-trained ear might detect which character was being revealed in each case. I am interested here merely in saying that form may be determined by the same impulses which lead a man to express himself in his own peculiar manner. And in that case the critic is directing his attention to the meaning of what he sees in the sense of what is behind it all. This will be deprecated by some critics who wish to restrict people to that which is isolated from everything else, the picture within the frame, the poem on the page. This is all very well if one maintains a stubborn silence, but the moment one tries to communicate what one sees or reads, one goes beyond the frame and the page willy-nilly.

If we know what the artist intended to do, we can presumably see whether he has succeeded in doing it or not. The form of the work of art then becomes the realization of the artist's purpose, as it might have been in Aristotle. But we also have a tendency to assume that all artists ought to have the same purpose. There have indeed been times when they did have the same purpose with minor deviations, but that time no longer exists and it is difficult to do more than guess under what conditions it will recur. Occidental societies at the present time are a mixture of people whose beliefs are diverse and frequently conflicting. This makes things hard for the critic who would prefer to write about a homogeneous society. In fact he acts as if it were his business in life to create enough homogeneity to produce agreement on what is good and bad. If he writes well enough to persuade a

large number of readers, he may succeed in building up at least
a small, though influential, group of followers and they will
become the aesthetic leaders of their time. But alongside of them
will exist larger and unorganized groups who will constitute
public opinion and who will in most cases pay very little attention
to what the leaders have to say. This is, I admit, an oversimplifica-
tion. Sometimes taste changes in obscure ways with no ostensible
push from the critics. The case of Van Gogh or Toulouse-Lautrec
is to the point. Van Gogh sold exactly two pictures during his
lifetime and now, eighty years after his death, he is one of the
most popular painters on record. It is unlikely that a retrospective
of Gérôme or Meissonier would draw the crowds which any exhibition of Van Gogh draws. We cannot go into all the reasons
for this change, partly because no one knows what they are and
partly because those which are known are so numerous that they
would require a volume to be expounded accurately. But the
romantic biographies of Van Gogh, the pathos of his life, the
drama of his suicide, the devotion of his brother, the publication
of his letters, to say nothing of our general interest in anything
abnormal, have all contributed to his present fame. Why the
vogue for biographies which are fifty per cent fiction should have
become so sweeping is another story, but that it has existed and
still exists needs no proof. A glance at the titles of popular books
is enough. Reading Van Gogh's letters tells us what his purpose
in life was and we can see for ourselves how successful he was
in achieving it. But somehow or other that purpose seems to be
one with which we can easily sympathize and our sympathy is
half the battle. But this is no specially peculiar case. Action
painting may not be so popular as figurative painting but it is
making headway against opposition, not in this instance because
of the dramatic biographies of its practitioners, but by the
infiltration into decorative design of the methods used by the
actionists. That has accustomed us to seeing their use of color;
we have become accustomed also to modern architecture with
its bare walls and clean structure, and against these as a back-

ground the nonobjective canvases take the place of the slabs of grained marble, the heavy brocaded hangings, the furbelows of the late nineteenth century, and in fact they introduce an element of drama into a coldly scientific setting. We are, I suspect, moved by these paintings much as by certain natural spectacles, and since they commit us to nothing as far as fellow men are concerned, we can enjoy them without moral involvement.

The question of why we are always so anxious to pass judgment on things is one to which I have no convincing answer. But the whole Judeo-Christian tradition suggests that good and evil are intricately woven into the texture of the universe. If one is brought up to think that the world and all that is in it was made by a beneficent God for man, man will try to find out why there should be so much evil and ugliness. But that is an unsatisfactory answer for it does no more than push the question back one step: why should we imagine that the universe is interested in our likes and dislikes? As for the ethical judgments themselves, they are for the most part inherited. We are educated from childhood to approve of certain things and to disapprove of others and no reasons are given for either attitude. We ourselves, if we went to confession, would have to admit that we did things of which we should disapprove. Otherwise there would be nothing to confess. We might be expected to confine our disapproval to our own acts and to let others take care of theirs, but this of course is not the situation in which we live. We are, I suspect most of us would agree, more ready to behold the mote in our brother's eye than the beam in our own. It is always a comfort to learn that our sins have been committed by others. For there lurks somewhere in our souls a suspicion that what is generally done is equivalent to what ought to be done. Moreover in a well-organized society with an articulate public opinion, we have little opportunity to show our solidarity with the tribe except through our words. For though in ethical matters we can manifest our agreement through conformity, in matters of belief we must express our opinions. To condemn the seven deadly sins by not committing them does not suffice. We must put our condemnation into words. And similarly when we are confronting a work of art which does not conform to our expectations, we feel bound to say so.

There is some question, however, whether works of art are produced in order to permit others to pass judgment on them. It is reasonable to believe that works of art which are made on commission or in order to win a prize in a competition or in the hope of fame or of making money must anticipate judgment. They stand on trial. If the client for whom a house is designed, a portrait painted, a commemorative ode written, or a string quartette composed, does not like it, the artist has failed and he does not want to fail for obvious reasons. Similar comments can be made, but will not be, about the other circumstances. And yet the existence of artists in all media who refuse to consider the public's tastes and the possible judgment of critics cannot be disregarded. There are just too many recalcitrant artists to be thought of as exceptions to the rules. It seems doubtful that the Fauves, for instance, painted as they did in order to curry favor with either the public or the critics. The same would be true of the early Impressionists, or Courbet, and, I imagine, of Caravaggio. I am not denying the pleasure which comes from mystifying people, from shocking them, or from simply defying them. But that pleasure does not suffice to explain the sacrifices which the artists whom I have in mind were willing to undergo in order to produce works of art as they themselves, and not others, saw fit. In their cases the spectator could not turn to traditional notions of form in order to judge them and he had little way of entering into the artist's intentions to judge them otherwise. He had two possible attitudes: to condemn the works of art in question as utterly unintelligible, or to look for some principle of order or form which, though novel, might nevertheless be found with a little good will. It is interesting now to read the sympathetic criticisms made by the few who were willing to risk their reputation for sanity by praising novel works of art. Men like Proudhon and Zola found things to praise in Courbet which Courbet, at least in his early days, had no intention of putting into them. But since a work of art has to be interpreted by someone if it is to be kept alive, part of its significance will be injected into it by those who look at it. A writer may use the vocabulary of the lower social orders because it comes naturally to him; it is his native speech. He may do so in order to reach a larger public. He may do so because he thinks it more suitable to his subject matter than polite or drawing room speech. He may do so because of his revulsion from speech which he thinks of as artificial, as Wordsworth and Coleridge in their "Lyrical Ballads" adopted the rustic speech of the English on the ground that it was more natural and sincere than that of the poetic tradition.[2] The relevance of a writer's speech may therefore be judged in four ways at least and the form of his poem, story, novel, or play might be determined by four different considerations. But when form is interpreted as the congruence of a work of art and something beyond the work of art, it is folly to maintain that the artist brought about that congruence deliberately. In the beginning of a man's career he will frequently, perhaps always, intentionally pursue a given course, but, as we have repeated in this study over and over again, as he grows in his career he will acquire habits of workmanship or artistry which become compulsive and therefore unconscious.

The fallacy of the critic is to infer that what he has discovered in a work of art was intentionally put there by the artist. And the error of the artist is to expect the critic to find in his work of art what he was conscious of putting in it. It took over two millennia for psychologists to wake up to the fact that even behavior which appears disorganized and random is nevertheless explicable and determined by theoretically discoverable causes. An artist might be asked to grant this and to permit the critic to point out what he finds in a work of art without first asking the artist whether or not he meant to put it there. But similarly the critic might be asked to permit the artist to forget that critics

exist and to produce whatever he in his own judgment thinks is
fitting. It is incredible that Leonardo should have thought of
Mona Lisa's smile as a symbol of enigmatic womanhood; women
were not enigmatic in 1503. It is similarly incredible that when
Shakespeare wrote *Hamlet* he should have known that he was
writing about the Oedipus complex. But at the same time when
women became enigmatic, it was normal, if not inevitable, that
people should begin to interpret the smile of Mona Lisa as a
symbol of the "great enigma," and that when people began reading Freud—to say nothing of Ernest Jones—they should see the
crux of *Hamlet* in the Prince's incestuous love for his mother.
New relevance is found in works of art when critics are enabled
to see new things in them. This ability is not attributable to any
change in human nature, to any shift in the *Zeitgeist*, to any
deeper insight into aesthetic values, but simply to that re-
orientation of interest which happens when a man learns something new. A new theory of history, psychology, or artistry will
start men looking for corroboration of its theses. Though it is
historically correct, for instance, to say that Easter is an old
Germanic festival and that Christmas has taken on many of the
characteristics of the Saturnalia, that in no way gives us the right
to impute to the celebrants of either festival any awareness of
their origins. But as long as a critic is frank enough to say,
"This is what I find in this work of art," he will be both telling
the truth and making the work of art more interesting. And since
the reason why he finds what he does find in a picture or some
other work of art is the same reason why others will agree with
him, the only problem which remains is why so many people
read the same books. No book which has been printed has ever
been read by only one person. Books like *The Golden Bough*,
The Decline of the West, *A Study of History*, and Freud's
various essays on psychoanalysis have been read so widely as to
create a definite climate of opinion. They have directed their
readers to look for things which their fathers knew nothing
about. As far as I know it is neither immoral nor stupid to profit

from one's reading. None of us knows the entire significance of anything which we do, and we may as well admit this and quiet down.

Furthermore, whether certain critics like it or not, works of art do have reference to things beyond themselves. They have reference to the artist's entire life to begin with, to the things and ideas which he admires, to those he hates, to his religious and political beliefs when he has any, to his sexual satisfactions, to his reactions to social approval or disapproval, in short to all relations in which he is one term. Works of art also contain comments on society, sometimes overtly as in the drama and the novel, and sometimes by implication. However restricted the society which a novelist depicts, he cannot deal with human beings in isolation from other human beings. Jane Austen's scene is about as narrow as any novelist's could be, and moreover what she omits is greater in scope than what she includes. But nevertheless she has given us a picture of more than a few isolated individuals. It has been pointed out that she says nothing about the Napoleonic Wars, that she derives her metaphors from trade, that her heroines are too submissive to their fathers and husbands, and these comments are supposed to be unfavorable. But there is no proof that in the social circles which she was describing the War was a constant source of worry, that commercial interests were not accepted as normal, and that the rule of husband and father was not generally accepted as right. Still, that it was possible for a novelist to overlook the War is important, and there is no reason why a critic should not point out where and how an artist has restricted himself.[3]

Works of art also have relevance to morality and to the economic order, in fact to every human interest. One can extend this as far as one wishes. That Shakespeare's princes are his heroes and his rustics comic relief may not indicate any economic theory on Shakespeare's part, but nevertheless the tradition in which he worked correlated seriousness with nobility and comedy with the lower orders. One has to accept this convention as one has to accept blank verse and the arias which occur every now and then in the form of soliloquies and rhetorical flourishes. An artist may attain verisimilitude but he will never reproduce truth. Once one has grasped the convention, the form appears. But it is absurd to assume a priori that one's own conventions must have been those of the artist. I recall showing a poem which I used to admire, Bridges' "London Snow," to a professor of English literature and asking him what he thought of it. "I can't see what meter he has used," was his comment. It was of course the meter of falling snow, which has not yet been given a name in the books on prosody. But my critic's assumption was that a poem must be written in one of the classified meters. If the form of a poem is in its meter and if its meter must be one which has already been ticketed, then "London Snow" is formless. But if a poet takes over the hesitating, swirling, retarding, quickening motion of snowflakes as they fall and uses that as his model, and if he does it successfully, the form, even if identified with the meter, is clear.[4] The fact that a poet has renounced comment on human life and has spent his time exclusively on nonhuman nature or on the world of artifacts determines to some extent what the form of his poem is going to be. The renunciation is itself of ethical relevance. A generation fed on poems in which nothing is said of moral problems will obviously not have the same attitude toward life as one which is familiar with the struggles and failures of men to be decent. A novelist like Henry James, whose only mention of economics is the schemes of parasites to live on their richer fellows, is, regardless of his intentions, saying something about morality and economics. At a time when critics did not see the influence of wealth on conduct, if there ever was such a time, it could not be expected that they would look to see how far the author was aware of the material determinants of behavior. When people thought—or at least said—that good would always triumph over evil, it was not surprising that novels ended happily for good men and unhappily for bad. These are the most elementary of considerations and should require no demonstration.

For even a picture, if only because of its size, may be excluded from the homes of the poor and if not costly enough, from those of the rich.

Now the objection to what I have been saying is twofold. First, it will be replied that references other than to the perceptual powers of man are irrelevant to aesthetics. They may be there, but they should not be mentioned. A work of art, it will be said, may be immoral or depressingly morbid or untrue to something called life, and yet be a great work of art. I am far from denying this. It is simply a judgment based on a very restricted notion of what constitutes a work of art. To separate one aspect of a work of art from all its others is a falsification of what one has before one. There is nothing in a picture or poem or what you will which does not contribute something to its nature and no one has the power to forbid one to look at it as a whole. If we are disgusted with the subject matter of a work of art, that cannot be denied nor should it be overlooked. Whatever else works of art are for, they are not to disgust us, unless the artist deliberately has chosen to do so for, let us assume, satirical reasons. In that case, for instance in some of Daumier's caricatures, we switch our point of view and we let ourselves be swayed by the message which the artist is trying to communicate. But usually we can tell whether the purpose of a work of art is social satire or not. No one would say, I imagine that Rubens in his "Garden of Love" or Ingres in his "Bain Turc" had disgust as his aim. If however, these squirming female nudes in the latter and those fat lolling women in the former do revolt us, why should we pretend to find them beautiful? A man cannot be asked, except for scientific purposes, to deny himself and disguise his real feelings. A zoologist may deal with animals which are disgusting to the ordinary man and, while he is doing zoology, he will deny his feelings of revulsion. The physician will examine a patient's stools and urine as part of his job, but that does not imply that he likes them.

In the second place, all the various aspects of a work of art exist together and influence one another. The artist may decide that his purpose is to weld them into a whole so that it demands analysis to distinguish among them. Fitness, though an old-fashioned requirement, will never be abandoned: no one would paint a "Crucifixion" with children playing gaily in the foreground, butterflies and birds floating overhead, and a happy color scheme. This of course is obvious. Yet the butterflies might symbolize the release of the souls from their bodies; the birds might symbolize Nature's joy at the Redemption; and the playing children might symbolize the happiness of the Innocents now to be born without inherited guilt. But, it will be observed, I have had to say "might," for no one without a symbolic tradition behind him would be able to read such a "Crucifixion." The one thing which a work of art can do which nothing else can do is to fuse together a great variety of references, to communicate an idea without evidence. I doubt that Chardin in his still lifes was trying to symbolize anything, but the quiet spacing of his loaves of bread and bottles of wine and all the other homely objects of the kitchen does to the minds of some observers vivify the peace and integrity of bread and wine. This does not ask for words and demonstration. One lives within the work of art while one is looking at it or reading it or listening to it, and translating it into some verbal formula is never successful. There is a kind of passionate absorption which these things exercise over us and the hackneyed phrase of losing ourselves in them is probably as accurate as any so far invented.

But here too, as elsewhere, the spectator is as much involved as the artist and his work. It is inevitable that some people will not fall in love with a given picture or musical composition or any other special kind of artistry. A person who is sensitive to pictures need not be also sensitive to music, poetry, or fiction.[5] I fail to see why this should be a problem unless one assumes that all people must be alike. It is not art as a whole to which we are reacting but to specific works of art. The whole history of critical opinion shows this. It is not that some critics are right and others wrong; at most it is that some critics are more con-

vincing or persuasive than others. But you cannot be just persuasive; you have to persuade human beings. The interpretation
which one critic makes may seem absurd to one reader and convincing to another. Surely this needs no proof. One need but
think of all the philosophic treatises which have been written to
demonstrate some little point and of how none of them has
convinced anyone other than their author. And yet philosophy,
being rational, one might think would have only to be written
in order to be convincing. Mathematics is more successful, but
even in that noble field there are disputes about the elegance
of proofs and as for the foundations of mathematics, they are
still being hotly debated. The stubborn individuality of human
beings cannot be eradicated as things are and has to be accepted
as one of those brute facts which cannot be explained away.

The question finally arises, if the form of the work of art is
that which makes it intelligible, to whom is it to be intelligible?
Is it to everybody, to the elite, to a jury, to a set of experts?
Well, it would of course be pleasant if a work could be so illuminated that everyone would understand it. But such a prospect
is very dim. People disagree for a variety of reasons, but one of
the most important is the differences in information. One could
hardly expect a Greek vase painter to appreciate Holman Hunt's
"Light of the World" or a provincial Christian to appreciate a
"Dance of Siva." But for that matter a man who will sit by the
hour watching the play of flames in a fireplace will stand aghast
before a Pollock. There may be no sense to this if by sense we
mean rigid consistency. Logic is verbally attractive perhaps but
it is not a schema with which to codify our emotional life. Our
minds are a complex of all sorts of memories, many of which are
very dim and all of which are likely to be infused with emotional qualities shared by no one else. If some people hate cats
and love dogs, that is not because cats are less lovable than dogs.
The answer lies in the persons, not in the animals. And the persons here are the total lives of the persons, their pasts as well as
their presents. It would be well if the whole field of art were

reconsidered as populated by individuals, not classes, individual artists, individual works of art, and individual spectators. In that case generalizations could be made, but they would be so abstract as to have very little content.

As a coda to this discussion it may be desirable to say something about the change which has come about since the Romantic movement in the relation between artist, work of art, and spectator. We may protest as much as we please, but we are the children of the Romantics and we cannot escape their heritage. One of the many things for which they stood in general was not only the fact of variety but its desirability. It was Herder more than any other one writer who persuaded men that national, that is, cultural differences were to be preserved and cherished. But by the 1830's one's times were substituted for one's nation, and it was not much later that writers like Gautier were preaching the right of every person to be different from every other. Originality then became a value, and in its train came the idea that there could be no common code of interpretation: each individual was forced to make his own interpretations in his own code. More and more was left to the critic, or the spectator, and the artist's responsibility for saying something which would be generally accepted was denied. Paradoxically enough the most subjective art could become the most universally acceptable, for it left everyone free to interpret it as he would. The less a work of art was tied to a specific subject matter, the better. Hence abstract, nonfigurative art became that which left the spectator freest to form his own judgments.

Schematically what happened was about as follows.

In the first phase, the artist differed from other men only in his congenital endowment. This was the period in which native genius was specially praised. Subject matter and treatment were prescribed by tradition and the spectator knew what to look for.

In the second phase, artists were not only believed to be different from other men, but from one another and each man's peculiar talent was emphasized. New subjects were introduced but technique on the whole was traditional. In painting there was of course a split between those men, like Delacroix, who thought that painting was more than colored drawing and those, like Ingres, who continued to put the emphasis on drawing. But with this exception, it was only the new subjects, landscape and "simple life," for instance, which puzzled people. This was as true of music and of literature as of painting.[6]

In the third phase, since everything experienced was believed to be a perceptual impression, at least in origin, one's objects came into existence only when a stimulus met a receptive mind and, though the impressions were admitted to be the one reality, as in the epistemological theory of sensory data, yet individual perceptions become more and more prominent. But when this point is reached, the spectator can have only impressions of the artist's impressions. Hence even if the painter or writer is dealing with natural objects, he can record only his own impressions of those objects, and the spectator or critic deals with his impressions of the work of art or artistry. But since each spectator is different from every other, no two spectators need agree on what they see except when psychological laws intervene. That is, there are certain occasions on which the normal eye will see what every other normal eye sees and that occurs in accordance with general laws. Hence here too there was a sort of objective reality which might be the target of the critic: that which was being represented.

But in the fourth phase, it was recognized that the artist's contribution to his work of art was paramount and, since traversing the perceptual screen was impossible, there could be no representation of any nonhuman reality. The work of art became thus an expression, rather than an impression, and it was an expression of something internal to, peculiar to, the artist. He was thus freed from any tie to the external world and projected into it through his artistry that which was enclosed in his own mind. This might be of two sorts: his unconscious fantasies, his dreams, his repressions, even his neuroses; and also his character as expressed in action, the sort of thing which might be expressed in calligraphy, gestures, the dance, free association, and doodling. Criticism in this case rested upon the spectator's sympathy with the expressive gestures of the artist. As in music terms naming emotional states of joy, sorrow, anger, peace, and the like are used by composers to suggest how a passage should be played, so in painting the names of pictures, when given, were names of emotions. But the more prudent painters pasted no labels on their canvases and left it up to the spectator to decide what was being expressed.

The result of this development was analogous in its effect to what happens when we enjoy natural objects, trees, the songs of birds, the dancing of willow trees, and sunsets. Art which began as an addition to nature and a better way of performing natural acts, ended as secondary nature, a sort of supernumerary nature. The work of art had as many meanings as there were people to see it and it took little time for accidental effects to be produced and left embodied in material form as a challenge to the spectator. Since reason is above all an interpersonal technique of interpreting things, it had to be discarded by critics, for whatever was interpersonal in works of art was in them purely by accident. The dialectic of this evolution was not unpredictable, for the moment that the aesthetic experience was defined as the pleasure to be got from sensation alone, it was logical that the artist strive for pure sensations unassociated with any stimuli. Such art is obviously the polar antithesis of arts which can be classified as painting, sculpture, music, or landscape, modeling, or sonatas. There must be no bonds to permanent material objects left, and the work of art becomes paradoxically a fleeting moment of sensation in material guise.

CHAPTER XV

Criticism as Interpretation

SINCE A distinction between terminal and instrumental values and between the spectator's point of view and the artist's makes possible eight judgments about a work of art and artistry, a critic must first decide which of eight things he means when he says that a picture, poem, or piece of music is good or bad.[1] These meanings are seldom kept apart, but on the contrary are usually fused together in such intimacy that neither the writer nor the reader knows precisely what is the subject of conversation. Few critics are willing to say that they are speaking for themselves alone and they customarily identify themselves with the entire human race. Few are willing to admit that their point of view need not be that of the artist and that the value which they find in a work of art need not be that which the artist found in it. Few are as frank as Tolstoi was when he identified moral values with aesthetic. Quite the contrary, most contemporary critics seem to believe that there is only one value properly called aesthetic and one point of view from which a work of art or bit of artistry can be seen. No one would deny, I think, that Berenson was one of the most competent students of Italian painting. Though some of his attributions and datings may have been wrong, he had as close an acquaintance with

Italian painting as any other man of his time. Yet we find him saying, in the conclusion to his book on *The Italian Painters of the Renaissance,* that all art produces what he called life-enhancement through tactile values, movement, and space-composition. But does he mean that the artist must—and does—have this in mind when he is painting? Does he mean that painting a picture enhances the life of the painter? Does he identify the feeling that one's life is enhanced with the perception of beauty? Is the feeling of life-enhancement produced by the three means of which he is speaking or does it come about after one realizes that tactile values, movement, and space-composition are present? Does a "Crucifixion" enhance life? An "Agony in the Garden"? El Greco's "Burial of Count Orgaz"? Is the quiet and serenity of Giotto less life-enhancing than the turbulence of Rubens? Is there anything else in a picture besides these three means to life-enhancement? In other words if both Courbet's "Burial at Ornans" and Poussin's "Amphitrite" are equally well painted, can they be substituted for each other when one has a yearning to see a beautiful painting?

In general it may be said that no single question will ever exhaust the possible problems which are aroused by any work of art or indicate all the possible sources of enjoyment. It is true that if we take the spectator's point of view, rather than that of the artist, and we usually have to, then there are only four questions which can be reasonably asked:

1. Has it terminal value for me as a work of art?
2. Has it instrumental value for me as a work of art?
3. Has it terminal value for me as artistry?
4. Has it instrumental value for me as artistry?

Translating these uncouth questions into more intelligible form, let us imagine that we are looking at Fouquet's portrait of Étienne Chevalier and Saint Stephen [Plate 4]. I can say truthfully that I think it one of the most beautiful portraits that I have ever seen; that it has produced in me the serenity and self-forgetfulness that I seek in all art; that its workmanship, color, drawing, composition, conception are so satisfying that I care nothing about whether Chevalier's likeness is true or not or whether Saint Stephen with that trickle of blood on his scalp is an adequate representation of the first martyr or not: I just find myself absorbed in all the intricacies of the workmanship which look so simple and straightforward at first glance; I do not raise the question of whether Fouquet was trying to impress a twentieth-century professor of philosophy and has chosen the right way to do so. It is clear at least to me that I have been first shocked into a deeply emotional state when I look at this picture. This state does not seem to involve any intellectual activity on my part whatsoever. I seem to be simply looking at something and finding it beautiful. I am no more aware of the causes of my condition than a billiard ball is when struck by a cue. I see at most the heads and shoulders of two men in profile, one of whom is behind the other. The man in the background has been wounded slightly in the scalp. He holds a thick book in one hand on top of which is a stone. My eyes then begin to move about within the frame and in all probability I read the label beneath it. This tells me what the subject of the painting is. But now I already know that Saint Stephen was the first martyr and that he was stoned to death. Had I not sung in chapel as an undergraduate the hymn:

> The martyr first whose eagle eye
>   Could pierce beyond the grave,
> Who saw his Master in the sky
>   And called on Him to save?

The stone then is what the books call an attribute, but in this case it is resting on the Bible and the outstretched hand with the book and the stone could have been used as an emblem of martyrdom, a hieroglyph the meaning of which is martyrdom. I can then answer the question, "What is this?" by saying that it is an emblematic presentation of the Protomartyr. But since

Étienne Chevalier is also there and in the foreground, it is clear that Saint Stephen was his patron saint, clear if the identity of names was not enough to show it. The double portrait then might be interpreted as a symbol of Chevalier's hope that, like his patron, he too might suffer for the Faith. On the one hand you have the earthly soul, on the other his heavenly counterpart. This lets loose a host of associations more or less random concerning a man and his heavenly patron, most of which could not have been present to Fouquet, but all of which are rooted in this picture before me.

Some of these associations also arise because of the similarity of the painting to others in the same tradition. I have to see in it something which runs through Catholicism, for such a work of art is not an isolated item without relation to predecessors and successors. Is it after all a portrait of Chevalier or an offering to Saint Stephen? Is Chevalier anything more than one of those donors who figure in so many religious paintings? This is a legitimate question, for the significance of the picture will shift according to my answer. But it will be observed that I cannot answer it unless I have memories of a number, more or less great, of other paintings. As long as I stay within the frame, I may be confronted with nothing more than two heads. Is the title a part of the picture? If without it the picture loses significance, then it is part of it. If on the contrary it is simply a label, like Opus 10, no. 3, in music, then it can throw no light on what the picture is about. But the moment that I know what it is about, I also *see* what it is about. And again, I ask what authority can prevent my indulging my curiosity and thus impoverish my experience. Why in short should I pretend that I know nothing about either Chevalier or his patron? Why should I make the futile attempt to be something that I am not?

If I know nothing whatsoever of the history of art, of iconography, of the technique of painting and drawing, I can neither enjoy nor fail to enjoy a painting. My mind will be absolutely vacant and, though certain colors and shapes may be pleasing or displeasing to me, or perhaps certain human faces or gestures attract or repel me, there will be nothing else in a painting which could stimulate the slightest interest. In fact not even faces could arouse pleasure or displeasure if I knew nothing of faces. I must at least recognize facial expressions and to do this demands experience of human beings. At the same time it must be admitted that if all that I have said is illegitimate, then the only paintings worth criticizing are visual patterns with no human relevance. The innocent eye is innocent of everything except sensations. And the sensation which it is capable of enjoying is meaningless. One can easily understand why critics and aestheticians who argue in defense of pure painting, identify it with painting which has no subject matter. Even those involuntary associations which we all have, when adult, with colors and shapes must be eliminated. And the agony of such mutilation just does not seem to me to be worth undergoing. I can derive a similar pleasure from watching waves breaking on rocks or the flight of a sea gull—provided that I do not know that the former are water and the latter a bird. Such ignorance may be bliss, but it is too dearly bought.

It all boils down again to the classifications which we make of works of art and to our preliminary definitions and assumptions. One can enjoy experiences without knowing much of what they mean. If this were not true, then the child or the savage would lead a pretty dull life. If I define a painting as a flat surface covered with colored areas, then it is obvious that subject matter is not part of a painting. Some pictures, abstractions and non-figurative paintings, clearly are nothing more than that. This does not make them ugly but it does make them thinner than paintings with equally beautiful design and also with subject matter. The Lorenzetti "Descent from the Cross" in the lower church at Assisi seems to me to be both beautiful in the design of its interlocking triangles and also in the adequacy of its design to its subject. Once you know what the subject is, and I imagine that everyone likely to see it does know at least this, then you can feel the adequacy of the design. The two are exquisitely fused into one work of art. Any interpretation of this will be based on analysis, but one can only analyze something which exists as a unit. When we interpret works of art, we untangle their various strains and lay them out, so to speak, side by side by means of our discourse itself, for one cannot speak of everything at once. When paintings were defined as imitations of nature, then the accuracy of imitation became a standard of excellence and design became less interesting; witness the academic paintings of the nineteenth century. And when only certain subject matters were believed to be worthy of presentation in works of art, then subjects which were low or vulgar or immoral were condemned without further ado. The criticism of Joshua Reynolds frequently dwelt upon the vulgarity of details in paintings and the criticism made of Veronese's "Marriage Feast at Cana" by the Inquisition was based upon its inclusion of irrelevant details. When the Council of Trent laid down the rules for appropriate religious paintings, it said nothing whatsoever about technical matters, taking technical excellence for granted; its target was simply the unsuitability of certain details. To say in reply that this target is not aesthetic is to substitute one definition of the aim of art for another. Should one re-examine the standards of Roger de Piles, one will find in them a conception which lands one in curious appraisals. But if one is willing to grant a man the right to use these standards, then his conclusions follow fairly well. It is true that most critics today would not rank Domenichino above Rembrandt, but that is because their standards are not those of Roger de Piles. They do not believe that painting is only colored drawing; but a very large number of their predecessors did.

There is of course a quite different approach to the matter. That is to recognize the individuality of each work of art and to try to discover what is in it, not to what degree it resembles others of its supposed class. This enterprise will not tell one whether the work of art is good or bad, but it will at least make it more interesting. Once something has captured our interest, we may then like or dislike it with more reason. Our liking and disliking will be felt before we know anything about it. But if we want to have reasons for our attitude, and we undoubtedly shall want some, then we shall discover various excellences which are shared by no other work of art of the same general type. Most of what we shall say in self-defense will be psychological nonsense, for none of us knows enough about the etiology of emotion to talk about it sensibly. But on the other hand, by turning the work of art into a subject of conversation, we shall inevitably be translating its peculiar qualities into words, none of which will be adequate but some of which may be illuminating. We are engaged in what Stendhal called crystallization. For it is doubtful whether our admiration for works of art is much different from our admiration for people. None of us really knows why we like certain individuals, some of whom we even disapprove of, and, whatever the force of attraction may be, it is so hidden beneath layers of symbolism that it is next to impossible to bring it to the surface. We may admire a person for his courage, or for his intelligence, for his spontaneity or for his balance, but he is always more than the incorporation of some moral trait and often alongside the admirable qualities lie others which are much less admirable. Of the latter, when we are aware of them, we are likely to say nothing, unless we dislike the person in question. In that case we may be objective enough to admit his possession of courage or intelligence or spontaneity, but we shall also point out when discussing him that in spite of these good qualities, he is a bore or a gossip or something else which people in general do not feel that they should admire.

But it may well be that the very combination of good and bad traits makes the man more interesting. How, we shall ask, can a person who is so charming in conversation, so witty, such a good raconteur, be such an abominable husband, faithless, improvident, volatile? If we do say this, we of course show our naïveté, for no one is all of a piece. And hence the logical thing to do would be to condemn, if we are given to condemnation, his bad traits and to praise his good. This, I grant, is very difficult. Life would be much easier if moral judgments were easier. But so would aesthetic judgments be easier if we could classify every picture, poem, statue, building, musical composition, and point out at once whether or not it conforms to the class-concept. To return to Roger de Piles, the artists who came out of his tests best were Raphael and Rubens. They were not faultless but nevertheless they ranked at the top of the list. Nor is it hard to see why. With painting considered as colored drawing, they were almost perfect, for color was thought of as no more than a vulgar stimulus to passion. And passion was thought of as something which must be subdued. Their color was just about right and their drawing well-nigh faultless. The Venetians were better colorists, it was admitted, but they were poorer draftsmen. That their particular kind of painting was not colored drawing did not make anyone given to such appraisals hesitate. If it was painting, pure painting in which the quality of the paint itself was of deep interest, that was their error. Such was said also about Rubens by the Poussinists and about Delacroix by Ingres. But above all what such an examination shows is that even if there are only four qualities to be examined in any painting, they will vary in excellence. There are of course more than four, but the principle is the same.[2]

To discover what any individual thing is comes down to discovering what it is for you. I am not saying that individuals are subjective creations, but they do not exist beyond consciousness. But nevertheless in the context of human experience their character is bound to be in part a projection of the minds of those who know them. Words are an excellent example of this. All words, with the exception of those whose derivation from some known language is immediately grasped or which are simply combinations of a prefix, suffix, and root, have to be understood as individual signs and their meaning cannot be inferred. We have to store up in our memories a vast quantity of such words, much as the Chinese have to do with their written characters. That is why we have to have dictionaries. They exist as the common memory. But, as we learn early in school, every word has both denotation and connotation and even if we know the former we do not necessarily grasp the latter. This is why translations often fail to communicate the precise sense of the original and why it is impossible to translate poetry, even if a translator is lucky or clever enough to match the meter and rhyme scheme. The total meaning of a verbal or any other symbol is apprehended by our total minds, conscious and unconscious, and is a nebulous atmosphere of perceptual, emotional, and intellectual suggestions. Whether I am dealing with a human being, a given picture or other work of art, or a definite historical event and want to communicate what I can only call its meaning, I must first name it, which unavoidably involves classifying it somehow or other; I must then describe it, which involves looking at it and seeing if possible its perceptual peculiarities; and, even if I refuse to like or dislike it—assuming that this is possible—my emotional attitude toward its class and its perceptual traits will in part determine what words I shall use to translate my experience of it. I am, let us say, trying to interpret the character of Abraham Lincoln. As I am an American, I had to be born either in the North or in the South. And as I am well beyond the age of adolescence, I have already been to schools and colleges and have read a few books on the Civil War. My attitude is therefore already directed toward some vague estimate of his character. Am I to think of him as the Great Liberator, the idealistic statesman, the Lincoln who set aside habeas corpus, the author of the Second Inaugural, the small town lawyer, the arbitrary and ruthless tyrant who deserved the bullet which finally got him, the poor boy who made good, the superstitious believer in dreams? He was obviously something of all these and more. But, like all great historical figures he has become a symbol of a set of values which are highly esteemed by some and depreciated by others. If I look at his portraits, I shall interpret them according to my own feelings about his role as it is given in the history books.[3] A Southerner could hardly be expected to see in that face what an abolitionist would see in it. Though no man can jettison his past, certain things float to the surface of his memory and others are buried. The historian will have to decide which are "important." But his definition of importance will depend on his appraisal of the situation in which he is interested. Even at this date, it is possible to believe that secession was a right reserved to each of the states and, if one shares this belief, then one's estimate of the person who did most to block secession will be different from that of a person who believes in unionism. To ask a man to be absolutely objective means to ask him to abandon his principles, and that is too much to ask of any man. So in judging works of art.

If, for example, I am confronted with Poussin's "Et in Arcadia ego," I first have to be able to read the Latin inscribed on the tomb and, unless I have read Panofsky on the subject, I shall probably read it wrong. There are probably more people who have not read Panofsky than have read him, and these people will render the Latin according to their lights. They may not even think that the inscription has any importance whatsoever and that the subject of the painting is two rustics looking at a tomb. This pastoral scene then loses its emblematic character and what will be seen in it will depend entirely on what the onlooker is used to looking for: drawing of the seminude shepherds, landscape, design, and all the other traditional properties of landscapes with figures. He will attend to the tomb with its inscription only if he has prior reason to believe that it may be the central detail of the composition. But that there is an inscription on the tomb might suggest only that it is a tomb. To make the inscription central is to transform the painting into what will be called with a curl of the lip, literature. Both versions of this picture have a certain fame and there is little, if any, doubt that to Poussin and his admirers the inscription was the subject matter of them, not the landscape nor the figures. This makes them both bad paintings according to some of our contemporaries and it makes their admirers bad critics.

An even more extreme example might be Gozzoli's "Saint Thomas Aquinas" in the Louvre [Plate 5]. Gozzoli was apparently so skeptical of his public's ability to read his painting that he inserted labels here and there to clarify it. Christ in His Heaven surrounded by cherubim and seraphim and the four evangelists below Him, each accompanied by his special attribute were not sufficient; there must be Saint Paul and Moses between them and the Lord, as well as a Latin inscription approving of the Saint's writings. Thomas himself is not only flanked by Aristotle and Plato, but they themselves are identified by labels. In fact, even Thomas is labeled on his halo and at his feet lies the prostrate figure of either Heresy or Error.[4] Below all this is a congregation of the righteous, both ecclesiastics and laymen with the pope on his throne, and these too have to be labeled by appropriate inscriptions. This rebus is easy enough to read and it is probable that it could be read even without the labels. My only thesis is that Gozzoli thought the labels were needed, that they are a help in interpreting the painting, that the details of the painting would be overlooked by someone who was not interested in this kind of picture, that it would attract the close attention only of those who are specially interested in Saint Thomas Aquinas and his place in the history of Church doctrine, and finally that one's liking or disliking for the picture would either be stimulated by one's first glance at it or by one's further study of it. A man passing through the Louvre knowing nothing of Saint Thomas would see only a collection of people of different sizes and in different positions on the canvas and would either walk away with a shrug of the shoulders or at most wonder what in the world it was all about. That pudgy large-sized man in clerical costume, holding a book on one knee, might perhaps arouse his curiosity, but, if I may judge from the files of tourists trudging through the galleries, not many pay the slightest attention to it. It may be wrong to say that they do not see it, but their seeing is that of a man who walks down a street and pays no attention to what is going on. There is to be sure another cause at work here. Tourists in the Louvre or any other large and famous museum look at what they have been told to be interested in. They are given this information by guidebooks and docents. They are halted in their parade before the recognized masterpieces and have little to say about where they should stop. But my example would be pertinent to the free man who is on his own.

There is a vague similarity between this Gozzoli and a number of other paintings, but its power of capturing the attention of visitors to the Louvre is a function of the visitor as much as it is a function of the picture. To a philosopher or a Catholic who knows something of Church dogma and its history, it is bound to be more attractive than it would be to a man who is innocent of such things. By an a priori decree, one can say that so literary a painting is not painting at all but, as we said of the Poussin, literature. Well and good; let it be called what you will. It is in a mixed mode, but the fact that there are words on it does not prevent there being also visual forms on it. The words "Ma Jolie" appear on a Picasso and, as a matter of fact, have definite historical reference to a song which was popular at the time the picture was painted. Moreover, why should words be illegitimate if attributes are not? The sword of Saint Paul and the tablets of the Law of Moses are also labels; so are the Eagle, the Ox, the Man, and the Lion of the four evangelists, the triple tiara of the pope and the costumes of the ecclesiastics. But presumably to a critic like Berenson all this is nonart as it would be to Clive Bell, Roger Fry, and, one imagines, to Sir Herbert Read. Let us call it then by a special name, an emblem or a hieroglyph. But hieroglyphs usually contain no words; emblems, at least in Alciati, contain both words and pictures. Why not forget this problem and simply call it Gozzoli's painting of Saint Thomas Aquinas? But to stop here is to abandon the search for quasi-scientific explanations and, what seems to be worse, for values. The painting has little, if any, value for the ordinary tourist. It has less for the seeker of pure painting. It also has none for the man who has not seen it. But similarly the anatomist who wonders how in the world Pegasus can beat his wings or a physiologist who wonders how the Centaur Chiron could find appropriate food, will hardly be moved by anything other than his liking for the ridiculous by pictures which include winged horses and centaurs. In the long run, all this comes down to the question of whether pictures are made for men or men for pictures.

The evolution of painting from 1800 down to our own times has been, as we have suggested in a previous chapter, in the direction of abstract and nonfigurative art. That abstract art is purer than figurative and literary painting cannot be denied. But why purity is any better than impurity has not been established. The adjective is question-begging since it has been used to qualify human beings who are supposed to be morally better than the average. But pure music, pure painting, and pure poetry acquire their purity through the purgation of sense. They are simpler than impure works of art. If poetry is only verbal music, music a structure of sounds produced by chance, painting colors and shapes without relevance to experience, each is simpler than works of art which "say" something. The purest poetry is obviously the babbling of children and the charms of nigromantics; the purest music is random sounds produced by capturing whatever happens to stir the air waves; the purest painting the accidental dribblings of a pot of paint. For these have not been restrained by the demands of communication; no rules of grammar or syntax limit their possibilities. But the irony of the situation is that their very simplicity and apparent haphazardness are more apparent than real, for the artist cannot escape the determinism of his unconscious and the spectator is free to interpret them as he will. There is undeniably great beauty in pure design, in spatial order, in the mere flow of a line or interplay of colors. But to restrict artistry to the creation of such things is bigotry. The cardinal sin of the nineteenth-century academic painter was not his feeling that he had to say something, but that what he had to say was trite, sentimental, and hence tiresome. The penalty he had to pay was that his pictures at best became quaint. They were perhaps too clear and left nothing to the spectator's imagination even when they illustrated an idea which was not false. But unfortunately many truths are embalmed in clichés and proverbs and one knows them by heart.

The purpose of interpretation is the communication either to oneself or to someone else of meaning. This assumes that what is before one is a sign, that one has a commonly accepted code of interpretation, and that both parties are agreed on the meaning of the word "meaning." Whether an artist wishes to create signs or not, what he creates will be used as a sign by the people who read it or see it. This is inevitable, or, if not inevitable, at least so usual as to be the statistical rule. For we cannot see even a face without attempting to read it, and the pathetic fallacy is just as often the very stuff of poetry. A metaphor is only a contracted simile, and the plainest statement of fact can turn into a metaphor if in the right context. In the case of our ordinary means of communication, we do have a code and for everyday business it does fairly well, though when one moves on to such subjects as philosophy and its branches, common meanings are missing. Much of the talk about such problems turns upon the meaning of the words being used, and indeed there is one school of philosophers which insists that the clarification of meanings is the sole task of philosophy. But however cloudy our vocabulary, it is the best means of communication which men have invented and the art of verbal communication is the oldest and most efficient art. Unfortunately there is even in this a disturbing complication.

That complication arises from the emotional aura which is attached to almost every word and symbol. Aside from decency and indecency, some words sound poetic, holy, commonplace, affected, naïve or vulgar and so on. And it is this phase of meaning which it is impossible to put into words. For it is the specific accompaniment of each word and the words with which we might try to illuminate it would themselves have different connotations. It is easy enough to quote a line of poetry such as

The light that never was, on sea or land

and give a straightforward definition of each noun that is in it. But the emotional aura of the whole line is attached to those nine words in combination and to nothing else. That being so, it is futile to try to paraphrase them in other words which cannot have the same emotional color. We might, of course, give some psychological explanation of why they should have this effect, but an explanation of something is not a re-creation of the thing in question. To see a sunrise is not to understand why the sun seems to rise, as to feel love for a woman is not the same thing as to understand in psychophysical terms why one has fallen in love. This is perhaps obvious, but none the less important because of that. Similarly, I may see a portrait of George Washington and know that it is his portrait and say so. But if the portrait excites me, depresses me, arouses sympathy in me for that square-jawed general, my saying so does not communicate my feeling at all; it simply tells someone that I have such and such a feeling. But to learn that someone has a specific feeling is not necessarily to share it. It is this side of symbols which might be called their significance rather than their signification. And in works of art which depict something, it is usually believed that their significance is as important as their signification. But for a group of people to feel the same emotions when looking at a work of art demands that they be very much alike. Their similarity, if complete, would demand that they be not only identical twins, but twins who had had precisely the same experiences, that is, the same education in the broadest sense of that term, the same language, the same likes and dislikes, the same sorrows and delights. This unfortunately is an impossibility. Nevertheless we can approach this degree of similarity as a limit and in people of the same social group, the same schooling, the same prejudices, we do approach it closely. There is no such thing as the American soul or mind, but insofar as Americans have been subjected to the same propaganda, victims of the same psychological warfare in advertisements, sermons, radio programs, newspaper editorials, and the like, they may be expected to share to a high degree the same attitudes of approval and disapproval. Uniformity of education—and not merely schooling—has produced a kind of emotional uniformity, especially in those Americans who have not ventured out of their own social groups. We have all heard of the perfect all-American boy; we know what he looks like with his cropped hair, sweater, and swagger; we know what jazz, swing, and twist programs he admires and how he hates those of his fellows who have long hair, do not wear his kind of clothes, and read what are called the little magazines. There will not be much individuality in such human beings and, as a group, they will share the same point of view about works of art. When periodicals like the *Saturday Evening Post, Life, Look, Esquire,* and the *Reader's Digest* have circulations running into the millions, one does not have to assume the existence of a national spirit to explain uniformity. One has simply to pick up the old slogan of giving the public what it wants, meaning by it, making the public want what you give them. There are, of course, not merely one public but several, and each of these publics will have its own standards of criticism. And within each group, however small, there will be some deviations from the norm. This just happens to be one of those stubborn facts which cannot be explained away. And in the existence of such deviants lies the potentiality of new modes of thinking and feeling. How such potentialities are actualized is a problem.

One can take a heterogeneous group of people to an exhibition of nonobjective paintings and reasonably expect them all to agree that the paintings are nonobjective. But from there on all is confusion. Many will confess that they get nothing whatsoever from them, though they usually say this in such a tone of voice that one infers that they have at least got some annoyance from them. The more sympathetic ones will admit that the color is pleasing or that they are reminded of windy streets or billboards covered with tattered posters. If the paintings resemble those of Mondriaan in their geometrical perfection, a few will see this and perhaps even admire it. If they resemble the dynamic swirlings of a Pollock, a few will feel the rush in their blood and even like it. Some will peer at the paintings in an earnest attempt to find something to like in them. Others will turn away with a snort and condemn them out of hand. Others will tolerantly say that they do not understand but admit that the painters probably knew what they were up to. Emotionally the spectators will vary from complete bewilderment to sympathy, running through various degrees of anger and apathy. This is not so atypical of human reactions to art that it should not be considered seriously. On the contrary, what is most interesting is that a flat surface covered with colors and lines should move anyone. But why then should a string of notes played on a flute move anyone? The anger and hatred might be explained as the effect of the unfamiliar which is always a threat to a man's security. But why should a few people be willing to accept the unfamiliar and actually make an effort to like it? Intellectually, the trouble is that one cannot classify the unfamiliar and it thus becomes unintelligible. Emotionally that which is unintelligible, if only unnameable, is a threat to one's peace of mind. It is like our fear of the dark.

What is needed obviously is a sound theory of the causes of emotion. No one, I suppose, is absolutely emotionless, and hence one finds it hard to explain the initiation of emotional states. Moreover, emotional reactions are observed in a child before he can express any ideas. He manifests his likes and dislikes by smiling and crying, by reaching forward and drawing back, by opening his mouth and firmly closing it. What ideas he may have in his head are unstated because he cannot talk, but in their rudimentary form of "This is good," and "This is bad," they are clear enough for practical purposes. By the time, however, he begins to read, to look at pictures, to listen to music, he has already stored up a good stock of aesthetic experiences and in them his ideas and emotions are indissolubly intertwined. But he also has been subjected to a host of influences from people whom he likes and dislikes and is probably not usually conscious of their source. He just *knows* that certain things are right and others wrong, certain good and others bad, certain to be accepted and others rejected. We know enough about psychology now to admit the causal importance of childhood experiences and the difficulty of liberating ourselves from their emotional effects. We do not stop developing at puberty, as everyone knows, but we amalgamate the experiences of our youthful and mature years with those of our childhood and the process goes on without our being conscious of it.

There are, however, certain hypotheses which might be considered at least tentatively. First, there is no denying that a person forms attachments, and of course their opposites, to his teachers. I mean by this to the person of his teachers. There are very few students who are so indifferent to the human race that they can sit before a teacher and have no feelings whatsoever about him. His appearance, his voice, his manners, his friendliness or coldness, all stimulate varying degrees of liking for him. If we like him very intensely, we transfer our liking for him to the things he likes. If he happens to like what we like, so much the better; that fortifies our judgment. But if he dislikes what we like and our liking for him is very great, we find ourselves trying to share his likes and eventually do share them.

Second, as we mature we become interested in the relevance of works of art, usually literature, to historical events and to the biographies of the men who made them. This is a beginning toward making them intelligible. We begin, as we say, to understand them. That in itself does not cause us to like them, but it creates a more sympathetic approach to them. When a person is told why an artist painted the picture which one is looking at, what he was trying to do, as we shall say, our psychology will be wrong in all probability, but it will throw some light on what puzzles us. When we first begin to learn something of musical harmony, music takes on a new interest; and when we first begin to learn something of pictorial composition in the old-fashioned sense of that term, we see that there is more to the picture than the reproduction of a face or historical scene. As we go deeper into such matters, our interest may be absorbed in artistry rather than in the

work of art and sometimes the mere difficulty of solving a technical problem excites our admiration. We may be, for instance, repelled by the exuberance of the Baroque, but we can still admire
its virtuosity. The next step may be the perception of the adequacy
of the artistry to the problem itself; we see that the exuberance of
the Baroque is a reasonable outcome of technical proficiency combined with a new and fairly widespread delight in motion. The
static seems to have given way to the dynamic; the opera, counterpoint, suspense in dramatic writing and the novel, painted vistas
on ceilings which seem endless, the interplay of light and shade
in paintings and architecture, all seem to be one with the new
physics. This sort of thing, though greatly exaggerated, excites our
admiration as the Newtonian cosmos excited the admiration of
those who first learned about it. It has been said, and it is probably
true, that when Giordano Bruno first used the adjective "infinite"
as a term of praise, a new attitude was prompted not only in
philosophy but also in art. The boundless was now good, not bad;
things need not have limits. Just as a building need not be
bounded by straight lines, but might push off into space uncon-
fined, so there was a possibility that poetry need not be confined
by logic and good sense, but might expand the imagination of the
reader as far as he wished to go. But then too painting need not
be confined either by illustration (the text) or the frame. On the
one hand, you could have the captured moment, as in impressionism; on the other, the restless dynamism of contemporary painting. Now all this is theorizing, an interpretation which need not
be an accurate account of the artist's intentions. But once a work
of art seems to fit in with an intellectual model, it becomes more
intelligible and our bewilderment lapses into satisfaction. We see
the relevance of what is before us to something larger and, even
if the relevance is tenuous, it suffices to create interest and out of
the interest enjoyment.

    This may appear in circles wider than that of an individual
biography. When Courbet exhibited his "Stone Crushers," as we
have suggested above, there were no complaints about its technical

correctness. In fact, it was a picture whose composition was about as rudimentary as it could well be, being only two figures against a backdrop. But the subject matter was believed to be vulgar, which of course it was in the sense that the people in it were working men. But this was painted before the slogan of the dignity of labor had been generally accepted. The subject matter of most paintings was usually some biblical incident, historical event, some myth of Greece or Rome, or some allegory. These were noble, edifying, and intelligible only to those with more than primary school education. But the nineteenth century saw the rise of various socialistic philosophies according to which the laborer was not merely someone to be pitied, but someone to be extolled. It was not long before the life of the middle classes supplanted that of the upper classes in all the arts. And since admiration for nature and for those who lived closest to nature grew, the peasant, as in the Barbizon School, supplanted the bourgeoisie. In the seventeenth century Louis Le Nain never had the success of Millet, though his paintings of peasants were just as serious. The reason was that there just were not enough people about to enjoy looking at such pictures in the seventeenth century. It took two hundred years, a bloody revolution, and above all the substitution of steam and water power for hand labor to give the laborer the beauty of the obsolescent. It is in fact one of the ironies of history that the movement in favor of the laborer began just as the laborer was disappearing and the machine was taking his place. A boy of the middle or lower classes, growing up in the nineteenth century in France, aware of the interests of his class and not ashamed of sharing them, could not avoid feeling the triviality of what he would have sneered at as the wasteful economy of the upper classes.

Let us take one more example of the pervasiveness of certain nonaesthetic ideas which have had an influence on aesthetics. The twentieth century, along with all its other innovations, has seen the spread of the new psychology, that of Freud and his school. This has taught all of us. We see the evidence in the widespread use of the Freudian vocabulary, talk about the Oedipus complex, repressions, the birth-trauma, the death-wish, to say nothing of our greater tolerance for homosexuality. It is almost current belief that a man's desires have precedence over his reason. The historian can see this beginning back in the eighteenth century in Herder and in those German philosophers who maintained that there was a kind of reason superior to the scientific reason, a kind of insight free from logic and more enlightening than logic. In Kant, Fichte, and Schelling, this began to make itself felt throughout the learned world. In Schopenhauer and Nietzsche, it gained popularity. In the various forms of pragmatism, it was beginning to win the battle. And in the whole theory of psychodynamics, regardless of the particular school, it became dominant. If the demands of the moral will in Kant had primacy over the pure reason, then as soon as the moral will was examined and found to be swayed more by desire than by evidence, the way was open for the Will to Live, the Will to Power, the satisfaction of the Libido, Cash Value, the Unconscious, and even the Call of the Blood. The twentieth-century artist, living in a time of universal schooling and free libraries, with advertising agencies only too happy to sell his works and create a public for them, could not but be influenced by the regnant ideas of his time. The result was works of art which gloried in their freedom from rational control: Dadaism, Surrealism, Action Painting, Tachisme, and Symbolism with sexual reference. The impact of such paintings was strongest upon people who had become willing to admit their sexual appetites. And this seems to have included the whole of the population. Where naughty boys drew genitalia on walls in the old days, Miró frankly puts them into his canvases. Where the nineteenth-century novelist drew the curtain over the bedchamber, the twentieth-century novelist makes the bedchamber the center of his stories. This is not because we are more obsessed with sexual relations than our grandfathers were. It is because we are more willing to talk about them. They have become less mysterious and in all probability will become boring within a few years. What will happen then to the art of fiction is anyone's guess. Lacking a subject, it may simply die or sink to the level of barroom entertainment whence it arose. Then we may expect to see the *Kama-Sutra* televised. And the élite will turn away with a yawn.

All such prophecies are dangerous and the human soul is capable of unpredictable shifts of interest. But at any rate it is unlikely for the time being that any critic will overlook the unconscious stimuli in works of art, whether he identify them with Freud's libido or Adler's desire for mastery or Jung's Collective Unconscious. A work of art will be seen as the expression of repressions, not as Croce's expression of impressions. If he knows enough psychology, he may say something which makes sense and what he says will give us an interpretation of works of art which will be entirely different from what the older critics used to say. For the work of art will not be enclosed within its frame or its book covers or the stage or its four walls; it will be suspended between the artist and the spectator, in elastic tension. It will be a field of exploration, a cipher whose message is the mind of the artist. The loss of a common code of interpretation was made clear the moment when artists began to write manifestoes explaining what they were trying to do. People have deplored the publication of manifestoes, thinking apparently that they should not be needed. But the fact is that they were needed and that works of art had ceased to be self-explanatory. For our younger contemporaries, the most novel forms of art seem to have become luminous and to them a manifesto is once again unnecessary. But we who were born in the entr'acte, between the old time and the new, still find ourselves confronted with puzzles which we cannot solve. But this may be simply because we are survivals from a culture that is dead. We are paying the price of increased longevity.

CHAPTER XVI

Cultural Relativism

STANDARDS in the nature of things can apply only to groups or to individuals as members of groups. It is possible to tell whether some bit of matter is a good piece of silver or lead, whether a tragedy conforms to Aristotle's definition of a tragedy, whether a man has normal eyesight or not, or is of average weight for his age and height, whether a tree is a maple or an oak. It is possible to tell whether George Washington was a good president or not, whether Stalin was a good Marxist or not, or whether Michelangelo's Christ in the "Last Judgment" conforms to the normal representations of Christ. But it is not possible to tell whether George Washington was a good George Washington or not, whether Stalin was a good Stalin or not, or whether Michelangelo's Christ was a good Michelangelo's Christ. In fact these sentences are nonsense. As members of classes with only one member, whatever they were is precisely what they were and to judge their goodness or badness forces us to apply to them standards of classes of which they were members. They were of course members of many classes but their entire nature could not be enclosed in any one of them. Washington was not only a president, but was also a general, a Virginia landowner, a slaveholder, an attendant of the Church of England, if not a fervent believer in its tenets, and a score of other things. Jefferson's estimate of his character differs from that of Parson Weems and Weems's estimate differs from that of Douglas Freeman. Analogous remarks could be made of each of the other individual beings mentioned. If the appraisal of a man is to be made on the basis of his whole nature and life, then it can never be exhaustive. It will have to be selective and hence partial. That is one justification for always taking motivation into account when praising or blaming a man for his acts. For two men may do what looks like the same thing and upon investigation it turns out that their motives, the circumstances surrounding their acts, the impulsions which eventuated in the acts, may be quite different. Insofar then as we are interested in works of art as individual things, in their differences from all other works of art, we cannot apply standards to them. We can enjoy them and we can interpret them. If, on the other hand, we are interested in what makes a work of art similar to other works of art, we shall have no difficulty in appraising them as satisfactory members of the class to which we have assigned them.

There are always two extreme points of view which a man may take about any experience. The first is scientific. It looks for common characters, wants generalizations, and puts a high value on conformity to a class-concept. Out of all this emerge scientific laws. The second is appreciative. It looks for the individual traits and cares nothing for common characters and, since one of the individual traits is the emotional or affective influence of the thing upon an observer, that has to be included in any appreciative description. The two points of view, I say, may be taken toward any experience. The difference is not resident in the experience itself but in the kind of information which the person having the experience desires. There is no inherent and compelling reason which forces a man looking at the stars in the sky to think of them in terms of stars, planets, galaxies, constellations, fiery masses of chemicals, and all the rest. He may look at the heavens as a spectacle. This may lead not to anything scientific but to something religious, as it did to Seneca. The heavens may declare the glory of God to an astronomer as they do to the Psalmist, but such a declaration is no part of astronomy. Similarly one need not read Shakespeare's *Henry* V as a drama, but as one man's interpretation of history. To take the scientific point of view on all occasions would be ruinous of much that makes life worth living: love would be a part of psychology, marriage a problem for economics, childbearing an incident in genetics. To take the appreciative point of view on all occasions would turn science into mythology or poetry.

It is the ineradicable individuality of things which causes all the trouble. How far it is possible to avoid individuality is problematic. The early Leonardo may have painted like Verrocchio, but as he grew older he developed a style which was marked by a personality which was unmistakable. Whether it would have been better for him to stick to his master's manner, thus smoothing the path for aestheticians and making it rockier for those who want to tack artists' names on pictures, I leave to others to decide. All critics would like to have a single standard of excellence by which they might judge all works of art or at least all works in what they have defined as a single genre. But if there is any contribution made to a man's personality by his genes, then it is unlikely that there will ever be such complete fidelity to a school or a set of rules that individual style can be eliminated. In so far as a work of art is individual, it is bound to be deviant: this is redundant. And whether or not such deviation is good or bad, some artists will be attracted by it and exhibit it. Thus new mannerisms and schools will arise and the innovations of a Beethoven, a Debussy, a Delacroix or a Monet, an Alberti or a Le Corbusier, a Wordsworth or a Whitman, will establish a new set of rules which may become as academic as those which they have violated. We see this happening in our own day in poetry, painting, sculpture, architecture, and dramaturgy. Now that Calder has invented the mobile, a thousand would-be Calders make mobiles. We see the imitators of Eliot and Auden on every bookstall, just as we see the imitators of Brancusi and Gabo in ever exhibition of sculpture. The moment Picasso began assembling *objets trouvés* and having them cast in bronze, every provincial sculptor did the same. The swing between submission and recalcitrancy has not ceased just because some innovations have become accepted. Impressionism, for instance, was a revolutionary technique in the '70's of the last century. Yet twenty-five or thirty years ago it had become the standard program of popular painters who felt that if they painted purple shadows, all pictorial problems would be solved. But the dribble and splash school is rapidly becoming as petrified as the impressionistic school became and it too will soon be thought of as academic. The moment an adjective such as "modernistic" becomes the name of a style, one can be sure that those who are appropriately named by it are conformists.

There have been times when it seems as if deviation, originality, innovation, recalcitrancy were more acceptable than at others. But even so apparently static an art as that of Egypt changed from time to time. We all know now that no artistic tradition is ever all of a piece. Nevertheless it is true that at times pressure had been brought to bear on artists to conform and there is no reason to suppose that artists are any less susceptible to such pressure than anyone else. I imagine, for instance, that what we call French academic painting of the nineteenth century was as homogeneous as any block of works of art could be. The pressure in this case came from the Ministry of Fine Arts which dealt out the prizes and bought the winning pictures for the national museums. "A governmental organization," says Dr. Eleanor Spencer in her essay on "The Academic Point of View in the Second Empire," [1] "provided for the education of the artist in various free city schools and for a limited number at the École des Beaux-Arts in Paris, and at the French Academy in Rome. It then provided a system for public recognition of the best of the mature artists through salons and expositions, with a variety of prizes and honors, and with funds for purchases and commissions. In addition to this the Hôtel Drouot, a public sales center, was sponsored by the same benevolent government in order to facilitate the private art market. In full control of this machine were the forty 'immortals' of *l'Académie des Beaux-Arts de l'Institut.*" What this organization asked of painters was no more than the Council of Trent or Cardinal Bellori or

Sir Joshua Reynolds, or in more recent times, Royal Cortissoz, asked of them. It was simply obedience to a set of rules which, first, seemed reasonable because traditional, and, second, would produce a stable official art for a society which was unstable. If one asks why certain times demand more conformity than others, we have no answer which will prove satisfactory in all respects. But it is probably true that a society which is cloistered, protected from the influence of outsiders, whether by act of God or of legislators, will be less tolerant of innovation than one which, like most modern Occidental societies, is in daily contact with others. So long as Japan was cloistered, its arts followed a set pattern which can be seen even in Japanese representations of foreigners. This was not because Japanese painters could not observe what lay before their eyes, for they have always been the most acute observers in the world. It was because they had accepted a formula as inherently right and they painted in accordance with its restrictions. But as soon as Europeans had free entry into Japan, the Japanese began to swerve from their own tradition and to follow the rules of the European tradition. Such buildings as the Museums of Tokyo and Kyoto are built in the style of the Second Empire. The late nineteenth-century Japanese painter who took to oils imitated his European contemporaries and today in any exhibition of contemporary Japanese painting one will see the same action paintings as are exhibited in the United States or France. The Japanese concert programs include the same classical pieces as are heard in New York or Paris or London. The novels again stick to Western themes translated into Japanese. We say truly enough that all this is attributable to the influence of Westerners on Japan. But why was this influence effective? In the United States, especially in domestic architecture, the influence runs the other way. Where the Japanese introduces at least one Western room in his house, the American takes over the whole Japanese house with only those modifications which Western ideas of hygiene and comfort necessitate. We have not yet accepted paper walls, cushions on the floor instead of chairs, one kakemono on the wall, and no central heating. And our Japanesque houses are as much a travesty on the Japanese house as the *Mikado* was on the Imperial court. Absurd as some of these details may seem, they do demonstrate how cultures interpenetrate. If the tonal structure of European music were in itself more beautiful and inherently more satisfactory to the human ear than the tonality of Oriental music, it would have originated in both East and West. For whatever the differences may be between Orientals and Occidentals, they are not such as to differentiate between the aural physiology of two species of man. All men are physiologically men and whatever may be attributable to common humanity will be found everywhere.

The differences must then arise out of the various patterns of culture, unless their rise is inexplicable. For there is no other source available. Therefore a cloistered culture will remain purer than one which is in touch with the world beyond its walls. We see this in isolated communities in the United States where we are told that eighteenth- and even seventeenth-century speech, old ballads, old dances, old superstitions, old ways of farming, of therapy, and of social intercourse remain. In the South Seas before World War I, much the same seems to have been true. In French Canada where an effort is made to keep families uncontaminated with modern ideas and ways of life, the same appears to be the case. Such facts are known to all and need no proof other than mention of them. But their significance is overlooked. We may say that the traditionalism of French Canada is due to the influence of the clergy and this is probably true. But the same clergy was making the same demands in sixteenth-century Europe and the demands were not fulfilled. There are some families, after all, in French Canada who, while remaining members of the Church, speak English as well as French, have less than fourteen or fifteen children, and move out of their native villages. One obviously cannot be affected by things of whose existence one is ignorant, but one can be unaffected by things with which one comes in daily contact. It all depends on how susceptible one is to novelty. The desire for change seems to be as strong as the desire for permanence, once there is a chance of satisfying it. It is the Orthodox Jew who frequents Gentiles who begins to taste forbidden flesh, but no one knows how many remaining within the spiritual ghetto have the same yearning. Even some Englishmen do what is not done. The history of the Occident could be rewritten from the point of view of the rebels.

Mixed societies are by definition heterogeneous. In the United States this heterogeneity is caused by survivals from the past, distant and recent, and by the influx of foreigners. In most European countries it is not immigration which has brought about diversity but acquaintance with neighboring cultures. The rise of the vernacular literatures and the consequent abandonment of Latin for serious writings, the development of the modern nations out of little principalities, the Reformation with consequent local sects, led the way for cultural diversification. But then the mutual interdependence of peoples for raw materials, as well as for consumers' goods, the spread of easy communications, made it essential that one people become acquainted with others. But when we say "people" here, we must make it clear that we are talking only of those men and women who are aware of the moment in which they live and defend or condemn it, people who are leaders of thought, whose words are listened to. In numbers they are very few as compared with the total population of a country. If we situate them at the top of the intellectual hierarchy, it will be found that there are several ranks below them, all of which have their own leaders too. All societies have been stratified, even if the strata are the chiefs and their lieutenants. But such stratification is not unique, for in so-called primitive societies the women form a class which is as differentiated by its labor as that of the hunters or priests. In our own society the class structure, intellectually speaking, is more complex, for we have those whose beliefs are on a level with that of savages, superstitious in religion, ignorant of science, feeling no ties to the community as a whole, and in art at most interested in the grocer's calendar and the Sunday supplements. At the top are the aesthetic and intellectual leaders, who write the books regardless of who will read them and paint the pictures regardless of who will see them. There is the class of the intellectual and aesthetic Tories, faithful to what they believe to be the tradition in religion, philosophy, science, and art, to say nothing of economics. They are to be found in our universities as well as in nonacademic circles. They are the professors who do no original work but continue in the way of their teachers, rationalizing their behavior with the notion that what is good is unchanging. They are the students who come to college not to discover what is new in learning but to get a degree for social and economic reasons. Then there is the densely populated stratum of people who support the radio and television programs, have the most modern kitchens and antiquated ideas, erect a cook-out in their backyards, buy gasoline mowers, send their children to the public schools as a matter of course but do nothing to improve their curricula, attend church regularly, are friendly and even hospitable, and don't want to be bothered. If they read at all, they read the most widely circulated magazines. They are the prey of all the advertisers and would rather suffer than not have what the advertisers tell them they ought to have. Now I am far from denying the mobility of the class-stratification in the United States: people move rapidly in and out of their strata and, as I have suggested earlier in this study, may belong to one stratum as far as their economic interests are concerned, and to another as far as their religious interests are concerned. It is in fact this mobility which makes the cultural anthropology of modern societies so difficult. But just as it is possible to look at England in the nineteenth century and find in it courtly art, popular art, and folk art, so in America of the twentieth century we can find the art of the *avant-garde*, nineteenth-century academic art, the popular art of the *Saturday Evening Post* covers and illustrations, and remnants of folk art. Moreover, on the principle of multivalence, sometimes the art of one stratum is adopted by the people of another through snobbishness and what Baudelaire called *nostalgie de la boue.*

A stroll through the streets of any old New England city will give one a longitudinal cross-section of the history of architecture since 1650. But also to enter into a contemporary house is not necessarily to find in it only contemporary furniture and paintings. I have seen an ultramodern house with Empire furniture in it and paintings by Matisse. There happens to be at the moment of writing these words a nostalgic vogue for Victorian furniture and decoration, where only a few years ago everyone was buying early American. But the Americans of the middle nineteenth century and colonial times did not try to be Victorian and colonial; they *were* it. They did not think that they were quaint and interesting; they were just themselves. Revivals, however ephemeral, draw out of the past qualities which were not in it for the men who lived in the past. The vogue for Greek and Latin names which was part of the classic revival may have had overtones of the Republican political philosophy, but when a real Roman was called Horace or Vergil or Julius, it was no more because of a political philosophy than when an Irishman is given the Hebrew name of Michael, it is because of a love for Hebraism. There is no mystery concealed in all this. People vary in their sensitivity to fashion, though some social groups make more of it than others. I am not minimizing the importance of what are labeled prestige values and status symbols, but am simply saying that someone creates them: they do not arise spontaneously. There were real people who sincerely admired Neo-Gothic architecture in America's romantic period, liked dark rooms, heavy hangings, gold frames, and plush. There are still people who admire these things, but not for the same reasons. It could not be for the same reasons, for no one in 1960 can possibly have the same mentality as anyone in 1840. For even if he consciously fights to preserve the past, he differs from his ancestors in that they were not fighting to preserve any past at all but were being modern.

Now when one says that tastes and standards of excellence are relative to cultures, it is immediately replied that this leads to chaos. Relativism in values is said to reduce to everyone's being as right as everyone else. This of course is nonsense. The difference between a relativistic and an absolutistic sentence is that the former is more accurate. The heights of mountains are measured relative to sea level, not to the center of the earth; weights are calculated relative to altitude and latitude; colors are usually determined relative to sunlight. It is the method used for such determinations which are absolute, not the findings. Any logical conclusion is relative to one's premises. Any laboratory investigation is relative to the instruments of observation and measurement. When an astronomer subtracts the observer's personal equation, it is because he does not want his results to be influenced by it. But if one is engaged in research in which the personal equation is integral to the problem, one cannot in justice subtract it. Recent developments in perceptual psychology have shown that what we perceive is in part determined by our emotional set, our expectations, our "hypotheses," our apperceptive mass, and so on. These are items from which no one can be liberated. Gombrich has shown how far this counts in our perception of works of art. The old standard impersonal perceptual object has gone by the board for the simple reason that it cannot be discovered. But aside from the contribution of the individual's congenital traits, if cultural forces influence a man's values to a detectable degree, then they cannot be omitted from one's calculations when values are in question. One can always, if one wishes, rise to a level of abstraction which neglects such factors, but the price is too heavy to pay, for when the appraiser vanishes, so do the appraisals.

The main premise of cultural relativism is the observation that individual beings in complete isolation are ineffable. But this isolation in itself is relative to the means chosen to produce it. Let us imagine a set of paintings by Giotto, Raphael, Leonardo, Titian, Fouquet, Van Eyck, Rembrandt, Poussin, Rubens, David, Géricault, Monet, Delaroche, Couture, Toulouse-Lautrec, Albert

Moore, Picasso, Tobey, Klee, and Kandinski; let us overlook the fact that they were painted in various countries at various times by various artists; let us then try to say something which will be true of all of them. Such a potpourri of pictures will have nothing more in common than their all being pictures. But we knew that to begin with. The property of their being pictures is what we started with and the problem which confronts us is why Giotto did not paint like Kandinski or even Van Eyck, why Italian painting of the fifteenth century is not like French painting of the eighteenth century, why Vermeer was forgotten and Van Gogh suddenly became popular, why Landseer is now only of historical interest and Constable a great master. These questions are not to be answered by saying that they were all painters or all human beings or all in search of the beautiful, for where there is no perception of difference there is no problem. There must have been something in, let us say, Fra Angelico and in the culture for which he painted which made his work different from that of Degas.

In mathematics the indefinables play the role of individuals. They are pointed to, not described. The definables are as they are relative to the indefinables. If one starts with points as indefinables, one defines lines as classes of points, planes as classes of lines, solids as classes of planes; but the reverse could be done just as well and solids could have been taken as our indefinables, their intersection defining planes, the intersection of planes defining lines, that of lines defining points. In the physical sciences where measurements are involved, lengths, velocities, weights, and so on, they are all, as we have said, relative to the observer's method, to such reference points as sea level, the fixed stars, the position of the sun, room temperature, even to average readings. When we are interested in classifications, and hence identifications, the pragmatic factor becomes of importance: what are we going to use the classifications for? We may want simply something that will be coherent with the traditional system. After all, the system of the four elements lasted well into the eighteenth century. After

Lavoisier it had to go, not because it would not work on the level
of uncontrolled observation, but because scientists had moved off
of that level. Sometimes coherence with theological, ethical, and
political presuppositions determine our classifications, as may be
seen in the history of geology, of biology, and of psychology. But
the very desire for system is itself supported only by the assumption that Nature is systematic. To lump all the Leguminosae together was a triumph of the taxonomic imagination. But that does
not mean that the man who wants a crop of beans should plant
wisteria. As the content becomes more complex, the investigator
has a choice of point of view. An acre of land may be discussed
from the geological, the pictorial, the religious (as in Wordsworth), the agricultural, and the economic points of view. But
the farmer does not have to think of its beauty before planting his
crops; he will stop at soil chemistry. It is true that sedimentary
soils have an agricultural value which granitic soils do not have,
but all the farmer wants to know is what the soil is like at the time
he is trying to get his living from it, not what its past history has
been. The lumberman is not concerned with the moral effects of
a vernal wood. And though a baby may be the hope of a dynasty,
the child psychologist does not care whether the royal name is
transmitted or not. Such remarks show, perhaps because of their
very triteness, that what something is, is relative to an observer's
interest at the time of observing it. It is admitted that the accepted points of view have themselves a history which is part of
the total history of culture.

When one speaks of the total history of culture, one has in
mind a rope of many strands which are intimately intertwined.
It is of course our custom to untwist these strands and to speak
of the history of science, of art, of philosophy, and of everything
else as if each thing could exist in isolation from everything else.
This is an important enterprise and should not be deprecated.
But nevertheless one should always keep in mind that the separation of human interests from one another is made for a definite
purpose, nothing more than facility of discussion. Each strand

has some effect upon its neighbors and they reciprocally on it. The lateral frontiers are very vague and as total history moves along, we find economics influencing politics and politics influencing economics, religion influencing art and art influencing religion, science influencing technology and practice influencing theory. There seems to be no way of declaring a priori what strain of human activity will be ineffectual in modifying the course of some other. For the methodological rules of a science are sometimes derived from ideas whose original source is no longer known. Is the rule *ex nihilo nihil* derived from the observation that artisans have to have pre-existent matter before they can make anything? From a bit of reasoning that if something can be made out of nothing, then anything can happen? From the desire to simplify, as an artist might, one's scientific theories? From the religious, or, if you will, theological, idea that creation *ex nihilo* is a prerogative of God alone? From the philosophical idea of two worlds, one of mystery, the inexplicable, and the other of reason? As it stands the statement looks like a description; in use it is an imperative. It says to the scientist, "When you are explaining an event, look for the antecedent events without which it would not have occurred, and check this by looking for those events in whose presence it will always occur—other things being equal." The situation is analogous to what one finds when one is writing a biography. A human being is what he is because of his ancestry as discovered in his genes, because of his relations with other human beings, both alive and dead, for most of their influences will come from what they have written or are reported to have written; because of the place where he lives, urban or rural, small town or large city; because of the prestige of the country in which his home is located, for this will determine the language which he speaks and the number of other languages which he has to read; because of the availability of theaters, museums, large libraries; because of that nebulous thing, the standard of living. And so it goes. Yet one cannot write a truthful biography which is devoted exclusively to any one of these important elements. For no cause operates upon a completely passive subject. Two men may read the same book, as is obvious, and react to it differently. To read, let us say, *Pilgrim's Progress* if one is a native of Siam and a Theravada Buddhist, is not to have the same experience as one would have who is a native of Boston and a Congregationalist. The various strains of influence obviously act together in combinations of different sorts and their effectiveness is going to alter in relation to differences in the individual.

The hope of the cultural relativist is to be able to discover just what the effect of culture is on a given individual. We know that certain cultural factors do have an important effect on the molding of a man's mind as a whole. A person first gets his language from the culture into which he is born; he also gets his initial standards of right and wrong, beautiful and ugly, from it; it circumscribes his experience of the past as its schools, libraries, museums, and theaters offer him opportunities to widen his knowledge. From these he cannot escape, even if he tries to. Now it is not yet possible to formulate reasonable scientific laws expressing all these relationships, but that does not prevent us from seeing their importance. One has only to imagine a man who has no language, no family, no school, no society whatsoever, and ask oneself what his standards would be. Such a monster could not exist; that is obvious. He would be like Condillac's statue before it was gifted with the sense of smell. Nevertheless we can in our imagination see what each of these relationships might contribute to his growth and thus escape from the error of positing a human being who is so generalized that he resembles everyone else and so detached from his historical moment that he is a mere formula. The pathos of the universal and eternal is of no help here. Works of art are not made by angels but by men.

However tiresome repetition may be, we must again repeat that we are not maintaining the utter difference of every man from every other man. We recognize that all men have something in common, that which is presumably described in biology and its ancillary sciences. But again, these are not the men who make works of art and live in a culture. It is all very well for ethnologists to point out that insofar as we are biological specimens we have similar needs; that is granted. But the problem is to find a society which permits its members to satisfy their needs in any way they wish. All societies, we are told, have incest-taboos; but the definitions of incest vary, even within the canon law.[2] All societies recognize that their members must eat; but what they can eat, when they can eat it, with whom they can eat it, vary. All societies recognize that people die and that their bodies must be disposed of; but they all also have rules about the proper way to die, the effect of dying upon one's future life, and the correct disposal of bodies. A dead body probably has no feelings about whether it lies in consecrated ground or on the slab of a medical school; but few men die without leaving behind them people who do care deeply about this. Ethnologists who are tempted to indulge in generalizations so broad that they would lump the Catholic, Jewish, Buddhist, Moslem, American Indian, Hottentot rites for the dead together, would do well to ask members of these religious bodies whether they too agree that all these rites are equally valuable. Or again, tell a Moslem or a Jew that the prohibition against eating pork is a food-taboo no different from the Egyptian prohibition against eating fish. Tell a Catholic that the sacrament of marriage is not essentially different from jumping over a broomstick in the presence of witnesses or from simply signing a book. Or tell him, if you dare, that Communion is a form of cannibalism. The experiments might not change the mind of an ethnologist, but they should prove useful to an art critic.

For even if the critic starts with differences in taste, he will soon find that bare liking and disliking are tied to cultures. If one were invited to a wedding and found the church hung with black crepe, no flowers near the chancel rail and a single taper burning on the altar, the bride entering in a long black gown and veil covering her, the organ playing the "Dead March" from *Saul*, one would wonder whether this was a macabre joke or simple evidence of insanity. It will surely be retorted that, though black may be suitable for very chic occasions, dinner parties for instance, it is not suitable for weddings. It will be admitted that suitability is determined by our associations with black, not with black itself. That suffices to show how a culture may determine the aesthetic effect of even a color, if one may call black a color. It is not black as a color which is being disliked; it is black as a color for a wedding dress. Once that is granted, the battle for absolutes is lost.

Does this then open the doors to chaos? Not at all. First, we are all members of some culture and the sense of belonging to that culture is a great satisfaction. Even the rebel wants to live with other rebels. Thoreau, the symbol of American individualism and rebellion, used to return from Walden to Concord to see his friends, to talk with them, and to eat their food. He also read books and, what is perhaps more significant, he wrote them too. He wrote his books either to fortify the feelings of those who were fellow rebels or to convert others to rebellion. Why this need for fellowship is so deeply ingrained in us may well come from our dependence on others for the satisfactions of all our needs. I say "may" because this does not happen to be one of those problems to which an answer can be found in any textbook. In any event man is not only a social animal, but he has to be one. Robinson Crusoe had to have his ship as a source of supply; the Swiss Family Robinson went into isolation as a family and, moreover, there was always the mother with her hoard of useful objects in her ever-present bag; all had been educated in a highly civilized society in Western Europe and had not lost their memories along with their possessions and shipmates. Hence the conjecture that the need for others has decided survival value. But it is one thing to need a grocer from whom one can buy bread and butter; it is another to need men with whose ideas and feelings one can sympathize. Even when a society within a society has been formed for specific purposes, its members will tend to stick together after those purposes have been achieved. Pleasure clubs, as they used to be called, exist everywhere and it would be foolish to maintain that they exist for any purpose other than that which their name suggests.

Luncheon clubs, dinner clubs, discussion clubs, art clubs, literary clubs, sports clubs, are not needed to provide luncheons, dinners, discussions, art, literature, and sport; such things can be had almost anywhere and in any company. They exist partly from habit and partly from the sheer pleasure of being in the company of people whom one happens to like. No more profound explanation is to be looked for.

Why is it that the eclectic is so scorned? Because he seems to have no single definite taste, no sharply defined principles, no ideas of his own. One is expected to belong to a church, to have been through a certain course of study, to accept certain rules of behavior in social affairs, to have read the great classics and been subjected to the best paintings and music, if only in reproduction. Each stratum of society or, if one prefers, each social group, will be cemented not only by its original program but also by its community of likes and especially dislikes. The tendency of men to form groups seems to be more than an appropriate target for satire. It would not be so common if it did not answer to some desire. Everyone cannot be abnormal. To be a man is a disease only if man ought to be an animal and nothing more. Normality is a statistical concept and, if men on the whole do something or are something or other, then that defines what normal humanity is. That being so, the differences among human beings in the respects which are in question here are differences not in conformity and nonconformity, but differences among what ideals, tastes, beliefs, customs, pursuits form the various groups. At the same time, it is folly to overlook the diversity of these groups and their reciprocal hostility at times. But that simply shows that within the larger group known as "society," there are smaller groups known as societies.

We have suggested that every art in its origin is magic. Magic is performed for a definite purpose, changing the course of history, including naturally one's personal history. A special social group exists in some societies, the priesthood, to perform the magic rites. But just as the silliest superstitions are retained in society, so are the magical rites. We laugh at the superstitions, unless we actually believe in them, but we do not laugh at the obsolescent rites. There is a very good reason for this, aside from the desire to preserve the past. To take the most obvious example, erotic feelings may be aroused as much by a picture or statue as by a woman. One may talk as much as one pleases about aesthetic distance, the fact remains that only a eunuch would fail to feel the stirrings of the flesh in front of certain paintings and statues. Otherwise there would not be this everlasting talk of pornography and immoral art. Moreover, people have been known to weep in the theater and even at the movies. The simplest percussive rhythms may set the feet tapping and the head nodding. But this is just as much magic as there is in the sympathetic magic of the savage. A picture becomes a substitute for real experience. This has been well-defined by E. H. Gombrich in his "Meditations on a Hobby Horse." [3] A work of art, whether pictorial or not, creates a second world for us, a world of illusion to be sure, but nevertheless more satisfactory in some way than the real world. Portraits, for instance, are clearly icons, but usually their painters try to bring out into the open some trait of character which others have failed to see or might forget. This is true even of photographs. The portrait, need I say, is not the person portrayed; it is a substitute for him. Its effect upon a spectator will be to make him admire, dislike, understand, question the person represented. It is in short a symbol, analogous to a relic, a lock of hair, a tooth, a bone, the grave, even if it be an empty cenotaph. Surely there is no need for me to enlarge upon the emotional power of such symbols and relics. We live surrounded by them: family possessions, family photographs, the flag, public monuments, the gowns of the presidents' wives, Lincoln's bed in the White House, battlefields, Plymouth Rock, flasks of water from the Jordan, urns of earth transferred from Normandy or the Argonne, old letters from friends, autographs, association copies of books, and even restored villages and towns. There will always be found someone to sneer at such things. His ridicule is based on what he will call the irrationality of it all. Of course it is irrational; that is its power. For all arts are fed by emotion and their rationality is the logic of feeling. Feeling requires no argument to prove itself; it just comes into being and vanishes the moment when it is examined.

A portrait of John Smith's great-grandmother may have no importance for anyone but him. A portrait of a village worthy, the founder of a college, the benefactor of a city, a national leader, king or queen or president, will exert its magic on more people simply because more people have been affected by the person depicted. So strong is this power that in the Soviet Union the portraits of Stalin have had to be removed and his embalmed body taken from Red Square to be put beneath the ground. The body cannot feel its disgrace, but the public can. One can perhaps wipe out the memory of a great man but not his existence. It was obviously the ceremony of disgrace in this case which was important. But such a ceremony is nothing more than a magical device. When a magician recites a meaningless verbal formula, the words have to be repeated in exactly the same form each time the ceremony is performed, just as in the Mass, the Latin words, *Hoc est corpus meum*, must be said in Latin. Meaningless words are about as far removed from rationality as any human gesture could well be. But that has nothing to do with the case. I know of no painting of Christ in which He is depicted as a Jewish peasant, son of a carpenter, except Millais' famous "Christ in the Carpenter Shop," which Dickens so heartily disliked. No one knows what Jesus looked like, but He was certainly neither the Pantocrator of Daphni nor the stern executioner of Michelangelo's "Last Judgment" nor the limp and spineless lantern-bearer of Holman Hunt's "Light of the World." It was in fact the artists' good luck that there were no authentic portraits or descriptions of Jesus; no one any longer accepts Josephus' description as authentic. Good luck, because it left the painter free to turn his portrait into a symbol of that side of Christ's teachings which seemed most important to him. As in early Buddhism, there were no portraits of the Redeemer; there were only aniconic symbols: the Cross, the

Fish, the sacred monogram. But these were more effective magically in that they did not commit anyone to accepting a concrete representation of a human being whose very concreteness and unavoidable individuality would lessen his symbolic value and power. What was wanted was a symbol of a set of beliefs and, if one thought that the Crucifixion was the central event in the history of Christianity, the Cross by itself would be more efficacious than a crucified body on the Cross. It is no refutation of what I am saying to point out that the cross is an ancient solar symbol; the meaning of a symbol is conferred upon it by those who use it. As a solar symbol the cross did not in anyway "mean" vicarious atonement, universal redemption, or inherited guilt, or suggest the incarnation and look forward to the resurrection. These meanings and associations were conferred upon it by Christianity and it would be absurd to deny this. If Jesus had been shot by arrows, as Saint Sebastian was, then it is true that the ancient solar symbol would not have been used. But the fact is that it was used and that two straight lines, one traversing the other at a right angle, took on a religious quality which they did not have before.

What this shows is that a simple geometrical figure can become invested with significance not inherent in it as a geometrical figure. The cross acquired this significance because of its resemblance to an instrument of torture which was actually used on a specific historical occasion. To an Eskimo, a Kaffir, or a Maori who had not been visited by Christian missionaries, it could not have had that significance. To a Buddhist or Hindu who might have suffered from missionary interference with his religious practices, it might well be an object of horror, as it is to some Jews and was to some English Puritans. To a Communist it is a symbol of superstition and therefore an object of derision, if not of contempt. It is therefore not its shape which gives it its magical power. It is its shape plus men's associations with it. If the world should be converted to Buddhism, the Wheel would take the place of the Cross. And if it should go Communist, then the Hammer and Sickle would take on the same kind of aura. It will, I think, be granted that in cases such as these the significance of the icon is relative to the culture in which it is used. What could the Lamb of God mean to a people who knew nothing of the Passover?

One can illustrate the same point from mythological paintings. Most mythological paintings and sculptures, as well as mythological metaphors, come to us from classical antiquity. How much the sophisticated Greek or Roman believed in what the myths related, I do not know. But it is at least possible, in view of Plato's attitude, that of Euhemerus, to say nothing of Lucian, that they believed in them in much the same way as a modern sophisticated Christian believes in the first two chapters of Genesis. At most he would follow Clement of Alexandria in saying that everything in the Bible had both a literal meaning and a symbolic meaning existing on various levels. To such people a representation of Venus and Adonis, for instance, was a picture of an actual goddess and her terrestrial lover. But it might also be an epigram on the vulnerability of Love. If the painting represented Venus and Mars, he might see it both as two deities who were in love with each other or as testimony to a scurrilous story in Homer. We may assume that any Greek or Roman likely to see such a picture would have read Homer. Now if a Florentine of the later fifteenth century, or a Frenchman of the sixteenth who had read Leone Ebreo, were to see such a painting, he would see Venus as a symbol of Love and Mars as a symbol of Strife and would then embroider on the theme of the reconciliation of two opposites, with references to Empedocles. The artist who had painted the picture, and there were plenty of Italians who did the theme, might well have seen it as an opportunity to paint two nudes, just as artists saw in Saint Sebastian a chance to paint Apollo in Christian form. This gives us three aspects of the painting, determined by the culture in which the spectator is living. The myth has taken on emblematic meaning. And the person whose imagination runs to such things could interpret the incident as Love conquering War or War conquering even Love. In short the work of art has turned into an impetus to the imagination to extend itself into fields which need not have been, and probably were not, in the artist's mind. Before one realizes what one is doing, one has gone well beyond the frontiers of the painting into a complex of ideas, emotions, attitudes, whose source was not the painting at all.

Now one of the features of magic is to turn things into something which they are not. Magic is the realization of the impossible. But nothing is impossible in art. The artist can create a world which is more intelligible, better, and more beautiful than the real world, if he wishes to. He obviously can transport us to distant times and places while we sit immobile in our armchairs. The magic in this is in the enforced surrender of our skepticism while we are within the picture, the covers of the book, or in the theater. But as in a magic rite, we have to give assent temporarily to what is going on. We have to participate in the ritual through capitulation, much as when at a spiritualistic séance, we must first be willing to believe before the spirits will perform. There is no physical contact between the magician and the effect which he is about to produce. What he does is scientifically irrelevant. So in religious acts, a man behaves as a magician when he prays before a statue and expects his thoughts to produce effects spatially remote from the object of his attention. Spatiotemporal details are of no importance. When one looks at Rembrandt's painting of Aristotle contemplating the bust of Homer, one does not first consult an archaeologist to find out whether that bust existed in Aristotle's time or not; one suspends criticism and lets the painting do its work.

The art of magic is of course highly ritualized. It will be effective, as we all know, only if the ritual is perfectly performed. Every detail must be ordered according to rule. But this has always been true of artistry also, up to very recent times. But even in the most accidental type of artistry, the submission of the artist to accident is a rule, and woe betide the painter who stops to think. Such an artist is like Plato's Ion, the Rhapsode, who had to be inspired, maddened by the god. It is the afflatus of his genius which creates his works of art. In our times our works of art have split off from the primitive complex in which they were born and have developed new functions of their own. But these functions too are successful only if the artist is, to use the words of Delacroix, as a serpent brandished in the hand of a Pythoness. The modern artist would not use such language. He would substitute the Unconscious for the divine afflatus, but the effect would be the same.

Finally, the artist like the magician forms a special class within society, is recognized as having the right to dress differently, to have his own code of behavior, and to demand special rewards. He will not think of his works of art as commercial products to be bought and sold and the very word "commercial" has taken on a pejorative meaning. So the priest and the shaman are peculiar people, have their own language, costume, manners, and privileges. The artist invests his business with mystery while demanding that everyone understand him. When he withdraws into himself and then expresses what he finds there, he expects his fellow men to be as interested in his discoveries as he is. His world may be that of the Collective Unconscious, the child within the womb, the wise innocent, the dreamer, and he assumes the right not merely to explore such worlds, which no one can deny him, but to insist that others share his enthusiasm for them. The procedure may well be more efficacious than one would imagine. For art is always an invitation to enter into the unknown and to enter into it without danger.

It may of course be contended that all this is irrelevant to our appreciation of art. But it is nevertheless relevant to human interests in art. Our fashion of stripping works of art of everything which does not conform to some aesthetician's theory is peculiar to one stratum of our society and is in no sense of the word obligatory on all of us. It would be absurd to object to the making of purely abstract painting, if such a thing is possible, but it would be equally absurd to maintain that only what is abstract in a painting is to be enjoyed. It is indeed doubtful whether the most abstract design can be seen only as that. For every shape, every color has some associations with a man's past and, when a person is moved by an abstraction, those associations are, as far as anyone knows, the cause of its magic. Such associations are partly personal but also in part attributable to the social milieu in which a man has been educated. And since what is loosely called Freudian symbolism has become part of almost everyone's background, those apparently meaningless shapes, movements, rhythms, and colors have taken on a meaning of which people were not aware before Freud, though they might well have been stirred by them. To urge a man to see nothing but form in a work of art, using the word "form" to mean design or order, is to urge him to overlook the humor and sometimes the pathos in Daumier, the tragedy in *Hamlet*, the philosophy in the *Four Quartettes*, and the religion in *The Brothers Karamazov*. Why we should be told to blind our eyes to the very things which turn us to the arts for solace, enlightenment, and simple pleasure, is a mystery to me. It is of course true that the cause of the effect of a work of art lies in its form, but we need not always be exclusively interested in causes. That is the road to emotional starvation and intellectual triviality. There just happens to be more in any work of art than its artistry, and we have a good reason for wanting to absorb as much of it as our capabilities permit.

Cultural relativism then is nothing more than a doctrine which insists first, on the fact that every man lives in some cultural environment; second, in the contribution of that environment to his ways of thinking, his standards of right and wrong, good and bad, beauty and ugliness. It is not a plea for everyone to ask himself what the influence of his culture has been on his likes and dislikes, his approbation and disapprobation. If it is any sort of plea, it is a plea for the understanding of disagreement in matters of taste, for abandoning aesthetic dogma, and for sincerity of judgment. It is only thus that the history of art and of criticism will make any sense, for it alone admits that everyone cannot be wrong. Even when false ideas about fact have been general, there is a reason for it. Changes in taste, like changes in ideas, are not the result of sin.

On Nonfigurative Painting

IF ONE WILL take the trouble to read *Artists on Art,* compiled and edited by Robert Goldwater and Marco Treves, New York (Pantheon), 2d ed. rev., 1945, one will see that the classic tradition, as formulated by the painters themselves, is that as far as subject matter goes, painting is an imitation of nature and that, as far as artistry is concerned, it is colored drawing.

Since about 1905, which I choose as the date of the first exhibition of the Fauves, a new kind of painting has evolved out of the old. Cubism, futurism, surrealism, dynamism, minimalism, abstractionism, nonobjectivism, and all the other modern movements in painting connote one thing in common: whatever else painting is, it is not an imitation of nature in the sense that one finds on a canvas recognizable objects. One sometimes finds pieces of a recognizable object, as in some of Picasso's Cubist paintings, or deformations of recognizable objects, as in the early Dali and Chirico, but in general it is safe to say that even when the painters use the word *Nature* in their manifestoes, they are not thinking of nature as a complex of people, trees, mountains, fish, and so on, the looks of which they transfer to a canvas as painters did up to and including the Neo-Impressionists. Though we cannot here discuss with any thoroughness the reasons for this revolution, one thing cannot, I think, be disputed: the painting is now projected upon the canvas from the artist's imagination unguided by anything which he sees in ordinary vision. It is either what he has imagined in a dream, or in fantasy, or thanks to the uncontrolled operations of his Unconscious. He has not reproduced what his eyes tell him about the visual aspects of the objective world. On the contrary, he has rejected the objective and impersonal world.

One has only to compare a photograph of a natural object with even the most careful pictorial representation of it to see that no painting has ever been photographic. Even when a photographer refuses to arrange the lighting, to compose his picture, to touch up his plates, the camera makes near things bigger than distant things with the result that sometimes feet or heads or hands are monstrously swollen. Such fidelity to linear perspective is never accepted by the painter. He knows that a foot, for instance, looks queer if it is painted to look bigger than it "ought" to look. He consequently reduces its size, regardless of perspective and the reports of the camera. Other arrangements, for the sake of design, both of shapes and of colors are too well-known to require any notice here. At most the naturalistic painter gives us verisimilitude, not factual truth. But ironically enough, he distorts to make things seem more natural.

Objectively there are only two things which can appear in any painting, shapes and colors. These may in themselves and in combination stimulate certain emotions, but that is beside the point here. Moreover they are never simply shapes and colors, but the shapes and colors of things and are seen with the things. The moment that a painter is convinced that he can produce only shapes and colors, and that he has no obligation to produce the shapes and colors of objective things, he will, if, like Picasso, he has some nostalgia for the natural world, abstract the shapes of natural objects and organize them on his canvas or abstract the colors and organize them, or do both on the same canvas.

By simplifying the human body, for instance, as Léger did, he may decide that the human head is an ovoid, the trunk and arms cylinders, and he will produce an abstract formula or pattern of the human body. So Bracelli did a series of "Caprices" in which human beings became compositions of cubes, springs, disks, all threaded together like the limbs of a lay-figure. This might be called abstraction through simplification. The results have sometimes been produced by the limitations of instruments, as when human figures are highly schematized in cross-stitching or animals in heraldry. Such results, however, are not those of the modern painter. Yet our acceptance of them shows that it is not the distortion which shocks us but the distortion in an unfamiliar context.

If we admit the legitimacy of abstraction through simplification, then one of the conclusions we shall draw is that the geometrical forms underlying the visual forms are of more aesthetic interest than the visual forms themselves. The fan-shaped elm tree, the pyramidal pine, the heart-shaped lilac leaf and the rondel of the daisy, to use examples which recall Ruskin, are presumably more beautiful when abstracted from the objects in which they are incorporated than the objects themselves. I say more beautiful, but any other eulogistic term would do within reason. We could say more emotionally satisfying, for instance, more stirring, or even more elevating since in a way they represent universal ideas rather than particular things. When they are used in applied ornament, in architecture, weaving, or carving, this is usually granted. And it might also be granted that in themselves they have a kind of beauty since they stand for order and harmony, for the pure intelligibility of geometry. Once it is admitted that what makes a human head beautiful is its oval shape, then why not simply substitute an oval shape for a head? And if it is these simple geometrical figures which delight us, why not construct canvases which like those of Bauer will be nothing more than geometrical assemblages? They would have no reference to physical objects but would rely entirely upon their purity of shape and line for their aesthetic effect.

But there has always been more to a visual object, whether a human being or not, than a shape or a set of lines. That something is of course motion. For even when a painting represents people in repose, the eye is induced to move about in the canvas, sometimes violently, sometimes quietly. What I have called in the body of my text the arabesques of Rubens illustrate this perfectly. There are times, as in the famous "Rape of the Daughters of Leucippus," where the subject represented is violent, but there are other times, as in his double portrait of himself and his first wife (in Munich), where the figures are in repose but the visual movement is nevertheless present. Even the most elementary books on art appreciation consent to emphasize this aspect of shapes and lines and Kandinski has shown us how much dynamism may be put on a canvas in which there are no recognizable figures at all. Hence a painting may be utterly without natural reference and yet have vitality in the sense of action. But when there are three possible foci of interest in a work of art, it is always possible that critics and artists as well will maintain that one of the three is essential and the other two accidental, or inessential.

Thus in the paintings of men like Mondriaan and Albers we find the dynamic element and color pretty well eliminated and spacing elevated to the rank of the essential. Color is present of course, especially in Albers, and he may think it of great aesthetic importance. But it is his simple squares superimposed which seem to catch the eye first and their color seems to function only as a means of differentiating one square from another. But in Mondriaan areas have given way to lines and only straight lines at that. Mondriaan here has done what the classic architects of the early Renaissance and of colonial America did, design façades which are flat and on which only the fenestration counts as creating a pattern. The spacing of the windows in a Florentine

palazzo or a New England farmhouse is admitted by all to be
very satisfying to the eye. If it is the spacing which has the
aesthetic value, then why not transfer it to a canvas and let
the eye enjoy it unimpeded by historical, religious, or other
similar associations?

But a painting by either Bauer or Mondriaan looks as if it had
been composed with ruler and T-square. The hand of man must
have been at work here but its work has been concealed. Such
paintings might be criticized as being too mechanical by people
who do not admire machines. No one to the best of my knowledge ever saw Giotto's O, but I suspect that what was so wonder-
ful about it was its having been drawn freehand. And if it was
drawn freehand, there would inevitably have been traces of the
hand which drew it visible in it. The calligraphic factor would
have been there just as it is in all drawings. The question which
naturally arises to one's lips is whether a beautiful manuscript is
more or less beautiful than a printed version of the same text.

If what is wanted in a painting is evidence of the man who
made it, and if the painting is to remain abstract, then the painter
will do everything in his power to impress his own personality
on his canvases. A painting may be just as abstract as another
and yet be tidy, neat, closely organized, and obviously controlled.
The amount of work which must go into a painting by Mark
Tobey is staggering. Those lines which move by centimeters, criss-
cross, tremble, shoot forward and retreat again, are not made
without deliberation. Their deliberateness is in the tradition of
Holbein or even Memling. It is a tradition which can be exaggerated into finickiness and absorption in detail, but since
Tobey's paintings are often the repetition of one detail, that
would not apply to him. On the other extreme is the forceful
hand which can express itself only in swoops, loads its wide brush
with paint and lets go. A great swoop from right to left, crossed
by an oblique from top to bottom, results in something remotely
resembling a giant Chinese character. It for its part continues
the tradition of such men as Frans Hals whose every brush stroke

seems to have been put down once and for all and afterwards has suffered no correction. In both these cases the hand is in control and the artist self-assertive. There is no overlooking the human character of such works.

To that extent they have to be rejected by those who have rejected humanity. For the doctrine has been advanced by such people as the Surrealists that conscious control of artistry is slavery. No one wants to be a slave. Liberation then must be sought and it will be found in forgetting plans, programs, and rules, and simply plunging into one's work and letting fortune take over. There have always been men interested in natural beauties. Leonardo, in a well-known passage, suggested that the artist look at stains and cracks in walls and elaborate them into faces. Baltrusaitis has studied works of art which have been made in similar ways. But neither Leonardo nor his disciples—if they were his disciples—ever suggested that the artist should abdicate as a conscious workman and submit entirely to accident. There were probably plenty of accidental effects in the paintings even of the cavemen, for how could they have been avoided? They were a welcome addition to the fruits of artistry. When by a happy stroke of the brush a satisfying effect is produced, it would be folly to eliminate it because it was not planned. But to turn a work of art into a happy accident and leave it at that, reduces the consciousness of the artist to zero.

That this does not necessarily result in an ugly or even an uninteresting picture is obvious. As a visual object, such pictures may surely be as beautiful as anything in nature. Unless one wants to speak of natural beauties as divine works of art, it has to be granted that physical and chemical forces alone are capable of creating things just as beautiful as anything made by man. This has been granted for centuries and became almost programmatic during the so-called Romantic period. But then no one, except when he was speaking metaphorically, ever thought of such sights as works of art. Moreover, everyone has always admitted that large areas of color, such as the blue sky or the ocean or a stretch of desert, are beautiful. But again there is a difference between the summer sky and a canvas covered with a wash of cerulean blue, even if the latter should perfectly reproduce the former. The difference of course is not in what is visual but in what the observer reads into it.

Aside from all that, what is of peculiar interest is the insistence upon reducing the artist to an ineffectual factor in creating works of art. He becomes simply the medium through which accident operates, no more important than the paint, the brush, the canvas, or any other of the accompanying circumstances among which a painting comes into being. His works of art turn into natural objects, in spite of their being made by a man and, though there is surely nothing wrong in this, what is right in it?

What is right seems at least to one observer to be the flat assertion of the individual's insignificance. One of the things which differentiates men from the beasts is art in the old-fashioned sense of that term, the sense which denotes conscious and deliberate control of one's medium and tools and possibly also a preliminary idea of what one is trying to make. This feeling of the triviality of the human will and the futility of its trying to produce anything is, if not a result, at least an accompaniment of a sheaf of ideas which have intimidated us since the rise of the natural sciences to the point at which we find them now. Some philosophers have for the last 150 years been drumming it into us that everything we do is determined first by our heredity and environment, then by physical and chemical laws, by economic laws, and finally by historical laws. A man does not, it is true, choose his genes, but he does modify his environment, sometimes by simply moving away from it, as Henry James and T. S. Eliot did. A billiard ball will be submissive to the Law of the Parallelogram of Forces, but the direction and velocity with which it hits another billiard ball are *its* direction and velocity and they are not entirely dependent on the force of the cue. Economic laws describe in part what men do and not merely what the nonhuman world does. And as for historical laws, no one has as yet succeeded in making them precise and, should someone accomplish this, he too would be describing human behavior in part at least. But none of that is so much to the point as the actual fact that some of us have become intimidated into thinking that we are nonentities and merely the butt of forces beyond our control.

It is one thing to be scared and another to act scared. Some of us during the two wars were scared, but we learned to conceal our fright and to combat it. This may have been silly and indeed hypocritical. But at any rate it was an attempt to solve a problem in characteristically human terms. I admit that if everyone had been scared and had acted scared, the wars would have been over almost as soon as they started and that would have been a highly desirable effect. But, as we all know, the incidence of fright, like the incidence of everything else, varies and whereas some of us submitted to our terror, others did not. It is the latter group who were the more typically human. Their very bravado was symptomatic of their humanity. The acceptance on the other hand of human impotence is the acceptance of death, and it is very interesting to observe the symbols of horror and death which have been read into the paintings of our times, not merely those which are painted in a semiautomatic manner by dribbles and splashes, but also in those the workmanship of which is exquisitely controlled.

None of this applies to the action-painters in the way it applies to unconscious and automatic art. It is true that our Unconscious is more potent than our Conscious, but no psychoanalyst ever thought that we should deny conscious controls. If he had, he would have thrown up the sponge as a therapist. An action-painter at least leaves a record of his power; an accidentalist, if I may use that term, leaves us a record of his impotence. Every artist of course bequeaths to posterity a self-confession, and it must be read by those who know the language. But nevertheless he leaves more also. And that more is the communication of positive feelings and ideas.

There is always the possibility that we have come to the end of the road and that painting is obsolescent. The crooning of a baby, like the singing of a bird, is charming, I suppose, but a little goes a long way. Similarly, doodles can be charming in what they tell us of the doodler. But again one exhausts their content after a few moments. To squeeze a tube of paint upon a canvas and let it ooze wherever gravity takes it may produce an emotional effect which is very deep. But we are not forced to satisfy the "excremental vision" twenty-four hours a day. We have all seen canvases of Vermeer, of Constable, of Seurat, of Utrillo, and of Picasso which are only a foot or two square and which hold our attention for hours. But a canvas five by seven on which a sponge of color has been thrown and allowed to drip soon wearies the eye and bores the imagination. It reminds one of the hum of traffic when one wakes up at night, a beautiful noise for a few moments but tolerable only if it soon drops out of consciousness. Perhaps the answer to this is that none of us have the time to look at a picture for very long, and that consequently what is wanted is something which will explode like a skyrocket and then fade away. But unfortunately pictures last. If painting is the art of producing a momentary impression, then it has become a new art which is the polar antithesis of that from which it evolved. For the frescoes which represent for us the origin of modern painting could not be seen in a glance and in fact had to be peered at and read.

That painting may after all be completely changed in its nature and in the direction which I have indicated is a comment on our culture and not depreciation of modern painting. In a sense when one frees the Unconscious, refuses to control repressions, and relies on accidents to communicate whatever one wishes to communicate, one testifies to the inadequacies of a culture insofar as human happiness is concerned. For happiness in part is the fruit of social ease. When a man fails to communicate in customary codes, it need not be due to any refusal on his part but to the inability of his fellows to understand him. We have all heard the hackneyed phrase, empty gestures, and it is true that the highly ritualized modes of communication become dumb through long usage. Platitudes are not merely wearisome, they may also be inane, worn out, and almost meaningless. The reckless destruction by the Cubists of natural objects which they then proceed to rearrange on a canvas may have been symptomatic of the meaninglessness of these objects when presented in literal fashion. Works of art, as we have insisted, do change their values and sometimes symbols lose their meaning and fail to take on a new one. It is not impossible that post-Cubist painting is made in a revulsion against that style of painting which had simply become intolerable through overritualization.

The ironical side of this is that when the critics stand in front of such paintings, they immediately translate them into literary terms. Thus we find J. K. in the *Art News* (January 1962) writing, "Helen Frankenthaler continues to work in the crisis area of freedom and necessity: more and more, internecine war flares where reason and unreason dance their padded knife-fight. She paints our case: how to be intelligently free under the Cheshire-cat smirk of self-consciousness. ["Black Shadow"] perhaps . . . demonstrates the savagery that obtains between the two: the black square braces against the kiss of an orange leech, while a waste of eggs and energy spumes from the jarred rigidity." Aside from the rhetorical obscurity of this passage, its specific sexual references and overtones of *Through the Looking Glass*, there can be no explicit symbolism of freedom and necessity in areas of paint on a canvas. Such a meaning can only be projected upon it from the critic's mind by an association of ideas which may be random for all one knows. Similarly, and in the same magazine, J. S. writes of one of Hopkins' paintings, "A further tension is in color: a clear yet muddied blue laid on flat with a dirtied yellow snarling down into it. . . ." Aside from such question-begging adjectives as "muddied" and "dirtied," when a color snarls down into another, the color has taken on animate traits which in the nature of things is no more rooted in it than the smile in a smiling sky or the babbling of a babbling brook. In short these critics are overworking the pathetic fallacy. If the question is asked why they do this, the answer is found in the words of one of their colleagues, N. E., who says, "Even in the most abstract drama or painting there should be some experience beyond the purview of the canvas." Whether there should or not may be questioned; but that there is, is indubitable.

Now this sort of inflated rhetoric, which goes back at least to Walter Pater's description of the "Mona Lisa," is not the specialty of those who admire contemporary art. A. Romanov, a Russian visitor to the Museum of Modern Art in New York, gave his impressions of Pollock's "Number 1" to his fellow Communists upon his return to Russia (same magazine, p. 30). He says first, "Regarding these works which dazzle the eye like a huge kaleidoscope, one can only say that their authors' irrepressible urge for the irrational leads either to a demonstrative rejection of the artistic image or to its deliberate annihilation, i.e., to the destruction of art." He points out that such paintings are "sterile and can neither delight nor move, instill joy or sorrow, but only leave the eye cold and indifferent." But then his cold and indifferent eye saw a canvas which was "an arbitrary and chaotic combination of color strains, abstract shapes and lines. . . ." It was, he continued, "futile to search for the artist's idea, his heart, his imagination and inner creative urge in that coldly premeditative conglomeration." Now a person who feels nothing at all in front of a canvas does not feel it to be chaotic, unimaginative, or coldly premeditative. He feels nothing whatsoever. It would look as if the enemies of action-painting, if "Number 1" is an action-painting, look, as N. E. does, for some experience beyond the purview of the canvas. In short, the most revolutionary techniques seem to land the critic in about the same position as the most traditional do.

I admit that writing of this sort is as confusing as the painting which it criticizes. I cannot be sure by any means of just what the critics are intending to say. But one thing seems probable:

such painting is projected upon the canvas from the mind of the artist as a slide is projected upon a screen. If it is painting *of* anything, it is painting of states of mind, of fright, of anxiety, of struggle, of joy, of despair, and the like, though as a matter of fact it is seldom painting of the more soothing emotional states. We have thus reached the point which the composers reached some generations ago and then abandoned for a generation: the point at which those emotions usually indicated by Italian terms, such as *allegro* or *energico*, indicate to the player the feeling which is supposed to be conveyed or stimulated by the composition. And it will be observed that if a spectator fails to feel the same emotion as another spectator confronted by the same canvas, that in itself does not prove that the canvas is emotionally neutral. For the same is true of music. The *allegretto* of Beethoven's *Seventh Symphony* does not sound even slightly joyful to all listeners. To some it may well sound wistful, if not melancholy.

Aside from the affective possibilities of such painting is the question of why the artist has turned his back on the external world and faced the internal alone. Could this not be attributable to the revulsion which many of us must feel toward a civilization bent on destruction and permeated with hatred? When one meditates on the amount of energy and imagination which is expended on weapons of devastation and vehicles of escape into interplanetary space, one sees that the disgust with life as it is lived at present is ubiquitous. It is true that while all this is going on, medicine, chemistry, psychology, and the humanistic disciplines are tackling, and indeed solving, more important problems, problems whose solution would enhance rather than destroy happiness. But the fact is that our attention is directed away from the program of health and well-being to that of warfare. The anxiety which is said to characterize our age is more widely felt by the reading public than by the great masses of our fellows, but it is the reading public which on the whole fixes the atmosphere in which we live. We live in terror of another war and we forget that wars are made by men and not by uncontrollable nonhuman forces. But we have also been drilled in the idea that we are impotent to change the course of history and are but playthings of the gods. No artist could feel at home in such a world, for that world has turned its back on all the arts, the arts being the one area in which man is free. The silence of John Cage and the electronic noises of Varèse cannot be sneered out of court since they are too eloquent witnesses to our contempt for humanity. When an art is negated by its very practitioners, the public can only acquiesce in the negation. What wonder then that artists have retreated into the Unconscious, the childlike, the savage, and the irrational? These happen to be the only remaining refuge.

Reference Notes

CHAPTER I: Art and Nature

1. The marvels of instinct are perhaps so well-known that they require no documentation. Professor Bergen Evans in his *Natural History of Nonsense* (New York: A. Knopf, 1946), Chap. 3, has exposed some of the absurdities which have been believed about instinctive behavior. Fabre in his *Souvenirs entomologiques* has both illustrated the marvels and shown the limitations of instinct, as far as insects are involved. S. W. Frost in *Insect Life and Insect Natural History*, now available in a paperback (Dover), discusses both the successes and the failures of instinctive behavior in insect life. Insects, he says (pp. 219 ff.), and this would probably apply to other animals as well, establish a routine which never varies and are unable to adjust to unusual conditions. The domestication of animals shows, however, that animals can adjust to some modifications of their normal environment, but how far this can be developed remains an open question. For that matter, the question may also be raised about man's ability to make analogous adjustments. For the idea that the beasts are more intelligent and happier than man, see A. O. Lovejoy and G. Boas; *Primitivism in Antiquity* (Baltimore: Johns Hopkins Press, 1935), Chap. XIII and G. Boas; *The Happy Beast* (Baltimore: Johns Hopkins Press, 1933).

2. At the present time artists whom I call great would be Schönberg, Bartók, and perhaps Hindemith in music. See, for instance, W. Mellers; *Romanticism and the 20th Century* (London: Rockliff, 1957), p. 181. This is confirmed by Professor Frederick Dorian in conversation. In painting, I should select as the inventors, Giotto, Raphael, Caravaggio, Cézanne, Picasso, and among Americans, Pollock. Raphael was not very inventive but did form a school. Sometimes an artist, like Browning, invents a new style but has few if any followers, whereas another, like Tennyson, follows a predecessor, in his case Keats, but makes noticeable modifications in his master's style and also forms a school.

3. I refer of course to the mares of Diomedes which were man-eaters. The best set of references to that legend is in J. G. Frazer's edition of *Apollodorus*, Loeb Classical Library (New York: G. P. Putnam's Sons, 1921), II, pp. 200 f.,

362 Reference Notes

n. 1 and 2. I am indebted to Col. Robert B. Ekvall for the information that Tibetans have been known to feed dried meat to their horses, for which see Sven Hedin; *Trans-Himalaya* (New York: Macmillan Co., 1909), p. 190. Col. Ekvall adds, "I myself have seen horses fed shavings or morsels of dried meat and recall that one Tibetan told me that wolf-meat—which the Tibetans do not eat—was specially good for horses: giving them special stamina and speed." Yet I note that the dictionary in its definition of "horse" says that the animal is an herbivorous mammal. This definition refers of course to the animal in its natural state.

4. See Alexander A. Goldenweiser; *Early Civilization* (New York: A. Knopf, 1922), Chap. V.

5. If one's imagination does not suffice to persuade one of the difficulty of chipping stones, see A. L. Kroeber; *Anthropology* (New York: Harcourt, Brace & Co., 1923), p. 144.

6. For support of the theory that the caveman's art is magic, see Count Bégouen; "The Magical Origin of Prehistoric Art," *Antiquity*, III (1929), pp. 5–19. It would require a visit to the caves themselves to see the overlapping of the images and the darkness which surrounds them. One needs no proof after such a visit that these men did not live in the caves, for they are wet and cold, their walls show no sign of being smudged by fire, and the kitchen middens, where they exist, as at Laugerie-Basse, are in the shelter at the entrance to the cave.

7. In spite of treating the Greeks as more savage than they actually were, Jane Harrison's *Ancient Art and Ritual* (London: Williams & Norgate, 1923), is still of great help in understanding the origins of Greek drama. That even in historic times the drama in Athens had its religious ties is denied by no one, as far as I know, and is eloquently shown by the place of the priest of Dionysos which still exists, clearly marked, in the Theater of Dionysos. None of the extant tragedies deals with anything other than the relation of men to the gods, and in one, witness *The Eumenides* of Aeschylus, there occurs a debate between Apollo and the Furies, on the rights and wrongs of the murder of Clytemnestra. If modern drama goes back to the mystery and miracle plays in origin, then it too has a religious source. Analogous remarks may be made about the origin of modern European music. Aside from the folk songs, European music begins with liturgy.

8. There may be some societies in which all members are submissive. But even where the sanctions against rebellion are severe, as in the armed services, and where the incentives to submission are very strong, as in religious orders, there exist from time to time cases of recalcitrancy. In so-called primitive societies there are laws, unwritten to be sure, but, like the British Constitution, efficacious nevertheless. Infractions are punished and in order to be punished they must exist. On punishment in early societies, see Paul Radin among others, *The World of Primitive Man*, particularly Part II, now available in a paperback, Grove Press, 1960. See also B. Malinowski's *Sex and Repression in Savage Society* (New York: Harcourt Brace & Co., 1927), especially those parts dealing with the incest-taboo. The late Ruth Benedict, whose *Patterns of Culture* (New York: Houghton Mifflin Co., 1934), seems to have given some readers the impression that everyone in a society conforms to the pattern, nevertheless denied this.

9. According to St. John Chrysostom; *Homilies on Genesis*, Chap. 4, there was no sexual intercourse in the Garden of Eden before the Expulsion. The

problem of how our primordial parents could "increase and multiply" without intercourse also interested the Father: see G. Boas; *Essays on Primitivism and Related Ideas in the Middle Ages* (Baltimore: Johns Hopkins Press, 1948), p. 70. It should be noted that along with praise of chastity, sometimes carried to disgusting lengths, went a love of self-inflicted pain and, of course, martyrdom. Two strains of thought are closely intertwined here: self-abnegation and the imitation of Christ. In the famous conversation between St. Francis and Brother Leo on perfect joy, we find what looks like praise of suffering for its own sake, but by the time we reach its conclusion we find that suffering unmerited punishment with joy is a duplication of what Christ suffered on the Cross.

10. I try to show later the sense in which all artistry is magic. Whether primitive man had any theories about sympathetic magic or not, all artistry has certain properties which resemble those of magical practices. In sympathetic magic, the work of art, wax doll, picture of the animal involved, and so on, is a substitute for that on which one wishes to effect a change. These things need not be more than rough symbols of that for which they stand, as the stripes in the United States' flag stand for the thirteen original states. The states do not look like stripes. But a lock of hair or the parings of fingernails of one's intended victim do not look like the victim either, and the doll or picture need not be an accurate image to operate effectively. For works of art as substitutes for reality, see E. H. Gombrich; "Reflexions on a Hobby Horse," in *Aspects of Form*, ed. by L. L. Whyte (London: Lund, 1951). Sometimes it is enough to give the object a name in order for it to be effective and naming is certainly a residual magical practice, whether it be the naming of children, of ships, or of pictures.

11. Huizinga in *Homo Ludens* calls any highly ritualized activity play. For though the purpose of the activity may be serious, the ritual itself has no genetic relation to the end in sight. A diploma, for instance, is just as good evidence of one's having got a degree if it is written in English as if it is written in Latin. Similarly one can draw a more accurate picture of something if one draws from a photograph rather than from the person or thing itself. But to draw from a photograph would not be considered cricket. *Homo Ludens* puts a high value *on the way* things are done.

12. I am now informed by those who know that wedding invitations are engraved to resemble printing, which carries the matter a step further toward the terminal value of the obsolescent.

CHAPTER II: The Temporal Dimension

1. On irreversible processes see E. Meyerson; *Identité et Réalité*, 3rd ed., Paris, 1926, p. 238. English translation by Kate Loewenberg (New York: Macmillan Co., 1930), p. 216.

2. The literature on identical twins and their behavior is very large. Much of it was written to prove if possible the separate contributions of heredity and environment. Since identical twins have exactly the same heredity, differences in environment ought to effectuate differences in behavior if environment could have any effect. Nathaniel D. M'ttron Hirsch in *Twins, Heredity*

and Environment (Cambridge: Harvard University Press, 1930), made such an investigation and came out with the conclusion that heredity was more important than environment, though he recognizes a fact which has been recognized by many others that sometimes one twin is right-handed and the other left-handed, a difference which might be of the greatest importance socially and hence psychologically (see p. 119). Of one pair of twins he says (p. 120), that they were alike in courtesy, play spirit, leadership, self-control, self-consciousness, aggressiveness, poise, posture, voice, enthusiasm, tastes in foods, games, and playmates; unlike in their spirit of co-operation, perseverance, patience, decision, and motor control. The twin who was superior in these last named traits was the right-handed one. The left-handed twin was "more often sulky . . . and stubborn; she at times resents having someone else so very much like herself." No one will fail to notice the possible correlation between these traits and her left-handedness and their relation to our subject. A more detailed examination of twins by H. H. Newman, F. N. Freeman, and K. J. Holzinger; *Twins, a Study of Heredity and Environment* (Chicago: University of Chicago Press, 1937), says (p. 36), "The two members of a pair are never truly identical but differ more or less with respect to all their characters and . . . they differ sometimes to a disconcerting degree." The degree of course would be disconcerting only if one expected them not to differ. The authors point out (pp. 125 ff.) that "the one point in which similarity is rare is handwriting," a conclusion also found as early as Galton. This whole study with its detailed statistical tables is of the greatest relevance to our topic. In a more recent work by Dorothy Burlingham; *Twins, a Study of Three Pairs of Identical Twins* (New York: International Universities Press, 1952), makes the point (p. 14) that even when mothers of identical twins try their best to treat them both alike, they find it difficult to do so, just as mothers who try to give them individual treatment fail. But she also points out that the relations between twins themselves may produce differences in character. "Dominant characteristics in one of a pair of twins tend to produce an active twin and a passive one. . . . What generally happens with a pair of twins in this period [infancy] is that one of the twins is the more vigorous one and it will bite, push, pull, or snatch things away from its weaker twin. The weaker one, as is usual with children of this age when attacked, will just cry over the hurt it has received, in no way try to defend itself but behave in a completely passive way" (p. 21).

3. See his essay "On the Discrimination of Romanticisms," now available in *Essays in the History of Ideas* (Baltimore: Johns Hopkins Press, 1948), pp. 228–53.

4. Going backward in time and taking only obvious pairs of conflicting manners, we have the Impressionists and the Academicians, the "romantic" Delacrusians and the "classic" Ingristes, the Poussinists and the Rubensists, the Caravaggeschi and the Mannerists, the Florentines and the Venetians. These, as I say, are only the obvious differences. One has only to make a list of painters contemporary with Botticelli to see how they differed individually.

5. One need only read Emile Mâle's *L'Art religieux après le Concile de Trente* (Paris: A. Colin, 1932), to see what the strictures of the Council were. First, there was to be no nudity in a religious painting (p. 2); second, there must be no useless details in a painting, for employing which Veronese

was called before the Inquisition (p. 4); there must be no vulgar figure in a religious painting, but all must be noble, wherefore the paintings of Caravaggio were not to be used (p. 6); there must be no erroneous ideas represented, nothing which might give rise to false religious views, wherefore the Virgin must not be represented as weeping or fainting at the foot of the Cross (p. 8). "When Rubens," said Mâle (p. 16), "undertook to decorate the church of the Jesuits in Antwerp, he agreed to paint thirty-nine panels 'in conformity,' says the contract, 'with the list handed him by the Superior.'" "The Jesuits were not men," he continues (*Ibid.*), "to leave the artists who were working in their churches without supervision; in the Gesù, Baglione assures us, the painter Gaspare Celio carried out what Father Valeriano had conceived. There is preserved in Austria a program prepared by the Jesuits for artists who were decorating their church in Brünn; a chapel was consecrated to the Cross, and it was ordered that there be exhibited there the symbols which pre-figured it in the Old Testament: Moses's rod, the pole from which the marvelous grapes were hung, the Tau carrying the bronze serpent." But the whole chapter should be read for its details. The general plan of the Council is translated in Elizabeth Gilmore Holt's *Literary Sources of Art History* (Princeton: Princeton University Press, 1947), p. 242, followed by the interrogation of Veronese before the Inquisition. Mâle also points out how some of the directions were evaded and makes the point that the directives concerned only paintings to be hung in churches.

6. Quietism was a doctrine expounded by Molinos (1640–1646) according to whom the individual must abdicate and leave all to God. It was condemned by Innocent XI in the bull *Coelestis Pastor*, November 2, 1687, for, as is clear, such complete abnegation relieved the individual of making any decisions whatsoever and therefore from any responsibility in doing either good or evil. Yet it might be thought of as an extreme application of Dante's thought in his famous verse, "Thy will is our peace." Any life of Mme Guyon will show to what lengths it might lead.

7. Cf. G. Boas; *The Inquiring Mind* (LaSalle, Illinois: Open Court Publishing Co., 1959), Chap. II and E. H. Gombrich; *Art and Illusion* (New York: Pantheon Books, 1960), *passim* in both of which books there are references to the psychological experiments on perception. The former was written as an introduction to epistemology, the latter as an explanation of what is seen in a painting. Both were written independently but agree in all essentials.

8. See J. Loewenberg; *Reason and the Nature of Things* (LaSalle, Illinois: Open Court Publishing Co., 1959), Chap. XIV for some of the consequences of this fallacy. It is not unlike what William James called "vicious intellectualism."

9. Cf. Albert L. Hammond's essay, "Idols of the Twilight," in his *Proprieties and Vagaries* (Baltimore: Johns Hopkins Press, 1961), p. 227. The *topos* itself goes back to the Greeks.

10. The limits of variation in ethical standards are discussed by Clyde Kluckhohn in his "Ethical Relativity: *Sic et Non*," *The Journal of Philosophy*, LII, no. 23, Nov. 10, 1955, p. 663. Though Kluckhohn was looking for as much uniformity as he could find, in reaction to the particularizing tendencies of his colleagues in anthropology, he did not find much in the way of common standards. "Every culture," he says (p. 672), "has a concept of murder, distinguishing this from execution, killing in war, and other 'justifiable

homicides.' The notions of incest and other regulations upon sexual behavior, of prohibitions upon untruth under defined circumstances, of restitution and reciprocity, of mutual obligations between parents and children—these and many other moral concepts are altogether universal." But this is simply an admission of what I have been contending: that each culture organizes the satisfactions of even basic drives. What should be shown by the man interested in proving uniformity of standards is that the same acts are approved and disapproved in all societies and the acts should be clearly defined. It is not enough to show that all societies regulate sexual behavior; one must also show that they all prohibit the same kind of sexual behavior, e.g., sexual experiences between people of the same sex, between people beyond the age of puberty and those below, between all people of both sexes below a given age, between a married man and the wife of another man, and so on. No relativist in his right mind would argue that any society allows complete freedom in all affairs, for that would amount to denying the possibility of any generalizations about anything.

11. For a full discussion of Schopenhauer's theory of music, see his *Welt als Wille und Vorstellung*, Bk. III, section 52; *Saemtliche Werke*, ed. Deussen (Muenchen: Piper, 1911), Vol. I, pp. 304 ff.

12. The distinction between notional assent and real assent is that of Cardinal Newman in his *Grammar of Assent* (New York: Longmans, Green & Co., 1947). Real assent is belief in the truth-to-fact of a sentence; notional assent amounts to little more in the long run than entertaining an idea as a useful hypothesis or possible truth-to-fact.

13. That we have feelings which are as persuasive as proved ideas needs perhaps no demonstration, but nevertheless it is a vague and misleading idea. I am not arguing that all feelings are to be trusted, but simply that we believe in hundreds of things for which we have no impregnable proof. To prove our own existence, the existence of other minds, and the existence of an external world—limiting ourselves to only three such beliefs—has seemed difficult to many philosophers who, it is true, begin their investigations with premises which create the difficulty. Regardless of why these problems arise, we all, I imagine, believe that we exist, that other people have minds, and that there is an external world. We simply have a feeling that these are truths and never bother to prove them. They are not even problems for most of us. Similarly when we have a feeling of hunger, we know it directly and need never ask anyone else what it is that we are feeling. The same is true of the sexual attraction which someone has for us. I am saying that when we feel that a work of art is beautiful, we do not have to ask a critic or other so-called authority whether it is beautiful or not. Its beauty hits us just as hunger or sexual attraction hits us. The question of whether we have the right feeling or not, assuming that the word "right" is appropriate, arises later. The obvious difference between beauty and hunger is that the latter may arise in the absence of any external object, unless the stomach with its contracting walls is external.

14. Near Aurangabad is a replica of the Taj Mahal and in Nashville is a replica of the Parthenon. Are they as "satisfactory" as the originals? If not, why not?

15. Cf. A. Foucher; *La Vie du Bouddha* (Paris: Payot, 1949), p. 36 f. Before his birth the future Buddha asks the divine assembly, "Under what form, my friends, shall I enter the bosom of my mother?" And the answer

is, "Under the form of a white elephant with six tusks." At this point Foucher adds, *Il nous est permis de rester au premier abord surpris de ce choix: toutefois notre étonnement diminuera sensiblement si nous faisons réflexion que nos symboles pourraient paraître non moins imprévus à des Indiens. Eux non plus ne verraient pas bien du premier coup d'oeil pourquoi nous nous représentons le Saint-Esprit sous l'aspect d'une colombe.*

CHAPTER III: The Arts and Society

1. Cf. V. Langevin and J. Lombard; "*Esthétique du dessin d'enfant*," *Revue d'Esthétique*, Vol. I and II (January–June, 1958), p. 5. See also Felix Deutsch; "Body, Mind, and Art," in *The Visual Arts Today*, ed. Gyorgy Kepes (Middletown, Conn.: Wesleyan University Press, 1960), esp. p. 44.

2. In fact, musical critics, as Nicolas Slonimsky has shown in his *Lexicon of Musical Invective* (New York: Coleman-Ross Co.; 1953), have poured out not only adverse criticism on composers from Beethoven to Wagner and Webern, but obscenity. This was especially true of German critics. Thus Heinrich Dorn (*Op. cit*, p. 235) says that Wagner thought *seiner Exkremente* were *den Ausfluss seiner goettlichen Eingebung;* Paul Schwers (*Ibid.*, p. 146) thought that the *Sonnenlaeufer* of Carl Ruggles was *Darmverrenkungen in atonaler Tristanekstase;* Berg's music is only *Brocken, Fetzen, Schluchzer und Ruelpser,* according to Paul Zschorlich (*Ibid.*, p. 53), and so it went. This book should be required reading for all who believe in either the universality of taste or the judgment of critics. All quotations from this book are printed with the kind permission of the publishers.

3. In spite of the Second Commandment, "In Rabbinical literature there seems something like the distinction made between a picture in the flat and an image in the round in the prescription in the Talmud that you may use, for sealing, a signet ring with the raised image of a man upon it, because when you seal with it, the figure in the wax will be concave and therefore not be so much an image as a hollow. The signet with the raised figure on it may not, however, be worn. On the other hand it is permissible to wear a signet with the figure sunk upon it, but you must not use such a signet for sealing," from Edwyn Bevan; *Holy Images* (London: Allen and Unwin, 1940), p. 53. See also note 1 on the use of seals during the 13th century among Jews. To this typically Talmudic distinction we might add the actual practice of putting frescoes on the walls of the Synagogue at Doura, frescoes which represented the Heroes of the Old Testament. An amusing rule was laid down for Catholics by Ansaldi in his *De sacro et publico apud ethnicos pictarum tabularum cultu: Nullam imaginem colendam esse, cuius nasum duobus digitis complecti.* Quoted in Bevan, *op. cit.*, p. 148, n. 2.

4. One outstanding example of this is the distinction between the *élite* and The Many in Athens, the *plebs* and the patricians in Rome, and in both places foreign residents who were in neither class and yet very influential in shaping the culture of these cities. In Shakespeare's plays, written for city audiences, we have the same type of distinctions, with the lower orders serving as comic relief to the tragedies of the upper. But what I say needs no documentation; it must have been noticed by everyone.

5. C. P. Snow; *The Two Cultures and the Scientific Revolution* (New York: Cambridge University Press, 1959). The alienation of the "intellectual" from the scientist is no more noticeable than the alienation of the artist from them both. Sir Charles could well have argued that there are three cultures at least.

6. Royce's clearest statement of the nature of the self as purpose is in his *Philosophy of Loyalty* and *The Problem of Christianity*.

7. Who could have prophesied that Debussy's *Clair de Lune* would be used as a signature for a radio program?

8. There are so many definitions of beauty that it would be absurd to try to list them all. Most of the important ones are discussed in K. Gilbert and H. Kuhn; *A History of Esthetics* (New York: Macmillan Co., 1940). But we can at least try a few samples. For Hegel, beauty is a sensuous manifestation of the Absolute; for Hogarth, it demands variety in unity; for Santayana, it is objectified pleasure; for Bacon, strangeness in proportion; for Descartes, it is based upon mathematical ratios; for Hutcheson, it is felt but not understood; and for Plato, it is supersensible. Supersensible beauty obviously cannot be found in any perceptible object. Mathematical ratios can be found only in works of art which can be quantified. Strangeness in proportion would not be found in literature except in poetic meters. How is the pleasure which we derive from music objectified? Is the beauty of a tragedy sensuous? Perhaps Hutcheson's idea is the most widely applicable because of its very vagueness.

9. What people find to appreciate in works of art may vary from nothing whatsoever to all sorts of occult beauties, symbolic references, and historical perspectives. It is only by fiat that one can declare some of these illegitimate. Whatever else aesthetic value may be, it is conferred upon the work of art by the person who feels it to be present. That is what gives plausibility to Santayana's theory of beauty as objectified pleasure. There are some people who can admire painting but not music, and others who admire music but not painting. And so it goes. See an amusing account of a musical evening attended by Wordsworth, Monkhouse, Rogers, and Coleridge in Henry Crabb Robinson's *Diary, Reminiscences, and Correspondence*, under the entry of April 5, 1832. See also note 5, Chap. XIV below.

CHAPTER IV: The Classification of the Arts

1. There are about 35,600 species of vertebrates against 815,000 of arthropods, and only 5000 of sponges. See Theodosius Dobzhansky; *Genetics and the Origin of Species* (3rd ed.; New York: Columbia University Press, 1951), p. 7. If I shy at the word "species" in the body of my text, it is because of disputes among taxonomists about just what a species is. For several meanings of the term, see Ernst Mayr; *Systematics and the Origin of Species* (New York: Columbia University Press, 1942), especially his references to Dobzhansky, pp. 115 ff.

2. One should check any tendency which one might have to think of Oriental civilization as more static than Western by reading Rhys Davids; *Buddhism* (London: Society for the Promotion of Christian Knowledge,

1917), p. 178: "The supposed immovability of the institutions and beliefs of the East has become almost a proverb; but as our knowledge of the East increases, the proverb will be likely to fall into disuse. There have been times, not far remote, when the rate of progress in India or China has been so slow, that, compared with the progress in England or America, it has seemed as nothing; but there have been times when Eastern Asia has moved faster than Europe. Except in a much more limited sense than the expression is usually meant to convey, 'the immovability of the East' is a delusion. As well might the Japanese talk of the unchangeable customs and beliefs of Russia and Spain." Had Davids lived a bit longer, he would have had to choose different examples.

3. The best collection of artistic manifestoes is given in Charles E. Gauss; *The Aesthetic Theories of French Artists* (Baltimore: Johns Hopkins Press, 1949). The folders and catalogues of current exhibitions will provide plenty of contemporary examples. The most charitable explanation of the gibberish printed in such manifestoes is that an artist in paint is not necessarily an artist in words. The art of exposition is not an inborn gift in most of us.

4. See G. Boas; *Wingless Pegasus* (Baltimore: Johns Hopkins Press, 1948). For the Realist Manifesto of Gabo see *Gabo: Constructions, Sculpture, Paintings, Drawings, Engravings*, with Introductory Essays by Herbert Read and Leslie Martin (Cambridge: Harvard University Press, 1957), p. 151.

5. For some specimens of fantastic American architecture, see the photographs from the collection of Clarence John Laughlin in the *Architectural Forum*, April 1956.

CHAPTER V: Functionalism

1. See A. B. Griswold; *The Arts of Thailand* (Bloomington: Indiana University Press, 1960), p. 32.

2. For Renoir's views of irregularity of nature, see Charles Edward Gauss; *The Aesthetic Theories of French Artists*, p. 36 f. "Observers know in effect," said Renoir, "that, in spite of the apparent simplicity of the laws which preside at their formation, the works of nature are infinitely varied, from the most important to the least, of whatever type or kind they are. The two eyes of the most beautiful face will always be the least bit dissimilar; even the nose is not found exactly placed over the center of the mouth. The sections of an orange, the leaves of a tree, the petals of a flower are never identical. It seems that the beauties of every order draw their charms from diversity. Upon examining from this point of view the most renowned plastic or architectural reproductions, one can easily see that the great artists who have created them, careful to proceed like nature of whom they are always respectful pupils, are on their guard never to transgress its fundamental law of irregularity."

3. The classic study of art from the psychoanalytic point of view is of course Freud's book on Leonardo, which discusses the subject matter of the "Mona Lisa" and its symbolic reference to the artist's life. This might well be supplemented by Norman O. Brown's *Life against Death* (Middletown: Wesleyan University Press, 1950), Chap. V, "Art and Eros." The erroneous

view that the artist must be a neurotic in order to paint, write, or perform any of the other arts, is combatted by Dr. Lawrence S. Kubie in his *Neurotic Distortion of the Creative Process* (New York: Farrar, Straus & Cudahy, Inc., 1958).

4. Whether Shylock was a comic character or not is still disputed and will continue to be disputed as long as *The Merchant of Venice* is played. Furness in his Variorum Edition of the plays (pp. 346 and 370) maintains that the comic Shylock is a creation of Lansdowne and that "there is no ground for the belief that Shylock was ever presented on the stage in a comic light. To assert it is to imply that Lansdowne's 'Shylock' and Shakespeare's Shylock are identical." "Macklin," he says (p. 346), "transformed Shylock from the grimacings of low Comedy to the solemn sweep of Tragedy." But Stark Young, who is surely not an insensitive play goer writes, "The seventeenth century comedy. with its light fable conceived in all the verve, vivid elaboration, brutality, and lyricism of its time, is turned into the tragedy of a suffering Jew, and the leading actor in the part is directed to wring it dry for its last drop of pathos, race problem, social injustice, and bitter edge." See his *The Theatre* (New York: Hill & Wang, Inc., 1958), originally published in 1927, p. 85. If one looks up the word "Jew" in Bartlett's *Concordance* to Shakespeare, one will find only seven occurrences of the word, five of which appear in the comedies in sarcastic or humorous lines. The two exceptions, from *Henry IV*, Part I, Act II, scene 4 and *Macbeth*, Act IV, scene 1, read respectively, "I am a Jew else, an Ebrew Jew," and "Liver of blaspheming Jew, Gall of Goat, and slips of yew," which express neither sympathy nor pathos. But to take a different example, I confess that *The Taming of the Shrew* has never struck me personally as funny, but as brutal and coarse. This may simply be because my sense of humor is dull; but if my dullness makes me see the play in this way, it shows that the spectator can project his own state of mind into the work of art. And that is all I am trying to show.

5. The most curious of such interpretations are in musical criticism, where one finds Bizet's *Carmen* castigated because "the heroine is an abandoned woman, destitute not only of any vestige of moral, but devoid of the ordinary feelings of humanity, etc. etc.," and *La Tosca* because it is "an alliance of a pure art with scenes . . . essentially brutal and demoralizing." "What has music to do," asks the author of this phrase, "with a lustful man chasing a defenseless woman or the dying kicks of a murdered scoundrel?" I take these gems from Slonimsky's *Lexicon of Musical Invective*, pp. 64 and 135 respectively. Recently (October 1961) I heard a radio announcer object to a jazz version of *Frankie and Johnnie* because it seemed to justify murder.

6. I refer of course to Boileau's "Art Poétique" and Reynolds' "Discourses." I have summarized the principles of the latter in "Joshua Reynolds as Arbiter of Taste," *Gazette des Beaux-Arts*, Juillet–août, 1961, pp. 93 ff.

7. Vaughan Williams in his article *Fugue* in Grove, p. 48, writes, "Bach rose superior to all rules and regulations with which Fux had hedged in the fugue, and evolved out of Fux's skeleton the living fugue, freed from all the impurities of pedantry."

8. Though the *Seven Lamps* exists in dozens of editions and my quotations can be easily found in any of them, the one which I used was printed in

1899, the 29 thousandth printing, published by George Allen. It contains Ruskin's own comments on his opinions. Page references are given in parentheses after each quotation.

9. The notion that Gothic architecture was irregular is discussed in A. O. Lovejoy's "First Gothic Revival and the Return to Nature," esp. sec. 2, pp. 155 ff. Similar ideas of irregularity will be found in his paper on "A Chinese Origin of a Romanticism," p. 101. Both papers are in his *Essays in the History of Ideas.*

10. I put in the qualification since after all the figures in many a Claude or Salvator Rosa or Gainsborough landscape were of no great importance.

11. On the beauty of obsolete instruments, see G. Boas; *A Primer for Critics* (Baltimore: Johns Hopkins Press, 1937); and *Wingless Pegasus, op. cit.* My opinion, as far as I know, has convinced no one, perhaps because I went too far in using a eulogistic term. I should no doubt have said that obsolete instruments become good-in-themselves, or sacred, rather than beautiful.

CHAPTER VI: The Arrested Moment

1. The most impressive instance of the source of scientific concepts in art is found in Aristotle's four causes: matter, that out of which a thing is made; form, that for which a thing is made; the agent, that which makes the thing; the essence, the kind of thing that is made. The first three are clearly derived from the making of artifacts; there may be some question of the fourth. Then there are certain criteria by which we select satisfactory hypotheses, such as simplicity and fertility, the former being an intellectual elimination of variety, the reduction of the observed multiplicity of things to unity, as in art the "inessential" is eliminated. The very word *cosmos* is in its origin an aesthetic term; we assume—we do not know—that things must be well-ordered and we look for that order and try to express it in a general description. So in portraiture, for instance, no one except Picasso has ever attempted to do more than paint one aspect of a man which stands for all his various aspects. But order itself is an aesthetic criterion; like the artist, the scientist introduces order into his experiences; he does not merely find it.

2. Ingres' devotion to Raphael is perhaps too well-known to need documentation. His notebooks, especially Cahier 7, are the source for our information about this, though his very technique proves the point. See, however, Norman Schlenoff; *Ingres, cahiers littéraires et inédits* (Paris, Presses Universitaires, 1956), p. 13. His "Vow of Louis XIII" includes a pastiche of Raphael's "Sistine Madonna" and his illustrations of the life of Raphael include the famous "Raphaël et la Fornarina" and "Le Cardinal Bibbiena offrant sa Nièce en Mariage à Raphaël," as if these incidents were on the same historical plane as his mythological subjects. He was not always Raphaelesque, as his portrait of Bertin shows, but it is fair to say as Jean Alazard says in his *Ingres et l'Ingrisme* (Paris: Albin Michel, 1950), p. 18, that in his later years he was *entièrement subjugué* by this painter. Ingres was a very stubborn conservative, even going so far as to insist on retaining his misspellings and grammatical errors as if his way of doing things were

self-justified. See, e.g., Schlenoff, *op. cit.*, p. 18. For those interested in Ingres' own words on the subject of Raphael, see Henri Delaborde; *Ingres, sa vie et son oeuvre*, Paris, 1911.

3. The Latin tag comes from Juvenal's *Satires*, X, 356 and is a prayer, not a description, and ends, as those who quote it seem to forget, with the notion that death is one of the *munera naturae*. But it is not infrequent to find that a context often weakens a quotation.

4. The great exception to this generalization is of course Wilenski. See his *The Meaning of Modern Sculpture* (London: Faber and Faber, 1932).

5. Even portraits which might be expected to retain all the individuality of the sitter have at times been "typed." See for instance Frances Blanshard's *Portraits of Wordsworth* (Ithaca: Cornell University Press, 1959), pp. 31 ff. and John Graham; "Lavater's *Physiognomy* in England," *Journal of the History of Ideas*, XXII, no. 4, Oct.–Dec., 1961, pp. 561 ff.

6. The dispraise of acquired learning goes back to ancient times. See *Primitivism in Antiquity*, p. 196, n. 8. In the Middle Ages it was related to the idea that Christ was speaking to the simple-minded as well as to the learned. See *Essays on Primitivism and Related Ideas in the Middle Ages*, pp. 24 ff. and 121 ff. In our own times it reappears in the cult of childhood.

CHAPTER VII: Art and History

1. For Winckelmann on the "Apollo Belvedere," see his *History of Ancient Art*, trans. by G. Henry Lodge (Boston: Osgood & Co., 1880), Ch. III, § 11, Vol. II, p. 312, where the statue is called "the highest ideal of art"; "an eternal spring . . . clothed with the charms of youth and the graceful manliness of ripened years, and plays with softness and tenderness about the proud shape of his limbs. . . . Neither blood-vessels nor sinews heat and stir this body, but a heavenly essence, diffusing itself like a gentle stream, seems to fill the whole contour of the body"; "this miracle of art. . . ." Victor Cousin in his famous *Du vrai, du beau et du bien* echoes all this. See the translation by O. W. Wight (New York: Appleton, 1857), p. 145. Cousin's influence in the United States was as great as it was in France, though he himself was not one of the most inventive minds.

2. Furness' list of criticisms of *Hamlet* in the Variorum Shakespeare cites Henry MacKenzie (1780) as the first critic to deal with the problem of the hero's hesitation. Before that time apparently no critic saw anything needing explanation in his failure to kill his uncle in the first act.

3. Matisse studied for about six weeks under Bouguereau and left in disgust.

4. Though Klee protested against the criticism of what he called infantilism in his paintings, he did say in 1902, "I want to be as though new-born, knowing nothing about Europe, nothing, knowing no pictures, entirely without impulses, almost in an original state." See Werner Haftmann, *The Mind and Work of Paul Klee* (New York: Frederick A. Praeger, Inc., 1954), p. 53. This may be interpreted as a desire to be less advanced than a child, but that would perhaps be unfair.

5. For the various speculations about the original condition of man in the

Christian Fathers, see *Essays on Primitivism and Related Ideas in the Middle Ages*, pp. 15 ff. and 54 ff.

6. The optimism in question might be attenuated in that any plan for reform is made by people who are not going to live under it once it is put into practice. At times like the present (1961), ten years suffice to make a plan obsolescent and it usually takes that long to put one into practice, at which point it is obsolete.

CHAPTER VIII: The Social Complex

1. "Practically every commentator has agreed that the helots of Laconia were the descendants of the original inhabitants of the land, non-Dorians, who had been reduced to serfdom by their conquerors," says H. Michell in *Sparta* (Cambridge, Eng.: University Press, 1952), p. 76. K. M. T. Chrimes, in *Ancient Sparta* (Manchester, Eng.: University Press, 1949), Chap. VIII, pp. 272 ff. gives the views of various scholars on this subject and concludes (p. 285) that "the majority were doubtless a lower stratum of the pre-Dorian population of the Eurotas valley, subjugated soon after the Dorian invasion; others were probably taken from other Laconian peoples (who had previously reduced the same elements to serfdom) when they in turn became subject to Sparta." Their situation was somewhat analogous to that of the Saxons after the Norman Conquest in England. As for the Indian castes, no scholar is sure of their origin. The original Aryans who came down into India apparently had no caste system. Later four classes developed: the Brahmans, priests; the Ksatriyas, warriors; the Vaisyas, merchants; the Sudras, cultivators and servants. The Sudras seem to have been half-breeds and black aborigines. Thus the division seems to be based on four different principles: function, racial origin, religion, and lineage. The original Hindu word for caste is *varna* which means *color* and that may lend some weight to the theory that the lowest caste was of a different color from the others. In that event they might have been the dark Dravidians. I take this information from Hastings' *Encyclopedia*, arts. *Caste*, by E. A. Gait and *Pariah*, by J. Jolly.

2. See *Courbet and the Naturalistic Movement*, ed. by G. Boas (Baltimore: Johns Hopkins Press, 1938), esp. p. 48.

3. See again Slonimsky's invaluable *Lexicon of Musical Invective*, pp. 205 ff. One of Tchaikovski's piano concertos, unidentified by Slonimsky, was characterized by the Boston *Evening Transcript*, October 25, 1875, as "formless void, sprinkled only with tinklings of the piano and snatchy obbligatos from all the various wind and string instruments in turn;" his music, said the *Wiener Fremdenblatt*, November 28, 1876, "in its hydrophobia, scorns logic, wallows in torpor, and time and again, collapses in dissonant convulsions." But the whole series should be read.

4. I recently read an open letter written by a Rabbi in Pittsburgh to the conductor of the local orchestra protesting against his playing the "St. Matthew Passion" on the ground that it was an anti-Semitic act. Where national, religious, or social pride is involved, there is no limit to the anger of people. Unfortunately pride may go before a fall, but the fall is often that of the person who offends one's pride.

5. See especially his *Biochemical Individuality* (New York: John Wiley & Sons, 1956).

6. In Paul Radin; *The World of Primitive Man* (New York: Grove Press, 1960), first printed in 1953, p. 113.

CHAPTER IX: Ideals and Values

1. I have discussed the conflicts between liking and approbation, together with their antitheses in both *A Primer for Critics* and *Wingless Pegasus*.

2. According to Réau, it is only in the sixth century that Christ appears on the Cross in human form. Up to the middle eleventh century He appears with eyes open and only later as dead. In the Catacombs He is represented by the Lamb, but never in person. The Cross erected by Constantine and Helena was a *crux nuda* studded with gems. Réau refers to L. Bréhier's *Les origines du crucifix dans l'art religieux*, Paris, 1904, for documentation. I have not seen this work. Edwyn R. Bevan, however, in his *Holy Images* (London: Allen & Unwin, 1940), says (p. 97), "No Christian representation of Christ upon the Cross is shown until after Constantine. The oldest picture of the Crucifixion known is the caricature scrawled by some heathen mocker on the walls of the Imperial Palace in Rome, in which the Crucified is given an ass's head and the figure of the Christian whom the mockery was intended to annoy was rudely sketched beside the Cross with the words below: 'Alexamenos worships God.' " He also maintains (p. 98) that during the first three centuries the Cross does not appear at all. He dates the earliest Crucifixion with Christ on the Cross from about 400 A.D. It appears on "a wooden door from Santa Sabina in Rome," as well as on a carved ivory box in the British Museum (p. 99). None of this, however, explains why the figure of Christ was omitted from the early crosses, why He was shown with open eyes, that is, alive, until the eleventh century, and why He was shown dead thereafter. But when one remembers Grünewald's "Crucifixion" in Colmar and literary descriptions of the Crucifixion itself in mystic writers, one sees that there is a definite progress toward emphasizing the human side of the Christ.

3. The archetypes of Jung exist in the collective unconscious and are not symbols of suppressed desires. In his Terry Lectures (1937), now published in *Psychology and Religion: West and East* (The Collected Works of C. G. Jung, Vol. 11), trans. by R. F. C. Hull (New York: Pantheon Books, 1958), he says (p. 50) that he means by archetypes "forms or images of a collective nature which occur practically all over the earth as constituents of myths and at the same time as autochthonous individual products of unconscious origin. The archetypal motifs presumably derive from patterns of the human mind that are transmitted not only by tradition and migration but also by heredity. The latter hypothesis is indispensable, since even complicated archetypal images can be reproduced spontaneously without there being any possibility of direct tradition." For an example of his own, see what he says about *quarternity* in the same volume (see Index *s.v.*). He emphasizes the hypothesis of their inheritance (p. 103) in contrast to their transmission from man to man. In "A Psychological Approach to the Trinity" (*op. cit.*, p. 150), he contrasts the collective unconscious with the personal unconscious and in-

sists that "archetypal ideas can never be derived from the personal sphere." One of his most impressive demonstrations of his theory is in his "Transformation Symbolism in the Mass" in the same volume, impressive if one is already convinced of the plausibility of the hypothesis. See also his article on "Psychotherapists or the Clergy," par. 533 (p. 345 of the same volume); his "Answer to Job," par. 648, p. 409; and "The Psychology of Eastern Meditation," *passim*. In his study of "The Tibetan Book of the Dead," par. 846, p. 519, we find him saying, "So far as I know, there is no inheritance of individual prenatal, or pre-uterine, memories, but there are undoubtedly inherited archetypes which are, however, devoid of content, because, to begin with, they contain no personal experiences. They only emerge into consciousness when personal experiences have rendered them visible." The historian of philosophy will be tempted to see in this a reflection of Kant's forms of perception as unified in the "transcendental unity of apperception." In ordinary language this would appear to mean that there are certain symbols which we inevitably use when we are confronted with those experiences which Jung calls, after Rudolf Otto (see p. 7), the numinous.

4. See Caroline Spurgeon; *Shakespeare's Imagery* (Boston: Beacon Press, 1958), originally printed in 1935, especially the charts. Dr. Spurgeon used the images to show the individuality of Shakespeare's mind in distinction to the work of Jung which tended in the opposite direction. For the use of Freudian symbols in criticism, see the various studies of Leslie A. Fiedler.

5. See Norman O. Brown; *Life against Death* (Middletown: Wesleyan University Press, 1959), Chap. XIV for Luther, and Chap. XIII for Swift.

6. Cf. Lawrence S. Kubie; *The Neurotic Distortion of the Creative Process* (Lawrence: University of Kansas Press, 1958), p. 38.

7. Erwin Panofsky; "The History of the Theory of Human Proportions as a Reflection of the History of Styles," in his *Meaning in the Visual Arts* (Garden City: Doubleday & Co., 1955).

8. See Denman W. Ross; *A Theory of Pure Design* (Boston and New York: Houghton Mifflin Co., 1907).

9. I have tried to clarify the problem of causation in my *The Inquiring Mind*, Chap. V.

CHAPTER X: The Orientation of the Critic's Eye

1. From Bacon's *Advancement of Learning* (London: Oxford University Press, 1956), II, xvi, 5.

2. See his "Answer to Job," in *Psychology and Religion, Collected Works, op. cit.*, par. 758, p. 469. For a fuller understanding of Jung's theory of archetypes, see Vol. 9, i and ii, containing respectively *Archetypes and the Collective Unconscious* and *Aion*.

3. For what it is worth, one might recall how for the first three centuries of Buddhism no representation of the Buddha was permitted and what Coomaraswamy called aniconic images alone were used, the Wheel of the Law, a pair of footprints, a lotus. So in the early centuries of Christianity one finds the Cross, the fish, and the Lamb. See note 2, Chap. IX above.

4. See "Courbet and His Critics" in *Courbet and the Naturalistic Movement* by G. Boas (Baltimore: Johns Hopkins Press, 1938), for hostile interpretations of "The Stone Crushers."

5. What theories Monet had are best found in G. Clemenceau's *Monet: les Nymphéas*, English trans. by G. Boas (Garden City: Doubleday & Co., 1930).

6. One of the most extraordinary accounts of the emotional values of color will be found in S. C. Pepper's *Principles of Art Appreciation* (New York: Harcourt Brace, 1949), p. 133, where he is discussing Picasso's "Absinthe Drinkers." After dwelling on the general blue tone of the painting which is depressing, according to this author, he says, "The unreal images of sadness float in blue, but if there is an item of hope anywhere, it tends to be picked out in yellow." The spot of yellow is the glass of absinthe. Was Picasso trying to say that absinthe is the one ray of hope in the lives of the poor? That is possible, but not purely visual. Moreover Degas did a pair of absinthe drinkers too and that picture is fully as depressing but in quite a different color scheme.

7. Professor Leslie Fiedler would be a good representative of the school which finds sexual symbols everywhere.

8. Koechel in his *Mozart Verzeichnis*, 3rd ed., rev. by A. Einstein (Leipzig: Breitkopf & Haertel, 1937), p. 585, *Die harmonischen Kuehnheiten des einleitenden Adagios haben mit der Revue musicale Fetis' und der Annus Z, xxxiii, xxxiv, xxxv, eine ganze Literatur hervor gerufen*. See also E. Newman, *A Musical Critic's Holiday* (New York: A. Knopf, 1925), pp. 131–50.

9. These quotations can be found in [Jacob Epstein] *Epstein, an Autobiography* (London: Hulton Press, 1955), pp. 257 and 259. They may be supplemented by Frank Rutter's comment, p. 261. The whole book is a gold mine of conflicting critical opinions, some furiously indignant, some friendly. Great emphasis is put on the indecency of the nudes in the hostile notices: they might be seen by children!

10. See note 9 above.

CHAPTER XI: The Hierarchy of Values

1. Literature against scholastic life in England, written by Englishmen is copious. Out of the mass of such works I select the following. First, Cowper's *Tirocinium* which is frequently cited; then Southey's reminiscences as given in his son's *The Life and Correspondence of Robert Southey*, Vol. I, p. 48, for instance, in which he says that his year at Corston held little profit and "a good deal of suffering," which should be supplemented by pp. 77 and 133 on his schooling at Bristol and Westminster; then Macready's *Reminiscences*, ed. by Sir Frederick Pollock, p. 9 on the abuse of power by the Praeposters at Rugby and p. 14 on corporal punishment; Sydney Smith in his essay on "Professional Education," originally published in the *Edinburgh Review*, in 1809, reprinted in *The Works of Sydney Smith*, Philadelphia, 1844, esp. p. 75; Crabbe's *The Borough*, Letter xxiv, and finally, to come down to our own times, Lowes Dickinson in E. M. Forster's *Goldsworthy Lowes Dickinson* (London: E. Arnold & Co., 1934), esp. p. 24 where Dickinson says, "I curse the time"—of schooling—"as I look back on it. It seems to me all evil and

no good." One sometimes wonders whether the copiousness of children's literature in English, as contrasted with French and Italian, is not to be explained psychologically as an attempt on the part of adults to create a happy childhood for themselves.

2. For the reception given to the *Eroica*, see Alexander Wheelock Thayer; *Life of Ludwig von Beethoven*, ed. by Henry Edward Krehbiel (New York: Beethoven Association, 1921), Vol. II, pp. 42 ff. The *scherzo* seems to have caused most of the trouble, for which see Marion M. Scott; *Beethoven* (London: J. M. Dent & Sons, reprint of 1951), p. 161. Cf. also Robert Haven Schauffler; *Beethoven, the Man Who Freed Music* (Garden City: Doubleday & Co., 1936), Chap. XVI, pp. 122 ff.

3. Dr. Solomon E. Asch in an article called "Opinions and Social Pressure," *Scientific American*, Nov. 1955, shows how even visual perceptions may be influenced by the opinions of other people present at the time of making the perception. If a man can be determined in this field, it is more than likely that he can be swayed in the field of aesthetics.

4. For these quotations see Peter Selz; *New Images of Man* (Garden City: Doubleday & Co., 1959).

5. Joseph W. Eaton and Robert J. Weil have made a study of a cloistered community to determine the incidence of mental disease in it. A report of their findings is in "The Mental Health of the Hutterites," *Scientific American*, Dec. 1953. The Hutterites are a small religious sect of German origin living in the western United States and Canada. They are inbred, 8,542 descendants (in 1950) of 101 original couples. They go to the public schools and speak English fluently, read the papers, and have telephones. They normally do not continue their scholastic education beyond the primary grades. This study was made to test the assumption that "insanity would diminish or disappear if mankind could return to a simpler life." The Hutterites lead "a simple, rural life, have a harmonious social order and provide every member with a high level of economic security from the womb to the tomb. They are a homogeneous group, free from many of the tensions of the American melting-pot culture." Yet in the history of the group there have been 53 cases of psychosis, 69 of neurosis, 51 of mental deficiency, 20 of epilepsy, and 6 personality disorders. The conclusion of the authors is that "the Hutterite culture provides no immunity to mental disorders. The existence of these illnesses in so secure and stable a social order suggests that there may be genetic, organic, or constitutional predispositions to psychosis which will cause breakdowns among individuals in any society, no matter how protective and well integrated." It should be observed that among the psychotic members of the group 39 were manic-depressive and only 9 were schizophrenic. One can draw one's own conclusions.

6. Mr. Eliot's opinion about Kipling will be found in his introduction to a volume of selections from Kipling's poems, called *On Poetry and Poets* (New York: Farrar, Straus & Cudahy, Inc., 1957), p. 265. For Proust on George Eliot see e.g., his letter to Georges de Lauris, in *Letters of Marcel Proust*, translated and edited by Mina Curtiss (London: Chatto & Windus, 1950), p. 159. The Index to the Pléiade edition of *A la recherche du temps perdu* gives references to her in the novel itself.

7. This is a bit exaggerated, for food-taboos among Jews are very elaborate and cause inconvenience to them as well as to their friends who happen not to be Jews. Moslems share some of these taboos and Catholics, of course,

have theirs as well. Hindus are even stricter about what they may eat and with whom. The relation between eating and religion can be explained only by a trained psychologist and I shall do no more than point to the importance of theophagy in Christianity. To affirm or to deny transubstantiation has been a capital crime at times, as we all know, and that would seem to indicate that the identification of one kind of nourishment was of a certain importance. But a thorough study of this matter would demand an examination of details both beyond my capacities and too long for a note.

8. For an interesting argument showing that art cannot determine action, see Mortimer Adler; *Art and Prudence* (New York: Longmans, Green & Co., 1937).

9. For an example of the influence of ignorance on public opinion, see Bernard and Judith Mausner; "A Study of the Anti-Scientific Attitude," *Scientific American*, February 1955.

10. Translation of W. R. M. Lamb in the Loeb Classical Library.

11. In the psychology of Freud, these could be associated with the erotic side of our nature, since they might become symbols of libidinous cravings which we have suppressed. There is perhaps no need to point out that Freud's definition of the *libido* makes it cover all our desires.

12. Dean A. P. Brogan of the University of Texas for some years presented a group of students with a list of ten vices and asked them to list them in order of viciousness. For his methods and results, see his "The Fundamental Value Universal," *Journal of Philosophy*, Vol. XVI (1919), pp. 96–104; "Urban's Axiological System," *Ibid.*, Vol. XVIII (1921), pp. 197–209; "A Study in Statistical Ethics," *International Journal of Ethics*, Vol. XXXIII (1923), pp. 119–34; "Group Estimates of Frequency of Misconduct," *Ibid.*, Vol. XXXIV (1924), pp. 254–71; and "Moral Valuations about Men and Women," *Ibid.*, Vol. XXXV (1925), pp. 105–24.

CHAPTER XII: Multivalence

1. The whole statement of Duchamps may be worth more than the few sentences which I have quoted. It runs, "In the creative act, the artist goes from intention to realization through a chain of totally subjective reactions. His struggle towards the realization is a series of efforts, pains, satisfactions, refusals, decisions, which also cannot and must not be fully self-conscious, at least on the aesthetic plane. The result of this struggle is a difference between the intention and its realization, a difference of which the artist is not aware. Consequently, in the chain of reactions accompanying the creative act, a link is missing. This gap, representing the inability of the artist to express fully his intention, this difference between what he intended to realize and did realize, is the personal 'art coefficient' contained in the work. In other words, the personal 'art coefficient' is like an arithmetical relation between the unexpressed but intended and the unintentionally expressed. . . ." Then follows the passage quoted. See *Visual Arts Today*, ed. by Gyorgy Kepes, *loc. cit.*, p. 112.

2. Tertullian; *De spectaculis*, ii.

3. See C. E. Gauss; *op. cit.*, pp. 60 ff.

4. Gustav Glueck in his *Das Grosse Brueghel-Werk*, Vienna, 1951, p. 45 quotes Sebastian Brant's *Narrenschiff* on the fall of Icarus and of Phaeton as follows:

> Hett Phaeton syn farren gelon
> Und Icarus gemaecher gton,
> Und beid gfolgt jrs vatters ratt,
> Sie wern mit jn der jugent dott.

My colleague, Professor Peter Salm, has put this into modern German as

> Haette Phaeton sein Fahren gelassen
> Und Ikarus gemaechlicher (behutsamer) gehandelt,
> Und (haetten) beide ihres Vaters Rat gefolgt,
> Dann waeren sie nicht in ihrer Jugend gestorben.

But no one looking at the picture need remember this any more than he need remember the story as told by Ovid. The picture could as well be used as it was by Auden.

5. My point should really be backed up by extensive quotation. But Eliot's works are available to all and, moreover, he has never said that poetry was a rebus.

6. See Werner Haftmann; *The Mind and Work of Paul Klee* (New York: Frederick A. Praeger, Inc., 1954), p. 53. Cf. Alfred H. Barr, Jr., in his introduction to *Paul Klee* (New York: Museum of Modern Art, 1945), p. 5 where he says that Klee's drawings have been compared "to the drawings of young children at an age when they draw spontaneously from intuitive impulses rather than from observation." But since he also compared them to the drawings of the insane, of palaeolithic man, Eskimo and Bushman drawings, and the pictographs of American Indians, many of which are not childlike at all, one wonders just what he means. Cf. Jean Lurçat on the childlike quality of Klee in Will Grohmann, *Paul Klee* (Paris: Cahiers d'Art, 1929), p. xxv. It goes without saying that the word "childlike" is in serious need of definition. As for equating it with the primitive and the insane, that is close to nonsense.

CHAPTER XIII: The Contribution of the Individual

1. Roger J. Williams; *Biochemical Individuality*, esp. pp. 37, 89, 95, 121, 127, and 167. This book should be supplemented with his more popular study, *Free but Unequal*.

2. P. B. Medawar; *The Future of Man* (New York: Basic Books, Inc., 1960), p. 37.

3. Medawar; *op. cit.*, p. 116, note 3 to Lecture 4.

4. For a discussion of Reynolds' criteria of good painting see G. Boas; "Joshua Reynolds as Arbiter of Taste," *Gazette des Beaux-Arts*, July 1961, pp. 93 ff.

5. Berenson, for instance, found all of Piero's paintings "impersonal" in the sense that, first, he carefully avoided reproducing his own feelings, and second, refused to express any emotion in his figures. The "Resurrection," he says, is painted with no thought given to what Christ actually looked like. "You feel the solemnity, the importance of the moment, as in perhaps no

other version of this subject," but you never ask whether "there is a fit expression on His face," *Italian Painters of the Renaissance* (London: Phaidon
Press, 1952), p. 110 f. Sir Kenneth Clark in his *Piero della Francesca* (Phaidon Press, 1951), p. 40, says "The 'Resurrection' . . . is above all a religious picture. Piero has used his mathematical science to create a sacred
image which will command our belief in a mystery. Masaccio's frescoes in
the Carmine are of miracles performed in the interests of humanity, charitable
works which are well within the range of human sympathy and understanding. But before Piero's risen Christ we are suddenly conscious of values for
which no rational statement is adequate; we are struck with a feeling of awe,
older and less reasonable than that inspired by the Blessed Angelico. This
country god, who rises in the grey light while humanity is still asleep, has
been worshipped ever since man first knew that seed is not dead in the winter
earth, but will force its way upwards through an iron crust . . . He . . .
has Himself the doomed and distant gaze of a somnambulist." This interpretation is shared by Charles de Tolnay in his article "La Resurrection du
Christ par Piero della Francesca," *Gazette des Beaux-Arts,* January 1954, pp.
35 ff. Van Marle in *The Development of the Italian Schools of Painting*
(The Hague: Nijhoff, 1929), Vol. XI, p. 66, dwells mainly on the fusion of
technical means and the religious significance of the painting. He says, "The
painting has been detached from the wall which it originally decorated and
transferred to its actual site. It is obviously the fresco technique which lends
itself to such a grandiosity of treatment, such a breadth of form and such a
blending of colours, all qualities which contribute to the inexpressible grandeur
of the work. Behind the four soldiers sitting leaning against the coffin, not
only sleeping but even personifications of sleep itself, appears the Saviour just
risen from His tomb, a supernatural figure with an all-knowing expression, full
of the comprehension of earthly suffering which, however, can no longer
touch Him. This splendid image of the resurrected Christ, from Whose mind
the anguish of the Passion has not faded, is shown in the centre of a landscape with hills in the distance, between trees, some of which are stripped
of foliage while others are in leaf," etc. etc. The iconographic significance of
the two sets of trees is not dwelt upon, perhaps because Van Marle thought
mention of them sufficient. Nor does he attempt to read into the painting the
three-day sojourn in Hell. John Addington Symonds, as might be expected,
dwells upon the emotions which the fresco stimulates in the observer. In
The Renaissance in Italy, The Fine Arts (London: Smith Elder, 1877), p.
234 we find him saying, "Those who have once seen his fresco of the Resurrection . . . will never forget the deep impression of solitude and aloofness
from all earthly things produced by it. It is not so much the admirable group-
ing and masterly drawing of the four sleeping soldiers, or even the majestic
type of the Christ emergent without effort from the grave, as the communication of a mood felt by the painter and instilled into our souls, that makes
this by far the grandest, most poetic, and most awe-inspiring picture of
the Resurrection. The landscape is simple and severe, with the cold light
upon it of the dawn before the sun is risen. The drapery of the ascending
Christ is tinged with auroral colours like the earliest clouds of the morning;
and his level eyes, with the mystery of the slumber of the grave still upon
them, seem gazing far beyond our scope of vision, into the region of the
eternal and illimitable." Wilhelm von Bode in *Die Kunst der Fruehrenais-
sance in Italien* (Berlin: Propylaeen Verlag, 1923), p. 59, perhaps for lack

of space simply says, *Das grossartige Fresko der Auferstehung Christi . . . ist ein Musterbeispiel seiner Meisterschaft sowohl in der Linien wie in der Luftperspektive,*" and leaves it at that. But J. A. Crowe and G. B. Cavalcaselle; *History of Painting in Italy*, Vol. V, ed. by Tancred Borenius (London: John Murray, 1914), p. 14, are definitely lukewarm. "The Saviour," we find, "Whose winding sheet is drawn over the left shoulder, leaving the torso and right arm bare, is at once realistic and colossal, and imposing as in the old Byzantine Sienese examples founded upon the antique. The parts are modelled with anatomical truth. But the type of face is Moorish, with full lips, straight broad-barrelled nose, and hollow eyes, whilst the extremities are coarse and common." The excerpts are not of course a fair sample of all judgments about this painting, but they do all come from writers whose opinions were influential in forming taste and who certainly had seen and studied a great many paintings. What they saw and failed to see, what they thought worth writing about, may therefore be considered as fairly illustrative of the divergences, due to individual interests, in critical attention. With the exception of Crowe and Cavalcaselle, they all admired the painting, but they admired it for a variety of reasons.

CHAPTER XIV: Form as a Standard

1. For a fine example of formal analysis, see T. M. Greene; *The Arts and the Art of Criticism* (Princeton: Princeton University Press, 1947), pp. 485 ff., in which Roy Dickinson Welch writes "A Discussion of the Expressed Content of Beethoven's Third Symphony."

2. But see Josephine Miles, *The Continuity of Poetic Language* (Berkeley: University of California, 1951).

3. I was in Düsseldorf on the eve of the German surrender in 1945 and, were I to describe what I saw, critics would say that it was improbable, if not false. Yet women were pushing baby carriages in the streets, marketing in the shops, gossiping and laughing at the corners; children were playing happily; everyone seemed well-dressed and above all comfortable. If it had not been for the destruction of the factory districts, one would never have known that a terrible war had been going on for five years and that a nation was crumbling. Within the little circle that I saw the War seemed like a minor event: these people were not in anguish or torment.

4. Cf. Bridges' *White Ship* in which the motion of the vessel is reproduced in the rhythm and meter.

5. The famous Dr. Arnold was frank enough to put down in black and white his dislike for both pictures and music. "I cannot bear," he said, "to stand for half an hour looking at pictures or landscapes that I know nothing about, or girls with fruit, or cottages, or schoolboys, or anything of that sort." And again, "Those who are musical can scarcely understand what it is to want that sense wholly; I cannot perceive what to others is a keen sense of pleasure; there is no link by which my mind can attach it to itself; and much as I regret this defect, I can no more remedy it than I could make my mind mathematical, or than some other men could enter into the deep delight with which I look at wood anemones or wood sorrel." From Arnold Whitridge;

Dr. *Arnold of Rugby* (New York: Henry Holt & Co., 1928), pp. 18 ff. If this seems strange, think of the sculpture which Balzac invented as a master-piece in *Cousine Bette*. He tried to give his readers the impression that Wenceslas Steinboch was a genius, but the masterpiece turned out by him sounds ridiculous to a modern reader. The Goncourt Brothers in their *Journal* (March 3, 1862) insist that the most famous of their literary friends de-tested music. The evidence could be extended, but I shall mention only Goethe whose indifference to music, especially to Beethoven's, is notorious.

6. See Wilfrid Mellers; *Man and his Music: Romanticism and the 20th Century* (London: Rockliff, 1957), on Debussy (p. 136); Chap. V, on Fauré and Strauss; the paragraph on Schönberg's row (p. 190); and the whole chapter on Stravinsky and Bartók. But after all there is nothing strange about this evolution. When there are a number of relatively independent elements pres-ent in a work of art, any of them may be changed with only minor changes being involved in the others. Thus one can find a good bit of Ingres' tech-nique of drawing in Degas, but the subject matter, except for one or two mythological and quasi-historical paintings, belongs to Degas alone. The sub-ject matter, ballet dancers, horse races, nudes washing themselves, could have been designed in the traditional manner and if Degas modified that manner as he indeed did, that was not because the subjects demanded it. One can draw a nude in a flat bath tub seen from in front on the level of the eye as well as from above. As everyone knows, he got a new feeling for design from Japanese prints and not from the inherent nature of the things he painted. From the point of view of design alone, he was thus very different from Renoir who accentuated the rhythm and flow of his subjects and made them the skeletal order of his canvases. If one thinks of nothing but that, Renoir becomes the father of Matisse. But of course there are other things to consider.

CHAPTER XV: Criticism as Interpretation

1. See "The Eightfold Confusion" in G. Boas; *A Primer for Critics*.
2. Roger de Piles's ranking of the painters is most easily found in Elizabeth Gilmore Holt's *Literary Sources of Art History*, p. 415. Each painter was graded on his composition, drawing, color, and expression. Of the painters listed those best known today rank as follows: Duerer, 36; Giovanni Bellini, 24; Domenichino, 58; Holbein, 48; Michelangelo, 37; Poussin, 53; Raphael, 65; Rembrandt, 50; Rubens, 65; Titian, 51. The highest grade on each count would have been 20. No painter was ranked above Raphael and Rubens and even they were not perfect.
3. Though the use of physiognomonics is out of style as a serious technique, it is still used by novelists and in ordinary conversation. For a guide to its use in fiction, see John Graham; "Lavater's *Physiognomy* in England," *Jour-nal of the History of Ideas*, Vol. XXII, no. 4, Oct.–Dec., 1961, pp. 561–72. I append for whatever interest it may have a reading of character based on physiognomy from an historian. Sir Lewis Namier in his *Vanished Suprema-cies* (London: H. Hamilton, 1958), says this of General Gourgaud: "It is enough to look at the man's picture, his garrulous, wide-open eyes, at his blabbing, argumentative mouth, at his forehead of a half-wit, at the excitable

stupidity of his face, to see what Napoleon let himself in for; it portrays a man who would have tried the patience of Job" (p. 5 f.). This is all the more amusing in that Sir Lewis did not have even a photograph to go on. He was interpreting an interpretation.

4. Réau in his *Iconographie de l'art chrétien* (Paris: Presses Universitaires de France, 1955), says that the prostrate figure is Averroës, which is probable, and that the whole painting is based on one by Francesco Traini, which I have not seen. There is also the possibility that it represents Guillaume de Saint-Amour, an enemy of the Mendicant Friars and Dominicans. But in either case it would symbolize error or heresy. Its ambiguity is interesting, as far as our present interests go, only insofar as it shows the necessity of knowing the meaning of certain symbols integrated into a work of art, before interpreting the work as a whole. Again, is the Pope in the lower part of the painting John XXII who canonized Saint Thomas in 1323 or Alexander IV, a contemporary of the philosopher-saint? If now we did not know the meaning of haloes, of the symbols of the Four Evangelists, of the triple tiara, and so on, what could we make of the picture?

CHAPTER XVI: Cultural Relativism

1. Dr. Spencer's essay will be found in *Courbet and the Naturalistic Movement*, ed. G. Boas, pp. 58–72.

2. As for incest, which is usually cited as a universal taboo, not even canon law made up its mind about the correct definition of this sin until several years had passed. Up to the time of the Lateran Council (1215) there were various opinions about the sin. Saints Ambrose and Augustine prohibited marriages between uncles and nieces; the Council of Ireland under Saint Patrick prohibited them between relations up to and including the fourth degree; the Council of Agde (506), between cousins german, second degree, and cousins issue of cousins german, third degree; Gregory III (731–41), up to the seventh degree; Innocent III, up to the fourth degree; and the Council of Trent put it back to the third degree. I take this from the *Dictionnaire de Droit Canonique*, ed. R. Naz, Paris (Letouzey and Ané), 1953, art. *Inceste*.

3. This will be found in *Aspects of Form*, ed. L. L. Whyte (London: Lund, 1951).

Index

Trianon, 100
"Triumph of Neptune and Amphitrite" (Poussin), 46
Truth, Lamp of, 89
"Turkish Bath" (Ingres), 50
Twain, Mark, 269

U

Unfinished Symphony (Schubert), 38
The Use and Misuse of Poetry (T. S. Eliot), 172
Utrillo, 116, 356

V

"La Valse" (Ravel), 191
Van Eyck, 284, 333
Vanity Fair (Thackeray), 283
Van Marle, 380
Varèse, E., 246, 360
Velázquez, 44
Venus of Melos, 128
Verdi, 118
Vergil, 14, 44
Vermeer, 333, 356
Veronese, 306
Verrocchio, 138, 324
Vézère, Valley of, 5
The Victorines, 248
The Virginians (Thackeray), 283
Vitruvius, 31
Vivaldi, 251
Vlaminck, 19, 243
"Vow of Louis XIII" (Ingres), 19

W

Wagner, 71, 108, 118, 234, 266, 367
Walpole, Horace, 108
Warburg Institute, 188
Washington, George, 245, 315
"Water Lilies" (Monet), 203
Watteau, 74
Watts, G. F., 201
Weems, Parson, 323
Weil, Robert, 377
Welch, Roy Dickinson, 381
Wellek, R., 108
Wells, H. G., 222
Whitman, Walt, 142, 325
Whyte, L. L., 363, 383
Wilde, Oscar, 61
Wilenski, R. H., 372
Williams, Roger J., 158, 255, 257, 379
Williams, Vaughan, 370
Williams, William Carlos, 155
Wilson, E., 108
Winckelmann, 84, 124, 372
Winnie the Pooh, 136
Wölfflin, H., 260
Wood, J., 102
Wordsworth, 262, 291, 325
Wright, Frank Lloyd, 78, 108

Y

Young, Stark, 370

Z

Zola, 84, 194, 197, 207, 266, 283, 291
Zschorlich, P., 367

UNIVERSITY LIBRARY
NOTTINGHAM